Early modern women and the poem

Manchester University Press

Early modern women
and the poem

Edited by Susan Wiseman

Manchester University Press

Published by Manchester University Press
Altrincham Street, Manchester M1 7JA, UK
www.manchesteruniversitypress.co.uk

British Library Cataloguing-in-Publication Data
A catalogue record for this book is available from the British Library

ISBN 978 1 5261 1684 0   paperback

First published by Manchester University Press in hardback 2013

This edition first published 2017

Typeset in Garamond by R. J. Footring Ltd, Derby
Printed in Great Britain by TJ International Ltd, Padstow

Contents

Contributors

Line Cottegnies teaches English early modern literature at the Sorbonne Nouvelle, Paris. She is the editor of the electronic journal *etudes-episteme. org.* She is the author of a monograph on Caroline poetry, *L'Eclipse du regard: la poésie anglaise du baroque au classicisme (1625–1660)* (Droz, 1997) and has co-edited several volumes on seventeenth-century literature. She is mostly interested in seventeenth-century women writers, in particular Margaret Cavendish, Aphra Behn and Mary Astell. She has been co-editor of Shakespeare's works for the bilingual Gallimard Pléiade editions (*Tragedies*, 2002; *Histories*, 2008; the comedies forthcoming) and is currently working on an edition of Shakespeare's *Henry IV, Part 2* for Norton. Her current projects involve a study of English seventeenth-century women writers and their relationship to French literature.

Margaret J. M. Ezell is Distinguished Professor of English and the Sara and John Lindsey Chair of Liberal Arts at Texas A&M University. She is the author of *The Patriarch's Wife: Literary Evidence and the History of the Family* (University of North Carolina Press, 1987), *Writing Women's Literary History* (Johns Hopkins University Press, 1993) and *Social Authorship and the Advent of Print* (Johns Hopkins University Press, 1999).

Helen Hackett is Professor of English at University College London. Her books include *A Short History of English Renaissance Drama* (I. B. Tauris, 2012), *Shakespeare and Elizabeth: The Meeting of Two Myths* (Princeton University Press, 2009), *Women and Romance Fiction in the English Renaissance* (Cambridge University Press, 2000) and *Virgin Mother, Maiden Queen: Elizabeth I and the Cult of the Virgin Mary* (St Martin's Press, 1995). She has recently written several articles on the Aston–Thimelby circle and their verse miscellanies.

Judith Hudson is currently completing doctoral studies at Birkbeck College, University of London. She works primarily in the fields of early modern literature and law, with particular research interests in miscarriages of justice, pamphlet culture and the representation of female criminality.

Edward Paleit is Lecturer in English Literature at the University of Exeter. He is interested in the reception of classical literature in early modern Europe, and the politics of early modern intellectual and literary culture in England. He has written *War, Liberty and Caesar: Responses to Lucan's 'Bellum Ciuile', ca. 1580–1650* (Oxford University Press, 2013).

Patricia Pender is Lecturer in English at the University of Newcastle, Australia. She is the author of *Early Modern Women's Writing and the Rhetoric of Modesty* (Palgrave, 2012) and the co-editor, with Sarah C. E. Ross and Rosalind Smith, of *Early Modern Women and the Apparatus of Authorship*, a special issue of *Parergon* (vol. 29, no. 2, 2012). She has previously published essays on Anne Askew, Mary Sidney and Anne Bradstreet in journals such as *Women's Writing, Studies in English Literature 1500–1900* and *Huntington Library Quarterly*, and currently coordinates, with Rosalind Smith, a three-year Australian Research Council project, 'Material cultures of early modern women's writing'.

Sarah C. E. Ross is Senior Lecturer in English at Victoria University of Wellington. She is the editor of *Katherine Austen's Book M: British Library, Additional Manuscript 4454* (Arizona Center for Medieval and Renaissance Studies, 2011) and the author of numerous articles on early modern women writers. She is currently completing a book entitled *Women, Poetry, and Politics in Seventeenth-Century Britain* and a teaching anthology of *Women Poets of the English Civil War* (with Elizabeth Scott-Baumann), and is the co-editor, with Patricia Pender and Rosalind Smith, of *Early Modern Women and the Apparatus of Authorship*, a special issue of *Parergon* (vol. 29, no. 2, 2012).

Paul Salzman is Professor of English Literature at La Trobe University in Australia. He has published widely in the area of early modern women's writing. His online edition of Mary Wroth's poetry (http://wroth.latrobe.edu.au) won the Society for the Study of Early Modern Women (SSEMW) award for best art and media project (2012). He is currently completing a book for Palgrave Macmillan entitled *Literature and Politics in the 1620s: 'Whisper'd Counsels'*, and editing Wroth's *Love's Victory* as part of the 'Material cultures of early modern women's writing' project.

Rosalind Smith is Senior Lecturer in English at the University of Newcastle, Australia, specialising in early modern women's poetry. She is the author of *Sonnets and the English Woman Writer, 1560–1621: The Politics of Absence* (Palgrave Macmillan, 2005) and the co-editor, with Sarah C. E. Ross and Patricia Pender, of *Early Modern Women and the Apparatus of Authorship*, a special issue of *Parergon* (vol. 29, no. 2, 2012). Her current work involves a monograph on women and true crime in the English Renaissance, and she coordinates, with Patricia Pender, a three-year Australian Research Council project, 'Material cultures of early modern women's writing'.

Suzanne Trill is Senior Lecturer in English Literature at the University of Edinburgh. Her research focuses on women's writing in England and Scotland (c. 1550–1700), especially devotional writing (poetry and prose). Her publications include *Lady Anne Halkett: Selected Self-Writings* (Ashgate, 2008) and, co-edited with Kate Chedgzoy and Melanie Osborne, *Lay by Your Needles Ladies, Take the Pen: Writing Women in England, 1500–1700* (Arnold, 1997) and *Voicing Women: Gender and Sexuality in Writing, 1500–1700* (Keele, 1996).

Susan Wiseman teaches in the Department of English and Humanities, Birkbeck College, London. She has written *Writing and Metamorphosis in the English Renaissance* (Cambridge University Press, 2014), *Conspiracy and Virtue: Women, Writing, and Politics in Seventeenth Century England* (Oxford University Press, 2006), *Aphra Behn* (Writers and Their Work Series, Northcote House, 1996, second edition expanded and revised 2007) and *Politics and Drama in the English Civil War* (Cambridge University Press, 1998).

Gillian Wright is Senior Lecturer at the University of Birmingham. She is co-editor of *Early Modern Women's Manuscript Poetry* (Manchester University Press, 2005) and has published on women's reading and letter-writing. Her book *Producing Women's Poetry, 1600–1730: Text and Paratext, Manuscript and Print* was published by Cambridge University Press in 2013.

Preface and acknowledgements

This collection is founded on an intellectual and organisational collaboration with Patricia Pender and Rosalind Smith. Together with Paul Salzman, we ran a conference on early modern women and poetry which was held by the London Renaissance Seminar in 2009. The conference was partly funded by the Australian Research Council's Network for Early European Research. Linda Grant, Kate Lilley and Michelle O'Callaghan also made important contributions at and after the conference. The essays here are not papers from that conference but stem from post-conference discussion, and Patricia Pender and Rosalind Smith have made very substantial intellectual contributions to thinking through the question of women and the poem. I want to acknowledge a substantial debt to their thinking and participation at all stages of the project.

At Manchester University Press the collection benefited from review by two challenging and precise readers and we have tried to respond to their excellent advice. We are grateful to Kim Walker for first taking on the project, and to Matthew Frost for commissioning the project and for grace and patience in the final stages. Above all, Ralph Footring, the production editor, brought the volume into shape with speed, precision and good humour, for which all the contributors are grateful.

Susan Wiseman

Researching early modern women and the poem

Susan Wiseman

Though by a sodaine and vnfeard surprise,
thou lately taken wast from thy friends eies:
Euen in that instant, when they had design'd
to keipe thee, by thy picture still in minde:
least thou like others lost in deths dark night
shouldst stealing hence vanish quite out of sight;
I did contend with greater zeale then Art,
This shadow of my phantie to impart:
which all shood pardon, when they vnderstand
    the lines were figur'd by a womans hand,
    who had noe copy to be guided by
    but Hales imprinted in her memory.
        Thus ill cut Brasses serue vppon a graue
        which less resemblane of the persons haue.[1]

THIS poem is almost certainly by Anne King. King (?1620s–?1690s) was part of the Great Tew circle, a group of aristocrats and church-men who attempted to preserve what they understood as prayer-book ways during the Protectorate of Oliver Cromwell. Among the Great Tew circle was Anne's brother, the bishop and poet Henry King. The 'Hales imprinted in her memory' was John Hales, a member of this circle, and the poem survives not in King's hand but in a manuscript by another writer intending to memorialise him – Izaak Walton. As Walton explains, in 1655 John Hales was to sit for his portrait but died before it could be done. Anne King then made a black and white image from memory – 'and very like him'. However, 'before she wood shew it to any that knew ether him or her selfe', she wrote the verse above and put it underneath – by way of 'an Apologie for her vndertaking it'.[2]

Anne King's poem puts before us some of the puzzles regularly en-countered when researching early modern women and the poem, including questions of authorship and authority; material traces; contextualisation in terms of circumstances, audience and traditions of writing; use of form and rhetoric; in what ways to weight the gender of the author in analysis; transmission and reception. The rest of this introduction discusses some of the ways in which scholarship has approached these issues. These puzzles are brought to life by the desire of scholars to know and understand; and how we attempt to articulate the versions of that desire is also foregrounded by the transmission history of Anne King's poem and of King as a writer.[3] The shaping of King as an author is particularly revealing because, at present, there are just enough material and intellectual traces of her work to know of her presence as a poet, and enough hints and suggestions that there are more of her poems to emerge.

The information concerning the authorship of this poem is, technically, fairly trustworthy – King's contemporaries understood this poem to be hers and they considered her talented at drawing and writing.[4] However, the situation it evokes suggests that a simple model of authorial control would not fit the situation and both the 'story' of the poem and the nature of its transmission invite comment. In responding to her friends, King has made a poem with several authors; the poem makes little sense extracted from the circle of friendship, thought, writing and transcription which it addresses and evokes. While we can only speculate about the fate of the original manuscript that Walton copied into his notes, the materials that exist invite investigation of the contexts of King's poetic production. In terms of preparing the poem for readers, it is evident that decisions about how the poem is edited and presented will strongly determine whether King is a sonneteer, a minor figure in a circle of male thinkers and writers, or a participant in a coterie culture of literary and creative exchange and circulation. The poem and Walton's account of its situation hint at a hinterland of quite specific, close, sociability and poetic culture while leaving much work to be done to tease it out.

The poem invites careful interpretation. It uses a sonnet form that allows it to end with a couplet crystallising the problematic that a flawed monument both fulfils the need for memorialisation and, it suggests, may compromise by giving a relatively lasting place to a partly realised, imperfectly representative, work of art. The genre of the poem is ambiguous, mixing elements of elegy, epitaph and occasional verse. Indeed, the narrative relates as much to its own creation as to its ostensible subject, Hales. The status of gender in that story is raised in the context of a drawing, from memory, circulating as a public memorial, 'lines ... figur'd by a womans hand'. In significant contrast, poetry is presented as justifying and explaining publication and circulation. In qualifying the terms on which the image is seen, it also supplies the excuse allowing it. Moreover, the poem uses its invoked context – of the circulation of a posthumous portrait from memory – to turn the conventions of modesty into a min-iature exploration of private and public, written and visual monument, lastingness and transience, and it is the modesty topos itself that King uses to suggest a philosophy of poetry and memorialisation.[5] The circumstances the poem presents may well be only part of the story. They tell us little about the mechanisms underpinning King's selection or self-selection as memorialist, for example. So, even as it apparently discloses the grounds of its production, King's poem is like many other manuscript texts in being enigmatic and only uncertainly placed in context, or contexts, which must have been literary, political, oral and written.

Finally, the question of how the poem, poet and context have been transmitted to us is significant. King's poem is representative in this, and transmission is something on which almost all the chapters in this volume comment. In 1934 the poem was transcribed and published by John Butt, a scholar working on Izaak Walton. However, King became a poet in a new sense when the poem was published in the anthology of 'seventeenth-century women's verse' *Kissing the Rod* (1988).[6] *Kissing the Rod* endeavoured both to establish a canon and to offer a treasury of poetry for a general reader through the Virago imprint. But although the editors worked hard to place King in her milieu, the two poems representing her make much less sense extracted and set against many others. An anthologised poem is not of course naked of associated material, but is recontextualised with new questions. Printed in such a collection, the poem has to be the main event and answer to the expectations set by the terms of the anthology. For King, *Kissing the Rod* brought her (two) poems recognition but, arguably, even though much grounding material was carefully supplied, left them without the context of circulation – all the factors in their environment that made them, from friendship to textual exchanges. Paradoxically, the terms on which the poem is widely circulated arguably place it under a pressure of isolation that shrinks its claim to significance. It seems, perhaps, like a smaller piece of evidence when organised under a single author rather than leading us to a complex nexus of literary, religious and political friendship, retreat and memorialisation. Anthologisation has been important in the recovery and transmission of poems authored by seventeenth-century women, and that many of the poets studied here feature in *Kissing the Rod* is in part testimony to that anthology's continuing significance. For King and for others, though, the canon-making process of anthologisation also has drawbacks in the loss of a sometimes all-important context and the equalising aesthetic implied in the process.

In 1988, King was available to most readers only through that single anthology. The situation is now very different, as all recent commentators acknowledge. The internet, with its creation of selective but instantly overlapping, if distracted, reading, is making available new versions of Anne King. For example, King appears in connection with a Henry King poem that is found on 'favourite poems' websites. King is, again, representative in the way access to her poems has been changed in the fast-changing world of online research and writing, and the chapters here engage with both the material texts and the internet. Google is, in many ways, a seventeenth-century poet's little helper – though what is not listed by that search engine is in danger of being lost in a new way.

One of the most important ways in which the Anne King under discussion appears on the world wide web is (along with many of the other women writing in the early modern period) as an entry in the *Oxford Dictionary of National Biography*. The author of King's entry, Vivienne Larminie, deftly balances the evidence that King was a writer and art practitioner against the absence of an extant body of made and written materials. The entry is long enough to strike a careful biographical balance. It represents the existing hints that King is worth consideration while not claiming so much that King's currently extant output looks slight in comparison. Moreover, Larminie represents the poetry in a way that allows for a picture of King's apparent place in her circle to emerge in some detail. The evidence suggests that her peers, largely male, held her in familiar respect as a talented artist and poet, valuing her enough to preserve at least some of her poems and images. In another context, of course, the materials on which such a judgement is based could be offered through a webpage. The 1934 article giving extracts from Walton's copying of the poem, the anthology and the biographical entry now shape King and in each her relationship to the poem is distinctly understood. A reader with access to the *Oxford Dictionary of National Biography*, the JSTOR digital library and *Kissing the Rod* can begin research from several angles. This range of materials, also, comprises a snapshot of how women and the poem have been understood in the twentieth and twenty-first centuries – as by-products of research, anthologised women poets, figures redressing an imbalance in a semi-national database of fame, and now as increasingly mobile objects of simultaneously archival and online investigation.

Anne King's poem and the shifting terms on which it has been offered to readers present us with some of the questions all the writers in this collection find in their encounters with primary material. These questions concern authorship, stories, material form, context, contacts, circulation, exchange and transmission – but also what processes to use to think about those factors in relation to women. However, as we see, such questions are inseparable from aesthetic, social and cultural forces. In order to see how these have been considered in recent decades let us turn to the critical writing on poetry and authorship, material context and media.

In her discussion of 'social authorship', Margaret Ezell examined the 'material conditions of being an author at the turn of the seventeenth century' and in doing so unpicked some long-held assumptions about how print and manuscript publication register the social formations of the period. Thus, Ezell makes an acute analysis of the critical consensus which locates the 1640s and 1650s as the time of the 'birth of a modern cultural era because of the "rise" of print', which became the 'norm for readers after 1660' because of the cornucopia of print in the 1660s; an enduring climate was established in which print culture became associated with literary production, driven by the market rather than the court, and which saw a more generalised use of 'print technology as a metaphor for the "new" ... associated with "modern" in a positive sense'.[7] As Ezell's careful history implies, the assumption that print was modern, and the visibility of its association with the market (through advertising, bookselling and regulation), put into play an understanding of print and the market as emancipatory in freeing authors and authorship from the constraints of aristocratic control. This understanding shaped critical assumptions without necessarily being made explicit and women's poetry was assessed in relation to them. However, as Ezell and others have indicated, the economies in which manuscript poetry circulated were diverse, and included, for example, both the compiled and the stored miscellanies of the Tixall family and the scriptoria in which manuscript copying took place commercially in the later seventeenth century. As Jane Stevenson has reiterated, the association between print publication and the market is far from ubiquitous or self-evident, there being many other motivations for print publication.[8]

At the same time, although for critics like Elizabeth Eisenstein the driver of modernity was technological development, for many other post-war writers on literature the priority was the diversely defined work of literary criticism. The producers' self-understanding as literary critics (whether New Critical, Leavisite or New Historicist), or as *more* a literary critic than a scholar or researcher, though with elements of the latter mixed in, had led to a naturalised prioritisation and discrimination of activities driven by aesthetic assessment over those associated with scholarship and research.[9] The question of the balance between research and critical evaluation in the activity of scholars of the early modern period in literature departments has fuelled many phases of post-war discussion, from the New Criticism to the New Historicism, or, within the study of women and poetry, projects such as the Perdita database and the New Formalism.

Within this wider discussion, Ezell's call for the recuperation of the manuscript has been heeded – the study of seventeenth-century manuscripts is no longer considered the investigation of a 'dead end' but is at the heart of current research in women's poetry.[10] As the work of Ezell and others shows, it is productive to analyse manuscripts and print materials at the same time as excavating the governing assumptions and metaphors which shape the way in which we, as workers in literary culture, approach and so determine that task. Ezell's attention to the nature of the material produced in the seventeenth century, from 'domestic papers' to presentation copies, combined with her responsiveness to the dynamics of transmission, has been enabling in terms of reflexive practice in literary work and has been taken up most energetically in the attention of feminist scholars to manuscript culture.

As Arthur Marotti reminds us, seventeenth-century writers regarded manuscripts as malleable and lyrics are interspersed among other materials. Similarly, arguing for a renewed attention to the contexts of texts made by women, Ezell notes that texts function as 'cultural ... documents', inviting investigation of the 'situation of the creation of the text', which is often bound up with its 'narrative', and both of which, in turn, affect how it might be read.[11] Attention to manuscripts in the study of sixteenth- and seventeenth-century women's writing, particularly poetry, has made the mode of 'publication' or record crucial to any account of the transmission of poetry by or associated with early modern women. Manuscript study has been immensely productive in developing ways to chart, investigate and sometimes interrelate unprinted works, and in interspersing literary with other concerns. Manuscript production has been recognised as both important and enduring. Although, obviously, the use of manuscript does not necessarily imply a preference over print, the relations between the two are specific and circumstantial; as George L. Justice writes, necessity and circumstance (as well as choice) drove the selection of media.[12]

The close study of manuscript and of print sources lends itself to the aggregation of conclusions and working hypotheses from cases studies. Insofar as the study of early modern poetry by women involves recovery, it is also canvassed in related but diverse genres; besides the monograph, some of the most significant work in the field is found in editions, electronic databases, essays and essay collections. It may be no accident that Justice and Tinker published a collection of essays, Ezell describes *Social Authorship* as essays, the findings of the Perdita project are issued in a database and books of essays, and Victoria Burke's important work on miscellanies often takes the form of evolving case studies.[13] Scholars are now also beginning to take on the quantitative issues associated with women's poetry and, alongside close studies, are investigating how many women wrote and what proportion of manuscript output that might represent.[14]

As Ezell articulates in the context of the history of authorship, the making and circulating of, and thinking about, texts involve complex processes in which such apparently identifiable opposites as production and consumption can turn into each other if we take seventeenth-century writers and readers (and, perhaps, in a different way, printers too, given the multiple printed texts instantiating alterations to the manuscript) as understanding texts, manuscript especially, as 'malleable'. Thus, Adam Smyth's discussion of print miscellanies starts with writers exchanging and using each other's poetry, ordering printed books and taking poems for manuscript copying from a printed miscellany; Smyth's writer-readers worked over, stored and exchanged letters, poems and printed books.[15]

At the same time that critical understandings of media have changed, so have understandings of authorship – both of women's poetry and more generally. The working model that prevailed for so long, of a text having a single author or point of origin, is not sustained by the evidence of manuscript or print publication. For example, while it seems beyond doubt that Anne King wrote the poem discussed above, at a deeper level perhaps was the sociability and memorial practices of the Great Tew circle that shaped its generation and publication. Publication, whether in print or manuscript, often involves the labour of many (or at least several) in the act of creation and the miscellany, the coterie and even the notebook (recording materials from many sources) are examples of this. Attention to the media of literary production has led to an understanding of the early modern text as complexly authored, multiply produced, remediated and reinterpreted rather than, necessarily, finished and 'fixed' in print, and each of the chapters here is attentive to the redactions of the texts it examines.

Addressing some of the same concerns that have occupied scholars re-searching seventeenth-century literary production in the last twenty years, particularly authorship, manuscript and print, this collection returns to two relatively basic (though not undisputed) categories in the field – 'women' and 'the poem'. Manuscript is significantly represented and so is print, sometimes in the same discussion; if authorship is important, so too are the terms in which the text was circulated or, in some cases, put out of circulation; if the evaluation of a text through transmission is investigated, so too are the terms and interests shaping literary and aesthetic evaluation in the seventeenth century. The chapters here concerned with manuscript and authorship are alert to the ways the authors they write about under-stand the terms of literary evaluation.

Accordingly, the chapters examine how the poems and poets under-stand the literary, classical and other inheritances poetry is working with in terms of the conventions of the presentation of texts by women. They examine how and why texts were and were not circulated, and what were the implications of reading texts, thinking about texts and exchanging texts. In their consideration of reading practices, the chapters tend to suggest that readers both read the texts to which they had access, as Jennifer Richards and Fred Schurink cogently argue, and use them in some of the ways discussed by Bill Sherman. These essays explore not only the reading of books but the complex and varying, sometimes contemplative, sometimes citational, ways single writers and groups respond to texts.[16] Finally, while attending to the production and circulation of texts, the chapters are also concerned with what stories these texts might want to tell. As D. F. McKenzie's work implies, the ways in which reading, writing and print work, and interact, are indices of attitudes to writing and reading. In the production of poetry, the interactions of reading, writing and print also give clues to understandings of literary and aesthetic value. These relationships are also, perhaps more deeply, significant because they hint at or even baldly show the ways in which social and economic as well as cultural dynamics were experienced at particular moments.[17] Responding to McKenzie, Matt Cohen's reconsideration of communication, working from the example of seventeenth-century New England, proposes publication as collaborative, indeed 'choral', whether or not the author function is prioritised. He sees it as a function of a 'series of producers' and consumers, constituting an 'embodied act of information exchange', in his terms a 'publication event'.[18] While Cohen's primary material is at a distance from the specific question of women and the poem, in terms of consideration of the material of texts, his prioritisation of the 'publication event' facilitates attention both to media and to the consumption or redaction of texts.

In the study of poetry of the seventeenth century, then, besides the media of publication, what is often at stake is how to assess and express the interplay of many factors (sociability, friendship, hatred, aesthetics, rage, economics, love and gender) that written forms, and poetry with an additional epitomising clarity, index, reshape and influence. Underpinning any particular assessment of women and the poem is an analysis of at least part of the society in which it existed. At present, the dominant understanding of a 'long' early modern period, say 1620–1760, is that poetry was at the centre of a process whereby a culture of social and then sentimental circulation gradually emerged. Such a narrative makes the Restoration a turning point at which, in the self-reflexive divisions of the social world, in tandem with the deliberate establishment of the aesthetic as a terrain of competition occupying both writers for profit and the elite, the conditions are set in place for the substantially later emergence of a culture of sentiment. This narrative of the social work of poetry in moving the subject and recounting the feelings of benevolence has only ever been partially true, and, as Simon Dickie has argued, the 'residual' cultures of the early modern period rage unabated in tandem with sentiment.[19]

Thus, while in the middle of the period explored by this collection the Restoration saw a deliberate transformation, even institutionalisation, of literary culture, the contributors are far from seeing this as instituting an emergent culture of civility. Rather, in the seventeenth century, these chapters suggest, poetry was at the service of many different kinds of social relationship. The contributors all see women and poems in a social and aesthetic context, and underpinning each chapter is an evaluation of economic and social factors. Thus, the Staffordshire miscellany compiled by Constance Fowler sits at the centre of a civil and collaborative, if socially instrumental, culture in which poetry was evaluated and swapped and, as Paul Trolander and Zeynep Tenger suggest, the status of the compiler (Constance) developed as an aesthetic arbiter.[20] Fourteen years earlier, as Paul Salzman tells us in chapter 6, Lady Mary Wroth and Edward Denny had had a violent poetic exchange, and Denny had acted as arbiter of cultural value, moral and aesthetic, in ensuring that only Denny's version of the exchange entered the developed network of satire exchange. Finally, examining fights over reputation and laureate status at the Restoration, Margaret Ezell brings forward material in chapter 8 which suggests relationships of rage and rivalry far, far indeed from the gentle sociability implied by Trolander and Tenger.

Poetry, then, is a specific set of modes and a part of events. Accordingly, responding to both the 'how' and 'why' of publication, the chapters here bring to the question of women and the poem an understanding of poetry as both actively made and situated. They see texts bound into circumstances in the world, and, in being written and preserved, reaching outwards from particular moments and circumstances. Such an understanding includes manuscript and print; women and men; stories of gender and stories of politics and war. Accordingly, the critical fields on which the chapters draw are those which recognise the interplay of textual situation (poetic, material, cultural); social situation and aim; intellectual engagement and influence; narrative and topic. In examining early modern women and the poem, this volume asks how women use poetry, and how poems use women, in England and Scotland in the period 1550–1680. Several decades of critical writing on 'women's poetry', 'gender and poetry', and the representation of women, or gender, in poetry have produced a rich and complex critical and scholarly field, and this context presents an opportunity to look again at the primary and secondary evidence concerning two key elements in the analysis of early modern women's writing – women and the poem.

The conceptual starting place of this volume, then, is the question of what are the many possible relationships between women and the poem in seventeenth-century Anglophone culture, and how these relationships might be investigated. The question is posed in the context of vigorous research and scholarship on early modern women's writing discussed above. This field is characterised by: overlapping critical questions about historicism and attention to the text; attempts to reinterpret the relationships between manuscript and print and simply to understand the nature and context of the manuscript evidence left by women; and attempts to understand in more nuanced ways the gendered production of poetry. In the light of this, the volume takes three categories as its framework for specific analysis:

- *Inheritance.* How did poetic genres come to women writers? How, and in what contexts, did women understand, interpret and select the genres, languages, modes in which they wrote?
- *Circulation.* How did poems, whether by men or women, circulate? What were the purposes and processes of networks and connections? How were poems and women bound into collaboration, gatekeeping, rivalry, friendship? How can we trace the writing relations of women whose texts initially come to us as apparently isolated manuscripts? What were the different forms of textual, and social, groups?
- *Narrative.* What story or stories does a text want to tell, and why? What tropes, tales or representations of gender mark it? How is gender told and read?

Part I explores the way women understood the poem in terms of the reception, influence and adaptation of past models and examples, working from the reception of classical texts by specific authors through the influence of European and classical models to the reception and reworking of literary form (chapters by Paleit, Ross, Cottegnies, Wright). Essays focus on the resources women writing poetry knew and encountered in chapters on classical inheritance, the religious sonnet sequence and the secular sonnet sequence. Using the work of Lucy Hutchinson, Elizabeth Melville, Lady Mary Wroth and Katherine Philips, these chapters explore the way these poets use both inherited texts and traditions and inherited poetic forms and conventions. Each of the chapters uses a specific example in order to ask us to reconsider the resources used in sixteenth- and seventeenth-century women's poetry and the cumulative effect is to shift our understanding to emphasise engagements that are neglected in contemporary analyses – the influence of Ovid and Virgil through humanist learning; the implications of the early development of the sonnet sequence in Scotland; the significance of the European resources available to women poets as mediators of poetic voice. Edward Paleit opens the volume with a discussion of women's relationship to classical learning and poetry. Situating Lucy Hutchinson in relation to her contemporaries, Paleit offers a detailed investigation of Hutchinson's relationship to the classical materials she works with. Taking the decisions about what she uses and how she uses it (Lucretius but also Ovid and, importantly, Virgil) Paleit extends the range of classical material with which we can see Hutchinson engages. His essay also articulates very fully the process whereby Hutchinson's poetic decisions subject the classical material to religious (theological and positional) dynamics to create a hierarchy of poetic articulation in which God's script, articulated in part in the book of nature, holds a prophetic sway. While Hutchinson is exceptional in her classical proficiency and the excitement of her involvement, at the same time she shares with others, perhaps more than is sometimes suggested, an awareness of the loaded implications of classical appropriation.

Examining both religious and Petrarchan inheritances, Sarah Ross analyses the innovative sonnet sequences of Elizabeth Melville, developing a case for the simultaneous influence of Petrarch and the Psalms on Melville's poetry, but particularly making the case that, in looking at Renaissance models for poetry, for both men and women, Scotland's court and religious poetry offers a scene both earlier than the English and innovative in specific ways that, in their psychological depth, are clearly manifest in the use of the sonnet. Taking up the question of women's reading and writing in relation to the sonnet sequence, Line Cottegnies turns to the significance of the European, reappraising the tendency of modern scholars to use sources, genealogy and elite family context as a way to indicate and expand the cultural value of Renaissance women poets while, in the process, erasing authorial agency and therefore obscuring other contexts more closely associated with the production of a female voice within the fraught field of masculine love poetry. Taking Wroth as a key example, Cottegnies examines the claim to genealogy made by both Wroth and her critics and returns us to the poet's specific claim and intervention as a 'female speaker and author of her own discourse'. Refocusing our attention on the European resources available to Wroth, in terms of both the reception of Ovid and the interventions of Louise Labé in the shaping of the European sonnet sequence and the female voice in the sonnet, Cottegnies traces Wroth's use of the *Heroides* as a way of modelling relations in the sonnet sequence and shows the importance of this influence for Wroth's simultaneously self-assertive subject position in *Pamphilia to Amphilanthus*. Thus, arguing for a renewed attention to Wroth's understanding of the specifically female voice and in consequence her relationship to a wider, European and classical, range of influence, Cottegnies also invites a similar reappraisal of the European dimension of elite and other women's poetry.

11

Sharing the preceding chapters' emphasis on a reconsideration of how women used the materials that came to them, Gillian Wright's contribution focuses on the implications of inherited literary convention and the masculine gendering of poetic form. Starting from Virginia Woolf's discussion of poetry coming to women in forms and sentences shaped as a shared masculine tradition, Wright turns to an early manuscript by Katherine Philips both to confirm and to challenge Woolf's hypothesis. Taking conventions as genre, or a horizon of expectation, Wright takes examples of Philips's poetry which articulate different ways of using, challenging and reinventing the masculine assumptions in the genres she inherited.

Hutchinson, Melville, Wroth and Philips all had readers and Philips, of course, was at the forefront of the literary sphere that emerged, indeed was in some ways created, at the Restoration. Taking up the question of circulation, Part II of the book examines the world of reading and readers, and looks at poems in terms of friendships, quarrels, competitions, coteries, networks and critical reception, both then and later. As Suzanne Trill argues, analysing the place of Mary Sidney in her collaboration with her brother Philip to produce the Sidney Psalter involves recognising and often unpicking the work literary critics have done. Much scholarship, both deliberately and through implication, not only distances the two collaborators from one another in terms of practice, but also systematically downgrades the work of Mary Sidney. As Trill argues, the close relationship between the sibling poets was recognised by, at the very least, John Donne in his discussion of the psalms as 'Sydnean' and possibly by other contemporary readers. Trill's chapter illuminates simultaneously the importance of collaboration as a model in the production and reworking of literary texts in the sixteenth and seventeenth centuries and the profound influence of scholarly and critical assumptions about the same activity – the production of literary texts – in shaping how they are understood to have been produced. As Trill also notes, a key factor in critical practice is literary value and, in the Sidneys' case particularly, the high value that modern scholarship has placed on authorship as the activity of a single subject, as well as, at times, on print publication as an index of success, and, above all, on masculinity as a norm (though not necessarily a good) in literary production. These values have worked unhelpfully to separate the Sidney psalms into 'his' (Philip's) and 'hers' (Mary's) and to lower the value of the work she did in revising and, in part, rethinking his. This work by Mary Sidney on her brother's psalms, Trill's analysis shows, evidences a consistent and sophisticated poetic labour and gift. Ultimately, she suggests, the collaborative models of Renaissance authorship and this collaboration between two important figures in the history of poetry and poetics should prompt revision of the hitherto parallel but separate consideration of men and women's poetry. The implication of the essay is that we might recognise that men and women worked together, and extend the model of collaborative authorship and to investigate men and women and the poem – together, in collaboration, competition, similarity and distinction.

Like Cottegnies in Part I, Paul Salzman investigates the way the male world shaped the reception of Mary Wroth's writing – in the way in which she circulated her writing and the way in which it, and therefore her point of view, was removed in the recirculation of scandal among men. Salzman takes as his starting place the exchange between Edward Denny and Wroth initiated by a suggestion in *Urania* that his daughter had committed adultery and Wroth's description of the father's violent reaction. Denny's vituperative poetic rejoinder provoked a response from Wroth. Salzman traces the circulation of this exchange, initially by Wroth herself and then later, in miscellanies of erotic and misogynistic verse of the kind compiled by young men of the Inns of Court. The initially paired poems were separated and Denny's attack on Wroth took on a transferable life of its own within miscellany culture. As Salzman's tracking of the many versions of Denny's verse indicates, the process of circulation is selective in relation to the categories and taxonomies which rendered certain kinds of verse desirable as offerings between men in the culture of literary and other exchange. Whereas Wroth's poem might have been suppressed for many reasons (hostile or protective), the attack on her was validated by extensive circulation.

The circulation of poetry in the Aston family, as discussed by Helen Hackett, discloses the multiple ways in which the copying, exchange and evaluation of poems became part of a familial mode of operation, but also a facilitator of social exchange and, as Hackett suggests, put women at the centre of forms of sociability in a family. Situated at the family base in Tixall, Staffordshire, home of the Catholic Baron of Forfar, Constance Fowler made a verse miscellany between 1635 and 1638, when, for much of that time, her father was away in Spain working for Charles I, taking with him her loved brother, Herbert. Constance, embedded in the Catholic Staffordshire elite, had a tight local network, comprising family and social connections locally and nationally, and communicated with her brother in Spain.

Margaret Ezell, taking up the question of communication and evaluation in two groups of poets who were very different from the Aston family, suggests the importance of recognising that competition and hostile criticism might motivate literary judgement, and her chapter extends the range of possible explanations for slurs beyond modesty, gender and sexual misconduct, to the importance of literary reputation. This essay focuses our attention on the emotions imbricated in literary and economic production and competition. This essay analyses competition and value in exchanges associated with Anne Finch and Anne Killigrew, examining them in terms of competition in literary and political spheres of the later seventeenth-century.

Part III of the book, 'Narrative', contains four chapters which emphasise the tales that poems tell, and how those stories both register and shape the understanding of women and the poem in the world of potential readers. Like Margaret Ezell, Patricia Pender invites us to reconsider the assumptions we bring to the worlds of seventeenth-century texts. Where Ezell invites us to reconsider expressions of praise and blame, Pender re-examines the modesty topos, using the example of Anne Bradstreet. In working closely with material often understood literally as apology for poetry or for gender, Pender precisely demonstrates Bradstreet's use of modesty as a claim to high achievement and an enduring status as a poet. Rather than simply acknowledging Bradstreet's importance, Pender accords her poetry the close attention paid to, for example Philips or Hutchinson, and finds at work a complex, tendentious and nuanced understanding of her own activity as a poet.

In examining women and the poem, the use of women as signifiers and bearers of meaning in poetry is as significant as women's literary production and, although it is arguably distinct from women's writing, in fact it provides the world of concepts and images into which women's poetry emerges. Accordingly, the stories poems tell of women is the subject of two chapters in Part III, by Ros Smith and Judith Hudson, who examine the shaping of femininity in the circulation of print material, approaching the question of women's relationship to the poem from the vantage point of the presence of women as subjects and objects in popular poetic forms. These chapters engage with a substantial tranche of material which, in being readily available to sixteenth- and seventeenth-century readers, shared and potentially spoken, is an important facet of the representation of women in poetic form. Such texts were a significant resource in which men and women can read and circulate the female voice and subject. Writing on the genre of female complaint, Smith notes that such popular poetic material invites reconsideration, particularly because it has been critically isolated from both complaint in elite texts and the use of complaint by women poets. Thus, reappraising the position of the material, Smith reframes the female complaint by turning to the specific example of the gallows confession to analyse the implications of 'popular complaint's rhetorical volatility'. The presence of the unmediated female voice in such verse emphasises the 'effect of authenticity' present in first-person lyric and particularly in complaint. As Smith argues, the ambiguous and persuasive nature of the female voice invites contextualisation in terms of the use of constructed, persuasive, proof in legal rhetoric, the understanding of the situation in terms of 'true crime', with the persuasive force of authenticity and the ambiguous status of female penitence. Her discussion clarifies that, while the voice of female complainant is not, obviously, necessarily or likely to be cognate with a 'real' woman, the reading context of such complaint instantiates an ambiguously persuasive, allowably self-justifying, 'heuristic possibility' in the female complaint which was, in certain instances, explicitly read as the authentic female voice. Thus, Smith's discussion emphasises the significance of female complaint like that of Mistris Saunders, or the sonnets attributed to Mary Queen of Scots, as offering speakers a chance to reinvent a world where values usually associated with female wickedness are rededicated as evidence of perverse virtue. Accordingly, the availability of such ballads and sonnets, their life in manuscript and in print, and the habit of reading aloud as well as circulation, makes them a resource that must be considered as circulating a volatile, poignant, first-person female poetic voice. Understood in this way, as she notes, the female complaint, whether written by men or by women, can be set alongside complaint literature by women including Isabella Whitney and Mary Wroth; and Lucy Hutchinson, too, copied ballad material into her commonplace book. As Smith argues, at least in the case of Mary Queen of Scots, this voice was, indeed, read by some as that of a woman writer; moreover, female exemplarity did not 'suddenly cease to bear complexity' when given to a female speaker.

The contemporary publications associated with the celebrated case of Anne Greene (1651) are the subject of Judith Hudson's chapter. Unfortunately made pregnant by her employer's grandson, Greene lost the baby and was hanged for its murder. Fortunately, she revived when taken down from the gallows and, her survival exonerating her, started a new life as a living paradox and medical marvel. As Hudson argues, the fact that all this took place in Oxford shaped the nature of the response in its attention to medical and philosophical problems and conundrums. And, as Hudson indicates, print as well as manuscript can delineate a readership and organise readers as a group – a process to which readers in the 1650s were particularly alert. As Hudson notes, Anne Greene came to be both a marvel and, through her extraordinary survival, a living critique of flawed justice. If, in Smith's essay, the female voice in poetry offers male and female readers heuristic identification, then the articulation of female crime and its reassessment in print culture also indicates the depth of possibilities, and the possibility of moral re-evaluation of female exemplary action in relatively popular poetic genres.

Finally, Sue Wiseman uses the example of a poem by Katherine Austen to explore the ways in which poetry can articulate land, labour and status and in doing so narrates a story of Restoration experience of property in which the estate poem is rewritten in terms related to the genres of prospect poetry and the idea of travel. Austen is understood as responding to some of the concerns explored in Part I, on inheritance, but also in Part II, on circulation (here, of ideas to tell a story of land), as well as to shifting poetic genres and a non-elite woman's relationship to literary circles from before and after the Civil War.

As this summary implies, the essays in this collection are detailed in their attention to the specifics of women and the poem. Many essays track exactly, or attempt to track, detailed relationships between poems and circumstances of production or exchange. In this, perhaps, they are products of a moment in critical understandings of early modern poetry and women when nuanced case studies allow us to begin to see women and poetry as, in different ways, strongly connected to the poetic, formal, social and political world in which their work was generated and read. Such precise connecting of women, poem and social and literary world is a crucial step towards the larger task of remapping the relations of early modern women, men and the poem, and this project underpins each essay. In the afterword, Patricia Pender and Rosalind Smith return to the question of this wider project of the continuing rethinking of the contributions of early modern women poets to literary cultures past and present.

Notes

1 J. Butt, ' Izaak Walton's collections for Fulman's life of John Hales', *Modern Language Review*, vol. 29, no. 3 (July 1934), pp. 267–73, at p. 271.

2 Ibid.

3 See Kate Lilley's illuminating discussion of the desires of scholars and the protocols of scholarship: K. Lilley, 'Fruits of Sodom: the critical erotics of early modern women's writing', *Parergon*, vol. 29, no. 2 (2012), pp. 175–92, at pp. 176–80.

4 V. Larminie, 'King, Anne [*married names* Anne Dutton; Anne Howe; Lady Howe], *Oxford Dictionary of National Biography*, online at http://www.oxforddnb.com/view/printable/68071 (accessed 9 August 2012).

5 See Patricia Pender, *Early Modern Women's Writing and the Rhetoric of Modesty*, Palgrave, Basingstoke, 2012.

6 G. Greer, S. Hastings, J. Medoff and M. Sansone (eds), *Kissing the Rod*, Virago, London, 1988.

7 M. J. Ezell, *Social Authorship and the Advent of Print*, Johns Hopkins University Press, Baltimore, 1999, pp. 1, 8, 9.

8 J. Stevenson, 'Women and the cultural politics of printing', *Seventeenth Century*, vol. 24, no. 2 (October 2009), pp. 205–237, at p. 208.

9 E. Eisenstein, *The Printing Press as an Agent of Change*, Cambridge University Press, Cambridge, 1980.

10 Ezell, *Social Authorship*, p. 11.

11 A. Marotti, 'Malleable and fixed texts: manuscript and printed miscellanies and the transmission of lyric poetry in the English Renaissance', in W. Speed Hill (ed.), *New Ways of Looking at Old Texts* (Papers of the English Renaissance Texts Society 1985–91), English Renaissance Texts Society, Amherst, 1993, pp. 159–173; M. J. Ezell, 'Domestic papers: manuscript culture and early modern women's life writing', in M. O. Dowd and J. Eckerle (eds), *Genre and Women's Life Writing in Early Modern England*, Ashgate, Farnham, 2007, pp. 33–48, at pp. 33–4.

12 G. L. Justice, 'Introduction', in G. L. Justice and N. Tinker (eds), *Women's Writing and the Circulation of Ideas: Manuscript Publication in England, 1550–1800*, Cambridge University Press, Cambridge, 2009, pp. 1–16, at pp. 5, 7.

13 Ezell, *Social Authorship*, p. 1; V. E. Burke and J. Gibson (eds), *Early Modern Women's Manuscript Writing*, Ashgate, Aldershot, 2004; J. S. Millman and G. Wright (eds), *Early Modern Women's Manuscript Poetry*, Manchester University Press, Manchester, 2005.

14 See 'Women writers in history: toward a new understanding of European literary culture' at www.costwwih.net (accessed July 2013).

15 A Smyth, *'Profit' and 'Delight': Printed Miscellanies in England, 1640–1682*, Wayne State University Press, Detroit, 2004, pp. xv–xxii.

16 J. Richards and F. Schurink, 'Introduction: the textuality and materiality of reading in early modern England', *Huntington Library Quarterly*, vol. 73, no. 3 (September 2010), pp. 345–361; William Sherman, *Used Books*, University of Pennsylvania Press, Philadelphia, 2007.

17 D. F. McKenzie, *Oral Culture, Literacy and Print in Early New Zealand: The Treaty of Waitangi*, Victoria University Press, Wellington, 1985.

18 M. Cohen, *The Networked Wilderness: Communication in Early New England*, University of Minnesota Press, Minneapolis, 2010, pp. 7, 17–18.

19 S. Dickie, *Cruelty and Laughter: Forgotten Comic Literature and the Unsentimental Eighteenth Century*, University of Chicago Press, Chicago, 2011.

20 P. Trolander and Z. Tenger, *Sociable Criticism in England, 1625–1725*, Rosemont, Cranbury, 2007.

Part I: Inheritance

Women's poetry and classical authors: Lucy Hutchinson and the classicisation of scripture

Edward Paleit

Introduction: the distant muses – early modern women poets and classical antiquity

EARLY modern women poets' search for cultural authority and poetic voice involved a vexed, sometimes contradictory relationship to literary models (as Sarah Ross and Line Cottegnies explore further in chapters 2 and 3). Classical poetry was especially awkward for women writers to accommodate and imitate, for a variety of social and cultural reasons. Greek and Roman literature – poetry, drama, oratory and historiography – was a central component of the education of high-status males in the early modern period. It was studied for an understanding of the Greek and Latin languages (grammar), and also to supply students with resources of discourse (rhetoric) and argument (dialectic). These skills could be put to use in the fields of employment open to educated men, whether administrative or diplomatic service or the professions of law, medicine and divinity. They could also, exceptionally, be perfected in a scholarly environment, facilitating enquiries into other areas of learning or elucidation of the texts themselves. But invariably they also served a social function, advertising gentility and membership of the ruling class. The writing of Latin or more rarely Greek poetry in the style of classical writers, a skill specifically taught and tested at grammar school and university, was an acknowledged means of performing educational attainment. Within this broad sociological context for the reception of ancient literatures, unsurprisingly much vernacular writing measured itself against classical models.[1]

Although women did not attend the great humanist institutions of grammar school and university, and were not expected to seek public employment, some clearly did receive what we now call a classical education. As well as princesses like Elizabeth Tudor, who were given a man's education to perform a man's role, a few English women, typically of high status, became accomplished readers and sometimes imitators of classical poetry.[2] Frequently these fortunate few were beneficiaries of a family tradition of educating daughters: the Mores and Sidneys, for example. It has also been suggested that in a marriage market peopled by humanistic-ally educated men, educated women had enhanced prospects.[3] Towards the end of the seventeenth century, arguments promoting the equal education of women began to appear alongside the development of girls' schools teaching some Greek and Latin; probably the two phenomena were related. However, even in the case of women who were, exceptionally, given access to classical literature, the ideological and social endorsement classical learning carried for men was still lacking.

Learned women poets, specifically, also faced other difficulties. When men surveyed classical literature, they instantly confronted a vast range of possible voices from which to draw *auctoritas* via imitation. Women did not. The names of several ancient women poets, to be sure, were well known. They were regularly rehearsed by pedagogues, from Juan Luis Vives onwards.[4] But with a few fragmentary exceptions, such as Sappho or 'Sulpicia', their actual writings did not survive. There were whole genres (epic, for example) in which there were no extant examples of ancient women's writing. The problem is encapsulated in Abraham Cowley's clever praise of Katherine Philips:

> Of Female Poets, who had names of old
>   Nothing is shewn, but only told,
> And all we hear of them, perhaps may be
> Male Flattery onely, and Male Poetry;
> [...]
> The certain proofs of our *Orinda's* Wit
> In her own lasting characters are writ,
> And they will long my praise of them survive,
>   Though long perhaps that too may live.[5]

Here, ancient literature's routine function as cultural legitimation and aesthetic standard is underlined yet, in the context of women's writing, ironised. Cowley's prophecy of immortality for Philips, given the mortal-ity of ancient women's writings and the possible mendacity of 'Male Flattery' such as his own, seems (at the very least) somewhat precarious.

Nonetheless, women writers who wished to enter the potentially com-promising spheres of print or manuscript publication often felt compelled to reach for whatever classical models were available to them, or have them imposed. A tradition of calling such 'published' women poets 'Sappho', which worked to restrict how they were perceived as well as what they could be expected to write, runs from the late sixteenth century through to the Restoration. Even later seventeenth-century female writers continued to filter engagements with classical literature through the prism of gender.

Aphra Behn's praise of Thomas Creech's translation of Lucretius, for example, conveys the distinct sense of treading on a male preserve; her renditions of Ovid's *Heroides*, another popular model for women's poetry, indicate similar constraints.[6] An equally good example is the posthumously published poetry of the writer and artist Anne Killigrew (1660–85), another 'Sappho'.[7] Killigrew also offers an imitation of the *Heroides*, but of greater interest is her unfinished epic on Alexander, which actually begins with a description of women Amazons. This promise of a feminised classical epic is not sustained, the editor declaring of the 'first essay of this young Lady in poetry' that 'finding the Task she had undertaken hard, she laid it by till Practice and more time should make her equal to so great a work'.[8] Thus, although by the Restoration increasing numbers of women read increasing amounts of classical literature, not least in translation, their ability to engage as male poets did with such works in their writings remained subject to obstacles and compromises.

The poetry of Lucy Hutchinson, née Apsley (1620–82), places this vexed relationship to the exemplary authority of mostly male classical authors in a particularly intriguing light. In some ways, Hutchinson is not representative of contemporary female poets: her pronounced Puritan political and religious prejudices, difficult to voice openly in the Restoration, ensured that the publication of her work was largely left until later centuries. Hutchinson was like other educated gentlewomen, however, in owing her learning to her parents' encouragement (and financial standing), and probably their wish to enhance her marital prospects.[9] That learning was considerable: according to Hutchinson herself, she was from an early age a gifted linguist and Latinist, easily outstripping her school-educated brothers.[10] She credits her husband's attraction to her to his chance discovery of her 'Latin books' (probably her commonplace or composition books) before he had even met her – only one of several anecdotes in her life writings to insinuate exceptional literary gifts.[11] Hutchinson's classicism is demonstrated by her verse translation of Lucretius's *De Rerum Natura*, the first complete example in English. It is also apparent in her commonplace book transcriptions, which included contemporary translations of Virgil by Denham and Godolphin. A fragmentary translation of book I of Ovid's *Metamorphoses* also survives.

The following discussion centres on Hutchinson's verse paraphrase on Genesis, composed in the 1660s to 1670s, although ascribed to her only in the late twentieth century.[12] It exists in two versions, a manuscript narrative of twenty cantos, stretching to Genesis 31:25 and apparently unfinished (and untitled), and a printed version of the first five cantos, published anonymously in 1679 under the title *Order and Disorder, or The World Made and Undone: Being Meditations Upon the Creation and*

Fall, as it is recorded in the beginning of Genesis. While the first five cantos do not differ hugely between versions, the printed text can be taken as a coherent work in its own right, a 'hexameral' epic on the Creation and Fall.[13] The manuscript, contrastingly, is neither obviously hexameral (it goes far beyond 'the beginning' of Genesis) nor indisputably epic; nor, strictly speaking, can it be termed *Order and Disorder*. Although neither version explicitly acknowledges female authorship, Hutchinson's moving discussion of the 'golden fetters' of matrimony – probably an intended classical reminiscence – and the punishing labours of childbirth strongly hints that the work is a woman's.[14] The decision to publish (part of) it remains curious: elsewhere, writing for her daughter, Hutchinson claimed 'I write not for the presse, to boast my owne weaknesses to the world'.[15] More research is still needed into its likely occasion and circulation: as Jane Stevenson points out, 'publication', when it comes to early modern women's writing, can mean many different things.[16]

Critical discussion often relates Hutchinson's Genesis work to her Lucretius translation, either identifying traces of quasi-Epicurean materialism in her theology, or stressing her affiliation to Lucretius's sublime poetics. A rather different argument is that it exemplifies Hutchinson's Puritan scripturalism.[17] While acknowledging there are links to the *De Rerum Natura*, I shall argue that Hutchinson does not use Lucretius differently or in a more privileged way than other classical authors. I will also contend that, despite its scripturalist assertions and recent attempts to see her as a neo-Epicurean, Hutchinson's work is that of an identifiably humanist poet, sharing literary techniques and a general concern for performed erudition with elite poetic approaches to scripture from the late sixteenth century onwards. After working through a number of examples, I conclude by arguing that the tension in her text between Calvinistic theology and a classicising poetics expresses also aspects of Hutchinson's situation as a woman writer.

Ovidian creation and Ovidian pathos: Hutchinson, Genesis and the *Metamorphoses*

In the 'Preface' to the published, five-canto *Order and Disorder*, the anonymous author we know to be Hutchinson explains the work as a reassertion of scripturalism ('I disclaim all doctrines of God and his works, but what I learnt out of his own word') against 'the account some old poets and philosophers give of the original of things', to which she had been attracted by 'youthful curiosity', and indeed sought to translate, but now vehemently rejects as 'blasphemously against God, and brutishly below

24

the reason of man', as 'vain, foolish, atheistical poesy'.[18] Critics interpret these words as disavowing Hutchinson's earlier translation of Lucretius, not least because they parallel her abusive discussion of the *De Rerum Natura* in dedicating her translation to the Marquis of Anglesey.[19] Her use of the word 'some' in the passage quoted above, however, indicates more than one pagan authority, while the attack on pagan creation mythology in general aligns Hutchinson's published text with reassertions of scripture's authority in the early Restoration by Anglicans such as Edward Stillingfleet or Calvinistic writers like John Owen, particularly against the claims of Cambridge Platonists that ancient (and especially Platonic or Pythagorean) philosophy could be used to unlock the 'mysteries' of the Bible.[20] The polemical suspicion of ancient philosophy and poetry expressed in the 'Preface' strongly parallels the eighth chapter of Owen's *Theologoumena Pandotapa* (1661), part of which Hutchinson translated as 'On theology', which treats pagan myths as a corrupted, potentially Satanic 'tradition' disfiguring divine truth, equating 'poetry' with suspect fabulation.[21] Hutchinson appears to imitate contemporary refutations of Platonist approaches to scripture within her Genesis text itself: 'lets waive Platonic dreams / Of worlds made in Idea, fitter themes for poets' fancies', she instructs, preferring 'what is true and only certain, kept upon record, / In the Creator's own revealèd Word'.[22]

Hutchinson's 'Preface' thus positions *Order and Disorder* principally as a contribution to contemporary debates over how to interpret scripture; any implicit critique of other poets, such as Milton, is only one aspect of this (and, as I shall show, Hutchinson's practice is closer to Milton's than some allow).[23] It is debatable what practical limits her assertions placed on her Bible reading. Asserting the primacy of God's word is one thing; determining what it actually means, another. Like other learned Protestants of their class, Hutchinson and her husband clearly consulted a wide array of sources, scholarly and otherwise, in pursuit of accurate scriptural interpretation. Their reading went beyond orthodox Calvinist commentaries, such as the *Annotations* produced by the Westminster assembly or Haak's *Dutch Annotations* (a summa of the doctrines confirmed at the 1619 Synod of Dort), which her husband requested on his deathbed.[24] In 1645–46, when Hutchinson was pregnant, the couple read widely in and were persuaded by contemporary polemics against paedo-baptism, 'which at that time came thick off the presses', including the works of Henry Denne and John Tombes (whom she champions unambiguously for having 'excellently overthrown' their opponents): an unorthodox stance which earned them the hatred, she recorded, of many Presbyterians.[25] This scholarly approach to interpretation of scripture can be detected in her Genesis narrative, as I show below.

Yet it is also evident (and more startling) that to make sense of the Bible Hutchinson turned to classical authors. Before the creation of the world, for example, she writes that 'the Earth at first was a vast empty place, / A rude congestion without form or grace, / A confused mass of undistinguished seed'; a marginalium describes 'Earth's Chaos'.[26] Such phraseology intersperses a brief biblical text ('And the earth was without form and void', Genesis 1:2) with the beginning of Ovid's *Metamorphoses* (1:7–9), which discusses the time before sea, earth and sky, when there was 'one face of nature throughout the whole world, which men have called Chaos':

> rudis indigestaque moles
> nec quicquam nisi pondus iners congestaque eodem
> non bene iunctarum discordia semina rerum.

> A rude and undigested mass, nor anything save a lifeless weight, and in like fashion congested and discordant seeds of not well connected matter.

Hutchinson's systematic echoes of Ovid ('rude', *rudis*; 'confused mass', *indigestaque moles*; 'congestion', *congesta*; 'undistinguished seed', *discordia semina*; 'Chaos', *chaos*) would have been instantly recognisable to learned contemporaries. In context, they offer a conceptually satisfactory and poetically vivid redescription of the 'earth' mentioned in Genesis (1:2). The latter is an obscurity: contemporary annotators were obliged to distinguish it from the 'earth' which God creates during the third day (Genesis 1:10) and refute the possible inference that it pre-existed God.[27] The phrase 'Earth's Chaos' seemingly attempts to hybridise scriptural and Ovidian concepts, potentially cutting through such difficulties.

Hutchinson's *impulse* to scriptural explication is unlikely to have troubled any biblicist contemporaries. But in turning to Ovid of all writers to satisfy it, her poetics seems out of line with contemporary reassertions of the primacy of scripture, and more like older (typically sixteenth-century) humanistic attempts to reconcile classical and biblical creation myths. Seventeenth-century discussions of the creation myth in the *Metamorphoses*, noting its selective similarity to the Bible's, connected it to the doctrines of Plato and earlier, Pythagorean cosmogony; they also tended to believe that scripture itself was, directly or indirectly, one of Ovid's sources. But while this might appeal to a neo-Platonist believing in a *prisca theologia* alongside the Bible – the position hinted at in George Sandys's translation of the *Metamorphoses* (1632) – the more orthodox Christian viewpoint, visible for example in a 'grammaticall' translation of the poem for schoolboys published in 1656, was that the relation-ship exposed Ovid's as an inferior, garbled and 'poetic' (and therefore untrustworthy) version of the scriptural truth.[28] This was certainly the view of John Owen, who, in a passage Hutchinson translated, claimed Ovid's was a schoolboy example of the corruptions to divine doctrine wrought by pagan philosophy and poetry.[29]

Hutchinson's use of Ovid to embroider the Bible is curious and problematic in this context; it also disabuses recent interpretations of her cosmogony as dependent ultimately on Lucretius.[30] But in terms of humanist poetic theory – particularly as practised some generations previously – it would have been less controversial. Earlier humanist poetics, following the doctrines of Horace's *Ars Poetica*, was extremely comfortable with 'mixing the false with the true', accommodating fables to sweeten and enrich didactic precept. Humanist rhetoricians advised similar fabular embroideries to improve persuasiveness.[31] The humanistic doctrine of verisimilitude had helped sixteenth-century poets to reconcile Ovid and scripture. Arthur Golding's dedicatory epistle in his 1567 translation of the *Metamorphoses*, for example, claims that:

> Not only in effect he [Ovid] doth with Genesis agree,
> But also in the order of creation
> … for what is else at all
> That shapeless, rude, and pestred heape which Chaos he doth call,
> Then euen that universall masse of things which God did make[?][32]

The account of pre-creation substance in Joshua Sylvester's translation of the *Deuine Weekes and Workes* of Guillaume Salluste, Sieur Du Bartas, also echoes Ovid's phraseology, although in a much more diffuse way than Hutchinson (whose appropriation is clearly direct, even if cognisant of Sylvester's translation).[33] Alistair Fowler notes both these earlier texts as legitimating John Milton's account of 'Chaos' in *Paradise Lost*, which also paraphrases Ovid's creation myth: 'even the most orthodox Reformers managed to reconcile the Platonic and Ovidian Chaos' with the Bible, Fowler claims.[34] This may well be true of sixteenth-century Reformist poetics, which Milton (who was suspicious of rigorous scripturalism, and not a Calvinist) may have been attempting to revive. Yet, by the mid to later seventeenth century, a changing intellectual and theological context made such reconciliations far more controversial. John Owen's repeated attacks on ancient poets and philosophers suggest that, for Calvinistic interpreters responding to neo-Platonist assaults on *sola scriptura*, being verisimilar was no longer enough. Hutchinson's frequent polemics against 'vain, foolish, atheistical poesy' leave little doubt that she agreed with him – officially. Her poetic *practice*, however, evidently has more in common with the elite Protestant verisimilar classicisations of scripture represented by Du

Bartas and Milton, and expressed by Golding, than with the Calvinistic scripturalism she appears to endorse.

A later allusion to the *Metamorphoses* further illuminates a tension between Hutchinson's humanist poetics and scripturalist theology. The occasion is the transformation of Lot's wife for looking back on the destruction of Sodom, given a single verse in the Bible (Genesis 19:26). Hutchinson significantly expands:

> While she with tears the glittering spires beheld,
> A sudden horror all her blood congealed.
> Her lips and cheeks their lively colours lost;
> Her members hardened with death's chilling frost;
> Her hands grew stiff, her feet stuck to the ground;
> Striving to cry, her voice no passage found.
> She would have turned her looks away from thence,
> But, to inform us what was her offence,
> Her neck stiff as the other parts was grown,
> Her disobedience in her posture shown
> Thus she, a lasting statue of hard salt,
> Became the monument of her own fault,
> And God's just punishment of that fond love
> Which she from that lewd place could not remove.
> Well suited, therefore, was her severe doom,
> There to remain her own long-lasting tomb,
> Which underneath Engaddis' high hill placed,
> For many ages suffered not time's waste,
> But for example to her sex remained,
> Teaching how curious minds should be restrained
> And kept within the Lord's prescribed bound,
> Which none e'er passed but swift destruction found.[35]

In the first nine lines Hutchinson, unlike the Bible, presents an image of *gradual* transformation, giving full weight to its miraculousness and the subject's painful experience of dwindling humanity. The technique is clearly Ovidian, and indeed her model is the petrification of Niobe (*Metamorphoses* 6:301–12), as is indicated by her use of the word 'congealed' (cf. *Metamorphoses* 6:307, *congelat*), by the details of her stiffening neck (*nec flecti cervix*, says Ovid, 6:308), the loss of colour from her face (cf. 6:304), her inability to speak (cf. 6:306) and, finally, the sequence from immobilised upper-body limbs to motionless feet (6:308–9). Niobe's story is of contempt for the gods causing her children to be annihilated by plague in punishment, paralleling Sodom's destruction. Renaissance commentary moralised her fate as punishment for the sacrilegious pride attendant on great wealth and power.[36] Like Lot's wife in Hutchinson's account, Niobe's frozen posture is preserved as an emblem of her transgression and transported to a mountain in her homeland (6:311–12).[37]

As Robert Wilcher demonstrates, working up a Bible story into a didactic emblem is part of Hutchinson's technique.[38] Nor is it theologically contentious in itself. But this passage does indicate that it is to classical texts as much as to theological ones that Hutchinson turned to craft such emblems. In this respect she was continuing an elite cultural tradition. As with Hutchinson's account of pre-creation matter, her use of Niobe as a model for Lot's wife is anticipated in (and must to some extent derive from) Sylvester's translation of Du Bartas.[39] The Du Bartas/Sylvester version uses several details from the Niobe myth, some later picked up by Hutchinson. Its 'The windes no more can wave her scattered hair', for example, renders Ovid's 'nullos movet aura capillos', while 'In her cold throat her guilty words congeal' paraphrases Ovid's 'ipsa quoque interius cum duro lingua palato / congelat'.[40] The Ovidian approach is explicitly signalled to the reader by describing it in the margin as 'Lot's wife *Metamorphoz'd*'; the last word is repeated in the translation itself (pp. 417, 418). Finally, Du Bartas/Sylvester anticipates Hutchinson in inferring from the episode a 'lesson' to 'Curious Spirits ... not to presume in Divine things to pry'; the orthodox interpretation was that she signified a 'caveat against Apostasie in the least degree'.[41]

As suggested above, Hutchinson is not copying Sylvester, however; her engagement with Ovid is linguistically direct and stylistically differentiated. Sylvester's version is prolix: the Lot's wife episode takes thirty-six lines, includes several distracting similes without Ovidian basis, such as a snared bird, and adds a coda translating the enigmatic verses often associated with Niobe, ascribed in the Renaissance to Ausonius.[42] Hutchinson's account has a rhetorical control and intertextual focus quite different from such abundance. Furthermore, while both draw on Ovid, it is only Hutchinson who seemingly registers his characteristic empathy for divine victims. In the *Metamorphoses*, Niobe's petrified body 'weeps nonetheless' (*flet tamen*) for her dead children, and her statue retains 'tears', *lacrimas* (6:310, 312). Although, in Sylvester, Lot's wife 'weeps and wails' and 'grieves' at losing her relatives – and perhaps more significantly her 'Iewels and habiliments' – the reader is not invited to share her tantrum.[43] The 'tears' Lot's wife sheds in Hutchinson, later attributed to her 'fond love' for the destroyed, are more plausibly moving. Such Ovidian empathy for Lot's wife may have something to do with a shared gender. Yet it reinforces rather than subverts Hutchinson's stern didactic message: compassion for the reprobate is a dangerous, particularly feminine, weakness.[44]

Significantly, Hutchinson's narrative accommodation of an Ovidian metamorphosis is licensed less by the authority of Sylvester's example than her knowledge of learned biblical commentary, itself drawing on extra-scriptural knowledge and speculation, and exemplified in her phrase 'a lasting statue of hard salt'. The term 'lasting' gestures to claims by ancient writers such as Josephus (*Antiquities* 1:2) to have actually seen Lot's petrified wife, while 'hard' refers to debates about the precise substance, clearly no ordinary salt, that could endure so long uneroded. The mineral resources of the Sodom region were typically brought in here: the *Annotations* of the Westminster assembly (besides citing Josephus) refer to the Elder Pliny's discussion of the Red Sea area.[45] Hutchinson's choice of the word 'statue' is also revealing. The Dutch and Westminster *Annotations* talk of a 'pillar', like the Geneva and authorised English translations. But the original Greek, *stele*, had different possible interpretations; Hutchinson's lexical choice is actually closest to the Vulgate's *statuam*. It is this choice which accommodates her Ovidian description of a human being finding her limbs turning to stone – becoming, that is, a statue rather than a pillar.

Hutchinson is not the only contemporary English poet to use such scholarly knowledge to perform a classicising paraphrase of Lot's wife's transformation. In fact, all the textual debates and scholarly material explaining her treatment can be found in Cowley's prose commentary to book III of his *Davideis* (first published 1656), where an ecphrasis of the Lot's wife episode, while not modelled on Niobe, also boasts an Ovidian touch.[46] It has recently been claimed that Cowley's playful, scholarly, erudite approach to the Bible is fundamentally opposed to Hutchinson's adherence to scripture as its own best interpreter.[47] It is true that Cowley reorders and transforms the biblical narrative much more obviously than Hutchinson. His prose commentary is a clearer exhibition of the learned seventeenth-century biblicism described in Killeen's recent study.[48] Hutchinson's text has no commentary, and her marginalia refer only to other parts of scripture. Her political and doctrinal differences from Cowley go without saying. But it is misleading to exaggerate such differences. To a learned contemporary (such as Cowley himself) Hutchinson's biblicist erudition and classicising approach would have been readily visible. Indeed, her Genesis text probably aims to *display* such qualities, advertising membership of an elite, Christian humanist tradition of poetically embroidering scripture with classical and scholarly reading.

Hutchinson, Virgil and the Carthaginian Babel bees

HUTCHINSON'S appropriations from the *Metamorphoses* – there are others in her Genesis narrative, besides the ones already discussed[49] – show her using classical literature to inform explicatory and emblematic expansions of scripture. What they less readily demonstrate is the large-scale imaginative compatibility of Hutchinson's world-view and that of some classical authors. In the tenth canto, for example, she compares the Tower of Babel's construction to the activities of bees:

> With these vain hopes the sons of men grew bold,
> And set upon the work: some carried mould,
> Some levelled ground, some the foundation laid,
> Some framed the doors and some the pillars made,
> Some burned the clamps and some prepared the bricks,
> Others with sand and slime the mortar mix.
> So when the bees a colony send out
> The new swarms soon disperse themselves about
> And several labours busy every one:
> Some search for honey, some expel the drone,
> Some suck the flowers, some carry their loads home,
> Some take what they bring in, some work the comb:
> All various toils with diligence intend,
> Yet in one public work their labours spend.
> So did these builders, who with blasphemies
> Extolled the pile which now began to rise.[50]

In familiar fashion, this passage intersperses details from a sparse biblical text (Genesis 11:3) with Virgil's description of the building of Carthage in the *Aeneid* (1:423–38), which also includes a bee simile.[51] The allusion's significance is enhanced by understanding its context. In the *Aeneid*, the city whose walls rise (*moenia surgunt*) belong to the bitterest and deadliest future foe of the Rome whose own 'lofty walls' (*alta moenia Romae*; *Aeneid* 1:7) are the poem's opening topic. Aeneas later discovers that his admiration for the Carthaginians – he even proceeds to help in the construction – simply delays his divinely commanded role to found the Roman race. His subsequent departure from Carthage and its grief-stricken queen Dido ignites the centuries-long, world-historical struggle between Carthage and Rome.

Hutchinson's allusion is topically appropriate. Her bee-like Babel builders (who copy Aeneas by glorying in the building works) also labour in the divine cause against divine will. Their Tower symbolises impiety and pride, which God punishes by destroying it and dispersing them. But the allusion is also enabled and intensified by a structural similarity between her world-view and that espoused in the Carthaginian books of the *Aeneid*. When, earlier on, she distils world history into an endless battle between light and darkness, she reaches precisely for a motif of two growing, rivalrous *cities*:

> Two empires here, *two opposite cities rise*,
> Dividing all into two societies:
> The little Church and the World's larger State,
> Pursuing it with ceaseless spite and hate.[52]

31

Hutchinson's vision of good and evil as opposed cities is of course principally Augustinian, not Virgilian. Theologically, ancient Rome was on the wrong side. But the *imaginative* identity with Virgil's foundation myth is clear to see. It was usual for seventeenth-century Puritans to see the elect in terms of Old Testament Israel. For the learned Hutchinson, however, the embattled but eventually triumphant 'little Church' is also, imaginatively, comparable to Virgil's threatened band of exiled Trojans, engaged in the difficult but divinely ordained task of founding Rome. Babel is, poetically, another Carthage, threatening to displace and rival the true city of God Christians are enjoined to build.

In the process of appropriating Virgil, Hutchinson is obliged, silently, to dispense with some awkward details of his original account. Babel, which Calvinist commentaries identified unambiguously with Babylon, is in her text the seat of Nimrod, and a symbol of tyrannical monarchy.[53] In Virgil's *Aeneid*, contrastingly, as well as building 'walls' (*muros*), 'foundations' (*fundamenta*) and 'pillars' (*columnas*) – details Hutchinson imitates – the Carthaginians also 'choose laws, magistracies and a sacred Senate'.[54] Carthage is thus identifiably a *res publica*, even if ruled by a queen. Indeed, as Renaissance commentaries on the passage make clear, Virgil's simile is itself an allusion, to his description of bees in the *Georgics* (4:8–314) in terms heavily recalling Roman society and political institutions. To seventeenth-century English interpreters, the *Georgics* bees, which live in an ordered political community under laws and value the common good, transparently constituted a *res publica* –'bees only live in common-wealths' as Thomas May put it in his 1628 translation.[55] They have kings (*reges*) – two of them – but elected ones.[56] This is not true of Hutchinson's Babel bees. They may unite in a 'public work', but they make no laws, magistracies or a senate, and the nature of their political constitution is not described. To identify Babel with monarchical tyranny, the 'commonwealth' associations of Virgil's bees, in both the *Aeneid* and the *Georgics*, are entirely effaced.[57]

Imaginative identification with her classical sources for Hutchinson, then, entailed transforming and sometimes amputating their political or philosophical content. This is also true of how she employs Lucretius. As scholars have often remarked, there are moments when Lucretian language, including references to atoms, can be found in Hutchinson's text.[58] There are also contiguities of voice and polemical stance (e.g. against superstition) between Hutchinson's Puritanism and the evangelical Epicurean.[59] Recently, however, Jonathan Goldberg and Alvin Snider have argued a more extreme case, attempting to locate in Hutchinson's Genesis narrative traces of an incompletely expurgated neo-Epicurean materialism.[60] Examining Hutchinson's actual practice suggests her use of Lucretius cannot really be differentiated from the way she reads and employs Ovid and Virgil: it has a poetic and rhetorical rather than a strictly philosophical rationale. In canto 19 of her manuscript text, for example, she takes the opportunity provided by Jacob's dream on the way to Haran of the ladder let down from heaven (Genesis 28:10–17) to launch a meditation of sixty-five lines contrasting the troubled dreams of the worldly, stirred up by the 'nimble Fancy', with the refreshing ones of the innocent, often homeless poor.[61] As Snider remarks, Hutchinson's catalogue of active dreams is drawn partly from a similar list in Lucretius.[62] Yet whereas the Roman poet is arguing that dreams derive from material impressions, and lack moral or metaphysical significance, Hutchinson is making the opposite case, following a didactic interpretation of contrasting dreams which Lucretius was endeavouring to challenge. She goes on to insist that God and sometimes Satan communicate through dreams, and entirely drops the materialist reduction underpinning Lucretius's dream discussion.[63]

Her satirical redeployment of Lucretius, moreover, is contained within a moralised rhetorical framework borrowed not from the *De Rerum Natura*, but Virgil. The passage's opening salute to those, like Jacob, deprived of shelter but blessed by calming dreams, 'O how are mean men, if they know it, blessed!' (19:9), alludes clearly to Virgil's 'O fortunatos nimium, si sua bona norint/agricolas!' (*Georgics* 2:457), which begins a long passage contrasting virtuous rural husbandry with the corrupt, typically urban pursuit of wealth and power, the latter also summarised with a satirical list (4:460–5). Hutchinson's allusion, however, here engages ironically with Virgil. As originally outlined in Maren-Sofie Røstvig's classic study, the *Georgics* passage, together with other classical poems like Horace's *beatus ille* epode (2:1), as well as the work of English poets such as Ben Jonson, was a constitutive element of a tradition of English writing in praise of the 'happy life' of rural retirement, free from the moral contaminations of public involvement.[64] Hutchinson was demonstrably aware of this tradition's conventions. A solitary poem, now often published after her *Memoirs* of her husband, and containing echoes of Jonson, Horace and Seneca, celebrates the liberty obtained by abstaining, in rural seclusion, from the pursuit of power, riches and pleasure.[65] This poem's emphasis on liberty, defined as freedom from want and disturbing appetite, is congruent with a number of mid-century writings on the 'happy life', notably Abraham Cowley's essays 'On liberty' and 'On agriculture', published in 1669. Ultimately, it celebrates the sovereign lordship of an estate-owning husbandman: 'What court can then such liberty afford', it concludes, 'Or where is man so uncontrolled a lord [i.e. as in the country]?'[66] As David Norbrook argues, certain lines in this poem praising untroubled sleep and mentioning also the 'active fancy' offer clear parallels with Hutchinson's

Genesis passage on dreams.[67] Yet the latter rejects the former's celebration of autonomous rural husbandry. Its list of those whose sleep is disturbed by dreams of their waking actions includes ploughmen, labourers, slaves and, finally, in what appears deliberately to echo Horace's *beatus ille* epode, tree-planters and vintners.[68] In rejecting either gentlemanly estate ownership or honest rural labour as the best route to dreamless nights, Hutchinson challenges the notion at the heart of much 'happy man' writing, including her own earlier poem. There, the 'rude multitude' are explicitly banned from the rural idyll: 'the vulgar breath doth not his [the happy husbandman's] thoughts elate, / Nor can he be o'erwhelmed by their hate'. But in Hutchinson's Genesis meditation, the truly blessed are precisely 'mean men' or 'the poor man', who lack even a home: even if, as Susan Wiseman contends, the earlier poem Christianises the classical 'happy man' ideal up to a point, Hutchinson's later work inverts its apparent social perspective.[69]

Such a dialectical, piously Christian confrontation with classical praises of a country life was not alone in seventeenth-century England. One finds it also, for example, in John Ashmore's 1621 translation of Horace, which presents Christian teachings on the blessed life, and especially the first psalm, beginning *beatus vir* and advocating the spiritual seclusion of the righteous, as preferential to the rural seclusion recommended by the *beatus ille* tradition.[70] Hutchinson's classicism is not therefore simply or always a performance of erudition. She sometimes alludes to authors to make points against them, or their contemporary reception, even if she shared imaginative congruities with their thought on other matters. But she does not do this consistently, taking up a *sustained* polemical position for or against a particular author. Indeed, the multiple intertextuality of such passages (which in this instance contains likely reminiscences also of Shakespeare) makes it difficult to argue for her affiliation to a single poetic figure, whether ancient or modern.[71] Hutchinson's political and religious views have induced certain scholars, notably Norbrook, to claim just such an affiliation: her Genesis text is presumed to possess a poetics that is 'consciously and polemically anti-Augustan', inviting her work to be read entirely and exclusively in relation to Latin poets like Lucretius or Lucan; allusions to Virgil or other Augustan writers are presumed to be confrontational.[72] Such aggressive demarcation of the seventeenth-century reception of Latin literature on grounds of political ideology finds only selective empirical support in the practice of seventeenth-century poets. Hutchinson, in common with Milton, certainly betrays an imaginative attraction to Lucretius. Both writers are also, however, imaginatively attracted to Virgil, Ovid and Horace, as an objective analysis of their habits of allusion amply reveals – indeed, often in the same passages of their texts.

Conclusion: Hutchinson, women's writing and the classics

THE above analysis suggests that, for learned contemporary readers, Hutchinson's work would appear strained between a theology rigorously adhering to God's word, and a poetics employing classical and indeed vernacular literary resources to explain and embroider it. The latter feature of her text, this chapter has suggested, is best explained by placing Hutchinson in a tradition of elite Christian humanist poetics, of the sort to which belonged contemporaries like John Milton and Abraham Cowley, or predecessors like Joshua Sylvester and Du Bartas. Indeed, it is somewhat easier to read Hutchinson's Genesis text as the work of a good humanist than of a good Calvinist, not only because her text in places seeks to display as well as use her classical erudition, but also because it is easier to allege a consistency of poetic technique for her writings than one of philosophical belief.

There may be methodological implications in this. Much recent analysis of early modern writings, particularly in the context of politics and religion, presumes the centrality of belief or doctrine and, having identified the nature of that belief, pieces together a coherent ideological world-view around it. Such an approach demands that we find ways of accommodating Hutchinson's classicism within the Calvinistic scripturalism presumed to be central to her outlook. It is certainly worth pointing out that, even in the prose works of committed scripturalists, rejection of classical doctrine did not rule out the rhetorical deployment of classical erudition. In *Theologoumena Pandotapa*, for example, John Owen frequently embellishes his own argumentation with polished citations of classical poetry, while considering the latter worthless (or worse) on theological grounds. The technique reflects and aims to display a rigorous humanist training, the mark of a gentleman commanding the right to be heard by other gentlemen.[73] At the same time, however, there are elements of double-think, of two not quite compatible strategies for truth-telling, within such a discourse. Understanding rigorous scripturalism and/or the rejection of classical culture as also a means of performing identity, particularly for dissenting writers, adds an extra layer of complexity to interpretation. A rejection of antiquity as youthful error, as Hutchinson performs in her 'Preface', had Augustine's ancient precedent. Christ's similar attack on classical culture in Milton's *Paradise Regained* shows that other contemporary poets also felt obliged to announce their conformity to an Augustinian template of Christian conversion/adulthood. One might nonetheless feel that even with Augustine, and certainly with Milton, much that was openly disavowed survives in the shape of linguistic and imaginative patterns. A hermeneutics making use of notions such as an 'unconscious' – recognising its status as only a heuristic device – might succeed better than a rationalistic commitment to the coherence of stated doctrines in explaining why Christian humanist writers rejected the classical inheritance which palpably and continuously shaped how they thought, imagined and wrote.

With such thoughts in mind, let us examine the problems of Hutchinson's classicising poetics in relation to her gender. In some ways, her claims of rigorous scriptural fidelity adhere to the 'author function' described by Hilary Hinds in relation to female prophets of the Revolutionary period: feminine weakness precisely occasions loquacity, on the basis that God is the true speaker.[74] Hutchinson's work contains similar effacements of her own authority before God's. In the 'Preface' to *Order and Disorder*, for example, she declares that her language is 'much too narrow to express the least of those wonders my soul hath been *ravished with* in the contemplation of God and his works', and immediately disavows her imagination: 'Had I had a fancy, I durst not have exercised it here; for I tremble to think of turning Scripture into a *romance*'.[75] Invoking English Protestant antipathies to romance for its racy subject matter and popish use of the supernatural, Hutchinson here denies actively mediating divine truth through imaginative composition, emphasising simply her reception of God's works. Significantly, she elaborates the same viewpoint in her celebration of God's creation of clouds in canto 2 of her Genesis narrative. Here, in familiar fashion, she develops a brief biblical text (Genesis 1:7) first by invoking cloud imagery from Psalms and Job, and then moving outside scripture to discuss:

> Those clouds which over all the wondrous arch
> Like hosts of various-formèd creatures march,
> And change the scenes in our admiring eyes;
> Who sometimes see them like vast mountains rise,
> Sometimes like pleasant seas with clear waves glide,
> Sometimes like ships on foaming billows ride;
> Sometimes like mounted warriors they advance,
> And seem to fire the smoking ordinance;
> Sometimes like shady forests they appear,
> Here monsters walking, castles rising there.
> Scorn, princes, your embroidered canopies
> And painted roofs: the poor whom you despise
> With far more ravishing delight are fed,
> While various clouds sail o'er th'unhousèd head,
> And their heaved eyes with nobler scenes present,
> Than your poetic courtiers can invent.[76]

Hutchinson again privileges receiving God's nature over imaginary artifice or invention, here attributing the latter to the deceiving surfaces of courtly aesthetics (and especially drama or the masque), which intervene between the viewer and divine truth. As in the 'Preface', a language of aesthetic rapture, 'ravishing delight', replaces authorship with reception, writing with reading. The argument presumes a particular understanding of visual perception: it is represented as ocular and passive, rather than active and mental. Cloud resemblances 'change the scenes in our admiring eyes', as if eyes are a sort of screen. Thus God's works can be perceived directly, without the need for mediation or interpretative reconstruction. In constructing this idea, Hutchinson almost certainly has in mind *De Rerum Natura*'s discussion of visual perception as a series of material impressions striking the eye, or, when the viewer is asleep, passing through the body to the mind, mechanically and involuntarily. Lucretius calls these impressions 'resemblances', *simulacra*, of the perceived object, and instances the striking likenesses formed by clouds, which, as Hutchinson translates, 'rise of themselves' (that is, without receptive agency) and lead us to 'behold figures of giants there, … mountains, and craggie rocks … another train of ayre-borne monsters'.[77]

While indebted to Lucretius, Hutchinson's employment of him here is, characteristically, transformative. She once again removes the atomistic underpinning of his argument. Despite an ostensible interest in the visual, her passage is really all about words and the way that, through poetry, they become images of 'ravishing delight'. Lucretius's visual *simulacra* become delightful *verbal* similitudes. And these, revealingly, turn out to accommodate all the suspect romance content supposedly banished by Hutchinson's disavowal of personal, imaginative authorship: castles, forests, monsters, ships in storms, battles all reappear in cloud formations. God, in fact, turns out to be the *ultimate* romance poet, giving to the unhoused poor the same kind of material found in court masques or comedies, only as nebular similitudes. The fact that God's comparisons are aesthetically superior does not eliminate the identity of content. Hutchinson gets away with reintroducing such anomalous 'romance' material into a poem on the Old Testament precisely because her neo-Lucretian idea of perception prevents such similitudes having any other origin but their Maker.

The theological manoeuvre is also indicative of Hutchinson's poetics. The divinely authorised trope of *similitudo*, together with the stress on the ravished reception of God's works against fancy-driven 'poetic' constructions, seems to be the way Hutchinson legitimates expanding her biblical narrative with precisely the sort of secular reading, be it in the classics or romances, she openly eschews. For of course a similitude is not a substitution; it preserves traces of the original. Untypically among contemporary women writers, Hutchinson's relationship with the classics is not explicitly filtered through gender. But this is partly because, through her manipulation of notions of authorship, she does not acknowledge that she is a poet in the creative sense at all. It is revealing and symptomatic that the displacement of her own poetic abilities onto God, occurring within one of the most vividly poetic passages of her text, betrays an imaginative dependence precisely on one of those classical writers whose 'vain, foolish, atheistical poesy' she publicly disclaims. Exactly when God is named the supreme and only poet, an attentive reader might detect a 'classical unconscious', so to speak, suggesting otherwise. In Hutchinson's text, such doubleness signifies and is constitutive of the paradoxes both of early modern female authorship and classicising bibliolatry.

Notes

1 For general accounts of humanist education, see P. Mack, *Elizabethan Rhetoric*, Cambridge University Press, Cambridge, 2002, pp. 11–75; Q. Skinner, *Reason and Rhetoric in the Philosophy of Hobbes*, Cambridge University Press, Cambridge, 1996, pp. 19–65; L. Jardine and A. Grafton, *From Humanism to the Humanities*, Harvard University Press, Cambridge, 1987.

2 J. Stevenson, *Women Latin Poets*, Oxford University Press, Oxford, 2005, chs 10 and 14.

3 Ibid., pp. 368–9.

4 J. L. Vives, *The Instruction of a Christen Woman*, trans. R. Hyrd, London, 1529, sigs D.iiir–D.iiiir.

5 A. Cowley, 'On the Death of Mrs *Katherine Philips*', in K. Philips, *Poems*, London, 1669, sig. c2v.

6 A. Behn, 'To the unknown *Daphnis* on his excellent translation of Lucretius', in T. Creech (trans.), *Titus Lucretius Carus the Epicurean Philosopher*, Oxford, 1683, sigs d2r–e3r.

7 *Poems, by Mrs Anne Killigrew*, London, 1686. John Dryden's dedicatory ode (sig. a2v) declares her a 'Sappho' by metempsychosis.

8 Ibid., pp. 81–2 ('Penelope to Ulysses'), 1–5 ('Alexandreis'), 5 (editorial comment).

9 As she hints herself: L. Hutchinson, 'The life of Mrs Lucy Hutchinson, written by herself: a fragment', in J. Hutchinson (ed.), *Memoirs of Colonel Hutchinson*, reprinted by George Bell & Sons, London, 1908, pp. 13–14.

10 Ibid., p. 14.

11 Hutchinson, *Memoirs*, p. 45.

12 For the ascription, see D. Norbrook, 'Lucy Hutchinson and *Order and Disorder*: the manuscript evidence', *English Manuscript Studies*, vol. 9 (2000), pp. 257–91.

13 See D. Norbrook, 'Introduction', in L. Hutchinson, *Order and Disorder*, Blackwell, Oxford, 2001 (henceforward *O&D*), pp. xxv–xxxi.

14 *O&D* 5:127–80 (p. 141). In Greek myth (e.g. Homer, *Iliad* 15:18), Zeus uses 'golden fetters' to punish his wife Hera after she plots against Heracles – hence, they symbolise the bonds faced by all wives (Hera/Juno is the goddess of childbirth and matrimony). See L. Giraldus, *De Deis Gentium Libri XVII sive Syntagmata* (1555), 105. On Hutchinson's attitudes to gender and patriarchy, see Norbrook, 'Introduction', *O&D*, pp. xxxv–xliii; S. Miller, 'Maternity, marriage and contract: Lucy Hutchinson's response to patriarchal theory in *Order and Disorder*', *Studies in Philology*, vol. 102 (2005), pp. 340–77.

15 L. Hutchinson, *On the Principles of the Christian Religion, Addressed to Her Daughter*,

ed. J. Hutchinson, London, 1817, p. 91; cf. Norbrook, 'Lucy Hutchinson and *Order and Disorder*', p. 288n.

16 J. Stevenson, 'Women and the cultural politics of printing', *Seventeenth Century*, vol. 24, no. 2 (2009), pp. 25–37.

17 For quasi-Epicurean readings, see J. Goldberg, 'Lucy Hutchinson writing matter', *English Literary History*, vol. 73 (2006), pp. 275–301; A. Snider, 'Hutchinson and the Lucretian body', in J. Hayden (ed.), *The New Science and Women's Literary Discourse: Prefiguring Frankenstein*, Palgrave Macmillan, Basingstoke, 2011, pp. 29–46. For scripturalist ones, see R. Wilcher, '"Adventurous song" or "presumptuous folly": the problem of "utterance" in John Milton's *Paradise Lost* and Lucy Hutchinson's *Order and Disorder*', *Seventeenth Century*, vol. 21 (2006), pp. 304–14; E. Scott-Baumann, 'Lucy Hutchinson, the Bible and *Order and Disorder*', in E. Scott-Baumann and J. Harris (eds), *The Intellectual Culture of Puritan Women, 1558–1680*, Palgrave Macmillan, Basingstoke, 2011, pp. 176–89.

18 *O&D*, pp. 3–4.

19 H. de Quehen (ed.), *Lucy Hutchinson's Translation of Lucretius: De Rerum Natura*, University of Michigan Press, Ann Arbor, 1996, pp. 23–8; for specific parallels, see e.g. Norbrook, 'Introduction', *O&D*, p. 3n.

20 E. Stillingfleet, *Origines Sacrae*, London, 1662; J. Owen, *Theologoumena Pandotapa*, London, 1661. Cf. S. Hutton, 'Edward Stillingfleet, Henry More and the decline of *Moses Atticus*: a note on seventeenth-century Anglican apologetics', in R. Kroll, R. Ashcraft and P. Zagorin (eds), *Philosophy, Science and Religion in England: 1640–1700*, Cambridge University Press, Cambridge, 1992, pp. 68–84. For an example of Cambridge Platonism's claims, see e.g. H. More, *Conjectura Cabbalistica*, London, 1653.

21 Owen, *Theologoumena Pandotapa*, pp. 73–105; L. Hutchinson, *On the Principles of the Christian Religion Addressed to her Daughter and 'On Theology'*, London, 1817, pp. 250–94.

22 *O&D*, 1:173–5, 176–8.

23 C. Moore, 'Miltoniana', *Modern Philology*, vol. 24, no. 3 (1926–27), pp. 321–9; cf. Wilcher, '"Adventurous song"', *passim*; Norbrook, 'Introduction', *O&D*, p. xxvi.

24 Hutchinson, *Memoirs*, p. 378.

25 Ibid., pp. 237–9.

26 *O&D* 1:301–3.

27 J. Downame et al., *Annotations Vpon All the Books of the Old and New Testament*, 3rd edn, London, 1657, sig. Av; T. Haak, *The Dutch Annotations Upon the Whole Bible*, London, 1657, sig. Bv (comments on Genesis 1:2).

28 See G. Sandys (trans.), *Ovid's Metamorphosis, Englished, Mythologiz'd, and Represented in Figures*, Oxford, 1632, p. 19; Anon., *Ovids Metamorphosis Translated Grammatically*, London, 1656, pp. 2–3.

29 'Quae initio operis scripserit *Ouidius* pueri norunt': Owen, *Theologoumena Pandotapa*, p. 74. Cf. Hutchinson, *On the Principles*, p. 251.

30 Goldberg, 'Lucy Hutchinson', pp. 292–3 – with passing reference to Hutchinson's Ovidian passage – claims that 'The Word is made to explain the creation of a Lucretian nature'.

31 See Horace, *Ars Poetica* 151–2, 338–9; T. Wilson, *The Arte of Rhetorike*, London, 1584, p. 198.

32 A. Golding, *The xv Bookes of P. Ouidius Naso, entytuled Metamorphosis*, London, 1567, sig. bi(v).

33 J. Sylvester, *Du Bartas His Deuine Weekes and Workes Translated*, London, 1611, p. 8.

34 A. Fowler (ed.), *Paradise Lost*, Longman, New York, 1971, p. 131 (note to 2:895–903).

35 *O&D* 13:155–76.

36 See Sandys, *Ovid's Metamorphosis*, p. 223.

37 Ibid., pp. 222–3.

38 Wilcher, '"Adventurous song"', *passim*.
39 Sylvester, *Du Bartas*, pp. 417–18.
40 Ibid., p. 418; *Metamorphosis* 6:303, 306–7.
41 Sylvester, *Du Bartas*, p. 418; Downame *et al.*, *Annotations*, sig. E3r (on Genesis 19:26); Augustine, *De Civitate Dei*, 10:8.
42 Sylvester, *Du Bartas*, p. 418. For the 'Ausonius' verses see the commentary by Sandys, *Ovid's Metamorphosis*, p. 223.
43 Sylvester, *Du Bartas*, p. 417.
44 Norbrook, 'Introduction', *O&D*, p. xxxn, argues that Hutchinson's warning to specifically female curiosity recalls personal experience.
45 Downame *et al.*, *Annotations* (1657), sig. E3r; cf. Pliny, *Natural History*, 31:17.
46 A. Cowley, *Davideis*, in *Poems*, London, 1656, pp. 90 (text), 114 (commentary).
47 Scott-Baumann, 'Lucy Hutchinson', p. 179.
48 K. Killeen, *Biblical Scholarship, Science and Politics in Early Modern England: Thomas Browne and the Thorny Place of Knowledge*, Ashgate, Farnham, 2009.
49 For example, *O&D* 14:47–85, for Ovid, *Metamorphoses* 11:592–625 (identified in Norbrook, 'Introduction', *O&D*, p. 181n).
50 *O&D*, 11:65–80.
51 Norbrook, 'Introduction', *O&D*, p. 148n, references only Virgil's bee simile (*Aeneid* 1:430–6), but the preceding lines on Carthage (1:423–9), and Aeneas's admiration of the rising walls (1:437–8; cf. 1:421, 'miratur molem Aeneas'), are also clearly imitated by Hutchinson.
52 *O&D* 5:87–90 (emphasis added).
53 See especially *O&D* 10:10–20.
54 *Aeneid* 1:426, 'iura magistratusque legunt sanctumque senatum'. Post-Renaissance editors sometimes consider these lines spurious.
55 See T. Farnaby, note to *Georgics* 4:153–6, in *Publii Virgilii Maronis*, Opera, London, 1634, p. 87; T. May, *Virgil's Georgicks Englished*, London, 1628, p. 119 (translating 4:154–5).
56 *Georgics* 4:200–1, translated by May, *Virgil's Georgicks Englished* (p. 121), as 'They all elect their king, / And little nobles'. Farnaby, *Publii Virgilii Maronis*, p. 89, elucidates the Roman political comparisons.
57 Contrast Norbrook, 'Introduction', *O&D*, p. 148n, who maintains that 'the bee simile was traditionally associated with monarchy' and argues for Hutchinson's 'republican revision'. This is somewhat misleading, not least as Norbrook omits all mention of the *Georgics* passage. May, for example, certainly describes Virgil's bees as a 'monarchike state' ('The argument', *Virgil's Georgicks Englished*, p. 111), but, as we have seen, also emphasises its commonwealth elements.
58 See e.g. D. Norbrook, 'John Milton, Lucy Hutchinson and the republican biblical epic', in M. Kelley, M. Lieb and J. Shawcross (eds), *Milton and the Grounds of Contention*, Duquesne University Press, Pittsburgh, 2003, pp. 37–63 (especially pp. 44–6); P. Hammond, 'Dryden, Milton, and Lucretius', *Seventeenth Century*, vol. 16, no. 1 (2001), p. 166, cited in Snider, 'Hutchinson and the Lucretian body', pp. 41–2.
59 R. Barbour, 'Between atoms and the spirit: Lucy Hutchinson's translation of Lucretius', in M. Suzuki (ed.), *Ashgate Critical Essays on Women Writers in England, 1550–1700, Vol. 5: Anne Clifford and Lucy Hutchinson*, Ashgate, Farnham, 2009, pp. 333–48; Norbrook, 'John Milton, Lucy Hutchinson', pp. 45–6.
60 See Goldberg, 'Lucy Hutchinson'; Snider, 'Hutchinson and the Lucretian body'.
61 *O&D* 19:9–64.
62 *O&D* 19:32–45; Lucretius, *De Rerum Natura*, ed. C. Bailey, Oxford University Press, Oxford, 1900, 4:966–79. Cf. Snider, 'Hutchinson and the Lucretian body', p. 41. Hutchinson's satirical dream catalogue possibly also recalls Shakespeare's Mercutio: *Romeo and Juliet* 1.4.72–88.
63 *O&D* 19:56–64.

64 M.-S. Røstvig, *The Happy Man: Studies in the Metamorphoses of a Classical Ideal: Volume I, 1600–1700* (2nd edition), Norwegian Universities Press, Oslo, 1962.

65 'Verses written by Mrs Hutchinson', in Hutchinson, *Memoirs*, pp. 385–6.

66 Ibid., p. 386 (its final couplet). S. Wiseman, *Conspiracy and Virtue: Women, Writing, and Politics in Seventeenth-Century England*, Oxford University Press, Oxford, 2006, pp. 212–16, persuasively reading the poem as partly a 'pastiche' of contemporary royalist Horatianism, places Hutchinson's ideal of rural sovereignty in the context of a quasi-republican freedom from monarchical direction.

67 Hutchinson, *Memoirs*, p. 385; Norbrook, *O&D*, pp. 24ff.

68 *O&D* 19:35–52 (51–2); Horace, *Epodes* 2:1.17–20.

69 *O&D* 19:9, 20; 'Verses written by Mrs Hutchinson', in Hutchinson, *Memoirs*, p. 386 (almost certainly echoing Horace *Odes* 3:1.1, 'odi profanum volgus et arceo'; for this poem's influence on 'happy man' writing, see Røstvig, *The Happy Man*, p. 22. Cf. Wiseman, *Conspiracy and Virtue*, pp. 215–16. Like Wiseman (ibid., p. 214) I rather doubt Hutchinson's 'poor man' celebration represents levelling social attitudes: it is in fact a literary/cultural trope signifying pre-social or non-social man (hence man in his natural state/man as he is to God/'everyman').

70 See J. Ashmore, 'Of a blessed life', *Certain Selected Odes of Horace, Englished*, London, 1621, pp. 91–6 (Psalm 1 in translation to close); ibid., 'The praise of a country life', pp. 81–7. Cf. Røstvig, *The Happy Man*, pp. 14ff.

71 The passage's references to care-worn, sleepless monarchs, tossing on their 'royal couches' out of guilt (*O&D* 19:11–20), recalls the Shakespearean trope of sleepless, guilty kings, notably Henry IV, who in *Henry IV, Part II* 3.1.5–17 similarly contrasts the innocent sleep of the 'vile', and insomniac rulers on a 'kingly couch'.

72 Norbrook, 'John Milton, Lucy Hutchinson', pp. 38, 41.

73 On the importance of gentility to having one's opinion respected in Restoration England, see S. Shapin, *A Social History of Truth: Civility and Science in Seventeenth-Century England*, Chicago University Press, Chicago, 1994, pp. 42–64.

74 H. Hinds, *God's Englishwomen: Seventeenth-Century Radical Sectarian Writing and Feminist Criticism*, Manchester University Press, Manchester, 1996, pp. 106–7.

75 *O&D*, p. 5 (emphasis added).

76 *O&D* 2:11–26.

77 *De Rerum Natura* 4:126–42; de Quehen, *Lucy Hutchinson's Translation of Lucretius*, p. 118 (4:133–6).

Elizabeth Melville and the religious sonnet sequence in Scotland and England

Sarah C. E. Ross

THE lyrics in manuscript that Jamie Reid-Baxter has attributed to Elizabeth Melville, the Scottish religious poet and author of *Ane Godlie Dreame* (1603), include three sequences of religious sonnets, a poetic genre around which there clusters a language of 'firsts' in literary-critical discussion of the period. Anne Lock's *A Meditation of a Penitent Sinner* (1560), a sequence of religious sonnets that paraphrase and expand on Psalm 51, has received extensive critical attention in recent years as 'the first sonnet sequence in English': to that distinction can be added (and frequently is) those of being a religious sonnet sequence, and of being by a woman.[1] Lock's *Meditation* is credited with 'introduc[ing] the religious sonneteer into English-speaking culture', and her text is a very early milestone in the emergence of original religious poetry more broadly in sixteenth-century England, a syncretic process of devotional language flowing into lyric verse of which the religious sonnet is just one, highly wrought, example.[2] To a critical narrative of that religious sonnet that begins with Lock's *Meditation*, we need now to add Elizabeth Melville's three sequences, which reveal a highly innovative engagement with multiple poetic influences and inheritances across the national borders of England and Scotland. Melville's newly recuperated religious sonnets consolidate the association of women with a poetic genre that reached its apotheosis in the religious sonnets of Herbert and Donne and, alongside the examples of Lock and Mary Sidney, exemplify the role that women could – and did – play in the emergence of an imaginative Protestant poetic in Britain.[3]

Elizabeth Melville's innovative engagement with the religious sonnet sequence occurs at a crucial moment around the turn of the seventeenth century. Anne Lock's *Meditation* predates very significantly any other known examples of religious sonnet sequences in Britain: the next to appear in print are those of her son Henry Lok and Barnabe Barnes in the 1590s, and those in manuscript by Henry Constable and William Alabaster occur at around the time of the authors' respective conversions to Catholicism, in the late 1590s.[4] Lok's *Svndry Christian Passions, Contained in two hundred Sonnets* (1593, republished 1597) and Barnes's *A Divine Centvrie of Spirituall Sonnets* (1595) are frequently cited as milestones in the development of an original devotional poetic in England, Ramie Targoff describing 'the emergence in the 1590s of Protestant sonnet series that are neither liturgically nor scripturally based, and that openly announce themselves as poems'.[5] Elizabeth Melville's sonnet sequences are likely to date from around this time, but they articulate a lyric subjectivity in relation to the divine that is strikingly inventive, and represent an individualised and psychologised experience of divine love that diverges markedly from the sonnets of Lok or Barnes. Even more strikingly, Melville's sonnet sequences work *as sequences* in new and distinctive ways. So what were her poetic inheritances and influences in the composition of religious sonnet sequences? Out of what poetic traditions do her religious sonnet sequences emerge?

These questions of poetic inheritance and innovation are, in this chapter, bound up more broadly with current critical reconsideration of the literary relationships between Scotland and England, and of cultural exchange between the two nations around the time of the union of the crowns. Deirdre Serjeantson has recently argued that the English religious poetic of Henry Lok owes much to his Scottish connections, and to an 'emergent literary self-awareness' in religious poetry that was more developed in Scotland in the 1590s than in England.[6] Elizabeth Melville drew, reciprocally, on English sources, but it is in the Scottish tradition of poetic pietism, cultivated by James VI himself as a poetic author, that the most important precedents for her sonnets are to be found. In this chapter, I will read Melville's sonnets alongside those of Anne Lock and Henry Lok, Barnes, James VI and I, and also alongside the 'Sundry Sonets' that appear at the end of a volume published by her Scottish Presbyterian contemporary James Melville, in 1598. James Melville's religious sonnets are likely to have been known by his compatriot, co-Presbyterian and distant relative, and they provide the most revealing point of comparison for hers. Together, the two Melvilles' religious sonnet sequences are illustrative of a Scottish religio-poetic culture that is itself in urgent need of fuller exploration, and that allows us to expand our understanding not only of women's relationship to the poem but also of the religious sonnet sequence as a poetic genre in early modern Britain.

Elizabeth Melville's three sonnet sequences, recently published for the first time in Jamie Reid-Baxter's *Poems of Elizabeth Melville, Lady Culross*, are preserved at the end of the 'Bruce manuscript', a volume of unpublished sermons by the radical minister Robert Bruce, one of James

VI's chief Presbyterian antagonists, now held in the New College Library, Edinburgh.[7] I follow in this chapter (and elsewhere) Reid-Baxter's attribution of the Bruce manuscript poetry to Elizabeth Melville, for reasons including style. The lyric poetry in the Bruce manuscript is not formally ascribed, but begins with two poems, a sonnet and a dixain, that are based, via an acrostic and an anagram, on Melville's name. This can safely be read as a technique of prefatory identification: the sonnet was a favoured form of liminary poetry in early modern Scotland, and acrostics and anagrams are techniques of inscription that we know Melville to have used.[8] Melville is also a known purveyor of the religious sonnet for spiritual succour in the first decade of the seventeenth century. Her sonnet to John Welsh of Ayr on his imprisonment at Blackness in 1605, preserved in a Wodrow manuscript, has long been known, and two comparable sonnets to the radical Presbyterian leader Andrew Melville, after his imprisonment in 1607, have recently been uncovered.[9] In each case, Elizabeth uses an acrostic or an anagram – or both – to inscribe her addressed subject into the form of her religious sonnet.

More problematic for our assessment of Melville's sonnets, and their place in the development of imaginative religious poetry in Britain, is their uncertain dating – particularly given that their writing may hover around the pivotal decade of the 1590s. The manuscript in which Elizabeth Melville's sonnets appear is occupied for the most part by twenty-nine sermons on Hebrews XI, which Robert Bruce preached at St Giles' Cathedral, Edinburgh, in late 1590 and spring 1591; these were never published, although Reid-Baxter believes that in the Bruce manuscript they are marked up for printing.[10] Bruce was exiled from Edinburgh in 1600, and it seems likely that the manuscript was compiled around, or shortly after, this date. It is entirely possible that the sonnets – and the poetry more generally – are much later, but the sermons and the poetry are transcribed in the same hand, and three further pieces of evidence suggest authorship in the 1590s or the first decade of the 1600s. Alexander Hume refers to Melville's 'compositiones so copious' in his dedication to her in 1598 of his *Hymnes, and Sacred Songs*, a likely reference to at least some of her lyrics preserved in manuscript; Melville refers in one of her sonnets to being 'young in yeirs'; and Melville's sonnets to Welsh and Andrew Melville, which are close in image and form to her Bruce manuscript sequences, date from around 1606–07.[11] On balance, it seems safe to conjecture that Melville may have written the Bruce manuscript sonnets between 1595 and 1610.

Elizabeth Melville's religious sonnets are, then, likely to date from some forty years after Anne Lock's *Meditation of a Penitent Sinner*, the foundational series of Calvinist, female-authored and sequential religious sonnets. Lock's *Meditation*, however, is not original in the terms that Targoff defines: the main text consists of twenty-one sonnets that paraphrase Psalm 51, in a style that Susan Felch describes as 'explicative paraphrase', and that is marked by repetition – of the words and phrases of the psalm, and in the iteration of the speaker's psychological relationship with the divine.[12] Lock prefaces her *Meditation* with five original sonnets that anticipate more clearly the imaginative devotional poetry of the later sixteenth century in their freedom from the template of the psalm in their creation of the speaker's voice: these five sonnets are prefatory preparations for the speaker's meditations, 'expressing', according to Lock's subtitle, 'the passioned minde of the penitent sinner'.[13] Felch describes a linear progression through these sonnets, as the speaker moves 'from the realization of sin, through confrontation with Despair, to a supplicant's posture'.[14] Lock's speaker is enmired, in her first sonnet, in 'The lothesome filthe of my disteined life'; she 'Can not enjoy the comfort of the light, / Nor finde the waye wherin to walke aright' (lines 5, 13–14). Repeatedly crying for mercy in all of the subsequent four sonnets, she falls to the ground 'With foltring knee' to 'Poure forth my piteous plaint with woefull sound' (5:5, 7), and to embark on the penitent sinner's expansion and reiteration of Psalm 51 that is the *Meditation*'s main text.

This nascent linearity notwithstanding, Lock's prefatory sonnet sequence is strikingly static in comparison with the sequences by Elizabeth Melville, in which a turn from worldly woe to a celebration of divine love and grace is a clear organising principle. Lock's speaker is a 'blinde wretch' who

> Finde[s] not the way that other oft have found
> Whome cherefull glimse of gods abounding grace
> Hath oft releved and oft with shyning light
> Hath brought to joy out of the ugglye place.
> (2:4–7)

Lock's speaker remains enmired, a stasis reflected in a poetic rhetoric of repetition that marks even the original, prefatory sonnets: she can only cry for mercy, the reiterated posture that concludes sonnets 2, 4 and 5. Melville's published *Ane Godlie Dreame*, in contrast, is structured around exactly the 'cherefull glimse of gods abounding grace' that eludes Lock's speaker, a vision of heaven that lifts Melville from her mire of despair and shows her the way to heaven (albeit a way that is 'wondrous hard' (line 337)). Melville follows a tripartite structure in the *Dreame* of lamentation, vision (Lock's 'glimse') and exhortation, and this structure of psychological progression is echoed in her second sonnet sequence. Melville's speaker is at first as enmired as Lock's, opening her sequence with a call to God, 'O louse me frome this lothsum lump of clay / my saviour sweit befoir I sink in sin!' (1:1–2). Her second sonnet, however, adopts a voice that addresses the first sonnet's 'Perplexit saull', assuring it of God's help and exhorting, 'Lift up thy hairt thou art to far cast doun / ovircum the ficht if thou wold wear the croun' (2:13–14). Melville resolves the sequence with an ecstatic confidence in God's grace and love that is entirely missing from the poetic experience of Lock's penitent sinner: 'O gratious god, so full of grace and love / how providentlie doth thow for thyne provyde!' (3:1–2).

Critical discussion of Lock's sequence has to a large extent focused on a sense of *limitation*, in its psalm-based rhetoric, in the extent to which it enacts an individualised Calvinist subjectivity, and in its use of the sonnet form.[15] Roland Greene discusses Lock's use of the sonnet for Calvinist devotional purposes in a terminology which is useful here: he explores the value that Petrarchan poetics places on 'invention' and on the individual psyche, describing these as deeply antithetical to Calvinist values of plainness, and he describes a Calvinist sense of identity that is less individual than it is defined by a certainty of sinfulness and a search for signs of election.[16] Greene defines Lock's sequence according to its *refusal* of Petrarchan invention, its expansion and reiteration of Psalm 51 representing a single and unequivocal turn to the Lord, according to the template of the psalm, rather than charting the multiple and fluctuating – even paradoxical – psychological shifts that characterise the poetry of Petrarchism. Greene describes the sonnet, in the sixteenth century, as 'practically a technology for representing *voltas* or "turns" of all psychic sorts', and Lock's almost non-existent use of the line 9 turn has also attracted comment. While it seems unlikely that she was 'not even aware' that she was using the sonnet form, as Michael Spiller suggests, Lock's lack of engagement with the technology of the psychological turn certainly underscores the stasis of her devotional lyric subjectivity.[17]

Anne Lock's *Meditation*, then, provides only a very partial precedent for Elizabeth Melville's sonnet sequences: there is a profound difference between Lock's reiterative paraphrases of 1560 and the rhetoric of poetic invention and originality that surrounds the religious sonnet, and the flourishing of British religious poetry, in the 1590s. Serjeantson's argument that an 'emergent literary self-awareness' in English religious poetry was 'already well developed in Scotland' in the 1590s is well supported by Scottish uses of the religious lyric, in which a sense of the poetic 'ingyne' is vital. James VI himself presided as an author over a flourishing religious poetic culture in Scotland, beginning with his *Essayes of a Prentise, in the Diuine Art of Poesie* (1584), which included a translation of Du Bartas's *L'Uranie*, the text in which Du Bartas establishes Urania as the muse of religious poetry. Du Bartas was admired deeply by the Scottish king, and he visited Edinburgh at James's invitation for six months in 1579, and on a diplomatic mission in 1587.[18] James's *The Uranie* was the first translation of Du Bartas in Britain, along with the translation of *Judith* by Thomas Hudson that was commissioned by James and published in the same year.[19] These texts founded a Bartasian tradition of original religious poetry in Scotland that was independent of – and more advanced than – the English one, in which Josuah Sylvester's translation of *Du Bartas: His Deuine Weekes and Workes* (1605) was so influential.[20]

'Ingyne', defined as 'mental or intellectual talent, natural intelligence or cleverness, ability, genius' in the *Dictionary of the Older Scots Tongue*, is a term that reverberates through Scots poetry, including religious poetry, from the 1580s onwards.[21] James VI's second published work on poetry, *Ane Schort Treatise Conteining some Reulis and Cautelis to be obseruit and eschewit in Scottis Poesie* (1585), contains a 'Sonnet Decifring the Perfyte Poete', in which the first quality described is 'Ane rype ingyne', as Deirdre Serjeantson observes. Serjeantson also discusses the use of the term by the pre-eminent Scottish court poet Alexander Montgomerie in his poem 'A godly prayer', where he reflects 'thou hes grantit me so good Ingyn / to Loif the, Lord, in gallant style and gay'.[22] James Melville, to whom I will soon turn, also uses the term in a dixain that praises James VI precisely by likening him to Du Bartas. The dixain is written in James Melville's hand in a British Library copy of Du Bartas's *La Seconde Sepmaine*; it describes the king as 'Gentle ingyne, pirreles in poesie' and invokes him to 'Imploy thy penne (I ken nane vther meit, / To match grait Bartas), as thow hes done before'.[23] James Melville's celebration of the Scottish king's religious poetic praises him in the terms of invention that the king regarded so highly, and it associates that quality with the religious poetry of Du Bartas himself, James VI's influential poetic model.

Essayes of a Prentise also contains a milestone example of sonnets used in sequential form: 'The tvvelf Sonnets of Inuocations to the Goddis', a sequence of James's own authorship. The volume is prefaced by five sonnets and three Latin poems of praise, each contributed by authors identified by initials; these are followed by James's sonnets of invocation, each of which addresses one of twelve pagan gods in turn. James's association of poetic inspiration with invention is reinforced throughout the sequence. He first addresses Jove, asking

> That thou my veine Poetique so inspyre,
> As they may suirlie think, all that it reid,
> When I descryue thy might and thundring fyre,
> That they do see thy self in verie deid,
> (1:5–8)

and he asks Mercury 'That for conducting guyde I may you haue, / Aswell vnto my pen, as my Ingyne' (11:3–4). James upholds in these sonnets a sense of poetic invention that coexists with his explication of divine poetics in *The Uranie*, where (via Du Bartas) he argues for the transferral of 'golden honnied verse' to the divine: 'Speak of that thryse great spreit, whose dow most white / Mote make your spring flow euer with delyte'.[24] Michael Spiller describes James's sonnets of invocation as 'categorical', in the sense that each sonnet deals in turn with one item from a category – here, the gods.[25] James's sequence is a precedent in this sense for Josuah Sylvester's 'Corona Dedicatoria' of sixteen-line poems, also categorical in describing the muses one by one, that prefaces his translation of *Du Bartas: His Deuine Weekes and Workes*, a book dedicated to James and which James owned.[26]

More distantly, James VI's sequence of invocatory sonnets is also perhaps a precedent for Elizabeth Melville's first sonnet sequence, a much more inventive tryptich which begins with a sonnet of invocation to 'great Jehovah michtie King of Kings' (1:1). Melville confidently invokes her own identity as a religious poet, asking both that God inspire her sacred writings and that her writing should not offend. Melville's second sonnet focuses on the godly work which she is able to undertake with her God-given talent:

> Lat hevin me blis with knowledge frome above
> to meditat upone thy hevinlie will
> poure doun on me the spirit of treuth and love
> that I may learne thy law for to fulfill.
> (1–4)

Her religious poetry becomes in this sonnet a 'scheild of faith' (7) to defend her against the trials of the world and against 'the dreidfull dairt / that Sathane schutts' (11–12); and in the triptych's third sonnet, she is able to adopt a stance of exemplary fortitude:

> I will be as ane elme that still doth stand
> and will not bowe for no kinkynd of blaist
> I will have my affectiouns at command
> and cause them yeild to reasoun at the laist.
> (1–4)

Like James VI's, Melville's first sonnet sequence is one of invocation to the muse(s) of religious poetry, and the ungendered confidence with which she claims the status of a religious poetic author is striking. Melville's sequence is, in fact, much more sophisticated than James's, charting a movement from apostrophe to God, to a more meditative reflection on the role of heavenly knowledge, to a confident assertion that she will 'hold fast' and 'Rejoyce in god' (3:5, 13). It is a movement predicated on a turn away from complaint; at line 9 of her third sonnet, Melville codifies her resolve to let 'earthlie cairs torment my mynd no more', declaring 'sould I lament I can not tell quhairfoir' (3:8–9).

Melville was strongly allied to the radical Presbyterianism of her distant relative Andrew Melville (and his nephew James), and to their religio-political opposition to James VI, which became more pronounced as his reign progressed. Poetically, however, the Melvilles and their pietist poetics owe much to the literary culture fostered by the king in the early years of his Scottish reign: James Melville's dixain of praise in the British Library's *La Seconde Sepmaine* attests to this, as does his dedication of *A Morning Vision* to James VI in 1598, in which he describes himself as 'Your Majesties maist humble Oratour and new prentise in Poësie'. It is this culture of Scottish religious poetic inventiveness that Deirdre Serjeantson has con-nected to the religious poetic aesthetic of Henry Lok, whose two religious sonnet sequences she describes as 'revolutionary in English poetry'.[27] Lok, it transpires, was in Scotland and at court in the early 1590s, employed by Lord Burghley, and later by his son Robert Cecil, as a messenger between the English government and the Earl of Bothwell.[28] And his presence there, as well as his awareness of the Scottish king's literary activities, is attested to by his authorship of a prefatory sonnet of praise to James VI's *His Maiesties poeticall exercises at vacant houres* (1591), just two years before the publication of Lok's own first sonnet sequence. It is also notable to find among the laudatory sonneteers to James's volume another Englishman and sonneteer, Henry Constable, who had a long-standing diplomatic association with the Scottish court.[29] Constable published a sequence of secular love sonnets, *Diana. The Praises of His Mistress, in Certaine Sweete Sonnets*, in 1592, several years before he is likely to have authored a religious sequence which remained in manuscript.[30]

Serjeantson's argument that the development of the English religious sonnet needs to be seen in the context of Scottish religious poetic culture is compelling, and it suggests a reciprocal question: to what extent do we need to read Elizabeth Melville's religious sonnets in the context of the English sequences published by Henry Lok and Barnes in the 1590s? Melville knew and wrote in response to a wide range of English, as well as Scottish, lyric poetry: she engages extensively in the practice of *contrafactum* or sacred parody, rewriting secular lyrics in sacred terms, and her *contrafacta* include sacred versions of several English poems. She rewrites Christopher Marlowe's 'The passionate shepherd to his love' (first published in 1600, although circulating widely in manuscript in the 1590s) as 'A call to come to Christ'; and the English lutenist Robert

Jones's 'Farewell sweet love' (published in 1600 and quoted by Malvolio in *Twelfth Night*) is the basis for her lyric 'Away vaine warld', published at the end of *Ane Godlie Dreame*. I have also argued elsewhere that Melville appears to parody, in one of her extended devotional lyrics, Philip Sidney's sonnet 5 in *Astrophel and Stella*, a parody that links her to the pre-eminent example of the English Petrarchan sonnet sequence of the 1590s.[31] While Melville's sacred parodies evince her familiarity with English literary and popular lyrics, however, the practice of sacred parody is itself distinctly Scottish (and continental), indicative of her religious lyrics' relationship to the Scottish *Gude and Godlie Ballatis*, and to the lyrics and sacred parodies of Alexander Hume, James Melville and Alexander Montgomerie. Montgomerie, 'already considered "maister poete," when [King] James's Renaissance began',[32] composed several influential spiritual lyrics, using the complex song form of two of his erotic poems for paraphrases of Psalms 1 and 2, and Elizabeth Melville herself wrote a sacred parody of Montgomerie's erotic lyric 'Solsequium'. A handful of sacred sonnets are found among the seventy or so sonnets that Montgomerie penned, but there is no religious sonnet sequence.[33]

It is also striking that Elizabeth Melville – an exclusively religious poet – writes more clearly in response to the secular lyrics of late sixteenth-century England than she does to its religious poetry. One possible connection (and indeed the only real connection evident to me) between Melville's religious sonnet sequences and those of Henry Lok and Barnabe Barnes is provided by the 'talent' sonnets that all three compose. Melville's 'great Jehovah' sonnet ends its invocation with a plea that God will guide her 'in writting of thy worthie word so sweit' and 'grant thy gifts may still growe more and more / That I ane tripill talent may restore' (12–14). Melville is drawing here on the parable of the talents (Matthew 25:14–30 and Luke 19:12–18) to describe her religious writing as a necessary act. Lok and Barnes utilise the same parable in their religious sonnet sequences, but there is little parallel evident beyond the use of the trope. This commonality, then, does little more than reveal that the parable of the talents was becoming something of a commonplace in religious sonnets, and in the original religious poetry of the period more generally.[34]

Lok's and Barnes's religious sonnets, and the sequences that they comprise, are also fundamentally different in kind from the tightly psychologised lyrics and carefully organised sequences of Elizabeth Melville. Lok favours the interlocking Scottish sonnet form used by Melville and her Scottish contemporaries, but his sonnets are typically more static than Melville's, operating very frequently on a single, almost emblematic, conceit, for example 'Within thy garden Lord I planted was, / And watred well with thy most carefull hand'.[35] Barnes's sonnets echo Melville's more closely in articulating a sense of 'inseperable combat betwixt earth and my sprite', although his style is most frequently descriptive rather than evocative ('I feel my soule in combat with the dust / Of sinfull flesh, and ready to break out').[36] Barnes's use of the classic Petrarchan sonnet form facilitates a prevailing turn in the sestet to a sense of divine resolution, but it is formulaic in comparison with the turns that Melville incorporates into her interlocking Scottish-form sonnets.

As sequences, both Lok's and Barnes's sonnets are defined – and suffer – by the ambition of their scale. Lok's *Svndry Christian Passions* is organised as two groups of 100 sonnets, and Barnes also invokes the numerological framework of the century. Barnes claims in his preface that his sonnets 'stand in my booke confused', and that this very disorder evinces the sonnets' spontaneity, that 'in earnest true motions of the spirite were they deuised'.[37] Lok distinguishes between his two centuries, describing the first as consisting 'chiefly of Meditations, Humiliations, and Praiers' and the second 'of Comfort, Ioy, and Thanksgiving'. Beyond these broad groupings, however, he, too, asserts the value of his sonnets' 'confused' arrangement: because 'their disorder doth best fit the nature of mankind'; because the sonnets were 'set downe by sundry accidents in my priuate estate and feeling'; and also because their lack of 'formall placing' befits 'the common inconstant forme of reading' by which readers peruse a book, that is, in fits and starts.[38] Helen Wilcox has observed of the religious sonnet sequence that 'in poetic terms it is often the smaller clusters of sonnets that function more effectively', and this observation is amply borne out in the contrast between Lok's and Barnes's loose-knit sequences and the tight psychological progression that defines those of Elizabeth Melville.[39]

Melville's third and longest sonnet sequence, a series of seven, operates according to a tripartite structure that is innovative and strikingly coherent, apparently owing little to the 'confused' sequences of Lok and Barnes. Melville's first and second sonnets express awe at the grace, love and care of God for His people; the third, fourth and fifth explore the 'deip distres' (6:4) of the speaker living in the flesh; and the sixth and seventh sonnets return to asserting a certainty in God's grace. 'Quho can conceave the wisdome love and grace / that did vouchsaif to creat us of noucht', the first sonnet opens, focusing on Christ's sacrifice as God's covenant with his elect; and the second sonnet is an explicit companion piece, its opening line echoing that of the first – 'Quho can conceave of godis great love and cair / to us quho live in these last evill dayis'. Sonnets 3–5, however, are permeated by a 'sence of sin void of all sence of grace' (5:1), and sonnet 3 echoes Anne Lock's sense of the speaker enmired in sin. The speaker compares herself to a 'sensuall sow' whose 'filth I far exceid', and 'quhois nature is to wallow in the myre' (1–2); she knows she should aspire to higher things, 'yit to the myre my nature still is bent' (8). Line 9, however, enacts a turn of the kind unmarked in Lock's sonnets: with an exclamation of 'o then quhat caus have I for to lament / my bypast life', Melville directs her focus to the knowledge 'that with Chrysts blude my blotts be wascht away' (9–12). Even within a sonnet at the nadir of this sequence, Melville turns *from* wallowing to 'avow and promeis by godis grace / not to turne bak bot fordward hold my race' (12–13).

It is in these central sonnets that the influence of secular Petrarchism on Melville's lyric subjectivity is most pronounced, paradox and juxtaposition, anaphora, repetition and internal rhyme expressing her sense that 'sin hes put me with my self at fead' (5:5).[40] Melville's sixth and seventh sonnets in the sequence, however, adopt the second-person imperative address that characterises many of her sonnets, as well as the exhortation at the conclusion of her *Dreame*. Sonnet 6 explicitly answers sonnet 5's 'sence of sin void of all sence of grace' with the reassurance that 'Though sence of sin do more and more incress / ... / hold Jesus fast and he sall send redress' (6:1–3). Line 9 of that sonnet asserts, 'If ye complaine he constant sall remaine', a declaration that not only illustrates the entwining of the Petrarchan and devotional genres of complaint in Melville's religious sonnets, but also enacts the certainty in God's love that concludes the sequence.[41] Melville adapts the complaint and the tortured lyric subjectivity of Petrarchan poetics to express the tumultuous worldly experience of the elect, and ultimately to rejoice, exhorting the reader, with a renewed and triumphant confidence in her last sonnet, to 'Tak courage then and be no more so sad / lift up your hairt your heritage is hie' (7:1–2). If, then, we are looking for answers to Roland Greene's pertinent question, asked of Anne Lock's *Meditation*, 'What are the logic and values of a Calvinist sonnet sequence?', the answers provided by Elizabeth Melville's longest sequence, which uses the sonnet to psychologise the Calvinist experience of divine love, are very different from those provided by the loose and extended sequences of Lok and Barnes.[42]

The most illuminating comparator for Melville's sequences is a set of ten religious sonnets published by her distant relative James Melville, the pastor-poet minister of Kilrenny on the east coast of Fife, in 1598. James was a staunch supporter of his uncle Andrew, the prominent leader of the Presbyterian party within the Kirk, and he was himself a leading Presbyterian spokesman; he was almost certainly personally known to Elizabeth, as a like-minded radical Presbyterian and as a poetic author.[43] Intriguingly, Elizabeth's recently discovered post-1607 sonnets to Andrew Melville are preserved in manuscript alongside anti-episcopal sonnets almost certainly composed by James, and an anti-episcopal Latin epigram by Andrew. James published, in 1598, two religious works as a single volume, *A Spiritvall Propine of a Pastour to his People* (a work of prose), and *A Morning Vision: or, Poeme for the Practise of Pietie, in Devotion, Faith, and Repentance* (a work of poetry, incorporating various catechetical poems).[44] *A Spiritvall Propine* features a number of liminary sonnets praising Melville's book, each bearing its respective author's initials; however, *A Morning Vision* concludes with a series of ten 'Sundry Sonets', all of which are unascribed.[45] It is these sonnets that I read to be authored by James Melville, and as forming a religious sonnet sequence.

That said, it has to be acknowledged that the 'Sundry Sonets' open with a sonnet that threatens to undermine both of these assertions. That first sonnet begins 'Svpreame essence, beginner, vnbegon, / Distinguish'd ane, and vndeuided three', paralleling in these lines and in those following a religious sonnet that is attributed in the Ker manuscript to Alexander Montgomerie, opening 'Svpreme Essence, beginning Vnbegun, / Ay Trinall ane, ane vndevydit three'. Melville's and Montgomerie's sonnets are, as Sally Mapstone and Roderick Lyall have explored, independent translations from the French of Marin Le Saulx's 'Supreme essence' sonnet, published in London in 1577.[46] Melville and Montgomerie are each working directly from the French, rather than one from the other, and it is unclear which translation came first.[47] This opening to the 'Sundry Sonets' draws invaluable attention to Montgomerie's prominence in Scottish poetic culture, and to the continental influences on Scottish religious poetry – sadly outside the scope of this chapter, except to note that James Melville's poetry also evinces close links to that of Theodore Beza.[48] James Melville's 'Svpreame essence' sonnet could also be seen to problematise his authorship of all ten 'Sundry Sonets', and Sally Mapstone cautions that they 'cannot be assumed in all cases to be Melville's'.[49] None, however, is attributed to another author, in contrast to the liminary sonnets at the beginning and end of *A Spiritvall Propine*; and while the sonnets are entitled 'Sundry', a term which perhaps cuts against a reading of them as tightly sequential, suggesting instead the looser arrangement of Henry Lok's *Svndry Christian Passions*, there is across them a pronounced spiritual development. These sonnets comprise, at very least, a sequence by dint of arrangement.

The 'Sundry Sonets' are arranged according to a psychological and devotional progression that is reminiscent of Elizabeth Melville's seven-sonnet sequence, at the same time as there are core differences between the two sequences that are reflective of the two Melvilles' individuated Calvinist poetics. James's opening sonnet (that is, the Le Saulx translation) is a declaration of God's supremacy – a sonnet imbued with a confidence comparable to Elizabeth's in her declarative opening. The next sonnet addresses not God but the reader, and marks a transition to three sonnets that exemplify a distinct aspect of James Melville's religious poetic: a catechetical style that defines much of the poetry in *A Morning Vision*, in which (in the words of its subtitle) 'the whole Catechisme, and right vse thereofe, is largely exponed'.[50] Sonnets 2–4 each contain points, numbered in the left-hand margin, on which the reader must dwell. For example, 'The substance of saluation' sets outs:

1 There is na gudnes in our selues inclos'd
2 All gud from God is into Christ our King.
3 And Christ be constant, faith is ay injos'd
4   And faith be loue is fallon weill disclos'd
5 The spirit thir works be word and Sacrament:
   To make the heart exceedingly rejos'd.
(6–11)

The sequence then moves into five sonnets that express the 'Restles care' of the heart and soul (9:1), before it concludes with a sonnet entitled 'A wish of true thank-fulnes', in which the speaker declares that 'My minde, my will, and mine affections all' are 'Illuminat by faith, and mortified':

My heart full hard, sa softly mollified,
My tongue sa tam'd, my lippes sa circumcis'd,
My thoughts reform'd, my language qualifi'd.
Mine actions all, in gudnes exercis'd.
(5–8)

James's sequence ends in a blaze of confidence and certainty of election comparable to the ending of Elizabeth's, both having traced a distinct devotional progression. Where the resolution to Elizabeth's sonnet sequence rests on a sacralised Petrarchan turn to the divine, however, James's sequence is catechetical to the end, as the lyric subject is tamed, reformed and mollified through the active, *linguistic* exercise of goodness.

James Melville's sixth and seventh sonnets operate as a complementary pair within the sequence, providing further insight into his intricate poetic reformation of the speaking subject. The sixth sonnet is entitled 'The melancholious Christian' and, in keeping with this description, it represents James's speaker at his most fretful, expressing a despair parallel to that of Elizabeth at her most enmired:

The melancholious Christian

I Cry, and call, with sighes, and sobs alas,
My sorrow streats, my sinnes this wo me wrought:
I pant, I pine, I feare Gods fierie face:

I die in dule, I dwine away for thought.
   Mirth sayes fare weil, & greeff hir newes hes brought
She loues to Iudge: Alas, I tyre for paine:
All joy is geane, that gladlie anes I sought.
Sen she hes seas'd, with all hir dulfull traine.
   Yet sall I thus (think I) in greefe remaine,
Sall heauines, my heart sa feare oppresse.
Confesse thy sinnes, confesse I say againe.
And mercie sall, with joy thy saule possesse.
   Thy countenance (O Christ) on me let shine:
   Refresh my heauie heart, with joyes diuine.

James's call, however, is immediately answered, in a companion sonnet on
'The sanguinean Christian':

The sanguinean Christian

I Shout, I cry, I loupe, I runne a pace,
My heart rebounds, this mirth hes mercie wrought.
I gaffe, I laugh, I loue, that pleasand face.
I liue, I lust, I grone in galland thought.
Greefe says gud night, & gladnes newes hes brought.
Na langer Iudge can I, nor paisan paine.
Now sorrow sighes, that feare vpon me sought:
Sen joy hes seas'd, with all her chearefull traine.
   I will na waies, in heauines remaine,
Nor suffer sadnes, pleasure till oppresse.
   Delite in Christ, delite in Christ againe:
Sa grace full gay, sall heart and spreit possesse.
   The Sunne of justice, on my saul dois shine:
   Whilk merrie makes, this mirthfull minde of mine.

This second sonnet remedies the complaints of the first on a word-for-
word, line-for-line basis. The cry, the call, the sighs and the sobs of 6:1
are matched by the joyful shout, cry, leap and running apace of 7:1; to
match the sorrow of 6:2, the 'heart rebounds' in 7:2; this is the work of
'mercie' that replaces the 'wo' of the previous sonnet. And this precise
rewriting continues throughout the sonnet: where the speaker declares
in 6:11, 'Confesse thy sinnes, confesse I say againe', he rejoices in 7:11,
'Delite in Christ, delite in Christ againe'. This is an intricate pair of
sonnets, deeply revealing of James Melville's religious lyric mode. 'The
melacholious Christian' is James's speaker at his most fretful, but even that
expression of fretful doubt is bounded, linguistically, within the iterative
and corrective binary structure of its pairing with the following sonnet.

   James Melville's melancholious and sanguinean Christian sonnets also
provide a comparison for a pair of complementary sonnets addressed by
Elizabeth to Andrew Melville after his imprisonment in 1607, recently

uncovered in manuscript (where they are preserved alongside three sonnets by James). Elizabeth ventriloquises her subject in the first of her two sonnets, addressing God in the voice of the oppressed and imprisoned Andrew Melville, as he dwells on his spirit's pain and the distress of the saints:

> Meik men ar vexed just saulls ar taine away
> And wel wer myne to flit among the rest
> Now lord mak haist and call me from this clay
> Deir Jesus cum, how long sall trouill lest?
> (1–4)

Elizabeth inscribes Andrew Melville's name into this first sonnet via both an anagram (And wel wer myne/Andrew Melwyne) and an acrostic; but the second sonnet is unmarked by these techniques and is written in her own voice, answering the ventriloquised Andrew's distress and exhorting him to a spiritual fortitude in his time of trial. Andrew appeals to God to 'End out my fecht' in line 9 of the first sonnet, an appeal that is countered by Elizabeth exhorting him to 'End out thy raice' in line 12 of the second. This example aside, Elizabeth's pair of sonnets for Andrew Melville are not related to each other phrase by phrase as James's are; rather, the second sonnet enacts a turn from Andrew's despair to Elizabeth's call to courage, and to her reassurance that 'Fair is that face that schortlie thow sall sie' (10). This is a progression from despair to fortitude, a turn from turmoil to a certainty of God's love, that also marks Elizabeth's second and third sonnet sequences.

Comparing Scottish and English secular sonnets of the period, Michael Spiller has argued that the Castalian speaker uses what he calls a 'forensic persona, exposing a case to the view and judgment of an audience by settling into a position which he then intensifies by repetition'; it is, in Spiller's view, the English fashion that 'gives the impression of a mind thrown about by its own passion'.[51] Spiller's descriptions resonate with the distinctions between James Melville's devotional sonnets, in which the lyric subject, as well as Christian doctrine, is 'couched into catechetick rime', and those of Elizabeth, who at once creates the impression of a mind thrown about, and resolves that passion via a Petrarchan volta and a declaration of the certainty of God's grace.[52] Elizabeth's and James's sonnet sequences reveal unique and distinct poetic voices, even as they were both deeply committed to Scottish Presbyterianism and immersed in a rich devotional lyric culture associated with that faith.

Elizabeth Melville is not a 'first' in her composition of religious sonnet sequences in Britain, but she is an early and innovative composer of strikingly individuated Calvinist sonnet sequences. Emerging out of a

Scottish religio-poetic culture that had been cultivated in the sixteenth century by James VI, but which flourished among a Presbyterian and pietist devotional community that found itself increasingly in opposition to the ecclesiastical policies of the monarch, Melville is representative of a Scottish strain of devotional poetics that warrants much more detailed exploration – both in its own right and in terms of its connections to the burgeoning of imaginative religious poetics in England in the years before Donne and Herbert. Elizabeth Melville's religious sonnets and those of her contemporary James Melville further correct and expand our sense of the religious sonnet in early modern Britain, and provide some preliminary insights into inheritances, influences and comparators through which these texts can be read. Elizabeth Melville, along with Anne Lock, is a notable addition to the roll of religious sonneteers, and a reminder of women's deep engagement in the emerging languages of post-Reformation piety – and in the development of the religious poem – in early modern Britain.

Notes

1 For example, M. Spiller, 'A literary "first": the sonnet sequence of Anne Locke (1560)', *Renaissance Studies*, vol. 11 (1997), pp. 41–55; and, most recently, H. Wilcox, 'Sacred desire, forms of belief: the religious sonnet in early modern Britain', in A. D. Cousins and P. Howarth (eds), *The Cambridge Companion to the Sonnet*, Cambridge University Press, Cambridge, 2011, pp. 145–65, at p. 146. For a discussion of the authorship question, see R. Smith, *Sonnets and the English Woman Writer, 1560–1621: The Politics of Absence*, Palgrave Macmillan, Basingstoke, 2005, pp. 15–26. Lock(e) is variously spelt with and without an 'e'; elsewhere in the chapter original spellings are retained, without any attempt to regularise (e.g. Josuah).

2 Wilcox, 'Sacred desire, forms of belief', p. 145.

3 For women and the development of post-Reformation languages of piety in England, see K. A. Coles, *Religion, Reform, and Women's Writing*, Cambridge University Press, Cambridge, 2008.

4 Wilcox, 'Sacred desire, forms of belief', pp. 156, 158. The next sonnet sequence published by a British woman is Lady Mary Wroth's *Pamphilia to Amphilathus*, a very different kind of text indeed (see chapter 3).

5 R. Targoff, *Common Prayer: The Language of Public Devotion in Early Modern England*, University of Chicago Press, Chicago, 2001, p. 74. Lok republished the *Svndry Christian Passions* with his verse paraphrase of Ecclesiastes in 1597, along with a further 100 *Svndry Affectionate Sonets of a Feeling Conscience*.

6 D. Serjeantson, 'English bards and Scotch poetics: Scotland's literary influence and sixteenth-century English religious verse', in C. Gribben and D. G. Mullan (eds), *Literature and the Scottish Reformation*, Ashgate, Aldershot, 2009, pp. 161–89, at p. 177.

7 J. Reid-Baxter (ed.), *Poems of Elizabeth Melville, Lady Culross*, Solsequium, Edinburgh, 2010. All quotations from Melville's poems are taken from Reid-Baxter's edition.

8 James VI advised in *Ane Schort Treatise Conteining some Reulis and Cautelis to be obseruit and eschewit in Scottis Poesie* (1585) that the sonnet should be used 'for compendious praysing of any bukes, or the author is thair of' – see J. Craigie (ed.), *The Poems of James VI of Scotland*, 2 vols, Scottish Text Society, Edinburgh, 1955, vol. 1,

pp. 65–83, at p. 81. See also J. Reid-Baxter, 'Liminary verse: the paratextual poetry of Renaissance Scotland', *Journal of the Edinburgh Bibliographical Society*, vol. 3 (2008), pp. 70–94.

9   The sonnet to John Welsh is in National Library of Scotland, MS Wod. Qu. XXIX (iv), fols 10–11; it has been anthologised in G. Greer, S. Hastings, J. Medoff and M. Sansone (eds), *Kissing the Rod: An Anthology of Seventeenth-Century Women's Verse*, Noonday Press, New York, 1989, and in J. Stevenson and P. Davidson (eds), *Early Modern Women Poets (1520–1700): An Anthology*, Oxford University Press, Oxford, 2001. The sonnets to Andrew Melville are in the National Library of Scotland, Crawford Collections, Acc. 9769, Personal Papers 84/1/1; see Reid-Baxter, *Poems*, pp. 119–20.

10   J. Reid-Baxter, 'Elizabeth Melville, Calvinism and the lyric voice', in D. J. Parkinson (ed.), *James VI and I, Literature and Scotland: Tides of Change, 1567–1625*, Peeters, Leuven, 2013, pp. 151–72, at p. 154 and note 12.

11   The dedication reads 'To the faithfvll and vertvovs ladie, Elizabeth Mal-vill, Ladie Cumrie'. Alexander Hume, *Hymns, or Sacred Songs, wherein the right vse of Poesie may be espied*, Edinburgh, 1599. See also Reid-Baxter, *Poems*, p. 40.

12   Targoff, *Common Prayer*, p. 74; S. M. Felch, *The Collected Works of Anne Vaughan Lock*, ACMRS, Tempe, 1999, p. lv. All quotations from Lock's sequence are taken from Felch's edition.

13   Ibid., pp. 62–4.

14   Ibid., pp. lv–lvi.

15   See, for example, Serjeantson, 'English bards and Scotch poetics', p. 173; and R. Greene, 'Anne Lock's *Meditation*: invention versus dilation and the founding of puritan poetics', in A. Boesky and M. T. Crane (eds), *Form and Reform: Essays in Honour of Barbara Kiefer Lewalski*, University of Delaware Press, Newark, 2000, pp. 153–70.

16   Greene, 'Anne Lock's *Meditation*', pp. 153, 165.

17   Ibid., p. 166; Spiller, 'A literary "first"', p. 49.

18   R. D. S. Jack, 'Imitation in the Scottish sonnet', *Comparative Literature*, vol. 20 (1968), pp. 313–28, at p. 314; Serjeantson, 'English bards and Scotch poetics', p. 165.

19   Alan Sinfield argues that Philip Sidney's translation of Du Bartas's *La Première Sepmaine* (in manuscript, now lost) postdated James's translation of *L'Uranie*, and that Sidney is likely to have encountered Du Bartas through Scottish connections, including James's tutor George Buchanan. A. Sinfield, 'Sidney and Du Bartas', *Comparative Literature*, vol. 27, no. 1 (1975), pp. 8–20.

20   See, for example, the influence of Du Bartas on Lucy Hutchinson, discussed by Edward Paleit in chapter 1 of the present volume.

21   See www.dsl.ac.uk (accessed December 2011).

22   Serjeantson, 'English bards and Scotch poetics', pp. 182–3.

23   Thanks to Jamie Reid-Baxter for drawing my attention to this poem, first discovered by Sally Mapstone.

24   *Essayes of a Prentise*, sigs Iiij, F.

25   M. R. G. Spiller, *The Development of the Sonnet: An Introduction*, Routledge, London, 1992, p. 104.

26   Jack, 'Imitation in the Scottish sonnet', p. 314.

27   Serjeantson, 'English bards and Scotch poetics', p. 184.

28   Ibid., p. 164, drawing on research by James Doelman.

29   Ibid., p. 162.

30   The datings of the Constable sonnets are Wilcox's: Wilcox, 'Sacred desire, forms of belief', pp. 156, 158.

31   S. C. E. Ross, '"Give me thy hairt and I desyre no more": the Song of Songs, Petrarchism and Elizabeth Melville's puritan poetics', in J. Harris and E. Scott-Baumann (eds), *The Intellectual Culture of Puritan Women, 1558–1680*, Palgrave Macmillan, Basingstoke,

2011, pp. 96–107, at pp. 99–100. Mary Sidney also parodies her brother Philip's *Astrophel and Stella* sonnet 5 in her paraphrase of Psalm 73, both women using the secular sonnet to inform their sacred poetry.

32 Jack, 'Imitation in the Scottish sonnet', p. 318.

33 This revises Ross, '"Give me thy hairt"', p. 102; see R. Lyall, *Alexander Montgomerie: Poetry, Politics, and Cultural Change in Jacobean Scotland*, ACMRS, Tempe, 2005, p. 302.

34 Lok's sonnets 1:87 and 2:4; and Barnes's sonnets 26 and 38. Melville's and Lok's uses of the talent trope revise the sense of uniqueness that caused J. L. Potter to suggest Barnes's talent sonnets as the precedent for Milton's, in 'Milton's "talent" sonnet and Barnabe Barnes', *Notes and Queries*, vol. 202 (1957), p. 447.

35 Lok, *Svndry Christian Passions*, p. 9.

36 'To the fauourable and Christian reader', sig. A3, sonnet 49.

37 Anthony Earl argues that groupings and a narrative progression can nonetheless be perceived, in 'Late Elizabethan devotional poetry and Calvinism: a re-evaluation of Barnabe Barnes', *Renaissance Studies*, vol. 11, no. 3 (1997), pp. 223–40.

38 'To the Christian reader', the preface to Lok's *Svndry Christian Passions* (1593).

39 Wilcox, 'Sacred desire, forms of belief', p. 151.

40 See Ross, '"Give me thy hairt"', for further discussion.

41 On the relationship between Petrarchan and psalmic complaint, see M. P. Hannay, 'Joining the conversation: David, Astrophil, and the Countess of Pembroke', in Z. Lesser and B. S. Robinson (eds), *Textual Conversations in the Renaissance: Ethics, Authors, Technologies*, Ashgate, Aldershot, 2006, pp. 17–49.

42 Greene, 'Anne Lock's *Meditation*', p. 165.

43 James Melville the poet is not to be confused with Elizabeth's father, Sir James Melville of Halhill, a courtier and also a memoirist.

44 *A Morning Vision* is, currently, missing from Early English Books Online (EEBO) (http://eebo.chadwyck.com/home), and James Melville's poetic texts are not widely available.

45 Reid-Baxter discusses the initialled sonnets in his 'Liminary verse'.

46 Marin Le Saulx, *Theanthropogamie*, published by Thomas Vautrollier in London in 1577. Vautrollier resided in Edinburgh from April 1580, as a bookseller and then printer, providing the avenue by which the two Scottish poets are likely to have read the *Theanthropogamie*. See Lyall, *Alexander Montgomerie*, p. 304, drawing on unpublished research by Sally Mapstone. See also Anne Kelly, 'Alexander Montgomerie and the corrections of poetry', in Parkinson (ed.), *James VI and I*, pp. 137–50.

47 Lyall, *Alexander Montgomerie*, pp. 302–6. Lyall provides the full texts of both Montgomerie's and Melville's versions, and his discussion of Montgomerie's devotional verse provides a useful comparative discussion of James Melville's lyrics.

48 Beza had direct links with several Scots Protestants, including Knox, Rollock, Buchanan and James Melville's uncle Andrew. Sally Mapstone explores the James Melville–Beza links in 'James Melville's revisions to *A Spiritvall Propine* and *A Morning Vision*', in Parkinson (ed.), *James VI and I*, pp. 173–92. Jack explores French influences on the Scottish Petrarchan sonnet in 'Imitation in the Scottish sonnet'.

49 Mapstone, 'James Melville's revisions', p. 177.

50 Mapstone emphasises James Melville's view of all of the material in this volume as a catechism. Ibid., p. 174.

51 M. R. G. Spiller, 'The Scottish court and the Scottish sonnet at the union of the crowns', in S. Mapstone and J. Wood (eds), *The Rose and the Thistle: Essays on the Culture of Late Medieval and Renaissance Scotland*, Tuckwell Press, East Lothian, 1998, pp. 101–15, at pp. 108–9.

52 J. Melville, *A Morning Vision*, p. 132.

CHAPTER 3

The Sapphic context of Lady Mary Wroth's *Pamphilia to Amphilanthus*

Line Cottegnies

IN 2006, Louise Labé passed away. She first died in 1566 but, in a recent study, Mireille Huchon caused quite a stir by claiming that the French poet, known as one of the first women to write a sonnet sequence, was probably the greatest literary hoax of all times. Basing her argument on internal evidence and on the praise poems published in Labé's 1555 volume of poetry, Huchon argues that the real Louise Labé (1524–66), who might actually have been a courtesan in Lyons, never wrote the poetry for which she was celebrated. Labé's oeuvre, Huchon claims, was written by a group of male poets, including Maurice Scève.[1] There is something almost perverse about the thought of a circle of conspiring men putting their heads together to ventriloquise a female voice in order to undermine a traditionally male-oriented genre, men who, by creating a woman in print, capitalised on the excitement caused by a shocking new voice – one of many early modern continental women poets who were celebrated for their poetry, including Pernette du Guillet (1520–45), Tullia of Aragona (?1510–56), Vittoria Colonna (1490–1547) and Gaspara Stampa (1523–54). Huchon's theory was bold, even fascinating. It gave a strikingly literal meaning to the structuralist mantra of the 'death of the author'; more fundamentally, it made light of attempts at reading Labé's poetry as the expression of her gender. Thankfully, Huchon's theory has not prevailed; the evidence has not been judged totally convincing by Huchon's peers.[2]

This instance of extreme revisionism is only one form of what can be identified as a contemporary uneasiness – whether conscious or not – with gender studies that start from and return to an identifiable woman writer, and their (at times) fraught negotiation with essentialism. One milder version of this revisionist drive, perhaps more insidious, comes as a side-effect of historicist contextualisation. It consists of approaching a woman writer from the angle of her sources, especially canonical ones, which are supposed to have 'authorised' her. While this quest for origins is necessary to assess the originality of any author, it can also lead to a dissolution of creative agency. Lady Mary Wroth has thus often been read as the product of an unusually brilliant literary genealogy rather than an individual author in her own right. This critical trend is exemplified by Michael Brennan in his introduction to Mary Wroth's *Love's Victory*, when he writes that we should view her 'not as an individual literary figure but rather as an important member of a talented network of writers drawn from the families of the Sidneys and the Herberts'.[3] This approach was in fact encouraged by Wroth herself. She made abundant use of her prestigious genealogy to fashion herself as an author, as the title page of her romance reminds us: 'Written by the right honorable the Lady Mary Wroath. Daughter to the right noble Robert Earle of Leicester. And neece to the ever famous, and renowned Sr. Phillips Sidney knight. And to ye most exele[n]t Lady Mary Countesse of Pembroke late deceased.'[4] As a consequence, both her romance and her sonnet sequence *Pamphilia to Amphilanthus* (published in 1621, at the very end of the sonnet craze in England) have been read as more or less successful *imitations* or offshoots of her uncle Philip Sidney's *Arcadia* and *Astrophil and Stella*. In her sonnet sequence, critics have also detected numerous echoes of the poetry of her father, Sir Robert Sidney, and her cousin (and lover) William Herbert, Earl of Pembroke.[5] The Sidney patriarchal line is impressive and unavoidable but also overbearing in its influence on both the contemporary reception and the critical evaluation of Wroth's authorship. The temptation is to overlook the fact that she might have flaunted her prestigious lineage only to authorise herself and speak in her own name. The sonnet sequence, in fact, indicates careful attention to and use of authorship – specifically female authorship. Thus, in *Pamphilia to Amphilanthus* Wroth presents herself, through the mediation of her persona Pamphilia, as an original *female* voice speaking to a male lover and presumably a male reader as well, in a genre – the sonnet – that was quintessentially coded as male in England.[6] Once we recognise the masculine lineage of the Sidney context as but one part of a picture, albeit an important one, the question of Wroth's use of this voice comes more clearly into focus. Accordingly, this chapter focuses on this self-consciously female stance in the sonnets, by looking at what it could have meant for an English early modern woman to position herself as a female speaker and the author of her own discourse, and to do so in the absence, contrary to what was the case on the continent, of a line of women poets publishing in the neo-Petrarchan tradition.[7]

Whose are the voices that Mary Wroth might have wanted to emulate or respond to? We know that she was raised at Penshurst Place, which had a well endowed library. Can we assess how Wroth's awareness of precedents – female authors and personas – might have framed her response to the neo-Petrarchan tradition? While Mary Sidney Herbert, her aunt, constitutes an obvious influence for Mary Wroth (although the former did not publish any original poetry), this chapter places Wroth's sonnets first in a more European context and, for comparison, it looks at Louise Labé, who, like her, but half a century earlier, wrote a neo-Petrarchan sonnet sequence from the point of view of a betrayed woman. This is turn involves examining the reception of other female voices or famous models that Louise Labé and Mary Wroth could have self-consciously emulated or seen as precedents, and principally Sappho and Ovid, for two reasons: first, because Labé explicitly claimed the patronage of Sappho; and second, because though not written by a woman, Ovid's widely popular *Heroides* offered a series of models for women's lyricism, including a version of Sappho herself. I would like to show that Mary Wroth's sonnets manifest an awareness, if not directly of Labé's poetry, then at least of Sappho's presence, in particular via her Ovidian persona. Once it is more fully established that an Ovidian persona was available to Wroth, it is also possible to contend, as this chapter also does, that Wroth uses the Ovidian model to subvert the poetic of the defeated female self that is central to the expression of the Sapphic subject, that is, to attempt to redeem the shame-ridden female subject from the stigma of self-expression.

Let us begin with the female voices around Wroth. There is no doubt that Mary Sidney Herbert was for her niece a model of female author-ship.[8] Mary Wroth was highly aware of the role played by her aunt in the completion of Philip Sidney's *Arcadia*, as well as of the works published under her own name. The title of her own romance, *The Countesse of Mountgomeries Urania*, is a deliberate echo of *The Countess of Pembroke's Arcadia*, which included Philip Sidney's sonnet sequence, just as *Urania* includes her own *Pamphilia to Amphilanthus*.[9] Wroth's title page also contains a tribute to her aunt, whose death almost coincided with the pub-lication of the *Urania* ('neece ... to ye most exele[n]t Lady Mary Countesse of Pembroke late deceased'). As Margaret Hannay has shown, Wroth took over Pembroke's role as a patron from 1610 onwards, as several poets of the period acknowledged.[10] Mary Sidney Herbert, however, rather than writing original poetry, had chosen translation from the French, Latin and Italian as her favoured mode of self-expression, a form of authorship that was deemed more acceptable for women.[11] Although she did write some occasional verse, very little of which has survived, she never wrote a sonnet sequence. The nature of Mary's Sidney's writing offsets Wroth's boldness and the extent of her own literary ambition, which went together with a certain social recklessness. In fact, Ann Rosalind Jones describes Mary Wroth as a 'declassée'.[12] To find a direct precedent, Wroth would have had to turn to the continent, mainly Italy and France, which had had several prestigious female poets, such as Vittoria Colonna, Gaspara Stampa and Louise Labé.[13] Labé was 'the first great female sonneteer of love' to write in French, a language which Wroth read,[14] but Labé was also one of the very first women to write about a female subject expressing her shame. It is unfortunately impossible to establish whether Wroth actually read Labé, but her *Pamphilia to Amphilanthus* presents interesting similarities with Labé's sonnets in terms of gender politics and self-fashioning. Both sonnet sequences show how a woman could express herself within a genre coded as 'male' and share similar strategies in the appropriation of Petrarchan grammar. Both explicitly stage a female lover-poet mourning her male lover's absence and inconstancy in a sequence that explores the complex – sometimes contradictory – psychology of desire and despair of the neo-Petrarchan model.[15] They both reflect, I argue, the ghostly resurrection of Sappho in the Renaissance, both as a famed poet and as an Ovidian persona.

There was no English translation of Labé's sonnets, but, as an aristocratic woman, Wroth would, as noted, have spoken and read French.[16] In fact, we know from a letter written by Lady Huntingdon that Mary Sidney (Wroth) was sent to the Netherlands, to Flushing and the Hague, where her father was posted as ambassador from 1589, to 'learn the French Tongue'.[17] No inventory of Mary Wroth's library has emerged. However, the library of the Countess of Bridgewater, which Margaret Ezell describes as representative of seventeenth-century women's learning in England, included about twenty French books, mostly literature.[18] Mary Wroth's uncle and aunt, Philip and Mary Sidney, also possessed an impressive library at Wilton; they spoke and read French, and translated several French works.[19] The library at Penshurst, where Mary Sidney (Wroth) was raised, would have been well stocked with French literature: according to a catalogue drafted in the 1660s, it contained between 700 and 800 French books, out of 4,500 volumes. They are mostly occasional and political works and were probably later purchased by Robert Sidney, second Earl of Leicester (1595–1677), while an ambassador in Paris, but there is nevertheless a fairly representative selection of earlier French literature, especially romances.[20] Louise Labé's *Euvres* do not feature in this catalogue, which includes surprisingly little poetry. But this should not surprise us: in the library catalogues of the period, lyrical poetry is usually mentioned (if at all) under such generic titles as 'French songs'. Mary Wroth could have been aware of Labé's *Debate Between Follie and Love*, originally published in the 1555 *Euvres*, which was translated into English by Robert Greene, a close friend of Sidney's, and appended to his romance *Gwendonius* in 1584. This title, however, is not mentioned in the library catalogue, but would probably not have been considered serious enough literature to be mentioned as a separate item. Published without the name of its author ('after the French'), the *Debate Between Follie and Love* is a curious allegorical dialogue. It went through two subsequent editions, in 1587 and 1603. Although Anne Lake Prescrott points to intriguing echoes of Labé's *Debate* in Wroth's pastoral play, which also included a debate between Love and Reason, she concludes that it is impossible to establish whether Wroth knew who its author was.[21] Although Wroth may have read Labé, it cannot be proved.

It is no coincidence, however, that new female voices thrived in the wake of the recent rediscovery of Sappho in Europe.[22] Although Mary Wroth does not actually mention Sappho directly, it is sufficient to look at Louise Labé's poetry to get a sense of the excitement the rediscovery of a female poet's voice from antiquity might have created about fifty years before the publication of *Pamphilia to Amphilanthus*. In elegy 1, which opens her 1555 *Euvres*, Labé explicitly claims to be emulating Sappho and singing 'the Lesbian love' ('l'Amour Lesbienne'),[23] defined here as unrequited love for a male lover. In the commendatory poems written in her honour by 'several poets' in the volume, Labé is repeatedly hailed as the 'Sappho lyonnaise' (the 'Sappho of Lyons'), the 'tenth muse' of France.[24] What was known of Sappho in those years? The period saw a flurry of scholarly interest in Sappho, which spawned a series of transcriptions and imitations in the European republic of letters.[25] Just a few years before Labé's volume appeared, Robert Etienne had published fragment 1 of Sappho's poetry, the so-called 'Ode to Aphrodite', with a poem whose attribution is questioned today, 'The moon has set' (fragment 168B), as part of his 1546 edition of the rhetorician Dionysius of Halicarnassus;[26] one year before Labé's *Euvres*, Henri Estienne included fragments 1 and 31 in Greek with Latin translation in his 1554 edition of Anacreon.[27] These fragments were the 'Ode to Aphrodite' (imitated by Labé in sonnet 5) and the 'Ode to jealousy' (sometimes known as the 'Ode to the beloved'), also popularised by Catullus in *Carmina* 51 long before it was imitated by Labé in sonnet 8.[28] These four poems contributed to establishing the image of Sappho as a mature woman pining for a young man by manipulating the gender of Sappho's lover, but Estienne also included an abridged version of her life by Lilio Gregogio Giraldi, which was fairly explicit about Sappho's alleged previous life.[29] Estienne published more of Sappho's poetry in 1560 in an edition of nine Greek lyric poets, again with Latin translations.[30] According to François Rigolot, it is quite possible that Labé had access to this material even before it was published. These influential editions fixed the image of Sappho, for most Renaissance readers, as a famous Greek female poet distinguished by Plato and later by Longinus, and whose oeuvre had survived only in fragments. She was henceforth presented as a matronly woman abandoned by her younger male lover. This is the image which Ovid also popularised in the fifteenth epistle from Sappho to Phaon in the *Heroides*, where she is just one of many women mourning for their lost lovers, on a par with Oenone, Dido, Ariadne, Hero, Hermione and others.

The significance of Labé's identification with Sappho has been studied in depth by François Rigolot and Joan DeJean, who have shown the importance of the Sapphic Renaissance for her self-fashioning as an author.[31] The publication of Labé's poems coincided with the publication of Pseudo-Longinus's Greek treatise on the sublime by Francesco Robortello in Basel in 1554.[32] This treatise also included Sappho's fragment 31 (the 'Ode to jealousy'), alongside an important commentary that made of the poem, described as 'the sublime Ode', a perfect illustration of Pseudo-Longinus's influential idea of the sublime. Sappho, the treatise argued, moved the reader by depicting the contradictory effects of passion in a way that was thought particularly convincing and lifelike:

> Are you not amazed how at one and the same moment she seeks out soul, body, hearing, tongue, sight, complexion as though they had all left her and were external, and how in contradiction she both freezes and burns, is irrational and sane, is afraid and nearly dead, so that we observe in her not one single emotion but a concourse of emotions? All this of course happens to people in love; but, as I said, it is her selection of the most important details and her combination of them into a single whole that have produced the excellence of the poem.[33]

Although it is not known whether Louise Labé was consciously emulating the Longinian notion of sublimity, Rigolot argues that Labé's poetry as a whole was read in this context as an illustration of the sublime, in that it aimed at moving rather than persuading the reader:[34] 'Ie vis, ie meurs: ie me brule & me noye./I'ay chaut estreme en endurant froidure:/La vie m'est & trop molle & trop dure.'[35] Some of these aesthetic principles were already part of the Petrarchan tradition and its neo-Platonic background, but one can argue that this contemporary context gave a renewed topicality as well as a theoretical basis for the fashionable Petrarchan poetics by emphasising not only the contradictory nature of passion, but also the 'moving representation of this passion'.[36] According to Joan DeJean, however, Labé consciously chose to emulate Sappho, and for reasons that had to do not only with her status as a celebrated poet, but also with the dynamics of desire her poetry displayed, whether Labé read Sappho in the Estienne edition in Latin or in Longinus in Greek (and Latin). In this, she argues, Labé proved a very perceptive reader of the Greek poet, for instance when in elegy 1 she describes the dynamics of desire as 'founded on eternal nonreciprocity', at a time when fragment 1 was, on the contrary, usually read as foreshadowing the eventual satisfaction of desire. DeJean concludes: 'Labé's vision of "Lesbian Love" could, therefore, be seen almost as a fiction of Sapphism that, on one major point at least, is also an uncanny prediction of the most recent theories of the functioning of the Sapphic desire'.[37] But if Labé had carefully read Ovid's *Heroides*, as is likely given how widely the text was read, she would have found ample emphasis both on Sappho's bold authorial stance and on the contradictory nature of her feelings, as will become apparent.

Had Lady Mary Wroth read Sappho? Although, contrary to Labé, she does not explicitly mention the Greek poet, she experiments with the verse form named after her, the sapphics, in the *Urania*, where one of her characters, the Duke of Brunswick, is made to sing lines 'in manner or imitation of Saphiks'.[38] As a poet herself, Wroth must have been aware of the presentation of Sappho as Venus's 'Poetess' in Ovid's immensely popular *Heroides*. Sappho's fragments were not published in English translation until 1749, in the translation by Ambrose Philips, but they would have been available, as seen before, in Estienne's Latin or, for fragment 31, in Pseudo-Longinus's *Treatise of the Sublime*. The latter treatise was accessible in Latin through several continental editions as early as 1572, and was well known in England at the beginning of the seventeenth century.[39] The British Isles, however, seem to have been only marginally concerned by the flurry of activity around Sappho herself in the sixteenth and seventeenth centuries. Philip Sidney was one of the few to have been very interested in Estienne's philological work, and he even corresponded with him.[40] Although the catalogue of the Penshurst library does not include the Estienne edition of Anacreon or his Greek anthology, it does include Estienne's Greek thesaurus.[41] Philip Sidney, Mary's uncle, knew Sappho's poetry well: he translated fragment 1, the 'Ode to Aphrodite', into anacreontics in the second Eclogues of the *Arcadia*. In the first Eclogues, Pyrocles, dressed up as Cleophilia, reads out 'Sapphics' to Philoclea – which, as Julie Crawford has recently argued, shows that Sidney was wittily playing with the homo-erotic implications of the lines.[42] Mary Sidney Herbert, Mary's aunt, also experimented with sapphics in Psalm 125.[43] Although we do not know whether Mary Wroth had access to the Sapphic fragments that had recently come to light, her poetry takes up two themes central to Sappho's poetry – although it must be granted that they were not totally specific to Sappho: nocturnal solitude (as seen in 'The moon has set') and the wild alternations of moods of the subject in love (as in fragment 31, the poem that was reproduced in Longinus, for instance). Wroth's sonnet P63 actually combines these two themes:

> In night may wee see some kind of light
> When as the Moone doth please to show her face,

...
Soe are my fortunes, bard from true delight
Colde, and unsertaine, like to this strang place,
Decreasing, changing in an instant space,
And even att full of joy turn'd to despite[.][44]

However, it might seem a little difficult to pinpoint a *direct* Sapphic influence in Wroth's poetry, given the paucity of sources and the rather unspecific nature of the themes in question. One of the reasons for Sappho's relative currency in the period (just like Pseudo-Longinus's) might simply have something to do with the domination of the Petrarchan influence, with its emphasis on the *voluptas dolendi* and its poetic of paradoxes – which implied a predilection for figures of oppositions such as antitheses, chiasmi and oxymora. Paradoxes and binary oppositions are indeed an essential part of Wroth's style, and of many sonnet sequences of the period, and this in a way reflects her familiarity with the literary context. But Wroth's poetry goes beyond the common heritage, radicalising these binary oppositions, which become vertiginously systematic in *Pamphilia to Amphilanthus*: 'From contraries I seeke to runn   Ay mee; / Butt contraries I can nott shunn   Ay mee' (P14, p. 93).

Can this radicalisation of stylistic effects be attributed to a Sapphic influence? Beyond the Sidney circle, it seems in fact that Sappho was mainly known in England through the Ovidian tradition. This is attested by Donne's curious epistle 'Sappho to Philenis', written around 1610, which calls attention to Sappho's discreet, but enduring, presence in early modern England. In the *Heroides*, translated into English by George Tuberville in 1567, Sappho is described as a whining matron pining for her lover.[45] That Donne set out to refute this version of a benign, more conventional Sappho by strikingly re-emphasising the gender of her beloved – following suit with Sidney, in fact – points to the fact that he also knew enough about the original Sappho to wittily set the record straight. It is quite possible, of course, that Donne knew of Estienne's work, where he could have found fairly explicit footnotes and a short biography of Sappho, but it would have been sufficient even to read Ovid's *original* Latin text carefully for him to garner all the necessary details about Sappho's early life.[46] Ovid's *Heroides* were in fact widely read across the school curriculum and used as material for Latin imitations in the sixteenth and seventeenth centuries.[47] Donne was thus only adapting a school exercise in order to write a *risqué* erotic piece. Recently, several scholars have reminded us of the importance of the *Heroides* as a collection of epistles by fictional *writing women*. Georgia Brown, for instance, has described Ovid's poems 'as repositories of forms of emotions [that] were read and sold as poems that readers could adapt to their own emotional purposes'.[48] Although they were in effect pieces of 'transvestite ventriloquism', they created convincing illusions of female authorial voices, and as such might have helped ease 'the stigma of print' for women.[49] In her perceptive study, Brown has shown that the craze for the epistle and the epyllion is essential for what she calls the 'generation of shame' as a dominant trait of early modern literature, with its new emphasis on individuality, intimacy and the value of personal experience.[50] Danielle Clarke has recently focused on creative imitation in Drayton's *Englands Heroicall Epistles*, but has also suggested that Ovid was carefully read by women writers like Isabella Whitney.[51] As Elizabeth Harvey has noted, however, Ovid used women's voices as a means of challenging 'conventional notions of tradition, of origins, of fathers, of paternity, of authority, of identity', but could write as a woman precisely because he was not one.[52] She nevertheless comments on the importance of Ovid's version of Sappho, which blurred the boundaries 'between "authentic" and constructed discourse'. While the *figure* of Sappho herself, as a celebrated ancient poet, offered women who desired to put pen to paper the empowering precedent of a female writer praised by the greatest poets and thinkers of antiquity, Ovid's *Heroides* offered ready-to-use models of women singing about their discontent in the form of the epistolary complaint.

Mary Wroth had most certainly read Ovid's *Heroides* in the 1567 translation by Tuberville, if not in Latin. In a poem inserted in *Urania*, she explicitly refers to the model of the Ovidian epistle by having her character Dorolina compare herself, in a complaint, to four of Ovid's heroines, Dido, Ariadne, Phillis and Penelope.[53] Here she clearly uses the *Heroides* as a repertoire of women singing in mourning for their plight. If it is the Tuberville version Wroth read, she might have been struck by the description of Sappho's wild alternation of moods: her assertive authorial stance, followed with her total, profoundly humiliating, lack of self-control. If the 'scandal' of her previous life was muted in this version, Sappho in Elizabethan garb was depicted as a defeated, discombobulated woman, alternately 'frantic', 'enraged' and prostrate, a formerly celebrated poet whose inspiration has petered in the face of her degrading obsession for the young Phaon:

> My wonted vaine in verse
> > Is overdry become:
> My lowring Lute laments for woe,
> > My Harpe with doole is dombe.[54]

Sappho is also depicted as an abandoned woman whose erotic yearning and sense of shame and guilt lead her to flagellate herself in *public* verse, to 'increase [her] shame' (p. 241): 'How there with open breast I stoode / the

Vulgar folke did see' (p. 241). This confirms again Georgia Brown's argument that the emergence of a new literary subject in the late Elizabethan era was intrinsically linked with the expression of shame: indeed, self-promotion and self-articulation are both 'sources of shame' (p. 220). If we read Mary Wroth's sonnet sequence in this perspective, then we see a female poet grappling with the necessary pursuit of (shameful) self-assertion. The sonnets can in fact be read as an attempt at redeeming the shame-ridden female subject from the stigma of self-expression, a stigma made worse by the fact that she was writing her poems in the context of her own socially improper situation. Her love sonnets, focusing as they did on a female poet abandoned by a lover, would inevitably have called to mind the scandal of her illegitimate affair with her own cousin. Both Labé and Wroth, then, present themselves (through their personas) as *fallen* women, whose sense of guilt is a central dimension of their experience of loss and of their lyricism. Not only do they depict themselves in the first person as having yielded to male courtship – the two sonnet sequences are explicitly about consummation and its aftermaths – but they both speak from the undignified position of the abandoned woman. The two principles of the neo-Petrarchan ethos, chastity and the emphasis on courtship, are thus turned into their opposites, promiscuity and post-consummation desolation. The sonnets for both Labé and Wroth imply at some basic level the exposure of a scandal.

Ovid obviously provided Mary Wroth with the title for her sonnet sequence, 'Pamphilia *to* Amphilanthus', which reads like the title of an Ovidian epistle; where a single name or the two lovers' names associated with the copula 'and' would have been more appropriate for a sonnet sequence, the 'to' evokes *The Heroides*. This choice is significant because, as a title, it frames the Petrarchan sequence and prompts the reader to locate it within an Ovidian form. The insistence in the poems on secrecy and coded exchange participate in the impression that we are indeed paradoxically dealing with semi-private public epistolary exchanges.[55] Addressing her own heart in sonnet P41, for instance, Wroth/Pamphilia emphasises the secret nature of her love: 'When thy chiefe paine is that I must itt hide / From all save only one who showld itt see' (p. 107). In sonnet P32, she describes her sacrifice as necessary: 'Since I must suffer, for an others rest' (p. 103). As we see, the Ovidian epistolary frame allows her to subvert the Petrarchan conventions in a subtle way; it evidences, I contend, that Wroth's sonnets show a strong awareness of the Ovidian ventriloquised female voice, which she reinterprets in a creative way. As will be apparent, she reacts most particularly against the dynamics of Sapphic desire that it reflects, with its emphasis on the intimate link between loss and the literary expression of shame.

Danielle Clarke offers an important caveat, warning us against taking the sonnet sequence as the direct expression of Mary Wroth's own feelings, given that Pamphilia in the sonnets is explicitly constructed as a persona by the Pamphilia of *The Urania* – who is herself a fictional character. The sonnet sequence, Clarke claims, is part of Pamphilia's strategy to conquer Amphilanthus in the romance. This implies that the speaker in the sonnets must be seen as created by Pamphilia, rather than by Wroth herself.[56] We must certainly keep this in mind, but, beyond this framing device, Pamphilia is also one of Wroth's personas, all the more so as the sonnet sequence might have been circulated separately as well, if we are to believe Josephine Roberts – and therefore out of the context of the romance.[57] Ovid's ventriloquised voices offer Wroth/Pamphilia a new take on the neo-Petrarchan emphasis on the contradictory nature of desire. Several critics have, in fact, commented on what they perceive as a masochistic, self-destructive drive in Wroth.[58] But the Ovidian context helps us understand the way in which Wroth turns the experience of loss and despair into an ethos which she calls 'the constant art' (P3, p. 86). Embracing the risk of repetition, the speaker thus repeatedly calls herself 'hapless me' (P6, P7, P10, P54…), a woman who 'nor can have hope, butt to see hopes undunn' (P25, p. 99). By describing herself as constant yet powerless, the 'hapless' subject displays herself negatively, as a void or an absence, hollowing herself out, as it were: in sonnet P52, she describes herself as almost schizophrenically haunted and 'possessed' by 'the hellish speritt absence' (p. 113). Jeff Masten astutely reads this paradoxical self-assertion as the affirmation of a female subjectivity 'only in terms of lack'.[59] Ann Rosalind Jones sees it as revealing, in more symbolic terms, an imaginative shift whereby Wroth turns loss of social status into amorous loss.[60] In fact, we could even go one step further: by staging her gradual self-annihilation, the speaker literally turns herself inside out – she *starves* herself, to use one of her favourite metaphors, in a form of literary anorexia, and ends up symbolically erasing herself in an ostentatious manner.[61] In doing so, she paradoxically exhibits her erasure, filling up the void with the spectacle of her suffering, disappearing self, poem after poem: 'dying I' (P49, p. 112), 'I might have binn an Image of delight, / as now a Tombe' (P67, p. 122).

Wroth's repeated self-obliteration offers a sharp contrast with the triumphant self-assertion of a poet such as Louise Labé. It paradoxically allows Pamphilia to finally transcend the pathos and powerlessness of both Ovid's shameful female characters and of the silent ladies of the innumerable sonnet sequences of the period. In the economy of loss and gain staged in the sequence, Wroth's persona can be seen to turn her loss ('poor me', writing to her 'dear', P42, pp. 108–9) into symbolic gain or 'profitts' (P37, p. 105), 'winning where ther no hope lies' (P21, p. 97), by virtue of a series

70

of *double entendres*. Wroth's sonnet sequence teems, in fact, with references to pecuniary exchanges as metaphors for emotional and sentimental exchanges: 'losses now must prove my fare' (P33, p. 103). It is clear that Wroth uses the potentialities of her name, which was spelt alternatively 'Wroth' or 'Worth', to play on the polysemy of the word 'worth', both as economic and as moral value or merit. Onomastic puns were inherent in the Petrarchan tradition, from Petrarch's *double entendres* on 'Laura' down to Philip Sidney's puns on the name of Lady Penelope Rich, the Stella of his *Astrophil and Stella*.[62] Several poets had also celebrated Lady Mary Wroth for her 'worth', such as Ben Jonson in his dedication to *The Alchemist*.[63] However, the economic metaphors rampant in *Pamphilia to Amphilanthus* all serve the strategy of symbolic exchange described above. Crucially, the sonnets allow the 'worthles rite' (P25, p. 99) of Mary Wroth's mournful songs to be turned into a celebration of her own 'worth', a reassertion of her constancy and virtue in the face of male inconstancy and promiscuity, as a way of redeeming the stigma of past immodesty.[64] Through the guise of her persona Pamphilia, Wroth thus spectacularly relieves herself of the shame attached to her situation as a woman seduced and abandoned by an indelicate lover.

By the same token, she also subverts the portrait Ovid had offered of Sappho in the *Heroides*, with her wild alternation of moods and her oscillation between shame and sorrow, and fury and despair. In contrast, Wroth/Pamphilia is made literally to belie another meaning of her name, by ostentatiously eschewing any predisposition to 'wroth' or wrath. In poem after poem Pamphilia stages herself instead as meek and patient, although this is not without revealing some tension: Mary Wroth's poetry has been described as tortuously fragmented and disjuncted, labyrinthine even. It is obscure at best, opaque at worst. In Roger Kuin's apt words, the text's 'body language' is 'one of crossed arms, crossed legs, hunched shoulders and a sidelong or downward look'.[65] For the critic, the language of spectacular self-abstention is a language that reveals inhibition and perplexity, 'the slightly strangled swan-song of a dying code'.[66] But there is a more positive way of reading this choice of a contorted style than as a symptom of failure. Wroth's poetry is radical in its innovations, drawing in the *Urania* upon a variety of poetic models.[67] *Pamphilia to Amphilanthus* shows an usual degree of sophistication in the way the neo-Petrarchan conventions are recuperated and recycled. According to Barbara Kiefer Lewalski, Wroth espoused the stereotypical feminine virtue – constancy – as a kind of 'camouflage' to divert the readers' attention away from the radical innovations of her sonnet sequence.[68] But it can be argued that Pamphilia asserts her own 'worth' by emphasising steady resolve and constancy not as camouflage, but as self-conscious strategy, aiming at sublimating the stalemate and at escaping from the sterile tropes of binary oppositions: 'winning, where ther noe hope lies' (p. 97).

To conclude, we see how Mary Wroth's lyrical voice in her sonnets emerges from her knowledge and revision of both neo-Petrarchan precedents and classical models such as the ones provided by Ovid's *Heroides*. It is clear that she saw in Sappho a famous female poet who could offer a model for self-expression, in particular for the expression of the contradictory nature of desire, described as the alternation between shame and the assertion of a female lyric voice. In *Pamphilia to Amphilanthus* the neo-Petrarchan trope of the defeated self is displaced by the Ovidian shameful female subject, who is revised and de-eroticised. The sequence thus obsessively stages the disciplining of shame by Pamphilia: the exposure, in print, of her own shame and failure to the reader's gaze is eventually turned into the affirmation of a new lyric female voice, a voice whose originality has to do with fragmentation and self-contradiction. What Wroth's sonnets exemplify is the metamorphosis of the hapless 'she' into a paradoxically powerful female subject who ostentatiously turns her weakness into a mode of assertion.

Notes

1 M. Huchon, *Louise Labé: Une Créature de Papier*, Droz, Geneva, 2006.

2 For a summary of the polemic, see M. McKinley, 'Louise Labé, "invention Lyonnaise" et polémique internationale', *Revue Critique*, vol. 737 (2008), pp. 748–54.

3 M. Brennan, 'Introduction', in M. Brennan (ed.), *Lady Mary Wroth's Loves Victory, the Penshurst Manuscript*, Roxburghe Club, London, 1988, pp. 8–9. Danielle Clarke comments, before showing how we should see Wroth as 'capitalizing' on the Sidneian heritage rather than 'capitulating' to her male relatives: 'Wroth is rightly viewed by most critics as a belated Sidneian imitator, whose diction and generic choices are ineluctably the product of her familial environment'. D. Clarke, *The Politics of Early Modern Women's Writing*, Longman, London, 2001, pp. 213, 214. William J. Kennedy reads 'an expression of totemic allegiance for the Sidney family's achievements' in Mary Worth's *Pamphilia to Amphilanthus*. W. J. Kennedy, *The Site of Petrarchism: Early Modern National Sentiment in Italy, France, and England*, Johns Hopkins University Press, Baltimore, 2003, p. 250.

4 *The Countesse of Mountgomeries Urania. Written by the right honorable the Lady Mary Wroath. Daughter to the right noble Robert Earle of Leicester. And neece to the ever famous, and renowned Sr. Phillips Sidney knight. And to ye most exele[n]t Lady Mary Countesse of Pembroke late deceased*, London, Printed [by Augustine Mathewes?] for Ioh[n] Marriott and Iohn Grismand and are to bee sould at theire shoppes in St. Dunstons Church yard in Fleetstreet and in Poules Ally at ye signe of the Gunn [1621].

5 See in particular G. Waller, *The Sidney Family Romance: Mary Wroth, William Herbert and the Early Modern Construction of Gender*, Wayne State University Press, Detroit, 1993; M. Quilligan, 'The constant subject: instability and female authority in Wroth's *Urania* poems', in E. D. Harvey and K. Eisaman Maus (eds), *Soliciting Interpretation: Literary Theory and Seventeenth-Century English Poetry*, University of Chicago Press, Chicago, 1990, pp. 307–35.

6   For a similar argument, see H. Dubrow, *Echoes of Desire: English Petrarchism and Its Counterdiscourses*, Cornell University Press, Ithaca, 1995, p. 135; M. E. Lamb, *Gender and Authorship in the Sidney Circle*, University of Wisconsin Press, Madison, 1990, ch. 4.

7   For the existence of a line of female religious poets, see chapter 2 of the present volume.

8   See for instance M. Hannay, '"Your Vertuous and Learned Aunt": the Countess of Pembroke as a mentor to Mary Wroth', in N. Miller and G. Waller (eds), *Reading Mary Wroth: Representing Alternatives in Early Modern England*, University of Tennessee Press, Knoxville, 1991, pp. 15–34; and M. Hannay, *Mary Sidney, Lady Wroth*, Ashgate, Farnham, 2010, pp. 229–30.

9   The 1621 edition of Wroth's *The Countess of Montgomery's Urania* seems very much modelled on the 1598 edition of *The Countess of Pembroke's Arcadia*, which also contained Sidney's sonnet sequence, as an appendix, just as Wroth included *Pamphilia to Amphilanthus* as an appendix to her romance.

10 See Hannay, *Mary Sidney*, pp. 153–7. Rosalind Smith points to connections between Wroth and radical Spenserian poets. R. Smith, *Sonnets and the English Woman Writer, 1560–1621*, Palgrave, London, 2005, pp. 99–100.

11 See for instance S. Trill, 'Sixteenth-century women's writing: Mary Sidney's *Psalmes* and the "femininity" of translation', in W. Zunder and S. Trill (eds), *Writing and the English Renaissance*, Longman, London, 1996, pp. 140–58, at p. 143 in particular; and D. Clarke, *The Politics of Early Modern Women's Writing*, Longman/Pearson Education, London, 2001, p. 13.

12 Lady Mary Wroth had to withdraw from society because of the scandalous situation in which she found herself, and Ann Rosalind Jones interprets Mary Wroth's *Pamphilia to Amphilanthus* as an attempt to 'rewrite her disgrace'. A. R. Jones, 'Designing women: the self as spectacle in Mary Wroth and Veronica Franco', in Miller and Waller (eds), *Reading Mary Wroth*, pp. 135–53, at p. 137.

13 Jones (ibid.) compares Mary Wroth to Veronica Franco.

14 Roger Kuin, 'More I Still Undoe: Louise Labé, Mary Wroth, and the Petrarchan discourse', *Comparative Literary Studies*, vol. 36 (1999), pp. 146–61, at p. 148.

15 Only two articles have briefly compared Labé and Wroth, without suggesting any direct influence of Labé on Wroth: Kuin, ibid.; and A. Lake Prescott, 'Mary Wroth, Louise Labé and Cupid', *The Sidney Journal*, vol. 15, no. 2 (1997), pp. 37–41.

16 For Wroth's knowledge of French, see N. J. Miller, *Changing the Subject: Mary Wroth and Figurations of Gender in Early Modern England*, University of Kentucky Press, Lexington, 1996, p. 45.

17 *HMC, De L'Isle*, II, 268, cited in J. Roberts, 'Introduction', in J. Roberts (ed.), *The Poems of Lady Mary Wroth*, Louisiana State University Press, Baton Rouge, 1983, p. 9. All subsequent quotations of Wroth's poems are from this edition.

18 M. J. M. Ezell, *The Patriarch's Wife: Literary Evidence and the History of the Family*, University of North Carolina Press, Chapel Hill, 1987, pp. 15–16. Heidi Brayman Hackel includes the catalogue of the library as an appendix in *Reading Material in Early Modern England: Print, Gender and Literacy*, Cambridge University Press, Cambridge, 2005. It contained eighteen books in French (out of 241 volumes) (p. 251). Incidentally, the Countess owned a copy of *Urania* (p. 262).

19 Philip Sidney translated Philippe de Mornay's *A Woorke concerning the trewnesse of the Christian religion, written in French*, published in 1587, and Mary Sidney translated de Mornay's *A Discourse of Life and Death*, with Robert Garnier's *Antonius*, both published in 1592.

20 I would like to thank Joseph Black for sharing the catalogue of the library before it was published. G. Warkentin, J. L. Black and W. R. Bowen (eds), *The Library of the Sidneys of Penshurst Place*, University of Toronto Press, Toronto, 2013. See also G. Warkentin, 'The world and the book at Penshurst: the second Earl of Leicester (1595–1677) and his library', *The Library*, vol. s6-xx (1998), pp. 325–46.

21 See Lake Prescott, 'Mary Wroth, Louise Labé and Cupid'.

22 According to Stella Revard, Sappho was interpreted as one of the leading lyric voices of erotic literature. See S. P. Revard, 'The Sapphic voice in Donne's "Sappho to Philaenis"', in C. J. Summers and T. L. Pebworth (eds), *Renaissance Discourses of Desire*, University of Missouri, Columbia, 1993, pp. 63–7.

23 L. Labé, *Euvres de Louïze Labé Lionnoize*, Lyon, Jean de Tournes, 1555, Elegie I, p. 100. See J. DeJean, *Fictions of Sappho 1546–1937*, University of Chicago Press, Chicago, 1989, p. 39.

24 Quoted in F. Rigolot, *Louise Labé Lyonnaise ou la Renaissance au féminin*, Honoré Champion, Paris, 1997, p. 44.

25 See Rigolot, *Louise Labé*, pp. 31–61.

26 *Dionysii Halicarnassei antiquitatum Romanarum lib. X*, Parisiis, ex officina Stephani, 1546–47.

27 *Anacreontis odae, ab Henrico Stephano luce et latinitate nunc primum donatae*, Lutetiae, apud H. Stephanum, 1554.

28 The first French translation of fragment 31, however, was published by Belleau in 1556 as appendix to his translation of Anacreon, *Les Odes d'Anacréon Teien traduites du grec*, Paris, 1556. Belleau is unusual in his 'decision to follow Sappho rather than her Latin successor for this scene of unrequited love' (DeJean, *Fictions*, p. 34), since he makes the person she loves female.

29 DeJean, *Fictions*, p. 30.

30 *Epigrammata Graeca, selecta ex Anthologia*, [Genevae], 1560. For the philological history of the publication of Sappho, see DeJean, *Fictions*, pp. 29–42. See also J. Crawford, 'Sidney's sapphics and the role of interpretive communities', *English Literary History*, vol. 69, no. 4 (2002), pp. 979–1007, at p. 1001, n. 32.

31 Rigolot, *Louise Labé*, pp. 54–67. See also M. B. Moore, *Desiring Voices: Women Sonneteers and Petrarchism*, Southern Illinois University Press, Carbondale, 2000, pp. 94–124. According to DeJean, 'she is the first … elaborately to stage her accession to authorship through an identification with the original woman writer, as the process by which she becomes a Sappho in her own right'. DeJean, *Fictions*, pp. 38–9.

32 *Dionysii Longini … Liber de grandi sive sublimi orationis genere [Texte imprimé], nunc primum a Francisco Robortello … in lucem editus ejusdemque annotationibus …*, Basilae, [n.s.].

33 Longinus, *On Sublimity*, quoted in D. A. Campbell (ed.), *Greek Lyric*, Harvard University Press, Loeb Classical Library, Cambridge, 1982, vol. I, p. 81.

34 Rigolot, *Louise Labé*, pp. 64–6.

35 Labé, sonnet VIII, *Euvres*, p. 115. 'I live, I die: I burn and drown. / I suffer extreme heat and yet am cold / Life is to me both too soft and too hard' (my translation).

36 Rigolot, *Louise Labé*, p. 65.

37 DeJean, *Fictions*, p. 41.

38 J. Roberts (ed.), *The First Part of the Countess of Montgomery's Urania*, Medieval and Renaissance Texts and Studies, Binghamton, 1995, p. 604.

39 *Anakreontos Teiou Mele Anacreontis Teii Carmina*, Londini, 1695. Longinus was published in England, with a Latin translation, only in 1636, by Gerard Langbaine (*Dionysii Longini rhetoris praestantissimi. Liber De grandi loquentia sive sublimi dicendi genere*, Oxford, 1636). It was translated into English by John Hall in 1652 (*Of the Height of Eloquence*). For the reception of Longinus in England, see T. J. Spencer, 'Longinus in English criticism: influences before Milton', *Review of English Studies*, new series, vol. 8, no. 30 (May 1957), pp. 137–43. See Chapman's hostile comment in his preface to *Homer*.

40 A. H. Upham, *The French Influence in English Literature from the Accession of Elizabeth to the Restoration*, Columbia University Press, New York, 1908, p. 48.

41 H. Estienne, *Thesaurus graecae linguae*, 5 vols, H. Estienne, Geneva, 1572.

42 See J. Robertson (ed.), *The Countess of Pembroke's Arcadia*, Clarendon Press, Oxford,

1973, pp. 81–2. Sidney also paraphrases Sappho's 'Ode to Aphrodite' in the second Eclogues, see pp. 163–4. See Crawford, 'Sidney's sapphics', pp. 979–80.

43 See M. P. Hannay, N. J. Kinnamon and M. G. Brennan (eds), *The Collected Works of Mary Sidney Herbert*, Clarendon Press, Oxford, 1998, vol. 2. Thomas Campion describes the 'English sapphic' in *Observations in the Art of English Poesie*, London, 1602, pp. 30–1.

44 Roberts (ed.), *The Poems of Lady Mary Wroth*, p. 119. Further citations are given in the body of the text.

45 *The Heroycall Epistles of the Learned Poet Publius Ovidius Naso in English Verse, Translated by George Tuberville*, London, 1567. Sappho's epistle is number 17 (pp. 108–17). On Donne and Sappho, see H. L. Meakin, *John Donne's Articulations of the Feminine*, Clarendon Press, Oxford, 1998, pp. 101–10.

46 See Revard, 'The Sapphic voice'.

47 For the importance of Ovid's epistles, see M. L. Stapleton, 'Edmund Spenser, George Tuberville, and Isabella Whitney Read Ovid's *Heroides*', *Studies in Philology*, vol. 105, no. 4 (2008), pp. 487–519.

48 G. Brown, *Redefining English Literature*, Cambridge University Press, Cambridge, 2004, p. 44 and, more generally, pp. 36–52 and 80–1.

49 E. D. Harvey, *Ventriloquized Voices: Feminist Theory and English Renaissance Texts*, Routledge, London, 1992, p. 50 and, more generally, pp. 15–53.

50 Brown, *Redefining English Literature*, p. 46.

51 See D. Clarke, 'Ovid's *Heroides*, Drayton and the articulation of the feminine in the English Renaissance', *Renaissance Studies*, vol. 22, no. 3 (2008), pp. 385–400; and Clarke, *The Politics*, pp. 194–5. See also her introduction to *Isabella Whitney, Mary Sidney, and Aemilia Lanyer*, Penguin, Harmondsworth, 2000, pp. xiii–xiv.

52 Harvey, *Ventriloquized Voices*, pp. 39–40. The quotation is from L. Kauffman, *Discourses of Desire: Gender, Genre, and Epistolary Fictions*, Cornell University Press, Ithaca, 1986, p. 61.

53 See U35, in Roberts (ed.), *The Poems of Lady Mary Wroth*, pp. 172–4.

54 F. Boas (ed.), *The Heroycall Epistles of the Learned Poet Publius Ovidius Naso* (trans. G. Tuberville), Cresset Press, London, 1928, p. 246. Subsequent citations are given in the body of the text.

55 According to Jeff Masten, Mary Wroth's sequence shows 'a woman's privatization of the genre towards other ends'. J. Masten, 'Shall I turne blabb? Circulation, gender and subjectivity in Mary Wroth's sonnets', in Miller and Waller (eds), *Reading Mary Wroth*, pp. 67–87, at p. 76.

56 Clarke, *The Politics*, p. 217.

57 See Roberts, 'Introduction', in *The Poems of Lady Mary Wroth*.

58 See for instance Waller, *The Sidney Family Romance*, p. 205.

59 Masten, 'Shall I turne blabb?', pp. 76 and 81.

60 A. R. Jones, 'Designing women: the self as spectacle', in Miller and Waller (eds), *Reading Mary Wroth*, pp. 135–53, at p. 144.

61 Elizabeth Hanson talks about autism in 'Boredom and whoredom: reading Renaissance women's sonnet sequences', *Yale Journal of Criticism*, vol. 10, no. 1 (1997), pp. 65–91.

62 Petrarch also punned on the inclusion of the word 'petra' (stone), almost magically present in his own name (Petrarca), to describe his psychological state as stupefied or turned to stone.

63 'To the Lady, most Deserving Her Name, and Blood: Mary, Lady Worth', in A. B. Kernan (ed.), *The Alchemist* [1612], Yale University Press, New Haven, 1974, p. 19.

64 Wroth seems to be aware here of how vital and ambivalent print publication could be for a woman's 'fame', both as a medium for self-preservation for a female author in the face of censorship, and as a source of public exposure. As Paul Salzman shows in chapter 6 of the present volume, manuscripts written by women could easily be suppressed and withdrawn from circulation, as was her answer to Denny, effectively.

65 Kuin, 'More I Still Undoe', p. 156. Danielle Clarke talks of a text 'which is constantly consuming itself, redacting all of its conflicts into an unstable self which cannot reconcile (or contain) all of these contrary impulses'. Clarke, *The Politics*, p. 219.

66 Kuin, 'More I Still Undoe', p. 157.

67 Clarke, *The Politics*, p. 214.

68 B. Kiefer Lewalski, *Writing Women in Jacobean England*, Harvard University Press, Cambridge, 1993, p. 263.

CHAPTER 4

Women poets and men's sentences: genre and literary tradition in Katherine Philips's early poetry

Gillian Wright

There is no reason to think that the form of the epic or of the poetic play suit a woman any more than the sentence suits her. But all the older forms of literature were hardened and set by the time she became a writer.[1]

IN *A Room of One's Own* (1929), Virginia Woolf meditated on the difficulties faced by women of earlier centuries in trying to imagine themselves into English literary tradition. For Woolf, these difficulties were epitomised by the literary sentence inherited by nineteenth-century women novelists such as Jane Austen, Charlotte Brontë and George Eliot from their eighteenth-century predecessors. This sentence, which enabled male writers such as William Thackeray and Charles Dickens to write 'a natural prose, swift but not slovenly, expressive but not precious', proved altogether more forbidding for aspiring women writers of the same period. The early nineteenth-century sentence, in Woolf's account, was 'a man's sentence', shaped by and redolent of the male stylists of the eighteenth century ('Johnson, Gibbon and the rest'). While facilitating the great male-authored novels of the Victorian age, it was utterly 'unsuited for a woman's use'.[2] Brontë 'stumbled and fell with that clumsy weapon in her hands', while Eliot 'committed atrocities with it that beggar description'. By contrast, Austen's astonishing success in reinventing the English novel was due to, and encapsulated by, her ability to ignore this prohibitively male sentence. Austen 'looked at it and laughed at it and devised a perfectly natural, shapely sentence proper for her own use and never departed from it'. Her example, in turn, helped ensure that the novel – still a young, 'soft' genre in the early nineteenth century – could be claimed and reworked by subsequent women writers for their own, inevitably gendered, purposes.

Following Margaret Ezell's influential critique in 'The myth of Judith Shakespeare', Woolf's imaginative rendering of women's literary history in *A Room of One's Own* has, rightly, been subjected to intensive scrutiny.[3] But although numerous aspects of Woolf's historiography are now known to have been factually inaccurate, many of her insights in *Room* none-theless remain both valid and critically productive. Most importantly, for present purposes, while Woolf was demonstrably wrong to imply that women writers, before Austen, were unable to write themselves into pre-existing, 'hardened' literary forms, she was right to identify generic engagement – in particular, engagement with poetic genres – as a matter for discomfort and anxiety among aspiring women writers of the early modern period.[4] If we examine the history of English-language women's poetry between the late sixteenth and mid-seventeenth centuries, it is striking how few female writers sought to engage with multiple poetic genres. Those who did, such as Mary Sidney and Mary Wroth, were very much the exceptions that prove the rule: both Sidney and Wroth were supported by their family's well established culture of poetic production and both worked principally in genres previously favoured by Sidney's brother, Philip.[5] Many of the women who lacked such familial support preferred to restrict the circulation of their writing to manuscript, or chose to devote their efforts to just one literary genre or subject. Finding the creative means to negotiate and rework a wider range of poetic genres seems to have been a challenge too far.

By the mid-seventeenth century, however, change was underway. In *Poems and Fancies* (1653), Margaret Cavendish (1623?–73) – supported, ad-mittedly, by a devoted and poetically knowledgeable husband – published verses on a wide range of subjects and in a wide range of genres.[6] Yet although Cavendish did work to some extent with established genres, such as dialogues, many of the forms and topics included in *Poems and Fancies* were of her own invention and owe little to pre-existing literary traditions. This generic independence – attractive though it has proved for twentieth- and twenty-first-century readers – means that Cavendish's poetry shows relatively little sign of the reception and reinvention of male-generated forms, tropes and motifs. To see how a woman of this period could respond – knowledgeably, creatively and diversely – to this problematic generic inheritance, we need to look elsewhere – in particular, to the work of Cavendish's younger contemporary, Katherine Philips (1632–64).

Philips is important to the history of English women's poetry for several reasons. One, most obviously, is that she wrote in a wide range of genres, showing a detailed knowledge and appreciation of pre-existing poetry, prose and drama, in both English and French. Another is that she – unlike Cavendish, as well as most other women writers of earlier periods – enjoyed a widespread and (mainly) favourable public reception in the seventeenth and early eighteenth centuries.[7] Philips's 1667 *Poems* (and its subsequent reprints) garnered admiration from both male and female readers, includ-ing John Dryden, George Farquhar, Aphra Behn and Jane Barker.[8] Indeed,

Philips's particular value as an authorising role model for other women does a lot to account for the much greater ease and confidence with which those female poets who emerged in the later seventeenth century – Anne Killigrew, Anne Finch and Mary Chudleigh, as well as Behn and Barker – were able to respond to literary genre. Thus, while Philips was not the first or only woman in the mid-seventeenth century to engage productively and diversely with generic forms (Anne Bradstreet, Lucy Hutchinson and Hester Pulter all offer instructive contemporary parallels), her evident awareness of her own literary inheritance (unequalled even by Bradstreet), her posthumous visibility as a woman poet and her formative influence on later women writers collectively signify her unique importance within women's literary history. Her engagement with literary genre marks a key foundational moment for English women's poetry.

Another reason why Philips is of especial interest as an early female reinventor of English generic forms is textual/biographical. Her poetry has survived in numerous and diverse textual witnesses: manuscript and print; autograph and scribal; formal and informal.[9] Among these witnesses, one of the most intriguing is an autograph collection of fifty-five of her early poems. Now known as the Tutin manuscript, this collection was almost certainly produced during the 1650s, when Philips was in her late teens and early to mid-twenties.[10] It thus provides unrivalled evidence for the young poet's experiments with pre-existing literary models and ideas. It shows how thoroughly, even at this early stage of her writing life, Philips had engaged with the challenges of literary tradition, and how diverse and distinctive her creative responses to these challenges could be. It also testifies to her own self-awareness both as a poet and as a reader of her own work.

In this chapter I will consider how Philips responded to traditional literary forms and ideas in the poems of the Tutin manuscript. My discussion will focus on the two genres for which she was later to become best known: retirement and friendship poetry.[11] Philips, as we will see, was more than willing to engage with the gendered challenges of literary tradition. In responding to men's sentences, she learnt to produce her own.

Philips's 'female' genres (1): retired spaces

PHILIPS's autograph manuscript is a 222-page quarto notebook, now held at the National Library of Wales, where it is catalogued as MS 775B.[12] Though its exact dates of compilation are unknown, it includes poetry dateable to between 1649, when Philips was seventeen years old, and 1657/58; it therefore includes none of her post-Restoration political or personal verse. Apparently intended for the poet's own personal use, it is a fair copy manuscript, with relatively few corrections and a small number of incomplete texts. The contents of the volume clearly show that, even by this relatively early stage of her poetic career, Philips was at ease in working with an impressively wide array both of genres – including elegies, epitaphs, songs, verse epistles, epithalamia – and of subjects – including friendship, politics, philosophy and religion. It is, moreover, likely that the volume in its original state may have included experiments in at least two further poetic forms. Elizabeth Hageman and Andrea Sununu have convincingly shown that the Tutin manuscript once included a copy of Philips's humorous travel narrative 'A sea-voyage from Tenby to Bristol', while Hageman has subsequently argued that 'A dialogue between Orinda and Lucasia', along with several other early poems, may have been excised from the volume after compilation.[13] Since still others of Philips's poems (such as 'On the 1. of January 1657' and 'Epitaph on her Son H. P. at St. Syth's Church'), though not included in Tutin, were almost certainly composed while it was under compilation, it is evident that the surviving contents of the manuscript, diverse though they are, provide only a partial representation of Philips's poetic activities up to 1658.

To demarcate a distinct category of retirement poetry among the contents of the Tutin manuscript is, in one sense, to draw a false distinction. Retirement from the travails and sorrows of public life is a frequent topic in Philips's early poems, including many which, ostensibly at least, belong within quite different generic groupings. Hero Chalmers, for instance, reads the Tutin elegies 'In memory of that excellent person Mrs Mary Lloyd' and 'In memory of the most Justly honour'd Mrs Owen of Orielton' as celebrating royalist withdrawal, while separation from worldly preoccupations is also implied in such religious poems as 'Happyness', 'Death' and 'The soule'.[14] A poem such as 'La Grandeur d'esprit', which praises 'A chosen privacy, a cheap content, / And all the peace which friendship ever lent', can equally be read as a study of friendship or of retirement.[15] In this chapter, however, the focus is on three poems which make the topic of retirement their central concern: 'Content to my dearest Lucasia', 'Invitation to the countrey' and 'A countrey life'.[16]

The Tutin manuscript, like many seventeenth-century miscellany manuscripts, includes textual sequences inscribed from each end of the volume. In the case of Tutin, the two sequences are distinguished by topic, with friendship and social lyrics predominating at one end, religious and philosophical poems at the other. Philips's early preoccupation with issues of retirement is amply demonstrated by her inclusion of poems on this subject at both ends of the manuscript. 'Content to my dearest Lucasia' is transcribed among the friendship poems (as are 'A retir'd frendship to

Ardelia' and 'In memory of ... Mrs Mary Lloyd'), while 'Invitation to the countrey', like 'In memory of ... Mrs Owen' and 'La Grandeur d'esprit', is included in the philosophical sequence.[17] While 'A countrey life' does not appear in the extant state of the Tutin manuscript, comparison with other early manuscripts of Philips's poetry strongly suggests that it, too, was once included among the philosophical poems, between 'La Grandeur d'esprit' and the elegy on Mrs Owen.[18]

The terms for modern scholarship on Philips's poetry of rural withdrawal were set by Maren-Sofie Røstvig in her classic study of seventeenth-century retirement literature, *The Happy Man*.[19] Røstvig's narrative, which associated the mid-century popularity of classically inspired retirement poetry with the royalist experience of defeat in the Civil War, readily accommodates Philips, whose self-identification with royalism is well known (though more problematic than is sometimes supposed).[20] In Røstvig's account, Philips's chief contribution to this topical genre was her portrayal of female friendship as the ideal state of, and condition for, virtuous retirement. However, Røstvig – despite the clearly masculine implications of her own title – did not fully explore the gendered aspects of Philips's involvement with retirement literature. As subsequent critics have pointed out, seventeenth-century retirement poetry had very different connotations for women than for men, both because of its classical origins and because of its socio-political premises.[21] The roots of retirement poetry in Latin poetry by Horace, Virgil, Martial and Claudian meant that most women, lacking knowledge of classical languages, had only partial access to the ideas and assumptions of this literary tradition. Such access would, in most cases, have been mediated by male writers, whether through the translation of classical texts or through original English-language contributions to the genre. Women's ability to engage imaginatively with the full range of 'retirement' tropes and presuppositions would thus, for the most part, have been subject to important limitations – as might their self-confidence in using such authoritative but culturally distanced literary forms.

Still more problematic for early modern women writers were the presuppositions about authorship and public engagement on which traditional retirement literature was implicitly premised. Male poets in this tradition could generally assume that involvement in public life – the option so virtuously rejected in most retirement poetry – was a valid and realistic possibility for them. The fact that royalist poets of the interregnum were, in effect, debarred from participation in public life did not undermine this assumption, but merely rendered their use of retirement tropes more paradoxical and poignant (ironically, helping to ensure the topicality of the genre in the 1650s). By contrast, no such assumption of political entitlement would have been available to (most) early modern women writers, whatever their political views or circumstances. As Sarah Prescott points out, 'women did not have anything to retire from in terms of public and professional life so [their] relation to the classical retirement genre is significantly different'.[22] Thus, while early modern women were evidently attracted to a genre which spoke to their own experience of restricted agency and exclusion from power, the significance of its implicitly masculine conventions would have undergone inevitable (if often subtle) change when adopted by female poets.[23] Since Philips, writing in the 1650s, was among the first Englishwomen to engage with retirement literature, her response to its gendered conventions is of particular interest.

'Content to my dearest Lucasia', 'Invitation to the country' and 'A countrey life' can be read as different answers to the same key question: namely, how could a seventeenth-century woman poet work with, or against, the male-generated norms of retirement poetry? Of the three, 'Content' represents the most obviously and explicitly gendered reworking of pre-existing conventions. The inscription of the poem to Lucasia (Philips's Welsh neighbour, Anne Owen) locates the text within a conversation between female friends – albeit a conversation in which Philips herself is the sole authoritative speaker. The subject, 'Content', is also (after the first stanza) consistently gendered female, and is portrayed as the object of persistent, if misguided, male searching. Though one might in principle wonder whether the 'men' who so fruitlessly attempt to locate 'Content' within a single conceptual, geographical or institutional space merely denote the generic masculine, rather than being specifically male, this possibility is anticipated and (probably) precluded by Philips's introductory stanza:

> Content the false world's best disguise
> The search and faction of yᵉ wise,
> Is so abstruse, and hid in night
> That like that Fairy red-crosse Knight
> Who treacherous falshood for cleare truth had got,
> Men think they have it, when they have it not.
> ('Content', lines 1–6)[24]

Philips's comparison of Content-seekers to 'that Fairy red-crosse Knight' figures the search for 'Content' as a heterosexual courtship in which 'Men', though deluded, are clearly the active agents. Her association of male seekers with Edmund Spenser's brave but foolish Redcrosse knight, while linking the feminised 'Content' with his knowledgeable and trustworthy Una ('cleare truth'), not only foreshadows the gendered roles outlined more fully in the remainder of the poem but also asserts her own authority to interpret one of the most canonical poems in English literature. The poet of 'Content', though not equipped to read Virgil or Horace in the original, is confident in citing *The Faerie Queene* to her own advantage.

In the central section of the poem, Philips discusses – and dismisses – the 'Content'-securing claims of courts and ambition (stanza 2), physical appearance, or 'bright outsides' (stanza 3), mirth (stanza 4), 'Liberty from Government' (stanza 5), military glory (stanza 6), university education (stanza 7) and solitude (stanza 8). Stanzas 2–4 focus on locations and qualities potentially available to both sexes, though stanza 2 may hint at gendered implications in its description of the flattery, riches and greatness of court life as 'things that doe man's sences cheat' (line 10). Stanza 5 develops and deepens these gendered implications, not only in its reference to 'Government' – a sphere in which only men, not women, could expect to be fully engaged – but also in its portrayal of subjection (whether to external 'Government' or to one's own 'passions') as a male condition (lines 27–28, 30). However, it is in stanzas 6–8 that the gendered aspects of Philips's argument become fully clear. Stanzas 6 and 7 address institutions ('the camp', line 31, and '[t]he schooles', line 38) which were, in Philips's day, exclusively male, while stanza 8 depicts solitude (represented by the 'sullen Hermit', line 43) as a specifically male experience. The army and university stanzas (6 and 7) thus see Philips rejecting key socio-cultural institutions to which she could never have hoped to gain access, while her construction of solitude both as lonely and as bad for the hermit's moral character (stanza 8) directly challenges a condition held up in much male-authored retirement poetry as the ideal state of human existence. Her conclusion that 'man was never made to be alone' (line 48) not only invokes scriptural authority for her rejection of solitude but also, in alluding to God's creation of Eve, suggests that the presence of women is essential to human contentment. But rather than developing this reference to Genesis into a celebration of heterosexual marriage (the obvious and predictable next step in the argument), Philips defies the logic of her own allusion and identifies the 'best' means of securing 'Content' not with matrimony but with friendship:

> Content her self best comprehends
> Betwixt two souls & they two friends
> Whose eithers Joys in both are fixd
> And multiply'd by being mix'd
> Whose minds & interests are so ye same,
> Theyr very griefs imparted loose y^t name
> ('Content', lines 49–54)

Though this initial depiction of friendly contentment does not specify the sex of the participants, a subsequent stanza – constructing Philips's speaker and her addressee, Lucasia, as exemplars of 'innocence and perfect friendship' – strongly associates this idealised state with women:

> Then my Lucasia we who have
> What ever love can give, or crave
> With scorn, or pitty can survey
> The triffles which the most betray
> With innocence & perfect friendship fir'd
> By vertue Joyn'd, & by our choice retir'd
> ('Content', lines 61–6)

For the Philips of 'Content to my dearest Lucasia', the highest state of human happiness is achieved through a combination of 'Privacy, & friendship' (line 70). Her own 'perfect friendship' with Lucasia is facilitated by their 'retir'd' location, which enables the mutuality and self-sufficiency of their relationship. Though Philips never claims that such friendship is uniquely female, the emotional logic of her poem consistently locates true contentment outside male-dominated public spaces, linking it instead with the retired spaces inhabited by women. Ironically, women's exclusion from public institutions helps to ensure that they, rather than men, are closer to knowing both true friendship and true contentment.

If 'Content to my dearest Lucasia' seeks to challenge and rewrite the values of traditional retirement poetry in implicitly woman-centred terms, 'Invitation to the country' and 'A countrey life' both represent a rather different way of reinterpreting the genre. 'Invitation to the countrey', though included among the philosophical poems in the Tutin manuscript, has strong associations with Philips's friendship poems: it is addressed to Rosania (the poet's coterie name for her school friend Mary Aubrey), who is urged to join the speaker in her remote country retreat. This time, however, though the importance of female friendship is everywhere assumed, the emphasis is on the opportunities for moral self-improvement afforded by rural retirement. Life in the country, physically removed from the corruptions and temptations of the urban world, can assist the individual both to achieve self-control and to gain true understanding of things earthly and divine:

> Kings may be slaves by their own passions hurld
> But who command's himself, command's the World
> A countrey-life assist's this Study best
> When no distractions doth the soule arrest
> There heav'n & earth ly open to our view
> There we search nature, and it's authour too
> ('Invitation to the countrey', lines 39–44)[25]

In contrast with 'Content to my dearest Lucasia', the argument of 'Invitation to the country' is only weakly gendered. This time Philips's masculine pronouns (e.g. 'himself', line 40) seem generic rather than specifically male; the figure who 'command's himself' is interchangeable with the female 'we' (Philips's speaker; Rosania, should she accept the invitation) who, benefiting from their retired environment, can 'search nature, and it's authour too'.[26] For much of the poem, the issue of whether men or women are better suited to country-style virtuous living does not arise. Yet the femininity of speaker and addressee are emphasised at the outset of the text, in the speaker's appeal to Rosania to endure the hardships of the country for their friendship's sake (lines 1–8). Gendered friendship also returns in the final few lines, as the speaker concludes:

> There (my Rosania) will we mingling souls,
> Pitty the folly which the world controuls
> And all those Grandeurs which y[e] most do prize
> We either can enjoy, or will despise
> ('Invitation to the countrey', lines 47–50)[27]

Though appreciation of the 'countrey' may not be available only to women, the special capacity of friends such as Philips and Rosania to 'mingl[e] souls' leaves them ideally placed to benefit from its pleasures. Less explicitly concerned than 'Content' with regendering the conventions of the genre, 'Invitation to the countrey' is equally clear in depicting rural retirement as congenial to women's friendship. It also lays still greater emphasis on the role of the country in stimulating women's spiritual and intellectual development. Remote rural locations may spell isolation and exclusion for men; for women they bring empowerment and opportunity.[28]

'A countrey life' represents yet another variant in Philips's complex response to the tradition of literary retirement. Unlike 'Content' and 'Invitation to the countrey', 'A countrey life' has no named addressee and reads more like a soliloquy than as an intervention within a conversation. Unusually for Philips, the central argument of the poem associates contented retirement not with women's friendship but with solitude. The speaker greets 'dearest Solitude' as '[m]y greate felicity' (lines 29, 30), and praises country life as facilitating that contempt for the world which is the best means of achieving happiness.[29] While others may seek a 'happy fate' (line 70) in knowledge or 'wayes of State' (line 72), her own preference is for balanced self-regulation and rural 'privacy':

> But I resolved from within
>   Confirmed from w[th]out
> In privacy intend to spinne
>   My future minutes out
> ('A countrey life', lines 73–6)

While the conclusion to the poem also acknowledges 'Freindship &
Honesty' as the only 'two things good' in earthly life (lines 82, 81),
this allusion to friendship is not only somewhat belated but seems all
but unrealisable in a poem which otherwise admits no companion into
the speaker's 'retir'd integrity' (line 85). Furthermore, the privileging of
solitude rather than friendship in 'A countrey life' also produces an ideal
of country retirement which, compared with 'Content' and 'Invitation to
the countrey', is strikingly ungendered. Though Philips, as in 'Content',
rejects the pretensions of public or social life to secure happiness, she does
not construct this rejection in gendered terms; feminine pronouns are not
used, and nothing within the poem itself marks the speaking 'I' as female.
When Philips declares 'Secure in these unenvyed walls / I thinke not on
the state' (lines 45, 46), she seems to be rejecting a genuine possibility – of
reflection on, if not necessarily participation in, the life of the nation.
Indeed, the accessibility of 'A countrey life' to both sexes – and to at least
one publicly experienced male reader – is amply demonstrated by its later
history of use by Charles II's son, the Duke of Monmouth. Monmouth's
manuscript notebook, allegedly recovered after his defeat at the battle
of Sedgemoor, includes a version of 'A countrey life' adapted to his own
circumstances; drastically excerpting and rearranging Philips's lines, it
nonetheless adds relatively little fresh material.[30] The heroic self-sufficiency
celebrated in 'A countrey life' was, apparently, an ideal to which both a
female poet and a would-be king could aspire. Monmouth's ready application of Philips's robust self-reliance to his own very masculine situation
demonstrates how thoroughly she had, in this instance, internalised the
conventions of male retirement literature. In 'A countrey life', effectively,
Philips is writing retirement poetry like a man.

Collectively, 'Content', 'Invitation to the countrey' and 'A countrey life'
demonstrate Philips's ease and confidence in working with the previously
androcentric norms of retirement poetry. They show her versatility in
responding to established literary forms, both through her skilful use of
three different metrical forms and through her varied application of ideas
of gender and friendship. More speculatively, these three poems may also
indicate that, over time, Philips grew more daring in her engagement
with the retirement genre. Though neither 'Content' nor 'Invitation to the
countrey' is dated in Tutin or any of the other early textual witnesses to
Philips's poetry, the emotional narrative implied by her 1650s friendship
poems makes it probable that 'Content', inscribed to Lucasia, postdates
'Invitation', addressed to Rosania. 'Invitation' is thus likely to date from
the early 1650s, 'Content' a little later, while 'A countrey life' is ascribed
to 1650 in the Rosania manuscript.[31] On this dating, the three poems
sketch out an increasingly assertive series of generic interventions, from

the gendered ventriloquism of 'A countrey life', through the gestures towards female self-assertion in 'Invitation', to the more systematic critique of masculinist literary values in 'Content'. Philips was developing her generic craft.

Finally, the physical location of 'Content', 'Invitation to the countrey' and 'A countrey life' within the Tutin manuscript testifies to Philips's skill as a reader and editor of her own poems. Though both 'Content' and 'Invitation to the countrey' attend to friendship as well as retirement, they differ in the relative importance ascribed to the two subjects. 'Content', which privileges female friendship, albeit as best realised in a retired setting, is appropriately placed in the friendship sequence. 'Invitation to the countrey' – primarily a meditation on the moral and spiritual advantages of country life, though structured within a friendship-based appeal to Rosania – more properly belongs within the philosophical sequence. Similarly, 'A countrey life', whose celebration of moral balance and self-sufficiency refers to friendship so very briefly, would have been thematically at home in the philosophical section of the Tutin manuscript. The Philips who planned and transcribed this early verse compilation did not merely know and understand the English retirement tradition, but also knew and understood her own poems.

Philips's 'female' genres (2): the construction of friendship

THE one topic that looms larger than retirement among the poems of the Tutin manuscript is unquestionably friendship. As well as the numerous poems addressed to Lucasia and Rosania, the manuscript also includes verses on and addressed to her friends Regina and Philoclea, as well as others entitled 'A friend' and 'Friendship'. The manuscript also includes two poems addressed to Francis Finch, each praising his treatise *Friendship*, privately published in 1653.[32] *Friendship*, addressed to the noble '*Lucasia–Orinda*' (that is, to Anne Owen and Katherine Philips), would be followed in 1657 by Jeremy Taylor's *A Discourse of the Nature, Offices and Measures of Friendship*, subtitled 'Written in answer to a letter from the most ingenious and vertuous M. K. P. [Mistress Katherine Philips]'. As early as the 1650s, friendship was key both to Philips's self-representation in the Tutin manuscript and to her modest but evolving public reputation.

Friendship is also among the central concerns of modern Philips criticism. In recent years, studies of Philips's friendship poetry have often focused on either its homo-erotic connotations or its political significance.[33] Less attention has, perhaps, been paid to the more technical aspects of Philips's friendship lyrics: namely how, at the level of language, form and imagery, they recast the gendered conventions of seventeenth-century love poetry. Philips's many allusions to Donne have been ably surveyed by Paula Loscocco and Elizabeth Hageman, while Hageman has also discussed her responses to poets such as Ben Jonson, Thomas Randolph and Abraham Cowley in her epigrammatic and complimentary verse.[34] Yet studies of Philips's sources, essential though they are, may nonetheless risk underestimating the extent of her engagement with earlier literature. Even where specific debts to previous poets are not overtly visible, the very act of writing in this highly conventional genre testifies to Philips's detailed understanding of its norms and values. Given that the traditions of the seventeenth-century love lyric she inherited were almost exclusively male-generated, even the most apparently technical aspects of her friendship poems – her use of form and structure, imagery and language – carry gendered implications.

Philips's carefully judged reworking of lyric conventions is perhaps at its most evident in her short poem 'To my excellent Lucasia on our friendship'. Located amid the first run of Lucasia poems in the Tutin manuscript, 'To my excellent Lucasia' is likely to have been one of Philips's earlier compositions, written when she was only nineteen or twenty years old.[35] Its commitment both to Lucasia and to the ideology of friendship is clear and emphatic:

> I did not live untill this time
> Crown'd my felicity
> When I could say without a crime
> I am not Thine, but Thee
> This Carkasse breath'd & walk'd & slept   5
> So that the world believ'd
> There was a soule the motions kept
> But they were all deceiv'd
> For as a watch by art is wound
> To motion, such was mine   10
> But never had Orinda found
> A Soule till she found thine
> Which now inspires cures and supply's
> And guides my darken'd brest
> For thou art all that I can prize   15
> My Joy, my Life, my rest.
> Nor Bridegroomes nor crown'd conqu'rours mirth
> To mine compar'd can be
> They have but pieces of this Earth
> I've all the world in thee.   20
> Then let our flame still light, & shine,
> (And no bold feare controule),
> As inocent as our design
> Immortall as our Soule.[36]

'To my excellent Lucasia' is written in the form now known as common metre, an iambic quatrain in which rhymed tetrameters alternate with rhymed trimeters. Despite her youth, Philips uses this deceptively challenging form with confidence and skill. She begins conversationally, with an early statement of the key before/after dichotomy around which the whole poem is structured: 'I did not live untill this time / Crown'd my felicity'. The use of 'Crown'd' in line 2 – inverting the expected iamb into a trochee – recalls both her predilection for royalist imagery and also her frequent tendency to subordinate her royalism to the priorities of private life; the latter can be glimpsed again in her claim to be happier than a 'crown'd conqu'rour' through her friendship with Lucasia (line 17).[37] The key argument of the poem is completed at the end of the first quatrain, as the poet directly addresses Lucasia for the first time, declaring 'I am not Thine, but Thee'. This complete identification between the speaker and Lucasia is typical of the rhetoric of mutuality between friends for which Philips is well known, and which contrasts so obviously with the unequal depiction of the sexes in many male-authored love poems of the period. Sceptical readers may note that this is a mutuality which is constructed exclusively on the poet's own terms and which, given Lucasia's spiritual and Anne Owen's social superiority over Orinda/Philips, is of much greater potential benefit to the speaker than to the addressee. Lucasia is given as little opportunity to speak as any mistress in a cavalier or metaphysical lyric; we cannot tell whether she, too, shares the speaker's 'felicity' in their newfound friendship.[38]

The subsequent twenty lines of the poem see Philips both enlarging on the life-changing narrative broached in the opening couplet and continuing to exploit the technical opportunities of her metrical form. Of the six quatrains in 'To my excellent Lucasia', all but one are formed of single sentences and constitute separate units in the argumentative structure of the poem.[39] Following the opening statement (lines 1–4), the second quatrain describes Philips's pre-friendship condition as merely an animated 'Carkasse' (line 5); the speaker's current detachment from this past self is emphasised not only by her use of past tense forms ('breath'd & walk'd & slept') but by her eschewal of the personal possessive ('This', not 'My', carcass). This section also introduces the characteristically Philipsian notions of 'the world' (line 6) and the 'soule' (line 7): the former watching but 'deceiv'd' (line 8), the latter inferred but absent. The third and fourth quatrains form a single syntactical unit, describing how the discovery of Lucasia's soul has transformed the speaker's existence. Paradoxically, the moment of transformation occurs at the break between lines 12 and 13, which also, as the mid-point of the poem, divides the text into exactly equal 'before' and 'after' sections. The image of the watch in lines 9–10 is one of Philips's many Donnean echoes; however, the comparison, rather than dominating the poem, is used only briefly to enhance the central before/after dichotomy, the empty, mechanised life symbolised by the watch contrasting with the enriched, joyful existence which follows her discovery of Lucasia's soul.[40] The emergence of the speaker as a named persona, Orinda, at line 11 is also associated with – by implication, made possible by – her self-identification with Lucasia.

Over the second half of the poem, Philips focuses on the 'after' section of her transformational narrative. As in the first three quatrains, her emphasis is on the benefits she has herself received through friendship with Lucasia, her 'Joy ... Life [and] rest' (line 16). The lumbering physicality represented by the 'Carkasse' is displaced by an etherialised mode in which the speaker's 'brest' (line 14) is spiritually sustained – 'inspire[d], cure[d] and supply[d]' (line 13) – by Lucasia's soul. The penultimate quatrain provides possible support for a homo-erotic (and somewhat anti-royalist) reading of the poem, through the speaker's favourable self-comparison with bridegrooms and conquerors (line 17), while also suggesting that, through her friendship with Lucasia, Orinda has become possessor of the world which once misjudged her (line 20, cf. lines 6–8). The final quatrain projects the women's friendship into eternity, albeit perhaps with a touch of anxiety; the curious allusion to 'bold feare' in line 22 may be less the confident disavowal it purports to be than a late attempt to reassure an apprehensive Lucasia.[41] Philips's use of 'controule' to rhyme with 'Soule' (lines 22, 24) has potentially worrying implications, while her description of their friendship's flame as 'inocent' (line 23) disturbs even as it reassures. However, the concluding simile – 'Immortall as our Soule' – not only re-emphasises the unity of the two women, but does so in the neo-Platonising language typical of Philips's philosophy of friendship in the Tutin poems.[42] An autograph emendation – 'Immortall', in Tutin, is a substitution for 'As deathless' – shows sensitivity to both sense and sound: though the two expressions are semantically and metrically equivalent, 'Immortall' avoids both the negative connotations of 'deathless' and the repetition of 'As'. Even after completing her fair transcription of the poem, Philips was prepared to improve it still further.

'To my excellent Lucasia' shows the young Katherine Philips at her most assured and idealistic – and, arguably, at her most manipulative. Her declaration of friendship for Lucasia is achieved through a complex reworking of lyric conventions; the resources of metre, verse form, rhyme, metaphor and diction are all exploited to produce her desired effects. A poem which pointedly excludes male society and disparages male emotions nonetheless depends on, and triumphantly transforms, male poetic conventions. One of the most forthright – and revealing – statements of her philosophy of friendship, it also, like the other friendship lyrics in Tutin, testifies to her skills and self-awareness as a literary reader.

Philips, readership and gender

THE poetry collected in the Tutin manuscript represents the apprentice work of an astonishingly capable and confident young writer. It also indicates that Philips, despite her lack of obvious cultural connections, was already beginning to gain a measure of public recognition. As well as the allusions to Francis Finch's *Friendship*, the manuscript includes her elegy 'In memory of Mr Cartwright' – the first of her poems to be print-published, in Cartwright's *Comedies, Tragi-Comedies with Other Poems* (1651) – as well as 'To the truly noble S^r Ed: Dering', a reply to a (now lost) poem in which Dering had ventriloquised, and thus complimented, her own work. It also collects four poems said to have been set to music by contemporary composers – 'To Mrs M. A. upon absence', 'Friendships mysterys to my dearest Lucasia' and 'On the death of my first and dearest childe, Hector Philipps', all set by Henry Lawes, and 'Against pleasure', set by Charles Coleman – and may once have incorporated 'A dialogue between Orinda and Lucasia', also set by Lawes.[43] Further evidence for the early reception and circulation of Philips's poems is provided by the reproduction of two Tutin poems in Lawes's *Ayres and Dialogues, the Second Book* (1655): the complimentary poem 'To the truly noble Mr Henry Lawes' among the prefatory matter and Lawes's setting of 'Friendships mysterys' among the 'ayres'.[44] Indeed, on the evidence of the Tutin manuscript, Philips seems to have been more impressed by the attention her poetry had begun to receive from contemporary composers than by its inclusion in print-published volumes. While her transcriptions of 'In memory of Mr Cartwright' and 'To the truly noble Mr Henry Lawes' make no reference to the fact that either poem had been printed, the musical renderings by Lawes and Coleman are carefully recorded. Even Lawes's setting of her epitaph on her own young son, Hector, is meticulously noted. Creative responses to her poetry seem to have mattered more to her than mere printed reproduction.

The retirement verse and friendship lyrics of the Tutin manuscript reveal the young Katherine Philips as an able reader of men's sentences. They also witness her ability both to work with and to interrogate the gendered assumptions of the literary traditions she had inherited. That other readers in their turn were able to enjoy and appreciate Philips's own diversely inflected sentences is demonstrated by the willingness of men such as Finch, Dering, Lawes and Coleman to reply creatively to even the most obviously gendered of her poems: her writings on friendship; her epitaph on her son. The 'older forms of literature' were indeed 'hardened and set' by the time Philips became a poet, but she found her own ways to respond.

Notes

I am grateful to Sue Wiseman and Kathleen Taylor for their thoughtful advice on earlier drafts of this chapter.

1   V. Woolf, *A Room of One's Own* [1929], Penguin, London, 1992, p. 72.
2   Ibid., p. 71.
3   M. Ezell, *Writing Women's Literary History*, Johns Hopkins University Press, Baltimore, 1993, pp. 39–65.
4   On early modern women writers and literary genre, see further: Ezell, *Writing Women's Literary History* (*passim*); B. Smith and U. Appelt (eds), *Write or Be Written: Early Modern Women Poets and Cultural Constraints*, Ashgate, Aldershot, 2001; and (for a slightly later period) P. Backscheider, *Eighteenth-Century Women Poets and Their Poetry: Inventing Agency, Inventing Genre*, Johns Hopkins University Press, Baltimore, 2005. Studies of particular relevance to the genres addressed in the present chapter include A. Messenger, *Pastoral Tradition and the Female Talent: Studies in Augustan Poetry*, AMS Press, New York, 1999; and A. R. Jones, *The Currency of Eros: Women's Love Lyric in Europe, 1540–1620*, Indiana University Press, Bloomington, 1990.
5   See chapters 3 and 5 of the present volume.
6   Cavendish claimed to have begun writing poetry during a temporary separation from her husband (*Poems and Fancies*, sig. A7r–v). William Cavendish would later, however, become the most faithful and enthusiastic supporter of her work.
7   Sidney and Wroth provide contrasting examples in this respect: while Sidney gained widespread admiration for her poetic paraphrases of the Psalter, Wroth was heavily criticised for venturing outside the suitably feminine space of devotional poetry. See M. Hannay, *Mary Sidney, Lady Wroth*, Ashgate, Farnham, 2010, pp. 240–1.
8   On the posthumous reception of Philips's poetry, see P. Thomas (ed.), *The Collected Works of Katherine Philips, The Matchless Orinda: Volume 1, The Poems*, Stump Cross Books, Stump Cross, 1990, pp. 23–39.
9   P. Beal (comp.), *The Index of English Literary Manuscripts, vol. 2, pt. 2, 1625–1700: Lee–Wycherley*, Mansell, London, 1993, pp. 125–81.
10 The name derives from a previous owner, John Ramsden Tutin, who first brought this important manuscript to scholarly attention.
11 My discussion of Philips's retirement and friendship poetry in this chapter complements my consideration of her political, religious and social verse in G. Wright, *Producing Women's Poetry, 1600–1730: Text and Paratext, Manuscript and Print*, Cambridge University Press, Cambridge, 2013.
12 The Tutin manuscript is described more fully by Beal, *Index*, p. 128.
13 E. Hageman and A. Sununu, 'New manuscript texts of Katherine Philips, The "Matchless Orinda"', *English Manuscript Studies 1100–1700*, vol. 4 (1993), pp. 174–219, at pp. 175–80; E. Hageman, 'Treacherous accidents and the abominable printing of Katherine Philips' 1664 *Poems*', in W. Speed Hill (ed.), *New Ways of Looking at Old Texts*, Arizona Center for Medieval and Renaissance Studies in conjunction with Renaissance English Text Society, Tempe, 2004, vol. 3, pp. 85–95, at pp. 91–2.
14 H. Chalmers, *Royalist Women Writers 1650–1689*, Oxford University Press, Oxford, 2004, pp. 110–13.
15 Tutin MS, p. 142, lines 1–2; compare Thomas (ed.), *The Poems*, p. 157.

16 For discussion of a further Tutin poem which foregrounds retirement ('A retir'd frendship to Ardelia') see G. Wright, 'Textuality, privacy and politics: Katherine Philips's *Poems* revisited', in J. Daybell and P. Hinds (eds), *Material Readings of Early Modern Culture: Texts and Social Practices, 1580–1730*, Palgrave, Basingstoke, 2010, pp. 163–82.

17 'Happyness', 'Death' and 'The soule' are also included among the philosophical poems.

18 Hageman, 'Treacherous accidents', p. 92.

19 M.-S. Røstvig, *The Happy Man: Studies in the Metamorphoses of a Classical Ideal: Volume 1, 1600–1700* (2nd edition), Norwegian Universities Press, Oslo, 1962, pp. 252–61.

20 On Philips's complex relationship with royalism, see R. C. Evans, 'Paradox in poetry and politics: Katherine Philips in the interregnum', in C. Summers and T.-L. Pebworth (eds), *The English Civil Wars in the Literary Imagination*, University of Missouri Press, Columbia, 1999, pp. 174–85; A. Shifflett, '"Subdu'd by You": states of friendship and friends of the state in Katherine Philips's poetry', in Smith and Appelt (eds), *Write or Be Written*, pp. 177–95; and my own discussions in Wright, 'Textuality, privacy and politics', and Wright, *Producing Women's Poetry*.

21 On women and the retirement tradition, see A. Messenger, *Pastoral Tradition and the Female Talent*, AMS Press, New York, 2001, p. 59; B. Price, 'Verse, voice, and body: the retirement mode and women's poetry 1680–1723', *Early Modern Literary Studies*, vol. 12, no. 3 (2007), online at http://extra.shu.ac.uk/emls/12-3/priceve2.htm (accessed July 2013), para. 5; and S. Prescott, '"That private shade, wherein my Muse was bred": Katherine Philips and the poetic spaces of Welsh retirement', *Philological Quarterly*, vol. 88, no. 4 (2009), pp. 345–64.

22 S. Prescott, '"That private shade"', p. 354. A few partial exceptions – royal and noble wives and daughters; mistresses; Restoration actresses – do not invalidate the point.

23 Retirement poetry – linguistic issues notwithstanding – would undoubtedly have represented one of the *more* accessible genres for women writers of this period. I owe this point to Sue Wiseman.

24 Quotations from 'Content' follow the Tutin MS, pp. 83–7; compare Thomas (ed.), *The Poems*, pp. 91–4.

25 Tutin MS, p. 174; compare Thomas (ed.), *The Poems*, p. 174.

26 For other masculine pronouns in 'Invitation to the countrey', see lines 33, 37 and 38.

27 Tutin MS, p. 174; Thomas (ed.), *The Poems*, p. 175.

28 See also Sarah Prescott's discussion of importance of rural Wales in Philips's poetic self-mythologisation. Prescott, '"That private shade"', p. 352.

29 'A countrey life' is quoted from the Clarke manuscript (Worcester College Oxford MS 6.13, pp. 24–5), which follows Tutin more closely than other early witnesses. See Hageman, 'Treacherous accidents', pp. 91–5. Thomas's text in Thomas (ed.), *The Poems*, pp. 159–62, follows the Dering manuscript (University of Texas at Austin, Harry Ransom Humanities Research Center, Misc *HRC 151 Philips MS 14,937).

30 On Monmouth's reworking of 'A countrey life', see Hageman and Sununu, 'New manuscript texts', pp. 209–12, and Beal, *Index*, p. 144, PsK 45.

31 Rosania MS (National Library of Wales MS 776B), p. 267; Beal, *Index*, p. 143, PsK 36.

32 'On M' Francis Finch (the excellent Palemon)', lines 25, 49–62, and 'To the noble Palaemon on his incomparable discourse of friendship', *passim*.

33 On Philips and homo-eroticism, see H. Andreadis, 'Re-configuring early modern friendship: Katherine Philips and homoerotic desire', *Studies in English Literature, 1500–1900*, vol. 46, no. 3 (2006), pp. 523–42; A. Stiebel, 'Subversive sexuality: masking the erotic in poems by Katherine Philips and Aphra Behn', in C. Summers and T.-L. Pebworth (eds), *Renaissance Discourses of Desire*, University of Missouri Press, Columbia, 1993, pp. 223–36; and E. Wahl, *Invisible Relations: Representations of Female Intimacy in the Age of Enlightenment*, Stanford University Press, Stanford, 1999, pp. 130–70. On Philips and politics, see C. Barash, *English Women's Poetry, 1649–1714:*

Politics, Community, and Linguistic Authority, Oxford University Press, Oxford, 1996, pp. 55–100; Chalmers, *Royalist Women Writers*, pp. 56–86; and C. Gray, *Women Writers and Public Debate in Seventeenth-Century Britain*, Palgrave, Basingstoke, 2007, pp. 105–31.

34 P. Loscocco, 'Inventing the English Sappho: Katherine Philips's Donnean poetry', *Journal of English and Germanic Philology*, vol. 102, no. 1 (2003), pp. 59–87; E. Hageman, 'Katherine Philips, *Poems*', in A. Pacheco (ed.), *A Companion to Early Modern Women's Writing*, Blackwell, Oxford, 2002, pp. 189–202. See also E. Scott-Baumann, *Forms of Engagement: Women, Poetry, and Culture 1640–1680*, Oxford University Press, Oxford, 2013.

35 Early witnesses variously attribute the poem to 17 July 1651 and to the same date a year later. In Tutin, the date has been corrected, and it is not clear whether '1651' or '1652' represents the preferred version.

36 Tutin MS, p. 49; compare Thomas (ed.), *The Poems*, pp. 121–2. Line numbers have been added for ease of reference.

37 See my discussion of Philips's moderated royalism in Wright, *Producing Women's Poetry*.

38 On this point see also K. Lilley, '"Dear Object": Katherine Philips' love elegies and their readers', in P. Salzman and J. Wallwork (eds), *Women's Writing 1550–1750*, Meridian, Melbourne, 2001, pp. 163–78.

39 Philips's punctuation in the Tutin manuscript is light and often erratic. My reading of the sentence structure in 'To my excellent Lucasia' is based on syntax rather than punctuation marks.

40 On Philips's use of Donne in 'To my excellent Lucasia', see Loscocco, 'Inventing the English Sappho', pp. 80–4.

41 Philips's early copyists – and perhaps Philips herself – hesitated over the expression 'bold feare': it appears as 'false fear' in both the 1664 and the 1667 *Poems* (pp. 105, 52), and as 'damp fear' in the Rosania manuscript (p. 320).

42 On the neo-Platonising elements in 'To my excellent Lucasia', see A. Brady, 'The Platonic poems of Katherine Philips', *Seventeenth Century*, vol. 25, no. 2 (2010), pp. 300–22, at pp. 312, 315.

43 Hageman, 'Treacherous accidents', p. 91; compare Beal, *Index*, pp. 144–5.

44 P. Beal, *In Praise of Scribes: Manuscripts and Their Makers in Seventeenth-Century England*, Oxford University Press, Oxford, 1998, p. 155. The prefatory matter to the *Ayres and Dialogues* also includes a poem by Charles Coleman, who may have become familiar with Philips's poetry through the Lawes connection.

Part II: Circulation

'We thy Sydnean Psalmes shall celebrate': collaborative authorship, Sidney's sister and the English devotional lyric

Suzanne Trill

AFTER Margaret J. M. Ezell published her ground-breaking essay 'The myth of Judith Shakespeare: creating the canon of women's litera-ture' (1990), many of us working on early modern women's writing rose to her challenge and began to re-examine the foundations upon which our putative 'canon' of women's texts was being fashioned. Thanks in large part to the influence of Ezell's work, we now know that, in contrast to Virginia Woolf's pessimistic assessment of sixteenth-century women's poetry, a large number of them were indeed able to pen both songs and sonnets.[1] Critical studies and edited volumes of such poems are now swelling our bookshelves; yet, as perhaps the need for this volume itself attests to, the prevailing assumption remains that women writers – especially women poets – were an endangered species in the sixteenth century. Among the many exceptions to this apparent rule discussed within this volume is Mary Sidney, Countess of Pembroke. Indeed, as Patricia Pender has recently convincingly argued, rather than being 'a marginalised and marginal literary figure', through her 'management of her brother's corpus, … her patronage, and her own literary self-fashioning', Mary Sidney played a 'crucial role in the construction of the English author function' and 'helped define the terms of early modern authorship and authority'.[2] Pender's argument builds on developments in authorship and attribution studies which have undermined the concept of the romantic, individual genius as the sole originator of a literary text and refreshed our recognition of the complex web of relationships by which literary texts are produced. Harold Love sums this up nicely when he states that any contemporary definition of authorship must be based on the assumption that an author is 'a repertoire of practices, techniques and functions' rather than 'a single essence or non-essence'.[3] In what follows, I argue that 'thy Sydnean Psalmes' represent an example *par excellence* of the complexity of 'author-ship' in the early modern period. While Pender's essay has a broad focus, here I want to concentrate on the pivotal role Mary Sidney played in the specific development of the English devotional lyric. In order to do so, I begin by re-examining the terms in which John Donne praises 'thy Sydnean Psalmes' in 'Vpon the translation of the Psalmes by Sir Philip Sydney, and the Countesse of Pembroke his Sister'.[4]

Although Donne's poem has been curiously marginalised until relatively recently, its eloquent encapsulation of the essential problematic of early modern devotional poetics is remarkable. Astonishingly, within the space of a spiritually significant seven sentences, Donne's encomium provides not only a succinct précis of the early modern debate on what constitutes an appropriate devotional poetics within Protestantism but also a very precise answer to this supposedly insolvable conundrum: the way to express the inexpressible or to 'name' God is, Donne asserts, to sing 'thy Sydnean Psalmes'. While I, and other critics, have made reference before to the seemingly simple phrase 'We thy Sydnean Psalmes shall celebrate', none of us has recognised its full implications for reformulating our understanding of the gendered narrative of the construction of the canon of English literature in general and the development of the English devotional lyric in particular.[5] Whereas our modern, critical divisions – between men and women, publication and manuscript, the sacred and the secular – have encouraged us to see separation and opposition, Donne invites us to recognise a more harmonious difference. Thus, it is my contention that Donne's extraordinary poem ultimately requires us to rethink our Woolfian-influenced tale of female *ex*clusion from literary history and revise it as a more *in*clusive story in which collaboration between the sexes is central.

This is, admittedly, a large claim to make apparently on the basis of six words, but let us pause here to look at them closely. With the possible exception of the adjectival noun 'Sydnean', none of the words used in this phrase are particularly challenging; however, the unusual syntactical order reinforces its peculiarly complex representation of possession, authorship and action. Most obviously, Donne's verbal violence disrupts the expected order of English grammar from subject–verb–object to subject(s)–object–verb. But, more particularly, this phrase is characteristic of Donne's overall style in this poem in its overabundant use of personal and possessive pronouns. In this way Donne powerfully underscores collaboration both between the human and the divine, and between two specific human beings. In its original context, 'We' most likely refers to those who comprise the English Church; whoever the precise referent, the speaker is definitely not an individual but is part of a collective. Donne's poetic licence subsequently delays the anticipated shift to a verb via two different kinds of possessive determiners: 'thy' and 'Sydnean'. He further disrupts our grammatical expectations by placing the object ('Psalmes') before the auxiliary and infinitive verbs ('shall celebrate'). Thus, the phrase respectively comprises a subjective pronoun, a possessive pronoun, an adjectival/possessive noun, a noun, an auxiliary verb and an infinitive. While this syntactical reversal could only be performed in a poetic context and remain comprehensible, Donne's precise phraseology is crucial to the point he is making.

Given that another feature of this poem is an acute interest in the effects of doubling, it is worth noting that the phrase comprises two pronouns, two nouns and two verbs.[6] The poem is centrally concerned with naming and with the relationship between the human and the divine, which is reflected in Donne's syntactical order: we (human), thy (divine), Sydnean (human), Psalmes (divine), shall celebrate (divinely inspired human action), that is, the human and the divine are distinct yet interwoven and balanced. Calling upon his contemporaries specifically to celebrate 'thy Sydnean Psalmes', Donne's choice of syntactical rearrangement places the emphasis on the object and its possessors. Crucially, the 'owners' of the object are doubled in more than one way: firstly, the Psalmes belong to *both* God and the Sidneys ('thy Sydnean'); secondly, Donne's use of the term 'Sydnean' here is insistently inclusive, as his adjectival noun denotes two people and thus he forms another kind of collective possessive. Indeed, here, as elsewhere in the poem, there are 'two that make one' (line 17): 'Sydnean' unambiguously refers to *both* Philip *and* Mary Sidney. Throughout his poem, Donne insists on the truly *collaborative* nature of early modern authorship. Bearing this in mind, I aim to explore how our sense of literary history might alter if 'we' – as modern, feminist, literary critics – follow John Donne and celebrate 'thy Sydnean Psalmes'.

I

POSSIBLY written by Donne to accompany a planned seventeenth-century publication of their Psalms, the poem's full title signals the collaborative production of the Sidneys' divinely inspired translation.[7] In explicitly identifying the subject of his encomium as the work of two specific, named individuals, Donne simultaneously invokes the paradoxical division and unity which is a central motif of the poem.[8] Donne definitively establishes both their separate identities and their interconnectedness. The Countess of Pembroke's position as Sidney's 'Sister' has powerful associations, some of which have been problematic for feminist critics, including me.[9] For now, I wish only to note that this clearly demonstrates that Donne is in no doubt that the 'Sydnean Psalmes' were *collaboratively* produced by *both* a man *and* a woman. Donne's awareness of the authors' sexual difference is reinforced by the reaffirmation of their sibling relationship within the rest of the poem: the Sidneys are alluded to as 'A Brother and a Sister' (line 15) and are aligned with the biblical example of 'thy *Moses* and this *Miriam*' (line 46).[10] What has not been commented on to date, however, is Donne's strategic use of names in this poem generally.

Given the poem is explicitly concerned with the problematic nature of naming in a devotional context, it is perhaps unsurprising that, although it opens with 'Eternal God', the speaker, anxious to avoid squaring the circle, refuses to elucidate further and claims instead, 'I would but blesse thy name, not name Thee now' (line 5). The reluctance to name God is reinforced by the poem's resistance to nouns in general; it is arguably overpopulated with non-specific naming substitutes and only four fore-names are used throughout. In addition to Moses and Miriam, the other names are David and John the Baptist; of all these, only David's name is used more than once. It is, of course, highly appropriate that all of these names are biblical. However, these names also provide Donne with an opportunity to invoke doubleness, as they have very precise typological connotations which place the Sidneys theologically. Although, in a poem praising psalm translation, the references to David would appear self-explanatory, the allusions to John the Baptist, Moses and Miriam are perhaps less immediately comprehensible. Having opened the poem by reference predominantly to Old Testament devotional poetics – David is initially alluded to as 'These Psalmes first Author' (line 9) – the first biblical figure actually named in the poem is John the Baptist: 'Two that make one *John Baptists* holy voyce' (line 17). Donne hereby repositions the Sidneys as New Testament harbingers of Christ's imminent arrival. This point is subsequently reinforced by Donne's direct quotation of '*Now let the Iles rejoyce*' (Psalm 97).[11] Taking into account Donne's sparing and meaningful selection of proper names, it seems to me that this places extra emphasis on the significance of the term 'Sydnean', as it is the only non-biblical, familial name to appear in the entire poem.

Strikingly, the distribution of Donne's extensive personal and possess-ive pronouns follows a potentially significant trajectory through the poem's progression. Broadly speaking, their usage moves from a specific set of possessive pronouns and determiners ('Thee,' 'Thy' and 'Thou', lines 1–18), through the third person ('they' and 'their', lines 23–9), towards an overwhelming emphasis on the plural ('we' and 'our', lines 43–56). For instance, the first-person singular is used only five times; in each case, the use of 'I' marks an associated sense of anxiety (as in line 5 quoted above). The other four usages appear in swift succession within the fifth sentence (lines 36–40), marking a curious disruption to collective continuity. In the previous sentence, Donne had evoked a utopian vision of cosmic harmony achieved through the mediation of Christ (lines 29–30) and the Holy Spirit's inspiration (who, as 'heavens high holy Muse' [line 31], 'whispers' the songs to both David and the Sidneys). However, in the next sentence he contrasts this idealised view with the rather more fragmented situation within the contemporary English Church: this disconnection is reinforced by the speaker's repeated use of the first-person singular pronoun 'I'. The lone speaker here laments both the disjuncture between 'English' psalms and indeterminate 'foreign' translations (line 38), and between the psalms used in the English Church and those used 'in Chambers' (line 39). Whereas here the individual is isolated and discouraged, the collective pronouns used elsewhere emphasise that relief and rejoicing are found within a community harmonised through communal, perhaps even congregational, singing of 'thy Sydnean Psalmes'.[12] Although the Sidneys have yet to be named within the poem, it is in this sentence that they are directly positioned as *'Davids* successors' (line 33) whose 'forms of joy and art doe re-reveale' (line 34) God's songs or psalms.[13] The Sidney's re-revelation is specifically linked with their capacity to promote reformation. In the space of two consecutive lines, the speaker uses the same abbreviated version of 'reform'd' twice: 'I can scarce call that reform'd, until / This be reform'd' (lines 40–1). Although used twice, this term is not merely doubled by repetition and through meaning but is also differentiated by function: firstly, as an adjective; and secondly, as a qualifying verb. While both uses allude to ecclesiastical reformation, I believe the second iteration is an unusual example of a rare usage meaning 'to correct, emend (a book, writing, etc.); to revise, edit; (also) to correct the writing of (an author)'.[14] Rewriting God's word – in the sense of translating it into various vernaculars – after all was at the centre of the Reformation.[15] And here, of course, Donne is celebrating the Sidneys' divinely inspired capacity to do exactly this with their psalms.

The precise context of the *English* Reformation is reinforced by the following rhetorical question which concludes the poem's fifth sentence: 'Would a whole State present / A lesser gift than some one man hath sent?' (lines 41–2). Although ostensibly contrasting 'a whole State' (England) with 'one man', Donne again manages to multiply a unity. On first reading, 'some' and 'one' seem to contradict each other. Is the referent here David? Or is it the Sidneys? And, if the latter, why use the singular? Disconcertingly, for modern readers, confusion is proliferated by Donne's typographical layout, 'some one man'. Is there more than one person involved here? Or is Donne's meaning closer to our modern 'someone'? There is at least one other early modern instance of the use of the specific 'some one' as a mode of limitation on the existential quantification of 'some'.[16] Either way, the main point remains that England should not offer 'A lesser gift' (line 42) but instead adopt the collaborative 'Sydnean Psalmes', whose achievements are specifically contrasted to the mass of others translated by a cacophony of 'some' people (lines 48–9). In another example of doubling, Donne's penultimate sentence again uses anacoenosis:

> And shall our Church, unto our Spouse and King
> More hoarse, more harsh than any other sing?
> (lines 43–4)

By invoking the collective, and appealing to his English audience's nascent sense of national pride, Donne prepares his audience to join him in agreeing with his conclusion in the final sentence; that is, God has provided the answer, as, through the Sidneys' Psalm translations, this 'is / Already done' (lines 46–7).[17]

The effect of the poem's strategic use of names (and therefore their implications for our understanding of collaborative authorship) reaches its climax in the final sentence, which begins:

> For *that* we pray, we praise thy name for *this*,
> Which, by thy *Moses* and this *Miriam*, is
> Already done; and as those Psalmes we call
> (Though *some* have other authors) *David's* all;
> So though *some* have, *some* may *some* Psalmes translate,
> We thy Sydnean Psalmes shall celebrate.
> (lines 45–50, emphasis added)

Donne's appellation here might appear to prioritise Philip's identification with Moses; however, such an interpretation sits uneasily with his obvious desire to praise the Sidneys' combined achievements. Moses may have been the 'author' of the Pentateuch, but Miriam is also famous for leading her people in songs of praise – or psalms.[18] Miriam is also the Hebrew form of the name Mary; thus, one might argue that Donne is emphasising Mary Sidney's contribution, as another woman associated with psalm authorship. More importantly, this point has to be considered in context. Donne's next line acknowledges that the attribution of the Psalms to David was a convention which might bear little relation to their actual origins: although 'we' use universal quantification in such attribution, that 'all' is qualified. Donne exposes the limits of our knowledge of the Psalms' authorship by pointing out that we know 'some have other authors' (line 48). Moreover, not only does he use the existential qualifier 'some' here, but he repeats it three times in the next line. In contrast to our lack of knowledge of the origins of 'David's' psalms, and despite Donne's awareness of the existence of a plethora of other contemporary, English metrical psalm translations, here, in direct contrast to the indefinite and indeterminate 'some', Donne is highly specific: 'We thy *Sydnean* Psalmes shall celebrate' (line 50).

According to the *Oxford English Dictionary* (*OED*), which cites only the two seventeenth-century usages (referenced below) as its examples, the adjective 'Sidneian' is defined as 'of, pertaining to, or characteristic of the life and works of Sidney'.[19] Sidney, here – as currently – is taken to refer solely to Philip. However, contextually, the gender specificity of these examples is not entirely clear: one refers simply to '*Sydnæan* showers / Of sweet discourse' and the other references Lady Mary Wroth as 'the happy starre, discovered in our Sydneian Asterisme'.[20] A full text search (including variants) on Early English Books Online (EEBO) produces only nine hits in eight texts between 1599 and 1663.[21] Donne is not cited in either source. As EEBO does not have a full text version of the 1635 edition of Donne's *Poems*, this is explicable. More curious is the *OED*'s omission of Donne's 'Sydnean', especially when Donne's poetry is otherwise cited 339 times. Although the 1635 edition is referenced only once, it is to provide the first cited usage of 're-reveale', which is in 'Upon the translation'. Significantly, it would seem that Donne's specific use of 'Sydnean' in this poem is also a neologism, as it clearly refers to *both* Philip and Mary.

Donne's attempt to connote both brother and sister by turning their shared familial surname into a unifying adjectival noun is meant to do more than simply illustrate how the Sidneys themselves epitomise the paradoxical connection between doubleness and unity so prevalent in this poem. As types, their example tells and teaches us how, why and what to do ourselves, as the poem closes with the communal audience imitating the Sidneys and creating a choir:

> And, till *we* come th'Extermporall song to sing
> (Learn'd the first hower, that *we* see the King,
> Who hath translated those translators) may
> These their sweet learned labours, all the way
> Be as *our* tuning, that, when hence *we* part
> *We* may fall in with *them*, and sing *our* part.
> (lines 51–6, emphasis added)

Donne envisages the English Church singing 'thy Sydnean Psalmes' both while on earth and on entering heaven. In this sentence, hammering home the collective nature of psalm-singing, Donne uses the first-person plural seven times.[22] As Hannibal Hamlin has observed, the fact that Donne concludes his poem with a homonymic rhyming couplet reinforces the unity through doubleness which animates the entire poem.[23] This balance is also indicated by the parallel use of 'our' and 'we', and 'we' and 'our' in the final two lines. The combined, yet dual, nature of the term 'Sydnean' is also emphasised by the use of 'them' in the final line. Overall, Donne's poem establishes a whole line of precursory authors into which the Sidneys are allocated their place: the ultimate authority is, of course, God, but, through God's spirit, the Psalms were initially presented to us by their 'first author in a cloven tongue' (line 9).[24] The recipients of Donne's praise are distinct but unified: 'Two, by their bloods, and by thy Spirit one' (line 14). While Donne clearly remains aware of the Sidney siblings' physical, sexual difference, by the poem's conclusion the pair become mutually 'Sydnean'. Donne's poem provides a cosmological gestalt in which the whole truly is far more than the sum of its parts. However, what was seemingly obvious to him has become rather less so for more recent readers: why is it, then, that the *collaborative* authorship of the Psalms, so highly praised by Donne, has seemingly become so problematic for readers of 'thy Sydnean Psalmes', at least since the nineteenth century?

II

AT first glance, it might appear that there really is no problem with the authorship or attribution question when it comes to 'thy Sydnean Psalmes', as it has long been recognised that Philip produced Psalms 1–43 and Mary was responsible for Psalms 44–150; furthermore, numerous modern critics have definitively established that Mary Sidney's active role in the writing of these psalms was well known by many of her contemporaries, not just John Donne.[25] However, by 1619, William Drummond reported Ben Jonson's hint that her role may have been merely declarative: 'Sir P. Sidney had translated some of the Psalmes, which went abroad under the name of the Countesse of Pembrock' and, by the mid-seventeenth century, John Aubrey's account of Wilton's library specifically mentions 'a manuscript very elegantly written, viz. all the Psalms of David translated by *Sir Philip Sidney*, curiously bound in crimson velvet'.[26] Such comments, together with the fact that nine out of the twelve extant manuscripts with title pages attribute the entire collection to Philip, lead Gavin Alexander to suggest that Mary was 'strangely reluctant to disseminate her major work in a way that made clear her authorship'.[27] However, in what follows I will suggest that the evidence indicates that it is Alexander's response which is strange and indicative of a misconception of early modern attitudes towards authorship, particularly in a devotional context.

Since Samuel W. Singer's 1823 edition of the Sidney *Psalmes*, it has become firmly re-established that Philip Sidney translated the first forty-three and Mary Sidney translated the rest.[28] Although aware of this fact,

Singer makes no comment upon it; however, later in the nineteenth century, Alexander B. Grosart wistfully remarks: 'I should gladly have welcomed more as Sir Philip's, for there can be no question that the Countess's portion is infinitely in advance of her brother's in thought, epithet, and melody'.[29] Albeit inadvertently, Grosart's higher evaluation of Mary Sidney's poetry appears to have resulted in a concerted effort to occlude her contribution to the collection. For example, in *Rock Honeycomb* (1877), despite having read Singer's edition of their Psalms and acknowledging that these poems are only 'attributed in part to Sir Philip Sidney' and selecting examples up to Psalm 72, John Ruskin does not mention Mary Sidney.[30] Indeed, although Ruskin admits 'the translations attributed by tradition to Sidney included many of the feeblest in the volume', he stubbornly insists on attributing *all* of his selections to Philip Sidney.[31] Where Ruskin printed Mary Sidney's poetry but ignored her authorship, subsequent, twentieth-century editors of the Psalms have acknowledged her authorship but have justified the exclusion of her poems because their studies focus on Philip.[32] The then dominant critical aim of literary studies being to establish authoritative editions of the 'complete works' of individual, male, canonical authors meant that the rest of 'thy Sydnean Psalmes' could simply be ignored. In addition, the early editors assumed that the revisions to the first forty-three poems were 'authorised' by Philip Sidney; however, it subsequently became clear that these were the work of his sister. For Sidney scholars, it had long been a source of regret that Philip had not completed the Psalms; the realisation that what had survived might not be securely 'his' was offensive to an editorial psyche which sought to recover authorial 'intentionality' and establish a 'clean' text which mirrored the individual's mind, uncontaminated by any other influence. This, and his annoyance with her 'inveterate tinkering', resulted in William A. Ringler's edition which 'freed' Philip's psalms from his sister's revisions: Ringler's edition remains the unchallenged standard.[33]

However, only one year later, another edition appeared which had quite the opposite intention: whereas 'Ringler has sought to reconstruct, as accurately as possible, the original wording of Sidney's Psalms 1–43', J. C. A. Rathmell's objective was to 'present the finally revised form of the text'.[34] Despite Rathmell's efforts, it took another twenty years before Mary Sidney's poetry became the object of sustained critical attention. The landmark publication of *Silent But For The Word* signalled the start of a shift which now means that Mary Sidney's writing is the subject of numerous critical studies, including the further biographical and editorial work of Margaret P. Hannay.[35] Despite this, Mary Sidney occupies an awkward position within the feminist literary canon, primarily because her 'major work' is in the broad genre of translation. Ironically, even the impressive *Collected Works* betrays the same individualist assumptions of earlier critical models, as it includes only Psalms 44–150. Very recently, the complete text has appeared in the World's Classics series, as *The Sidney Psalter: The Psalms of Sir Philip and Mary Sidney* (2009); however, as its title illustrates, reuniting the siblings in this way still does not result in a celebration of 'thy Sydnean Psalmes'. For better or worse, the proper noun 'Sidney' will always be read as signifying Philip, so this title inadvertently privileges his contribution. Furthermore, the use of the conjunction 'and' in the subtitle reinforces a sense of sequential authorship, in which the Psalms remain divided into two 'parts'. Although the recent editors cite Mary Sidney herself as the most definitive source for the collaborative nature of this project, they ultimately position her as 'the principal author and editor of the Sidney Psalter'.[36] Our modern investment in individual ownership and authorship apparently precludes a full appreciation of what a truly collaborative project might mean. But what happens if we take both Donne and Mary Sidney seriously and read 'thy Sydnean Psalmes' as a divinely inspired, collaborative project?

III

As the editorial investments above indicate, somewhat paradoxically, the most contentious aspect of the collaborative nature of this project remains Mary Sidney's revisions to her brother's translations. The nature of this challenge is epitomised by Henry Woudhuysen's admission that he excludes the Psalms from his otherwise exhaustive study of the circulation of Philip Sidney's manuscripts because 'successive revisions by the countess of Pembroke ... made his own work on the text difficult to separate from hers'.[37] Clearly, there is not space here to analyse all of Mary Sidney's revisionary work, so, as a test case, I am going to focus on her alteration of her brother's endings of Psalms 1, 16, 22, 23, 26, 29 and 31.[38] Although Rathmell commented that Mary Sidney was 'understandably cautious' when 'recasting her brother's work', since then the only other critic to have examined these revisions in any detail is Gavin Alexander. While I agree with Alexander that the consistency with which Mary Sidney revises these poems is significant, unlike him I do not think this is because she 'does not understand that asymmetry can give greater poetic closure'.[39] Whatever their other differences, all commentators agree that the most outstanding feature of 'thy Sydnean Psalmes' is their poetic variety; thus, it simply does not make sense to suggest Mary Sidney did not understand a particular poetic effect. Alexander also asserts that Mary Sidney's awkward 'condensation' of the conclusion of Psalm 23 indicates that 'addition to Sidney is here subtraction from him'.[40] Unfortunately, contextually, this comment appears to position *all* her revisionary poetics negatively in relation to her brother's 'originals'. Conversely, focusing my attention on Mary Sidney's revisions to Psalm 26, I, somewhat polemically, asserted that, there, her 'compression ... manifestly improves her brother's poetics'.[41] Both positions highlight the perils of selective exemplars. Thus, although I will look in some detail at what Mary Sidney did when revising Psalms 31 and 1 below, I want also to suggest that it is possible to identify patterns to her process across all seven revisions; rather than working from the basis that such 'additions' necessarily represent either a 'loss' or a 'gain', what might this reveal about collaborative authorship?

Alexander bases his case for Mary Sidney's 'subtraction' from her brother on the assumption that Philip's use of half-stanza endings was partly influenced by his reading of the Marot-Bèze psalter and his interest in such endings is evidenced in his other poetry. However, Alexander cites only two instances from *Certaine Sonnets*, whereas he notes such forms account for 'around a fifth of' the first forty-three psalms.[42] A further complication to this justification of Philip's poetics is that, strictly speaking, three of these poems do not end in 'half-stanzas' at all. According to Ringler's edition, Psalm 1 concludes with a quatrain rather than a sexain, and Psalm 16, again predominately written in sexains, concludes with an extra couplet. Ringler's edition of Psalm 29 does not identify stanzas. In different variants, however, this psalm is alternatively displayed in sexains or tercets but, whichever stanzaic layout is used, the psalm concludes with an extra couplet. Furthermore, six out of seven of these 'half-stanzas' also disregard the rhyme scheme established in the rest of the poem, substituting instead a mono-rhyme scheme. It is also worth noting that the distribution of those half-stanzaic endings is disproportionately represented within the final third of the psalms attributed to him (22, 23, 26, 29). The proportion of poems ending in such 'formal deviation' is both extraordinarily high and highly inconsistent in practice: from such evidence it seems appropriate to speculate that perhaps Philip did not think of them as 'finished' at all.

Alexander finds it 'extraordinary and significant' that Mary Sidney 'identified each case and worked hard to regularize them all'.[43] But what I find truly remarkable is that in none of these revisions does she ever choose to *add* to the poems; that is, she never extends her brother's extant 'half-stanza' into a full stanza but always condenses what he had already written. As a general rule, regardless of original line length, Mary Sidney's revisions reduce her brother's word count by at least a third. Clearly, this is not because she could not expand them, which means it had to be her choice. Interestingly, in all cases she also retains specific words or phrases from her brother's text: working collaboratively, Mary restyles these into the pattern he himself had established in the previous part of the particular poem. This is demonstrated in the siblings' variant conclusions to Psalm 31, of which the first below is Philip's:

[22] Yet I confess in that tempestuous haste	a	
I said that I from out Thy sight was cast;	a	
But Thou didst heare, when I to Thee did moane.	b	
[23] *Then love him ye all ye that feel his grace,*	c	
For this Our lord preserves the faith full race	c	65
And to the proud in deeds pays home their own.	d	
[24] *Bee strong I say his strength confirm in you,*	a	
You that do trust in him who is still true,	a	
And he shall your establishment renew.	a	

In order to underline how Philip Sidney breaks his own pattern, I have added a line break to emphasise how this poem ends; in this case, specifically in a half-stanza mono-rhyme. Unlike the conclusion of Psalm 23, the half-stanza here makes the poem seem unfinished; especially when compared with his sister's revision:

[22] Yet I confess in that tempestuous haste	a	
I said that I from out Thy sight was cast;	a	
But Thou didst heare, when I to Thee did moane.	b	
[23] **Then love** the **Lord all ye that feel his grace;**	c	
Who paires **the proud, preserves the faithfull race:**	c	65
[24] **Be strong in** hope, **his strength shall you** supply.	d	

This version ensures the poem concludes as it began in both rhyme and stanza form. The numbers in square brackets on the left-hand side identify the verse of the biblical psalm to which the main text corresponds and the line numbers on the right confirm its concision, which reduces the fifty-four words highlighted in italics above to twenty-seven. However, the bold text demonstrates that, of those twenty-seven words, only five of them are 'new' to Mary. She is as deft with her brother's words as she is – both here and throughout – with her biblical and other sources. In Rathmell's terms, no doubt this would be classified as 'cautious': indeed, it is the most extreme among the seven revisions in retaining Philip's wording. While in this instance Mary Sidney retained 81 per cent of her brother's words, at the other extreme, her rewriting of Psalm 26 uses 80 per cent of her own. But, as with Donne's poem, repetition here is not slavish reiteration: indeed, Mary doubles the meaning of single words to carry the full sense of her biblical sources. Her use of 'to pare' primarily signifies pruning or trimming but also carries a sense of diminishment.[44]

The aural pun on 'pair' also invokes a sense of this result as an appropriate complement and neatly encapsulates John Calvin's suggestion that this means 'the proud' will get the 'reward ... they deserve' while alliteratively reflecting his appreciation of the elegance of the original Hebrew.[45] Her choice of 'hope' for 'trust' invokes the now obsolete biblical meaning of a 'feeling or trust or confidence' along with 'an expectation of something desired'.[46] And her selection of the final verb 'supply' connotes not only support and assistance but a promise of completion or supplement.[47] In this example, I submit that, through concision, clarification and carefully chosen alliteration, Mary's subtraction becomes a form of amplification. Furthermore, the slight but significant alterations she makes here reinforce the generally accepted view that one of her main theological sources was Calvin's *Commentaries*. This influence is also evident in some of the terms she chooses to alter in her revision of Psalms 16 and 22, in which the words 'knowe', 'joies' and 'service' are directly traceable to Calvin. This 'reliance' upon her sources has troubled critics who fetishise 'originality'. Mary Sidney's studious engagement with theological authorities has been viewed as an indication of her indecisiveness, a trait which is further exacerbated by the sense that she was 'congenitally incapable of leaving a poem alone long enough to produce a definitive copy'.[48] Such attitudes reveal a modern misconception of the process in which Mary was involved; after all, the whole point of the Psalms is to encourage the believer to meditate on God's word day and night.

This message is encapsulated in the second verse of the first psalm, which, in the Geneva version, reads 'But his delite is in the Lawe of the Lord, and in his Lawe doeth he meditate day and night'. Arguably this is the most important psalm in the collection; for, as Calvin explains, 'He who collected the Psalms into one volume ... appears to have placed this Psalm at the beginning, by way of preface, in which he inculcates upon all the godly the duty of meditating upon the law of God'.[49] Given the crucial significance of this psalm, it is particularly vital to examine the revisionary process here. As a form of control, here, first, is the prose text of this psalm from the Geneva Bible:

4. The wicked are not so, but as the chaffe, which the winde driueth away.
5. Therefore the wicked shall not stande in the iudgement, nor sinners in the assemblie of the righteous.
6. For the Lorde knoweth the way of the righteous, & the way of the wicked shal perish.

In Philip's version, this becomes:

[4] Such blessings shall not wycked wretches see: a
     But lyke vyle chaffe with wind shal scattred be.   a

109

[5] For neither shall the men in sin delighted	b	15
Consist, when they to highest doome are cited,	b	
Ne yet shall suffred be a place to take,	c	
Wher godly men do their assembly make.	c	
[6] For God doth know, and knowing doth approve	a	
The trade of them, that just proceeding love;	a	20
But they that sinne, in-sinfull breast do cherish;	b	
The way they go shal be their way to perish.	b	

Thus, formally, Philip sets up a pattern of six-line stanzas comprised of rhyming couplets predominantly in iambic pentameter. In both these stanzas and his preceding two, Sidney establishes a deviation to this pattern insofar as the third and fourth lines contain an extra syllable and, therefore, end in feminine rhyme. Sidney's and Spenser's use of feminine rhyme is well known but, generally characterised as 'weak', it is an unusual choice for the conclusion of such a significant psalm.[50]

Although apparently happy to retain the feminine endings in the middle of the stanza, it is striking that Mary Sidney's revision works particularly hard here to ensure this poem does not end in this manner:

x / x / x / x / x /		
[4] **Not** soe the **wicked; Butt like chaff with wind**	a	
x / x / x / x / x /		
[5] **Scatt'red, shall neither** stay in *Judgement* find	a	
x / x / x / x / x / x		
Nor with the **just**, bee in their meetings placed:	b	15
x / x / x / x / x / x		
[6] For good mens waies by God are knowne and *graced*.	b	
x / x / x / x / x /		
Butt who from *Justice* sinfully doe stray,	c	
x / x / x / x / x /		
The way they goe, shall be their ruins **way.**	c	

This is achieved not only by adhering to the formal patterns initiated by her brother but by a potentially perilous departure from the biblical original. Like Calvin and the Genevan translation, the final word in Philip Sidney's translation is 'perish'. The decision to alter this term is particularly problematic insofar as it also appears in Psalm 2 (verse 12). As Psalms 1 and 2 arguably construct a pairing which sets up the direction of the entire Psalter, not using 'perish' could easily be construed as heretical. However, given the way stress works in English pronunciation, Mary Sidney cannot conclude the poem with 'perish' without also finishing on a 'weak' accent: daringly, her solution is to substitute it with 'ruins way'. While for modern readers, 'ruin' might seem a less threatening choice, it arguably indicates

Mary's acute sensitivity to early modern nuance and inflection, as it could mean: 'to inflict great and irretrievable damage, loss, or disaster upon'; 'to destroy, extirpate, eradicate'; 'to incur spiritual death'; or to be brought 'to damnation'.[51] Elsewhere, her choices once again reflect her awareness of Calvin's *Commentaries*, as the words italicised in the above are directly traceable to this source. While these emphasise justice and judgement, Mary's inclusion of 'graced' serves to remind the reader of the typological manner in which the psalms are to be read, that is, with an awareness of Christ's redemptive sacrifice. Finally, her concluding rhyme on 'stray' and 'way' skilfully both reminds the reader of 'the straying steppes' of her brother's second line and reconnects the use of the term 'way' in both the second and the final verse of the Genevan version of this psalm. In so doing, Mary creates her own version of this psalm while continuing to engage with her main collaborators: her brother and God.

IV

O N the basis of the evidence discussed above, it is my contention that our separate – and separatist – traditions of critical editing and scholarly studies have created an artificial distinction between two of the most influential figures in the historical development of the canon of English literature. Indeed, I find myself reflecting that a wholly unsubstantiated critical assumption has driven the study of 'thy Sydnean Psalmes' to date – that is, the conjecture that Philip Sidney always intended to translate all 150 psalms. Curiously, no critic I have consulted offers even a shred of evidence that this was the case and, as with his sister, uncertainty remains about when Philip wrote the translations which are ascribed to him.[52] Ultimately, the idea that he intended to translate the complete Psalms seems to derive primarily from the fact that his sister manifestly *did* do so. Over the centuries, a myriad of patterns to the narrative structure of the Psalms has been posited but there is a general sense that the trajectory of the collection moves from a focus on the individual towards the community and the cosmos.[53] Bearing this in mind, it is interesting that at least one critic notes the individualistic and introspective qualities of Philip's Psalms and suggests that, stylistically, they are reminiscent of a sonnet sequence.[54] Although Psalm 43 may seem an odd place to stop, according to *The Book of Common Prayer*, this is the final psalm to be read on the evening of the eighth day of the week. What appears arbitrary may well be more appropriate than was previously thought; in fact, it could be argued that completing the book of Psalms seems at odds with Philip's aesthetic interests.

Whatever his intentions, it remains a fact that it was Mary Sidney who chose to complete their translation and therefore, due to the narrative trajectory of the biblical text, the majority of the poems attributed to her have an increasingly communal perspective. Yet, as has been noted, she ultimately chooses to conclude the volume by translating Psalm 150 as a 'Sydnean' sonnet.[55] My speculations above flag the collaborative nature of this gesture, which is further intensified by the possibility that, if she was still working on the *Psalmes* in 1599, she could simultaneously have been editing *Astrophel and Stella* for the 1598 edition of *The Countess of Pembroke's Arcadia*.[56] In combining God's word, her own words through translation and her brother's favourite sonnet form (more usually associated with individualistic expression) into an expression of communal praise, Mary Sidney's sonnet perhaps epitomises the truly collaborative nature of 'thy Sydnean Psalmes'. As indicated earlier, Donne's poem also emphasises the communal function of this text. Its macrocosmic significance having been established early in the poem, Donne heightens its microcosmic importance for the English Church. This point is reinforced by his citation of Psalm 97, 'now let the Isles rejoice', which, although 'a plaine prophecy of the spreading of the spiritual kingdome throughout the whole world', was peculiarly apposite to Donne's awareness of the need for this in England.[57] Interestingly, Mary Sidney's version of Psalm 97 draws attention to 'you Isles with waves enclosed' (line 3) and displays a similar reticence to Donne in 'naming' God (using Jehova, the Romanised version of Yahweh). Also, whereas R.-J. Frontain notes that Donne's phrase 'make all this All' (line 23) can be traced to I Corinthians 5:28, it is also uniquely used in Mary Sidney's translation: 'the lord of all this all' (Psalm 97, line 16).[58] Thus, this intertextual reference reinforces a central point made in Donne's poem: that singing 'thy Sydnean Psalmes' will reinvigorate the English Reformation.

In drawing this chapter to a conclusion, I want to look once again at the much commented upon Simon van de Passe portrait of Mary Sidney. Over the years, many have drawn attention to the way in which this engraving's iconography emphasises her 'Sidneian' connections and poetic aspirations; however, usually, the term 'Sidneian' is used as in the *OED* definition (above). Only very recently, Alexander noted the possible significance of 'the repeating motif of the outer lace' being 'a swan shaped like an "S"'.[59] Alexander points out that many of the 'University Latin elegies for Sidney play on the proximity of the Latinized "Sidneius" to the Latin *cygnus*' and argues that its appearance on Mary Sidney's lace is 'a memorial of her brother' and 'a badge of her own writing', which he characterises as 'a "swanne-like dying song"'.[60] This connection is significant but in focusing on how this associated her specifically with her brother, Alexander overlooks the broader, literary significance of the swan as a metaphor for the early modern poet. According to Patrick Cheney, a poet's association with a particular bird places the poet in a very specific position. Significantly, Cheney's book includes emblematic images of 'The Prophetic Swan' and 'The Swan as a Sign of the Poet', and he argues that these connections merged 'the scriptural myth of the prophet or divine singer with the classical myth of the poet in order to reveal the prophetic authority of his art'.[61] Importantly, however, in the van de Passe engraving the poet is, of course, female. By aligning herself with the figure of the swan, then, Mary is making a different kind of 'Sydnean' allusion, one which, like John Donne's, includes both her brother and herself as divinely inspired poets. Here it is necessary to reiterate that the book she holds in her hands in the picture is clearly entitled '*David's* Psalms'. While, of course, this does allude to the 'Sydnean Psalmes', it also reinforces the collaborative nature of this endeavour, as suggested by Donne. As indicated in my introduction, engaging with already established critical accounts of the alternative models for an early modern poet's career path enabled Pender to highlight Mary Sidney's fundamental role in the creation of her brother's literary career and, by extension, in the establishment of the foundations of the canon of English literature. It used to be lamented that, if only Philip had completed the Psalms, we would have access to a missing link in the evolution of this genre.[62] Of course, that text does exist but in order to recognise this fully, along with Mary Sidney's role in the development of the English devotional lyric, we need to set aside our separatist traditions and embrace the collaborative model of 'thy Sydnean Psalmes'. Early modern, feminist, literary critics have spent a long time searching for the elusive figure of 'Shakespeare's sister'; perhaps it is time to consider whether she has been hidden in plain sight for over 400 years but that she should, in fact, be styled 'Sidney's sister'.

Notes

In addition to Sue Wiseman, I would like to thank Marilyn Booth, Dermot Cavanagh, Natasha Simonova and Greg Walker for their comments on earlier drafts of this chapter.

1 M. J. M. Ezell, 'The myth of Judith Shakespeare: creating the canon of women's literature', *New Literary History*, vol. 21, no. 3 (1990), pp. 579–92; V. Woolf, *A Room of One's Own* [1929], Panther, London, 1985, p. 46.

2 P. Pender, 'The ghost and the machine in the Sidney family corpus', *Studies in English Literature*, vol. 51, no. 1 (2011), p. 65.

3 H. Love, *Attributing Authorship: An Introduction*, Cambridge University Press, Cambridge, 2002, p. 33.

4 All references to this poem are to G. A. Stringer, 'Donne's dedication of the Sidney Psalter', *John Donne Journal*, vol. 27 (2008), pp. 197–8. That issue contains a series of articles from a colloquium on this poem – see pp. 145–96.

5   R. E. Pritchard, *The Sidney Psalms*, Carcanet Press, Manchester, 1992, p. 18; B. Quitslund, 'Teaching us how to sing? The peculiarity of the Sidney Psalter', *Sidney Journal*, vol. 23, nos 1–2 (2005), p. 99; S. Trill, '"In Poesie the mirrois of our Age": the Countess of Pembroke's "Sydnean" poetics', in K. Cartwright (ed.), *A Companion to Tudor Literature*, Blackwell, Oxford, 2010, p. 430.

6   See H. Hamlin, 'Upon Donne's "Upon the translation of the Psalmes"', *John Donne Journal*, vol. 27 (2008), pp. 175–96, at p. 187.

7   There has been some debate over the dating and purpose of Donne's poem. For a summary of the differing perspectives see Hamlin, 'Upon Donne's'; and R.-J. Frontain, 'Translating heavenwards: "Upon the translation of the Psalmes" and John Donne's poetics of praise', *Explorations in Renaissance Culture*, vol. 22 (1996), pp. 103–25.

8   R-J Frontain, 'Translating heavenwards', p. 105.

9   S. Trill, 'Spectres and sisters: Mary Sidney and the "perennial puzzle" of Renaissance women's writing', in G. McMullan (ed.), *Renaissance Configurations: Bodies, Voices, Spaces, 1580–1690*, Macmillan, Basingstoke, 1998, pp. 191–211.

10 See M. P. Hannay, '"This Moses and this Miriam": the Countess of Pembroke's role in the legend of Sir Philip Sidney', in M. J. B. Allen *et al.* (eds), *Sir Philip Sydney's Achievements*, AMS, New York, 1990; Frontain, 'Translating heavenwards', p. 106. Emphases here and below are original unless stated otherwise.

11 Calvin comments that this psalm 'contains a prediction of [the] kingdom of Christ'; R. J. Anderson (ed.), *Commentary on the Book of Psalms by John Calvin*, 5 vols, Calvin Translation Society Publications, Edinburgh, 1845–49, vol. 4, p. 53.

12 M. White, 'Protestant women's writing and congregational psalm singing: from the "Song of the Exiled Handmaid" (1555) to the Countess of Pembroke's *Psalmes* (1599)', *Sidney Journal*, vol. 23, nos 1–2 (2005), pp. 61–82.

13 M. P. Hannay, 'Re-revealing the Psalms: the Countess of Pembroke and her early modern readers', *Sidney Journal*, vol. 23, nos 1–2 (2005), pp. 19–36. See also M. P. Hannay, 'Re-revealing the Psalms: Mary Sidney, Countess of Pembroke, and her early modern readers', in L. P. Austern, K. B. McBride and D. L. Orvis (eds), *Psalms in the Early Modern World*, Ashgate, Aldershot, 2011, pp. 219–35.

14 'Reform', *adj*[1], *OED*, II.5.b.

15 See S. Trill, 'Sixteenth-century women's writing: Mary Sidney's Psalmes and the "femininity" of translation', in W. Zunder and S. Trill (eds), *Writing and the English Renaissance*, Longman, Basildon, 1996, pp. 140–58; M. White (ed.), *English Women, Religion, and Textual Production*, Ashgate, Farnham, 2011.

16 'Some: 6. Followed by *certain* or *one* with limiting force'; see T. Cooper, *Thesaurus*, '*Vnus aliquis*, some one man' (1565); 'some', *adj*[1], *OED*, B.I.6.

17 As many critics have noted, Mary Sidney emphasises the Englishness of the Sidneian *Psalmes* in her dedicatory poem, 'Even now that care', addressed to Queen Elizabeth. See H. Hamlin *et al.* (eds), *The Sidney Psalter: The Psalms of Sir Philip and Mary Sidney*, World's Classics, Oxford University Press, Oxford, 2009, pp. 5–7 (especially stanzas 4 and 6).

18 See Exodus 2:1–10; 15:20–1; see also M. Osherow, 'Biblical women's voices in early modern England', in A. Poska and A. Zanger (eds), *Women and Gender in the Early Modern World*, Ashgate, Farnham, 2009, pp. 11–43.

19 See, for example, Richard Hillyer: 'though many Sidneys exist … I usually point to him when writing of Sidney'; R. Hillyer, *Sir Philip Sidney, Cultural Icon*, Palgrave Macmillan, New York, 2010, p. xviii.

20 R. Crashaw, 'Wishes. To his (supposed) mistresse', *Steps to the Temple*, 1646; and G. Chapman, trans, *Homer: Complete Works*, 1616, sig. Gg 6v.

21 Of these, five relate to women: Chapman; Thomas Moffett's *The Silke Wormes and Their Flies* (1599) and *Sir Philip Sydney's Ouránia* (1606) by Nathanial Baxter, which are all dedicated to Mary Sidney; and two are to references to James Howell's

celebratory sonnet prefacing Anna Weamys's *A Continuation of Sir Philip Sydney's Arcadia* (1651).

22 Although Frontain notes the communal conclusion, he also suggests 'the final image is … of the speaker'. Frontain, 'Translating heavenwards', p. 117.

23 Hamlin, 'Upon Donne's', p. 187.

24 For further discussion of the significance of 'cleft' and 'cloven', see J. Baumgaertner, 'Harmony in Donne's "La Corona" and "Upon the translation of the Psalmes"', *John Donne Journal*, vol. 3, no. 2 (1984), pp. 142–3.

25 M. P. Hannay, *Philip's Phoenix: Mary Sidney, Countess of Pembroke*, Oxford University Press, New York, 1990.

26 R. F. Patterson (ed.), *Ben Jonson's Conversations with William Drummond of Hawthorden*, Blackie and Son, London, 1923, p. 19; R. Barber (ed.), *John Aubrey: Brief Lives*, Folio Society, London, 1975, p. 146 (emphasis added).

27 G. Alexander, *Writing After Sidney: The Literary Response to Sir Philip Sidney, 1586–1640*, Oxford University Press, Oxford, 2006.

28 S. W. Singer (ed.), *The Psalmes of David translated into divers and sundry kindes of verse … Begun by … Sir Philip Sidney … and finished by the … Countess of Pembroke*, Chiswick, London, 1823, online at http://archive.org/stream/psalmesdavidtra01singgoog#page/n10/mode/2up (accessed April 2012); A. Feuillerat (ed.), *Sir Philip Sidney: Complete Works*, 4 vols, Cambridge English Classics, Cambridge University Press, Cambridge, 1912–26, vol. 3, p. ix.

29 A. B. Grosart (ed.), *Sir Philip Sidney: Complete Works*, 3 vols, London, 1873–77, vol. 2, 1873, p. 209.

30 J. Ruskin (ed.), *Rock Honeycomb: Broken Pieces of Sir Philip Sidney's Psalter*, Ellis and White, London, 1877, online at http://ia600404.us.archive.org/26/items/rockhoney combbrooosidn/rockhoneycombbrooosidn.pdf (accessed April 2012).

31 Ibid., p. xii.

32 Feuillerat, *Sir Philip Sidney*, vol. 3, p. ix.

33 W. A. Ringler (ed.), *The Poems of Sir Philip Sidney*, Clarendon, Oxford, 1962.

34 J. C. A. Rathmell (ed.), *The Psalms of Sir Philip Sidney and the Countess of Pembroke*, Stuart Editions, New York University Press, New York, 1963, p. xxxii.

35 M. P. Hannay (ed.), *Silent But For The Word: Tudor Women as Patrons, Translators, and Writers of Religious Works*, Kent State University Press, Kent, 1985; M. P. Hannay, *Philip's Phoenix: Mary Sidney, Countess of Pembroke*; M. P. Hannay, N. J. Kinnamon and M. G. Brennan (eds), *The Collected Works of Mary Sidney Herbert, Countess of Pembroke: Poems, Translations, and Correspondence*, 2 vols, Oxford English Texts, Clarendon, Oxford, 1998; M. P. Hannay, N. J. Kinnamon and M. G. Brennan (eds), *The Collected Works of Mary Sidney Herbert, Countess of Pembroke: The Psalmes of David*, 2 vols, Oxford English Texts, Clarendon, Oxford, 1998.

36 Hamlin *et al.* (eds), *The Sidney Psalter*, p. xvii, and also p. xvi.

37 H. R. Woudhuysen, *Sir Philip Sidney and the Circulation of Manuscripts, 1558–1640*, Clarendon Press, Oxford, 1996, p. 2.

38 For the purposes of this chapter, I will therefore refer to the 'standard' editions of the Sidney Psalms 1–43, in Ringler, *The Poems of Sir Philip Sidney*, and Rathmell, *The Psalms of Sir Philip Sidney*.

39 Alexander, *Writing After Sidney*, pp. 92, 94.

40 Ibid., p. 94.

41 Trill, '"In Poesie the mirrois of our Age"', p. 434.

42 Alexander, *Writing After Sidney*, p. 92.

43 Ibid.

44 Pare, *v.* I; Pair, *v.* 1, OED.

45 Anderson, *Commentary on the Book of Psalms*, vol. 1, p. 520.

46 Hope, *n¹*, 2, OED.

47 Supply, *v* 1. 3 †b; *Obs.* 7. a, OED.

48 C. Freer, *Music for a King: George Herbert's Style and the Metrical Psalms*, Johns Hopkins University Press, Baltimore, 1972, p. 74. See also Alexander's comment on Psalm 42; Alexander, *Writing After Sidney*, p. 94.
49 Anderson, *Commentary on the Book of Psalms*, vol. 1, p. 1.
50 M. Quilligan, 'Feminine endings: the sexual politics of Sidney's and Spenser's rhyming', in A. M. Haselkorn and B. S. Travitsjy (eds), *The Renaissance Englishwoman in Print: Counterbalancing the Canon*, University of Massachusetts Press, Amherst, 1990.
51 Ruin, *n.* 1; *Obs. Rare* 4. a; 7a. Ruin, *v.* 2; †5. *trans. Obs, OED.*
52 A. C. Hamilton states that 'it is not known whether Sidney, together with his sister, translated the Psalms early or late in his career'; however, he also suggests they represent an 'early exhibition of virtuosity'. A. C. Hamilton, *Sir Philip Sidney: A Study of His Life and Works*, Cambridge University Press, Cambridge, 1977, p. 71. By contrast, Ringler suggests a composition date of 1585. Ringler, *The Poems of Sir Philip Sidney*, p. l.
53 P. W. Flint and P. D. Miller (eds), *The Book of Psalms: Composition and Reception*, Brill, Leiden, 2005.
54 R. Greene, 'Sir Philip Sidney's Psalms, the sixteenth-century psalter, and the nature of lyric', *Studies in English Literature, 1500–1900*, vol. 30, no. 1 (1990), pp. 19–40; see especially pp. 27–34.
55 Alexander, *Writing After Sidney*, p. 121; Trill, '"In Poesie the mirrois of our Age"'; K. A. Coles, *Religion, Reform, and Women's Writing in Early Modern England*, Cambridge University Press, Cambridge, 2008, p. 99.
56 M. Brennan, 'The date of the Countess of Pembroke's translation of the Psalms', *Review of English Studies*, vol. 33, no. 132 (1982), pp. 434–6; M. Brennan, 'The Queen's proposed visit to Wilton house in 1599 and the "Sidney Psalms"', *Sidney Journal*, vol. 20, no. 1 (2002), pp. 27–53.
57 A. Gilbie (ed.), *The Psalmes of Dauid truely opened and explained by paraphrasis, according to the right sense of euery Psalme ... by that excellent learned man Theodore Beza*, London, 1580, p. 234.
58 Frontain, 'Translating heavenwards', p. 105.
59 Alexander, *Writing After Sidney*, p. 78.
60 Ibid., pp. 78, 81.
61 P. Cheney, *Spenser's Famous Flight: A Renaissance Idea of a Literary Career*, University of Toronto Press, Toronto, 1993, p. 72.
62 Greene, 'Sir Philip Sidney's Psalms', p. 27.

CHAPTER 6

Mary Wroth and hermaphroditic circulation

Paul Salzman

I want to begin by rehearsing a story about Mary Wroth's publication of *Urania* that will be familiar to many people, but that I recount here in order to set the scene for an analysis of the circulation and recirculation of her vituperative poetic exchange with Edward Denny. Among a number of thinly veiled depictions of Jacobean court scandals in *Urania*, Wroth gave an account of the violent responses of Edward Denny to accusations that his daughter Honora, married to James Hay, Viscount Carlisle, had committed adultery. In the romance, Denny, who is portrayed as the father of Seralius's wife, reacts even more furiously to the suspicion (not justified, as the romance has it) than his son-in-law. Wroth writes:

> her father a phantasicall thing, vaine as Courtiers, rash as mad-men, &
> ignorant as women, would needs (out of folly, ill nature, and waywardnesse,
> which hee cald care of his honour, and his friends quiet) kill his daughter, and
> so cut off the blame, or spot, this her offence might lay vpon his noble bloud,
> as he termed it, which by any other men must with much curiositie haue been
> sought for, and as rarely found, as Pearles in ordinary Oysters. (I.ii.3)[1]

Denny's response to this confirmed the accuracy of Wroth's analysis of his character. The image of his honour being as rare as pearls in ordinary oysters especially piqued his imagination; he wrote a poem attacking Wroth in the style of misogynistic libel which had become quite a popular genre, sliding from the almost respectable slurs of some of Donne's love poetry through to the scurrilous attacks on Frances Howard's sex life provoked by her divorce from the Earl of Essex and marriage to the King's favourite, Robert Carr.[2] In the 1620s amid growing resentment at scandals that accumulated during King James's reign, the circulation of libels increased in manuscript culture, including libels written much earlier in the reign. Denny's poem sets up an image of Wroth as a monster, a 'hermophradite in show', who has produced an 'idell book' and struck at 'some mans noble bloud'.[3] In an image that is so often turned against women, especially women writers, Denny links sexual laxity with pretensions to authorship, creating an extremely nasty reworking of the oyster image: 'Yet Common oysters such as thine gape wide / And take in pearles or worse at euery tide'. Denny also uses the image of drunkenness against Wroth and concludes by demanding she return to more seemly feminine pursuits than authorship: 'worke o th' workes leave idle bookes alone / for wise & worthier women haue writt none'. This last seems a rather dangerous line to take against the niece of Mary Sidney, Countess of Pembroke, and perhaps Denny did repent it in the cold light of day, as in his follow-up letter to Wroth he backtracks and suggests she should write 'heavenly lays' not 'lascivious tales', and follow the 'rare, and pious example of your virtuous and learned aunt'.[4]

Far from being cowed by this attack, initially Wroth responded in kind, writing a fierce letter to Denny stating that his verses must have been written by a 'drunken poet', claiming disingenuously that she did not 'intend one word of that book to his Lordships person or disgrace', but also enclosing a reply poem (reproduced here as Figure 6.1, and also in the Appendix to this chapter, along with Denny's first poem), with, as she puts it, Denny's own lines 'reversed'.[5] She pities Denny's 'rash folly' and, like all smart writers of satire, says her response has been only 'a mornings work'.[6] Wroth does indeed reverse Denny's poem, line by line. Denny becomes the 'Hirmophradite in sense in Art a monster', who has produced 'railing rimes ... against a harmless booke'.[7] He is an 'ass', and his revised oyster image is revised again:

> Can such comparisons seme ye want of witt
> > When oysters haue enflamed your blood wth it
> But it appears your guiltiness gapt wide
> > & filld wth Dirty doubt your brayns swolne tide

From 15 February 1621/22 Wroth and Denny exchanged two letters each, and their two poems, before the correspondence seems to have come to an end, and Denny's attack on Wroth was curtailed after she rallied some powerful friends to her cause, labelled by Denny, in his last extant letter to her, as her 'noble allies'. These included those to whom Wroth evidently sent the correspondence: William Cecil, second Earl of Salisbury, and Buckingham's brother-in-law, William Feilding, Earl of Denbigh. I want to explore the way this exchange circulated and how, despite her best efforts, Wroth seems to have been unable to infiltrate the male, not to say misogynistic, culture of Stuart libels, satires and misogynistic/erotic verse.[8] There is no doubt that *Urania* caused a stir which Wroth may not have anticipated, although the romance seems to

118

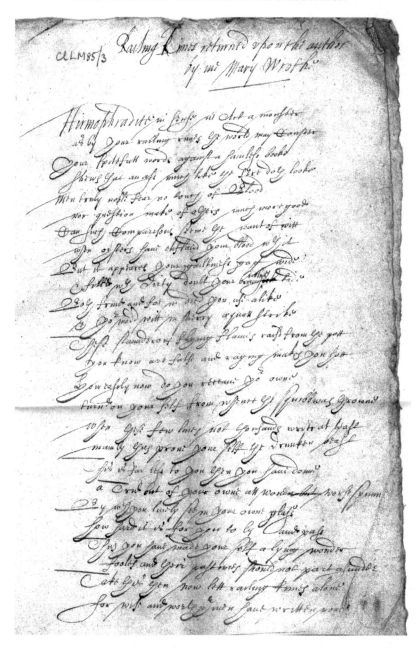

Figure 6.1 Mary Wroth, poem. Courtesy of University of Nottingham, CL LM 85/3.

me to demand exactly the kind of reading process that led to Denny's denunciation, as the allusions to current social, personal and political scandals and controversies, rather than being concealed, are easily detected by those in the know, as evidenced by Denny's rapid recognition of his own story. Similarly, Denny's reading and Wroth's response circulate in a manner which represents a struggle over the interpretation of *Urania* itself, and of Wroth's writing practices.

On 9 March 1622 (the date is significant because it indicates how quickly the ripples of this exchange began to spread) John Chamberlain wrote to Dudley Carleton as follows:

> The other paper are certain bitter verses of the Lord Dennies upon the Lady Marie Wroth, for that in her booke of Urania she doth palpablie and grossely play upon him and his late daughter the Lady Hayes, besides many others she makes bold with, and they say takes great libertie or rather licence to traduce whom she please and thincks she daunces in a net: I have seen an answer of hers to these rimes, but I thought yt not worth the writing out.[9]

This is, I think, a significant moment in any attempt to understand how Wroth's poetic scope was circumscribed by at least some of her contemporaries. It is the start of a process whereby Denny's demand that she not write 'lascivious tales and amorous toyes'[10] was in a sense imposed upon her by the way that the poetic exchange with him was played out in the manuscript circulation of poetry that was so vibrant in the 1620s, 1630s and 1640s. Denny's poem was sent by Chamberlain to Carleton, but Wroth's was not worth writing out, let alone circulating. So, as it turned out, Wroth's poem survives in a single exemplar, while Denny's was not only passed on with the exchange of letters but also circulated separately within the manuscript poetry miscellanies and commonplace books of the 1620s to 1650s. In order to tease out further the implications of this situation for any reading of Wroth's feisty, libelous poem, what follows looks in some detail both at this circulation of Denny' demand, and at the initial and subsequent effects of Wroth's strategy of sending the pair's entire exchange to influential court figures.

The sole remaining copy of Wroth's poem survives, together with the complete exchange of letters and Denny's poem, in the Clifton papers.[11] These are scribal copies almost certainly sent by Wroth to Sir Gervase Clifton (1587–1666). Clifton was a moderately influential man who had interesting connections with Wroth. He was married seven times; his first wife was Penelope Rich, illegitimate daughter of Penelope Rich and Charles Blount, Baron Mountjoy. The younger Penelope was raised within the household of Robert Rich, Earl of Warwick, her mother's then husband, as though she was a legitimate daughter of the marriage, although her mother's liaison with Blount was an open secret. It is tempting to speculate about a sympathy this might have created for Wroth in Clifton, given Wroth's affair with her cousin William Herbert and her own illegitimate children.[12] Clifton's first wife died in 1613, and when Wroth sent the exchange with Denny to him, Clifton was married to his second wife, Frances Clifford, the daughter of Francis Clifford. Francis was the uncle of one Anne Clifford, and Anne seems to have been a close friend of Wroth; further, her second husband was Wroth's cousin, Philip Herbert (William Herbert's brother); it is true that Anne Clifford's uncle was instrumental in keeping her from the estates she claimed as her inheritance, but that would not necessarily have prevented his daughter from having a connection with Wroth.[13] Perhaps Wroth's poem remains with the letters sent to Clifton because he would have been sympathetic to her situation as well as to her literary work, but it is simply not possible to be sure of this.

The most influential recipient of the exchange Wroth was able to call upon to defend her was William Cecil, second Earl of Salisbury, who was in King James's favour in the early 1620s, though he never rose anywhere near to the heights of his father, Robert Cecil. The letters between Denny and Wroth are preserved in the Cecil papers at Hatfield House, but neither of the poems is now with the letters, though they may have been included when first sent.[14]

A similar situation exists with the set of letters sent to William Feilding, first Earl of Denbigh, where the poems were almost certainly included with the letters, sent by Wroth as part of what I would describe as not only her campaign for vindication against Denny's slurs, but also her circulation of her poem in response to Denny as an example of her literary prowess, and of her stinging rebuke to his misogynistic put-down. Feilding was Buckingham's brother-in-law, married to Susan Villiers; given that Wroth also wrote directly to Buckingham protesting disingenuously that she cannot understand the 'strange constructions' made of her book and offering to recall copies of it,[15] Feilding may have been enlisted because he would have had Buckingham's ear. But by offering the whole exchange to Feilding, Wroth could be seen as reinforcing rather than disowning the idea that her book did indeed have personal and political reverberations. In her covering letter to Feilding, Wroth significantly says she sends 'thes things unto you, unfit for your most iudisiall eyes to behold, and goodnes to read; and unseemly for mee to pubblish *if innocensy guarded mee nott*'.[16] Wroth is indeed embarking upon further *publication* of her work, intended to show Denny 'his error', which here means his error in daring to take her on in a poetic contest. This process might be compared to what Line Cottegnies, in chapter 3, calls the 'economy of loss and gain staged' in *Pamphilia to Amphilanthus*.

With this kind of publication, Wroth is calling the shots; she is sending copies of poems and correspondence to a select audience, while at the same time she must have been aware that people like Chamberlain were circulating the exchange as well, though I wonder how she would have felt knowing that her poem had been suppressed by Chamberlain. And in the wider sphere of manuscript publication, it was Denny's poem that circulated, detached from the correspondence and from Wroth's poem in reply. Denny's poem appears in three extant manuscript miscellanies. In the initial exchange of letters, Denny entitled his poem 'To Pamphilia from the father in law of Seralius'.[17] This has the effect of embracing his own identification with the character in *Urania*, while also identifying Wroth with Pamphilia, her principal avatar in the romance and in her poetic sequence *Pamphilia to Amphilanthus*. In response, Wroth titled her poem 'Railing rimes returned upon the author'. These titles make sense within the exchange, but Denny's changes completely when his poem appears on its own; in all three manuscript miscellanies it is titled 'To the Lady Mary Wroth for writinge the Countes of Montgomery's Urania'. The three copies also share a variant of the last couplet, possibly indicating a common source.[18] In each case the poem is also attributed: in the British Library manuscript it is 'By ye Ld Denny', in Huntington it is 'By the L:D', in Beinecke Osborn it is 'By the Lord Denny'. While the three manuscripts are all different in nature, they share a common interest in collecting, within a considerable range of poetry, political satires, libels, love poetry and misogynistic erotic verse.[19]

The placement of Denny's poem in British Library additional manuscript 22603 illustrates the way it has been assimilated into the rather jejune misogyny of this kind of collection.[20] It is placed just after the extremely popular poem 'Nay phew, nay pish'; spoken in the voice of a woman, this is a poem of 'reluctant' seduction which is present, in Joshua Eckhardt's analysis, in over thirty-eight manuscripts.[21] Denny's poem in this manuscript is followed by another piece of eroticism, 'Venus sports', which begins 'Come sit thou on my knee'.[22]

The presence of the poem in Huntington manuscript 198 is especially interesting. This is a two-part manuscript, and the first part, an independent miscellany, has been examined closely by scholars because of the large number of Donne poems it contains.[23] Once again, the Denny poem is collected together with erotic verse and libels. Eckhardt notes that when this compiler paired Donne's 'The curse' and a particularly vicious libel directed at Frances Howard, he 'accentuated each poem's acerbic tone ... and crudeness'.[24] On the flyleaf of this manuscript the name Edward Denny is written twice in what appear to be two different hands.[25] While Peter Beal and Eckhardt (following Beal) declare that this is a different

Edward Denny to the Earl of Norwich who is the subject of this chapter, I think it is an odd coincidence that the miscellany should contain a copy of Denny's hermaphrodite poem, especially with the more reduced signature of 'L:D'.[26] Regardless of who compiled this manuscript, it is similar to the other two instances of the collection of Denny's poem as an exemplar of misogynistic spite, placed in the context of an entire genre of this kind of verse, without Wroth's reply.

The final example of this circulation of Denny's poem is its previously unnoticed inclusion in the Beinecke Library Osborn manuscript b.197.[27] This is the commonplace book of Tobias Alston, who died at the age of nineteen. It is a large collection and it has been suggested that a number of Herrick poems and poems relating to Cambridge University may have been passed on to Tobias by his half-brother Edward, who was a contemporary of Herrick at Trinity Hall, Cambridge.[28] Alston's compilation had a brief moment of fame when Gary Taylor claimed that he had identified a 'new' poem by Shakespeare, 'Shall I die?', attributed to Shakespeare in Bodleian manuscript Rawlinson Poet.160, the only other copy being in Alston's manuscript.[29] Once again, Alston surrounds Denny's poem with a typical mixture of topical, what the catalogue describes as 'light', erotic verse, and satirical/libellous poems on subjects like the Spanish match.[30] And while Alston does not include Wroth's poem, it is perhaps worth noting that his miscellany does contain the text of a masque performed for King James at Sir John Croft's House at Little Saxham.[31] The masque, *The Visit of the Nine Goddesses*, with its speaking parts for nine female characters, is described by Alison Findlay as breaking 'the circuit of silence' for court women, so while Wroth's voice is absent, some female voices are represented.[32] It is intriguing, too, that John Chamberlain suggested that this masque was 'invented' by Croft's daughters.[33]

The approximate dates associated with these three manuscript miscellanies indicate that Denny's poem circulated into the 1640s at least.[34] One can only speculate how Wroth may have felt about this, given that the circulation of her own work seems to have been curtailed after the publication of *Urania* in 1621. Her lengthy manuscript continuation of *Urania* exists in only a single copy, although *Urania* itself continued to be read with an eye to its depiction of scandals like that associated with Denny, as evidenced by the letter to Wroth written in 1640 by George Manners, Earl of Rutland, 'meetinge with your Urania', asking her to 'interprete unto me the names as here I have begunne them'.[35] If we as readers restore Wroth's poem to its dialogue with Denny within the 'boys' own' world of the poetic miscellanies I have been discussing, we are able to read it as answering not simply Denny's individual slurs, but also the attitudes towards women expressed in many other poems.

When Denny labels Wroth a 'Hermophradite in show, in deed a monster', he is likely to gain assent from the readers of his poem in the anthologies, which assert that female sexuality is monstrous (as is the case with the Frances Howard libels), or a joke.[36] But in yoking this to Wroth's literary activities by saying that she is a monster in deed, Denny is trying to short-circuit her achievement, something emphasised by the circulation of his poem as, standing alone, a chastisement directed at Wroth for daring to write *Urania* (it is worth noting that it is not the publication but the writing that is criticised). Wroth recasts Denny as the hermaphrodite, and a poor writer who has produced 'railing rhymes'. Suddenly literary judgement has replaced sexual politics. Wroth also shows just how skilled she is in the libel form, which was almost invariably associated with men as writers, women as subjects – or objects.[37] This becomes clear when she twists Denny's pained assertion of honour (noble blood) into a further analysis of his hot-tempered revelation of the very lack of a quality he is so anxious to claim: 'Men *truly* noble fear no touch of blood' (emphasis added). Taken as a whole, from this point on Wroth's poem is a libel as fierce and as telling as anything written in the period. Might that be why Chamberlain, who was in the habit of sending pretty much everything topical he could glean to Carleton, including a quantity of poetry ranging from verses by the King through to libels like Denny's, was not prepared to help it circulate as he happily copied Denny's poem to send to Carleton?

Wroth turned the 'squib' upon the author by aiming unerringly at his most vulnerable points, especially his excessively touchy sense of honour. Even the oyster image, so reminiscent of sexual slurs in libels such as those assailing Frances Howard, is reversed, as the oysters enflame Denny's blood so that his mind becomes dirty. Denny was especially sensitive to the accusation of drunkenness, writing in one of his letters to Wroth: 'your Ladyship pleases to tax me with the odious vice of drunkenness which, I utterly abhorre'.[38] Wroth really digs away at this in her poem, replying to Denny's unimaginative couplet 'Both frind and foe to thee are euen alike / Thy witt runns madd not caring who it strike' with 'Both frind and foe in deed you use alike / & yor mad witt in sherry aequall strike'. The vivid image of Denny's wits clouded with sherry is extended later in the reversal of his reference to a 'drunken beast'. Denny's images as applied to Wroth are lame, but in fact they reveal him as in a glass (that is, a mirror). Wroth accuses Denny of making himself a 'lying wonder' because of how he has, in circulating his poem, only succeeded in confirming the accusation which he protests against. Denny is left looking like a fool, rather than Wroth, and perhaps the key moment occurs when Wroth defies Denny's attempt to circumscribe what a woman might write: 'Take this then now lett railing rimes alone / For wise and worthier men haue written none'. Of course, men did indeed indulge in writing and collecting railing rhymes, and Denny's poem duly became part of that process.

By adding her own libel to Denny's in a process that turned his poem inside out, Wroth created a kind of literary hermaphrodite: a conjoined poem that spliced her defence of her female authorship onto his misogynistic slur. In his poem, Denny called Wroth a 'Hermophradite in *show*', attempting to figure her as the 'monster' he claims she has become because of her 'deed' in writing her romance. Her monstrousness is made visible by Denny in the figure of the hermaphrodite, but he is responding to a process whereby Wroth's visibility in writing and publishing has made Denny's scandal visible to the world, despite the fact that she has teasingly concealed it beneath romance names that apparently fooled no one. Wroth's reversal of this accusation involves labelling Denny a hermaphrodite 'in sense' – he is a monster in art whose brain produced a kind of emptiness, as opposed to Wroth's own significant literary achievement. In Wroth's telling pun, Denny's fury makes him a hermaphrodite *incensed*, as well as one in thrall to his *sense* of outrage, which betrays his lack of sense, as exemplified by his propensity to bodily malfunctions like drunkenness and murderous rage directed against his own daughter. One might even see, if we return to the description in *Urania*, a rather disturbing kind of hermaphrodite image of Denny in the phrase 'rash as mad-men, & ignorant as women'.

Wroth's conjoined poem may have turned hermaphrodite from slur into new creation, but the process of circulation, as it turned out, undid this positive hermaphroditic quality, folding Denny's poem back into an all-male context in which women's bodies and their writing produced anxious satire. Wroth's dangerous supplement, which transformed Denny's male poem into a positive, hermaphroditic hybrid, was repressed. So in the seventeenth century, there was, I would argue, a concerted attempt to render Wroth's unsettling poem invisible, and it was kept out of the very process of circulation that would have, in a lasting way, unsettled the whole notion of hermaphroditic writing. We need to restore this poem to a more prominent position in her oeuvre, especially as it is such a dramatic contrast to the style of the rest of her poetry – though there are what we might call ideological resemblances to the defence of women enacted throughout her work. The poem libelling Denny complicates our view of her subtle interrogation of Petrarchanism, and her cynical view of court sexual politics, in *Pamphilia to Amphilanthus* and her other poetry; had it been collected along with Denny's poem, it might have provoked a reconsideration of how the figure of the woman who is libelled can write back. Indeed, this chapter, along with others in the present volume, is part of a general reconsideration of the process of how women's writing circulated, or in the case of Wroth's poem, had its circulation anxiously closed down, as it challenged a genre like the libel which male writers had complacently felt to be their preserve.

Appendix

Transcriptions of the 'hermaphrodite' poems from copies sent to Gervase Clifton (Nottingham University Library, MSS CL LM 85/3).

1. Edward Denny's poem

Hermophradite in show, in deed a monster
  as by thy words and works all men may conster
Thy wrathfull spite conceiued an Idell book
  brought forth a foole wch like ye damme doth look
Wherein thou strikes at some mans noble blood
  of kinne to thine if thine be counted good
whose vaine comparison for want of witt
  takes up ye oyster shell to play wth it
Yet Common oysters such as thine gaype wide
  and take in pearles or worse at euery tide
Both frind and foe to thee are euen alike
  Thy witt runs madd not caring who it strike
These slanderous flying fames [*sic* = flames] rise from the pott
  for potted witts inflamed are raging hott
How easy wer't to pay thee wth thine owne
  returning that wch thou thy self hast throwne
And write a thousand lies of thee at least
  & by thy lines discribe a drunken beast
This were no more to thee then thou hast done
  A Thrid but of thine owne wch thou hast spunn
By wch thou plainly seest in thine owne glass
  How easy tis to bring a ly to pass
Thus hast thou made thy self a lying wonder
  fooles and their Bables seldome part asunder
worke o th' workes leaue idle bookes alone
  for wise & worthier women haue writt none

    To Pamphilia from the father
    in law of Seralius

2. Wroth's reply

Railing Rimes returned vpon the author by Me [*sic* = Mistress] Mary Wrothe

Hirmophradite in sense in Art a monster
　As by your railing rimes ye world may conster
Your spitefull words against a harmless booke
　Shows that an ass much like ye sire doth looke
Men truly noble fear no touch of blood
　nor question make of others much more good
Can such comparisons seme ye want of witt
　when oysters haue enflamed your blood wth it
But it appears your guiltiness gapt wide
　& filld wth dirty doubt your brains swolne tide
Both frind and foe in deed you use alike
　& yor madd witt in sherry aequall strike
These slaunderous flying flames raisd from ye pott
　You know are false and raging makes you hott
How easily now do you receaue yor owne
　Turnd on your self from whence ye squibb was throwne
When these few lines not thousands writt at least
　mainly thus proue your self the drunken beast
This is far less to you then you haue donne
　A trid [*sic* = thrid] but of your owne all wouen but worse spun
　[Roberts reads as 'all wordes worse spun']
By wych you liuely see in your owne glass
　How hard it is for you to ly and pass
Thus you haue made your self a lying wonder
　Fooles and their pastimes should not part asunder
Take this then now lett railing rimes alone
　For wise and worthier men haue written none

Notes

1　I quote directly from *Urania* but see J. Roberts (ed.), *The First Part of the Countess of Montgomery's Urania by Lady Mary Wroth*, Arizona Center for Medieval and Renaissance Studies, Tempe, 1995, p. 516.

2　See the analysis in J. Eckhardt, *Manuscript Verse Collectors and the Politics of Anti-Courtly Love Poetry*, Oxford University Press, Oxford, 2009, ch. 3. Michelle O'Callaghan places the Wroth–Denny exchange in the context of libel, and compares it with an exchange between Eleanor Davies and Christopher Brooke over an apparent slur cast by Davies against Brooke's wife, Lady Mary Jacob; see M. O'Callaghan, '"An uncivill scurrilous letter": "womanish brabbes" and the letter of affront', unpublished paper. I am grateful to Professor O'Callaghan for allowing me to read this paper.

3　The poetic exchange is in J. Roberts (ed.), *The Poems of Lady Mary Wroth*, Louisiana State University Press, Baton Rouge, 1983, pp. 32–5; at this point I quote directly from the copies and letters sent to Sir Gervase Clifton, Hervey Jukes Lloyd Bruce manuscripts, preserved at Clifton Hall, Nottingham University Library, MSS CL LM 85/1–5. Full transcripts are provided in the Appendix to this chapter, with some corrections to Roberts; the poems do not appear to have been referred to directly since Roberts reproduced them as part of her introduction to *The Poems*.

4 Roberts (ed.), *The Poems*, p. 239.

5 Ibid., p. 237.

6 Ibid.

7 In her use of the term 'railing rimes', which was common currency for rough and by implication at this stage satirical/derisive verse (possibly with origins in Skelton, 'Colin Cloute', with Skelton derided by Puttenham as a 'rude railing rimer' – thanks to Andrew Zurcher for this reference), Wroth echoes King James's attack on libels, 'O stay your tears, you who complain': 'That Kings designes darr thus deride / By railing rymes and vaunting verse' – quoted from A. McRae and A. Bellany (eds), *Early Stuart Libels*, online at http://purl.oclc.org/emls/texts/libels (accessed July 2013).

8 As well as Eckhardt, *Manuscript Verse Collectors*, see the authoritative study by A. McRae, *Literature, Satire, and the Early Stuart State*, Cambridge University Press, Cambridge, 2004; and also A. Marotti, *Manuscript, Print, and the English Renaissance Lyric*, Cornell University Press, Ithaca, 1995, ch. 2.

9 N. E. McClure (ed.), *The Letters of John Chamberlain*, American Philosophical Society, Philadelphia, 1939, vol. 2, p. 427. It is worth noting here that Wroth had close ties with Dudley Carleton, as did her aunt Mary Sidney, Countess of Pembroke. Two letters of Wroth to Carleton – who was at the Hague and a strong supporter of Elizabeth of Bohemia, as was Wroth and the rest of the Sidney family – from 1619 are extant, written with considerable affection; in one of them Wroth notes that she has presented Carleton with 'some rude lines', which casts an ironic light on Chamberlain's failure to send Carleton a copy of the Wroth's hermaphrodite poem; for the letters see Roberts (ed.), *The Poems*, pp. 235–6.

10 Roberts (ed.), *Poems*, p. 239.

11 As noted above, the Clifton papers are held in Nottingham University Library, having been inherited by Hervey Juckes Lloyd Bruce in 1869; Juckes's son changed his name to Clifton and the family donated the papers (which stretch from the twelfth to the twentieth centuries) to the University of Nottingham in 1948 and 1958; the library's online catalogue has detailed information about the manuscripts and the family.

12 For Wroth's affair and detailed information about her children, William and Elizabeth, born in 1624, see M. P. Hannay, *Mary Sidney Lady Wroth*, Ashgate, Farnham, 2010; the older Penelope Rich, of course, was the object of Wroth's uncle Philip Sidney's passion, as described throughout *Astrophil and Stella*.

13 See R. T. Spence, *Lady Anne Clifford*, Sutton, Stroud, 1997; Clifton and Frances named a daughter after Anne and another daughter after Margaret, Anne's mother, which seems to indicate a cordial relationship.

14 The letters are in the Cecil papers, Hatfield House: 130/117; 130/118; 130/120; and 130/121. It is worth noting here that the Cecil letters are in a different hand to the Clifton letters and poems, although both are scribal, whereas the letters sent to Denbigh are written by Wroth herself. I have been unable to determine anything further about the identity of the two scribes, although Wroth would have had access to secretaries both within her own household and at Penshurst, which may account for the differences.

15 For the letter to Buckingham see my discussion in P. Salzman, *Literary Culture in Jacobean England: Reading 1621*, Palgrave Macmillan, Houndmills, 2002, pp. 66–7; and R. Smith, *Sonnets and the English Woman Writer, 1560–1621: The Politics of Absence*, Palgrave Macmillan, London, 2005, pp. 88–92.

16 I quote from Warwickshire Record Office, CR2017/C48/2/1; see the letter in Roberts (ed.), *The Poems*, p. 242 (emphasis added). The letters sent to Denbigh are all written by Wroth herself (as was the letter to Buckingham), which makes it particularly frustrating that copies of the poems sent to Denbigh do not survive.

17 This is the title of the poem as found in the Clifton manuscripts.

18   Collation of the four manuscript instances of the poem points to a probable common
source for the British Library, Huntington and Beinecke versions, which would have
been substantially different to the source for the version in the Clifton manuscript.
The most significant difference is the final couplet, which in Clifton reads 'Work o th'
workes leaue idle bookes alone / for wise <u>and</u> worthier women haue writt none', and
in the other three manuscripts reads 'worke lady worke, lett idle bookes alone / For
wisest women sure haue written none'. In terms of the later circulation of Denny's
poem it is worth noting that Margaret Cavendish quotes a slightly different version of
the final couplet, but one that seems derived from the version common to the three
miscellanies: 'Work lady, work, let Writing Books alone. / For surely wiser Women
nere wrote one'. Cavendish uses this couplet twice, in *Poems and Fancies* (1653), sig.
A3v and *Sociable Letters* (1664) sig. b; in neither case is there a specific ascription to
Denny. Again, this is an interesting instance of the currency of Denny's poem and the
invisibility of Wroth's reply. A significant pointer to a common source for the British
Library, Huntington and Beineicke Osborne versions is a shared error in line 17 caused
by eye-skip: these manuscripts all read 'And write a thousand lynes of the at least / And
by thy lynes describe a drunken beast', where Clifton has 'And write a thousand *lies*
of thee at least / <u>And</u> by thy lines discribe a drunken beast'. Collation also indicates
some slight variations in the Beinecke manuscript from readings in British Library and
Huntington, such as 'slanderous flames' rather than 'slanderous flying flames' in line
13, but these are relatively insubstantial and are more likely to be caused by Alston's
slips or alterations in transcription than by a different source.

19   The manuscripts fit neatly into Marotti's categorisation of the popularity of erotic
verse as stemming in part from the identity of most compilers as young men at
university or inns of court; see Marotti, *Manuscript*, p. 75.

20   This manuscript is noted by Philip Bliss as being in the same hand as Bodleian manuscript Rawlinson Poet.147; the identity of the compiler is unknown. The manuscript
has a poem dated 1643 and one dated 1644, and was probably compiled soon after that.

21   British Library additional manuscript 22603, fols 64–64v; Eckhardt, *Manuscript Verse*,
pp. 173–4, includes a text of the poem; see also Marotti's comment on this manuscript,
including his noting of Denny's 'misogynistic poem': Marotti, *Manuscript*, p. 78.

22   65–65v; this poem seems to be unique to this manuscript.

23   This is also referred to as the Haslewood–Kingsborough manuscript; see the account
in Eckhardt, *Manuscript Verse*, pp. 87–8; and also C. M. Armitage, 'Donne's poems
in Huntington manuscript 198: "New Light on The Funerall"', *Studies in Philology*,
vol. 63 (1966), pp. 697–707.

24   Eckhardt, *Manuscript Verse*, p. 88.

25   I am grateful to Mary Robertson, William A. Moffett Curator of Medieval and British
Historical Manuscripts at the Huntington Library, for answering my queries about
this manuscript.

26   P. Beal, *Index of English Literary Manuscripts*, Mansell, London, 1980, vol. 1, part i,
p. 253; Eckhardt, *Manuscript Verse*, p. 88. Beal offers no explanation for his view that
the manuscript is signed by a different Edward Denny; Armitage ('Donne's poems')
feels that Denny is a likely candidate. See Beal, *Index*, p. 698. It is possible that there
has been some confusion between Denny and his uncle, also Edward Denny, who died
in 1600 and has a monument in Waltham Abbey, where the Edward Denny under
discussion here was also buried. Armitage and some other sources give 1630 as the
year of Denny's death, which would make it unlikely that he had an association with
Huntington 198, but he definitely died in 1637, which makes such an association at
least possible. It is perhaps significant that the poetic exchange between Wroth's lover
William Herbert and his friend Benjamin Rudyard is included in this manuscript –
this seems to be a unique appearance prior to the publication of the exchange and
it is at the very least ironic that they should be present in this manuscript alongside
Denny's poem – the exchange is on folios 138–47. The association is also strengthened

by the inclusion of Thomas Carew's poem on the death of Denny's grand-daughter, a poem which appears in only a small number of extant manuscripts. (I am grateful to Professor Mary Ellen Lamb for pointing this out to me.)

27 Roberts seems not to have known of the poem's presence in this manuscript when she collated the other instances of Denny's poem for her edition of Wroth's poetry.

28 See the catalogue entry for the manuscript. It shares a few poems with the British Library manuscript that are comparatively rare; for example, a poem first published by Richard Johnson in 1620 in *The Golden Garland*, 'Fond wanton youth makes love a god', is copied only in these two manuscripts.

29 Virtually all scholars then rejected Taylor's ascription; for an acerbic summing up, see B. Vickers, *Counterfeiting Shakespeare*, Cambridge University Press, Cambridge, 2002, preface.

30 See the libels gathered together in *Early Stuart Libels*, http://www.earlystuartlibels. net/, which has twenty-four that are included in Osborne b.197.

31 See C. E. McGee, '"The visit of the nine goddesses": a masque at Sir John Croft's House', *English Literary Renaissance*, vol. 21 (1991), pp. 371–84.

32 A. Findlay, *Playing Spaces in Early Women's Drama*, Cambridge University Press, Cambridge, 2006, p. 131.

33 McGee, 'The visit', p. 374, although McGee rejects this suggestion in favour of authorship by Thomas Carew.

34 This would seem to be the most likely date for British Library additional manuscript 22603; the Beinecke Osborn manuscript b.197 would seem to date from the late 1630s, given that Alston died in 1639; Huntington 198 was probably compiled in 1630. See Armitage, 'Donne's poems', p. 698.

35 Roberts (ed.), *The Poems*, p. 245.

36 While more complex associations with the image of the hermaphrodite were possible, especially within Ovidian poetry, as outlined in J. C. Mann's important article, 'How to look at a hermaphrodite in early modern England', *Studies in English Literature 1500–1900*, vol. 46 (2006), pp. 67–91, Denny's explicit link of hermaphrodite and monster narrows these down to the overarching notion of a monstrous female sexuality manifested in unworthy pursuits.

37 See O'Callaghan's summing up ('An uncivill scurrilous letter'); G. Alexander memorably says that 'Wroth goes as far as a woman can to give Denny the lie and challenge him'. In G. Alexander, *Writing After Sidney: The Literary Response to Sir Philip Sidney, 1586–164*, Oxford University Press, Oxford, 2006, p. 286.

38 Roberts (ed.), *The Poems*, p. 238.

CHAPTER 7

Sisterhood and female friendship in Constance Aston Fowler's verse miscellany

Helen Hackett

CURRENT work on early modern women and poetry – including the present volume – is illuminating the relations between poetry and its social contexts. We are discovering that women's poems were frequently produced in the family, the friendship group, the neighbourhood, or communities defined by shared political or religious affiliation, and that creative interactions within such communities took diverse and complex forms. We are also learning that early modern poetry did more than just reflect pre-existing relationships; rather, poems performed social functions, and actively forged, defined and promoted relationships. Moreover, these social functions were achieved not only by the internal rhetoric of the poem, but also by processes of transmission, circulation and reception.

We therefore need to extend the concept of 'women's poetry' beyond merely poems authored by women. It may be difficult and even inappropriate to isolate the authorial agency of an individual woman in a collaborative process, as Suzanne Trill shows in chapter 5. Furthermore, participation in literary culture could take forms other than authorship, including collecting, selecting, transcribing, editing, juxtaposing, endorsing and exchanging poems. Such were the activities of Constance Aston Fowler, who apparently never authored a poem, but was very active in poetic culture and a poetic community.

Some time in the mid-1630s, when probably in her mid-teens, Constance[1] began compiling a manuscript verse miscellany, now in the Huntington Library (MS HM 904).[2] She was one of five children of Walter Aston, Baron of Forfar, a Catholic who enjoyed the favour of Charles I, and whose family seat was at Tixall in Staffordshire. Lord Aston had spent much of the 1620s in Madrid as an ambassador; while Constance was compiling most of the miscellany, from 1635 to 1638, he was in Spain again, now accompanied by Constance's brother Herbert, with whom she exchanged letters and poems. Around 1635, Constance had married Walter Fowler, the heir to a neighbouring Staffordshire estate, St Thomas's Priory, an established centre of recusant activity, but according to inscriptions on her letters to Herbert she was not as yet living with her husband, residing instead with her mother at another Aston house, at Colton, not far from Tixall and St Thomas's.[3]

Constance's miscellany contains the hands of several scribes. Most of the poems are in her own hand (hand A); the other main scribe, probably an itinerant priest, wrote in a semi-secretary hand (hand B) and inscribed Catholic devotional poems into the gaps between Constance's transcriptions at a slightly later date.[4] For the purposes of this chapter, I will not discuss the additions in hand B, but will concentrate on Constance's own transcriptions, which form the bulk of the volume. They offer a significant example of female participation in verse miscellany culture, combining poems by conventional miscellany favourites such as Ben Jonson and Henry King with 'coterie' poems by and about Constance's family and friends.

In chapters 4, 5, 6, 8 and 12 of the present volume, respectively Gillian Wright, Suzanne Trill, Paul Salzman, Margaret J. M. Ezell and Susan Wiseman all explore diverse ways in which family and immediate milieu influenced women's participation in poetic culture. In the case of the 'coterie' poems compiled by Constance, sisterhood and female friendship function both as subject matter and as social bonds created and affirmed by poems. Both acts of composition by Constance's friends and relations and acts of selection and transcription by Constance were social transactions, fashioning identities and relationships within a particular set of social coordinates. These included: familial identity as Astons; political affiliation as royalists; class status as an aristocratic/gentry family with an interest in court culture; local identity as Staffordshire landholders, an identity accentuated by the absence of the head of the family in Spain; religious identity as Catholics; and affiliation with a network of friends and relations.

There are no full-length poems attributed to Constance in her own miscellany or other surviving Aston sources, although she clearly enjoyed and valued the many poems produced by her literary family, and assigned herself a crucial role in circulating and preserving them. Her father had been a patron of Michael Drayton and also wrote verses of his own.[5] Constance's brother Herbert and sister Gertrude were poets too, as were Constance's close friend Katherine Thimelby, who in the late 1630s became Herbert's wife, and Katherine's brother Edward Thimelby. Although Constance may not have composed verses herself, there is ample evidence of her creative gifts in her letters to Herbert, in which she writes fervently of her love for him, her passionate friendship with Katherine and her support for their courtship. She vividly describes vignettes such as a dinner at Tixall where she and Katherine enjoyed conspiratorial exchanges: 'she would sometimes give a looke to me as if bechence her eye had so wander'd, and then she would steale the prittiest words to me ... (Oh) she would softely say (That I might speake my thoughts to you,) and then againe, (Oh what worlds would I give I might possess you but one halfe howre to my selfe!)'.[6] On the outer sheets of her letters, Constance inscribed ciphers and mottos, often artfully written at angles to one another to create patterns and designs. On the wrapper of the letter just quoted, for instance, she drew a true love's knot (used in her miscellany as a cipher for Herbert)[7] and surmounted it with a crown (her cipher for Katherine), with the inscription 'methinkes I se you set this on', to represent the wished-for success of Herbert's courtship. Beneath the true love's knot Constance wrote, in a triangular formation, 'She is K T the queine of sweetnesse', and curving around the whole design she inscribed the endearing couplet, 'Oh thinke what a hapynes tis that M[ist]r[es]s Thimelby is'.[8]

Constance, then, brought artistic talents to her letter writing, and her miscellany compilation was also a creative act, deploying personal and aesthetic choices to produce a distinctive and self-expressive literary artefact. Her letters to Herbert frequently solicit poems: 'Send me some verses for I want some good ones to put in my booke'.[9] Her criteria for 'good' verse reflected her desire to participate in current fashions in miscellany compilation, and she included poems generally popular on the miscellany scene. However, they also included assertion of the royalist politics, the Catholic faith and the court-oriented aesthetics of her circle; and, in many cases, acquaintance with, and affection for, the author and/or addressee of a poem. Constance evidently understood herself to be exercising autonomous taste and literary judgement.

She was also more than merely a passive receiver of verses: she sent them out to Herbert too, complaining, 'pray see how hardly you deal with mee, when I have sent you all the verses that I could gett perpetuly, never omietting the sending of any, that I could get, that wer good ones'.[10] She also passed Herbert's own poems on to others: 'They are much commended by all, as they deserve; and you have ganed the English ladyes' harts extreamely by them, to see you so constant a favorite of ther miritts'.[11] Constance was thus a kind of literary agent or 'voucher', using her participation in networks of literary exchange to establish both her brother's reputation as a poet and her own judiciousness as a critic.[12]

Aesthetics and affection intertwined in Constance's principles of selection to invest special value in Herbert's own compositions. 'I have written to you I know not how often,' she chides him, 'and beged of you most pittyfully that you would send me some verses of your owne makeing and yet you never would when you know I love them more then can be expressed'.[13] The context for their literary exchanges is always Constance's sisterly love, which she frequently and fervently avows: 'I shall ever bee unable to exsprese the true and serius Dearenes of my ever constant Love to you'.[14] As for a number of the other women discussed in the present volume, Constance's engagement with poetry was at once constituted by and constitutive of personal intimacy and familial identity.

A sister editing a brother

AT around the same time that Constance was compiling her verse miscellany, Herbert was making one of his own, inscribed with the date 1634 and including topical references running into the 1640s (it is now in the Beinecke Library, Yale). At least 70 per cent of the contents of Herbert's miscellany also appear in other seventeenth-century sources, including manuscript and print miscellanies and song-books, demonstrating his participation in mainstream miscellany culture.[15] Some are miscellany favourites such as Sir Walter Raleigh's '[Like to an] hermit poore in pensive place obscure' and Sir Henry Wotton's 'Your meaner beauties of the night';[16] others are songs from plays.[17] The predominant themes are love and courtship, with some poems bordering on the obscene: 'If amasd at Beauties wonder I presume your breast to touch / Or attempt a little under would you thinke I do too much / Ono, no ono &ᵃ' (folio 4v). Others satirise the inconstancy of women with a casual misogyny (e.g. folio 33r). There are political poems too, especially later in the volume, satirising Puritans and parliamentarians. Only one poem in the collection refers to Herbert's family and his Staffordshire origins: 'A Rurall panegrigg on the Lady southcots wedding day', which commemorates the wedding of Herbert's niece and locates the celebration at Tixall (folio 51v). However, the poem is not in Herbert's hand, and appears late in the volume, suggesting an addition after a change in the volume's ownership and use. Otherwise, the miscellany shows no interest in Herbert's family ties or local roots, instead strongly suggesting a young man aligning himself with the court and with London, fashioning himself as a slightly rakish man-about-town, and participating in 'cavalier culture'.

Yet the Herbert who appears in Constance's letters and miscellany is a devoted brother intimately bound into the family circle. Among the eight poems by Herbert that Constance transcribed into her own anthology are 'To the Lady Mary Aston' (their elder brother Walter's wife) and 'To My Honer'd sister G A', a eulogy to their sister Gertrude.[18] The latter poem specifically celebrates Gertrude's gifts as a poet, and even defers to them.

Herbert aptly invokes the muses – poetic sisters – to assist the praise of his own poet-sister (lines 1–2), then invokes Donne, aspiring to sing 'in verse as high,/As strong lin'd donne; the soule of poetry/Exprest his progresse; and Anatomy' (lines 4–6). It is not the 'masculine persuasive force' of Donne's elegies or songs and sonnets that Herbert is emulating here,[19] but the female-inspired hyperbole of the *Anniversaries*: just as Elizabeth Drury's death, according to Donne, bereaved and reconfigured the cosmos, so Gertrude exceeds earthly praise. It is her own skills as a poet that call forth Herbert's highest veneration: 'no subject's fit/For you to write of but your selfe, no witt/Able to comprehend you but your owne;/To write none worthy but your selfe alone' (lines 39–42).

Herbert firmly sets Gertrude's poetry in a familial context: 'by this you tye/Eternall luster to our familye' (lines 101–2). Her surviving poems indeed mainly commemorate family ties and family occasions. A number of Gertrude's compositions appear in *Tixall Poetry*, an anthology compiled from family manuscripts by a nineteenth-century descendant, Arthur Clifford. They include 'On the death of her only child', 'To her husband, on New-Years-Day, 1651', 'Uppon the returne from our friends in Stafordshire' (after her marriage, Gertrude lived in Lincolnshire) and 'To my brother and sister Aston, on their wedding-day, being absent'.[20] Even her poems on non-occasional themes often form part of dialogues within the family circle, such as 'To Mr E—T—, who holds selfe-love in all our actions', which participates in a verse debate with her brother-in-law Edward Thimelby.[21] Gertrude, then, was mainly a poet of family themes. Constance's selection and transcription of poems by Herbert into her miscellany fashions him, too, as a family poet, like Gertrude, emphasising his affection for and even deference to his sisters in a way that is entirely absent from his rakish self-representation in his own miscellany.

Constance was not disconnected from the 'cavalier' miscellany culture in which Herbert participated: she transcribed poems by miscellany favourites such as Robert Herrick, Ben Jonson, Henry King and Thomas Randolph, and various anonymous poems which appear in other manuscript and print sources, such as 'Eyes gaze no more' and 'with bowed thoughts lowe as this hollow cell'.[22] While Herbert included an elegy for Francis Villiers, son of the Duke of Buckingham, killed in 1648, Constance included an elegy for Buckingham himself, assassinated in 1628; both alike are statements of royalist allegiance.[23] She was evidently 'plugged into' miscellany culture, unsurprisingly, since she evidently looked to Herbert as one of her main suppliers of verses. Especially interesting is her transcription of 'O love whoes powre and might could never be withstood', which, as Adam Smyth has noted, also appeared in a number of other manuscripts (Margaret Crum lists thirteen) and in print miscellanies, including *The Marrow of Complements* (1655), *Wit and Drolery* (1661) and *Folly in Print* (1667).[24] Constance's version omits many of the coarser lines that appear in the printed texts, including 'A Turd in Cupid's teeth' and 'I'll rend her smock asunder'. Smyth surmises that these emendations to produce 'a relatively decorous verse' may have been made by Constance herself, and raise 'important questions about the degree to which Fowler's transcriptions were in fact active, even creative acts, rather than simple mechanisms of duplication'.[25] Alternatively, if, as seems likely, the poem was among those supplied to Constance by Herbert, he may have edited it to make it suitable for his sister.

Whoever edited the poem, it illustrates that, whether by choice or by compliance with convention, female miscellany compilation proceeded under different principles from those applied to men.[26] This appears restrictive; yet we also see that the role of miscellany compiler allowed Constance to 'edit' Herbert, constructing him as a devoted, home-centred, and sister-worshipping brother rather than the dashing young blade of his own preferred self-image.

Sending sisterhood: home thoughts to abroad

THUS Constance's miscellany emphasises the circle of affection formed by herself, Gertrude, and the absent Herbert. Among the poems that she sent to her brother in Spain were two by Richard Fanshawe, their father's secretary in Madrid, who visited the Aston women at Colton during a trip to England in 1636.[27] Constance explained in a letter to Herbert that one of these poems was 'made in particular to my sister Gatt [Gertrude]' and that 'The occasion of making them was this: We had bin one eavening at bowles, and when we caime in, my sister was opening her hayre with her fingers, and bid him tell you that she would not curle her hayer no otherwaies then it curled itselfe till she saw you againe'.[28] Fanshawe accordingly wrote: 'Celia hath for a brothers absence sworne / (Rash oath) that since her tresses cannot mourne / In blacke, because uncutt Apollos hayre / Darts not a greater splender through the ayre / shee'l make them droope in her neglect'.[29] He went on to explain that despite Celia/Gertrude's renunciation of artificial curling, her hair curled naturally anyway (lines 21–2).

The poem constructs a relationship in which the three companions in Staffordshire – Constance, Gertrude and Fanshawe – are bound together not only by mutual affection and esteem but also by their affection for Herbert, and his role as imagined reader. Gertrude's vow expresses her love for Herbert; Fanshawe celebrates it in verses as Herbert's colleague and a family friend; and Constance shows sisterly affection in transcribing the poem and sending it to Herbert. These four individuals are connected by a web of relationships, and each interpersonal bond in this web is reinforced by the circulation of the poem. Gertrude's golden curling hair seems to have been a notable personal feature, and also received extended praise in Herbert's encomium 'To My Honer'd sister G A', discussed above.[30] An unattributed devotional poem transcribed by Constance into her miscellany, 'On the Passion of our Lord and saviour Jesus', also mentions hair-curling, and may well have been by Gertrude. The female speaker vividly imagines being present at the scourging and crucifixion of Christ, and dwells on her personal culpability for his sufferings: 'My curious Diett Hungar to him brought / My foolish Joyes presented him sad thoughts / My pleasurs in vaine glory breed his scorns / My often curlinge weav'd his crown of Thorns'.[31] The poem concludes, 'My will and understandinge I resigne / unto the crosse: and to his crowne of Thorns / And peirced head bequeath all that Adorns / My useles haire'.[32] This poem thus shares concerns with Fanshawe's poem and Constance's letter about Gertrude's renunciation of hair-curling: all three concern a similar act of sorrow and self-castigation, although Fanshawe's poem and Constance's letter transpose this from a sacred context to the secular context of love for a much-missed brother, elevating sisterly love almost to a holy cause.

Fanshawe's poem vividly evoked for Herbert in Madrid his local roots in Staffordshire. The writings of the Aston circle were frequently generated by interaction between their local and international contexts; hence Constance's accompanying letter, quoted above, further emphasised the domestic and familial: 'We had bin one eavening at bowles...'. During the same visit Fanshawe also composed 'A dreame', a sonnet imitating Spenser's 'Prothalamion', which similarly idealises Staffordshire and sisterhood for the absent Herbert. Spenser's poem in celebration of the double betrothal of the daughters of the Earl of Worcester had represented them as a pair of swans gliding down the River Lea or Lee, a tributary of the Thames, to join the main river: 'With that I saw two Swannes of goodly hewe, / Come softly swimming downe along the Lee; / Two fairer Birds I yet did never see'.[33] Fanshawe echoed Spenser to represent Constance and Gertrude as a pair of swans, but relocated the scene to the River Trent in Staffordshire: 'I saw two swans come proudly downe the streame / Of Trent, as I his silver curles beheld, / To which the doves that drawe fayre venus Teame, / And venus selfe must beauties scepter yield'.[34]

In Spenser's 'Prothalamion' the poet finds in his riverside vision of the swans relief from 'discontent of my long fruitlesse stay / In Princes Court'.[35] His is very much a London poem, using the Rivers Lea and Thames to create a pastoral idyll within the city. By transposing the vision to the Trent, Fanshawe removes it completely from the city to the country, from the metropolitan to the provincial and parochial, and uses idealised pastoral description to place the Aston sisters in their local setting and to recreate this for their brother. Again, Constance's letter to Herbert explains the circumstances of composition: she, Gertrude and Fanshawe

> wer all walking in the owld halle, and looking upon Trent, and I was speaking how you used to course your boy Dick about that medow, and talking of many such things. But the next morning he came out with these verses, which I doe not think but you will like very well, for methinks they are very prity ones, if they had bin made of better subjectes. Wee made him beleeve that you should fight with him when he came into Spaine againe, for abusing your sisters so, in flattering of them so infinightly as he has don in these verses.[36]

Home is recreated for Herbert by nostalgic evocation of 'the owld halle' with views over the River Trent, of carefree younger days in the 'medow' and, above all, of his paired sisters, personifying his family origins and identity and the affectionate sanctuary that awaits him on his return.

Arthur Clifford titled his anthologies of his Aston ancestors' writings *Tixall Poetry* and *Tixall Letters*, emphatically identifying them with the ancient family seat. However, it is evident from Fanshawe's poems and Constance's accompanying letter that in fact this circle's writings were rarely merely local, but were shaped by the separation of family members over long distances. As years passed, these scattered family members would come to include not only Lord Aston and Herbert in Madrid, but also several Aston and Thimelby women – including Gertrude – who joined the English convent in Louvain. It is largely because they were dispersed that the Astons were so invested in ideas of family and home, so that, paradoxically, their writings were often most local when they were most international.[37] It is also worth remembering that although until the 1640s the Astons seem to have been exempted from the usual penalties for Catholicism because of their father's friendship with King Charles, English Catholic gentry families lived under constant threat of sequestration of their estates.[38] Constance's transmission of Fanshawe's poem to Herbert, and her composition of the letter enclosing it, create and affirm a textual fantasy of home as safe, sure, innocent, unsullied and timeless, a place where memories of past shared happiness and hopes of future reunion converge. 'Home' is constructed in writing, and in the transmission of writing, for Constance as much as for Herbert, for sender as much as for recipient.

An important ingredient in this textual construction of home was the assertion and idealisation of sisterhood. Gertrude's renunciation of hair-curling expressed sisterly devotion; Constance's transmission of poems and letters to her brother maintained sibling intimacy though physically apart; and the symmetrical pairing of the two sisters in Fanshawe's 'swans' poem formed an emblem of the harmony and pastoral tranquillity of home. Spenser's 'Prothalamion' had exploited the aesthetic appeal of female doubles, as had Shakespeare in *A Midsummer Night's Dream*, when Helena reminded Hermia of their 'sisters' vows, ... schooldays' friendship, childhood innocence': 'we grew together / Like to a double cherry: seeming parted, / But yet an union in partition, / Two lovely berries moulded on one stem'.[39] In *As You Like It* Celia even described her sisterly intimacy with Rosalind as swan-like: 'We still have slept together, / Rose at an instant, learned, played, eat together, / And wheresoe'er we went, like Juno's swans / Still we went coupled and inseparable'.[40] Such works created a tradition of sisters, or sisterly friends, as pleasingly symmetrical and touchingly reciprocal, personifying balance, harmony, serenity and also pre-sexual innocence. Fanshawe mobilised this tradition in his poem to evoke for Herbert the tranquillity, affection and security of home.

Constance and her siblings probably knew Spenser's and Shakespeare's idealisations of female bonds: an 1899 sale catalogue of the library at Tixall records a 1611 edition of Spenser's works and a 1632 second folio of Shakespeare.[41] It also included a 1638 edition of Sir Philip Sidney's *Arcadia*, offering another model of loyal and virtuous sisterhood in Pamela and Philoclea.[42] Moreover, the family owned a manuscript of the Sidney Psalms.[43] Suzanne Trill shows in chapter 5 that although later scholars have sometimes underestimated the skill and scale of Mary Sidney's contributions to these psalm translations, her contemporaries understood them as a true collaboration and joint production. As Trill discusses, Donne acclaimed the Sidney siblings as united by God in shared poetic creation: 'Two, by their bloods, and by thy spirit one; / A brother and a sister, made by thee / The organ, where thou art the harmony'.[44] The copy of the Sidney Psalms owned by the Astons included the elegy by Mary for Philip, 'To the angell spirit of the most excellent Sir Philip Sidney', celebrating the sister–brother bond; while beyond the Psalms, Mary also collected, edited, preserved and circulated her brother's other works. Constance's situation differed in several respects: her brother, happily, was not dead; she did not write compositions of her own; and she did not seek print publication of his works, as Mary Sidney did for the *Arcadia*. Nevertheless, Mary Sidney may have offered Constance an example of the many collaborative, creative and influential roles – not only authorship – that a woman could perform in a context of sibling intimacy; and of how sibling intimacy could be constructed and idealised by means of various kinds of literary act.

As well as sending Fanshawe's two poems to Herbert, Constance also transcribed them into her miscellany. Their function, then, was not merely to project idealisations of sisterhood and home across the ocean to Herbert, but also to serve Constance herself as commemorations of an intimate domestic scene, designations of her place in a network of relationships, and affirmations of her identity as sister, muse and purveyor of poems. Another poem in her miscellany concerning sisterhood is 'upon castaries and her sitters [i.e. sister's or sisters'] goinge A foote in the snow'.[45] This is one of two unattributed poems on 'Castara' that Constance transcribed; the other is 'on castaraes sittinge on Primrose banks'.[46] They may be by the Catholic poet William Habington: they resemble poems in his print volume *Castara* (first published 1634), and Constance included another poem from this collection elsewhere in her miscellany.[47] If they are Habington's then the Castara referred to here, as in his print poems, is Lucy Herbert, daughter of William Herbert, first Baron Powis (1573?–1655), whom Habington married clandestinely in 1633,[48] and the sisters in the snow are Lucy and her sister Katherine. However, these two unattributed 'Castara' poems may be imitations or adaptations of Habington by Sir William Pershall, husband of Constance's sister Frances. They are subscribed with a cipher of cross-hatched lines which is associated with Pershall elsewhere in Constance's miscellany.[49] In this case Castara and her sister or sisters could be any combination of the Aston sisters, Constance, Gertrude and Frances. Whichever is the case, the 'sisters in the snow' poem certainly sits comfortably alongside Fanshawe's poems on the Aston women, and is consistent with the emphasis throughout Constance's volume not merely on poems inspired by sisterhood, but on the construction and idealisation of sisterhood in poetry. Her transcriptions define the role and identity of 'sister', elevate sisterhood as a virtuous and idyllic state, and reinforce sisterly bonds.

Female friendship

THE Aston circle enjoyed poetic dialogues, and it was often the women of the group who engaged in this highly sociable form of composition. Gertrude composed 'To Mr E—T—, who holds selfe-love in all our actions' as part of an exchange with her brother-in-law Edward Thimelby, while Katherine Thimelby composed a reply to William Habington's 'To the honourable G T'.[50] Constance also transcribed into her miscellany a female–female verse dialogue, between Katherine Thimelby and Lady Dorothy Stafford. Lady Dorothy's parents were Robert Devereux, second Earl of Essex, and Frances Walsingham, widow of Sir Philip Sidney, so she offered the Astons a line of association back to the Elizabethan court and the Sidneys' literary circle. Born in 1600, in 1615 Lady Dorothy married a Catholic baronet, Sir Henry Shirley; he died, and in 1635 she married William Stafford of Northamptonshire, but died herself the following year.[51] Her acquaintance with the Astons is attested by Constance's inclusion in her miscellany of two poems by Lady Dorothy, as well as poems by others on her marriage to Stafford and her death.[52]

The dialogue begins with a poem headed 'upon the L[ady] D[orothy] saying K[atherine] T[himelby] could be sad in her company'.[53] Katherine opens, 'Madem you say I am sad I ansure noe/unlesse it be because you say I am soe' (lines 1–2), then protests, 'Ther is no Joy if not by me possest./when in your conversation I can find/Ther be all treasures to delight the mind' (lines 17–19). The poem at once commends Lady Dorothy's conversation and itself participates in ongoing conversation, to conclude, 'Therfore by these your favors I intreate/you will beleeve my Joy in you complete' (lines 27–8). 'The L[ady] D[orothy's] ansure' opens, 'Deare cosen pardon me if I mistowke/I thought the face had bin the truest booke' (lines 1–2).[54] It proceeds through similarly elegant and complimentary couplets: 'I feare'd you sad because that smileing grace/which oft hath Joye'd me was not in your face' (lines 7–8). Lady Dorothy thanks Katherine for her commendations, modestly protesting that friendship makes Katherine view her as better than she is, and is a 'multipling glasse' which enhances the one beheld (lines 13–14). She closes by aspiring to deserve Katherine's high opinion of her: 'But this beleeve you canot favore shew/To one more yours and will be ever soe' (lines 23–4).

In some ways this exchange resembles other celebrations of sisterhood and female friendship in Constance's miscellany: the closing lines by Lady Dorothy imply similitude and reciprocity between herself and Katherine, and thus sit comfortably alongside Fanshawe's 'two swans' poem and the poem about Castara and her sister (or sisters) in the snow. Yet the parallelism between Katherine and Lady Dorothy is attained only at the end of their poetic exchange and is something that Lady Dorothy concertedly works towards. Margaret J. M. Ezell in chapter 8 cautions against assuming that literary coteries in which women were active were always sisterly and supportive. There is no reason to doubt Lady Dorothy's goodwill towards Katherine, but at the same time we should be wary of reading this exchange at face value, as a simple expression of friendship conducted on equal terms. Closer inspection reveals that it is underwritten by a distinct hierarchy. Katherine addresses Lady Dorothy twice in her poem as 'Madem', and refers to herself deferentially as 'your servant', who is 'unworthy' of the 'blessing' of Lady Dorothy's friendship (lines 1, 7, 15, 19, 23). It is Lady Dorothy who introduces the more intimate term 'Deare cosen', and concludes her poem on a note of mutual affection and obligation.

She is in fact condescending magnanimously. Lady Dorothy was born in 1600, Katherine in 1617 or 1618,[55] and their poetic dialogue was probably composed a little before Lady Dorothy's death in 1636, making Katherine at most eighteen years old, while Lady Dorothy was in her mid-thirties. Lady Dorothy, then, writes as a thrice-married older woman; as the daughter of an earl who was mourned as a chivalric hero and of the widow of a literary icon; and as a mentor figure rather than a friend of equal status. Equality and intimacy are graciously constructed in her answer poem – 'tis you that have inriched mee / For whoes sake I did wish to steale From thee' (lines 21–2). The genre of answer poem implies dialogue and partnership, but what we observe here is not the simple expression of a pre-existent balanced relationship; rather, the poem strenuously crafts likeness and mutual regard. The pair of poems, taken together, constructs female symmetry out of underlying asymmetry. At the same time, Constance's transcription of the exchange between Katherine and Lady Dorothy triangulates the relationship: by copying and preserving the two poems, Constance places herself, too, within the embracing circle of female intimacy that they form.

Lady Dorothy may well have fascinated the Aston women because of her connections with court culture. She was the dedicatee of *Changes, or, Love in a Maze* (1632) by James Shirley, who was favoured by Queen Henrietta Maria, and was described in 1633 by Lucius Cary, Viscount Falkland, as 'one of the fairest, wittiest and newest widdowes of our time'. In this year Walter Montagu wrote *The Shepherds' Paradise*, his elaborate masque of Platonic love, for performance by the Queen and her ladies, and according to Falkland, Lady Dorothy 'longs extreamely to read it, and hath sent to beg a sight of it'.[56] The Astons acquired a manuscript of the play, perhaps via Lady Dorothy: according to the 1899 sale catalogue of the Tixall library it was inscribed 'the Lady Pearsall's Booke 1653', probably referring to Frances Aston Pershall, Constance's sister.[57] Lady Dorothy thus connected the Astons to the neo-Platonic courtly fashion for idealised love and friendship that was cultivated by Henrietta Maria,[58] and this may have influenced their literary idealisations of passionate and ennobling female friendships and sibling affection.

Some of the most remarkable examples of such idealisation of female friendship are in Constance's letters to Herbert in Spain. Perhaps influenced by the court fashion for passionate intimacy, Constance wrote fervently of her love for Katherine Thimelby, the woman Herbert hoped to marry: 'I love her above my life, and vallew her infinitly ... ther was never any more passionat affectionat lovers then she and I ... you never knew two cretures more truely and deadly in love with one another than we are'.[59] It is difficult for a modern reader to encounter such passages without thinking of homo-eroticism; clearly, Constance's primary affective bond at this time was with Katherine, while her own recently acquired husband never features in either her letters or her miscellany. Yet Constance's relationship with Katherine was also triangular, in that her adored brother was a constant presence. Constance signs herself to him as 'Your ever most afectionat sister and most true lover CF', and explains that, while Katherine is 'the onely wonder of this age', 'you two are deare partners in my hart, and it is soe holly devided betwixt you'.[60] She seems to have understood herself as Herbert's proxy in courting Katherine, while at the same time performing to him the warmth and intensity of affection between herself and Katherine. Thus three kinds of intimacy – distinct, yet interlinked – are in play: same-sex friendship; brother-sister affection; and heterosexual courtship directed towards marriage. Constance and Katherine bond and mirror each other as female friends; Constance and Herbert are bonded and mirror each other as siblings; Herbert and Katherine bond as lovers. These three pairings form a triangle, or intertwine to form a true love's knot, Constance's cipher for Herbert.

The knot would be bound tighter by Herbert's marriage to Katherine, which in effect made her a new sister to Constance. The Astons, in common with the general practice of the time, understood sisters-in-law simply as sisters: in a poem to his brother's wife Mary, Herbert addressed her as 'Ever most Honour'd Sister'; while Lord Aston wrote to welcome Katherine into the family, addressing her as 'Good Dawter' and signing himself 'Your loving father'.[61] The roles of friend, sister-in-law and sister merged in this social network, creating a community which valued female agency and was largely held together by female bonds. It was in written exchanges that these female identities and bonds were defined, enacted and perpetuated.

Conclusion

THE Astons' writings were socially produced, where the term 'social' encompasses a number of meanings. These include: the Astons' affiliation with the Catholic community, royalist politics and court culture; their sense of elevated class status; and their local rootedness in Staffordshire, always in tension and in dialogue with their international connections and perspectives. They also include various intersecting relationships – family ties, same-sex friendships and courtship – which not only inspired the Astons' poems and letters but were also actively fashioned and developed in these writings. Constance's transcriptions into her miscellany both record and create intricate social patterns, including symmetrical and asymmetrical partnerships, triangles, four-way formations and intertwined knots. Even texts which at first sight look like one-to-one transactions often involve third or fourth parties as implied recipients or transcribers, constructing an elaborate geometry of communication and exchange.

In this writing (and written) community, women enjoyed a variety of roles: as inspiration, subject matter and addressees of poems; as authors of and respondents to poems; and, in Constance's case, as procurer, transcriber, editor, collector, preserver and purveyor of poems. Constance's verse miscellany, and her commentary upon it in her letters, highlight the diversity and complexity of relations between seventeenth-century women and poetry. They place female identities and relationships at the centre of the Astons' poetic community, and thereby foreground sisterhood and female friendship as both productive of poems and produced by poems.

Notes

This chapter is dedicated to the memory of Jinty Hackett, a beloved sister-in-law and friend. I am grateful to Susan Wiseman for her helpful and productive comments on earlier drafts of the chapter.

1 Because this chapter refers to a number of members of a few families, it would be confusing to refer to individuals by their surnames; first names are therefore used instead.

2 Evidence for dating includes: inclusion of a poem from William Habington's *Castara*, first published 1634; inclusion of poems attributed to Lady Dorothy Stafford, a family friend, who died in 1636; also a poem on her death; and a poem on the return of Constance's father, Lord Aston, from Spain in 1638. C. Aston Fowler (ed.), manuscript verse miscellany, Huntington Library, MS HM 904 (c. 1634–39), folios 32v–3r, 136r–v, 152v–3v, 158v–9r, 196r–200v; D. Aldrich-Watson (ed.), *The Verse Miscellany of Constance Aston Fowler: A Diplomatic Edition*, Renaissance English Text Society, Tempe, 2000, pp. 63, 105, 124–5, 134, 157–63; K. Allott (ed.), *The Poems of William Habington*, Liverpool University Press, Liverpool, 1948, pp. 81–2.

3 Aston papers, British Library additional manuscript 16452, folios 21–5; A. Clifford (ed.), *Tixall Letters: Or, the Correspondence of the Aston Family, and Their Friends, During the Seventeenth Century*, 2 vols, Edinburgh, 1815, vol. 1, pp. 85–106.

4 H. Hackett, 'Women and Catholic manuscript networks in seventeenth-century England: new research on Constance Aston Fowler's miscellany of sacred and secular verse', *Renaissance Quarterly*, vol. 65, no. 4 (winter 2012), pp. 1094–124; H. Hackett, 'Unlocking the mysteries of Constance Aston Fowler's verse miscellany (Huntington Library MS HM 904): the Hand B scribe identified', in J. Eckhardt and D. Starza Smith (eds), *Miscellanies in Early Modern England*, Ashgate, Farnham, forthcoming.

5 Fowler, verse miscellany, folio 188r; Aldrich-Watson, *Verse Miscellany*, p. 146; Aston papers, folio 21v; Clifford, *Tixall Letters*, vol. 1, p. 89.

6 Aston papers, folios 26r–8v; Clifford, *Tixall Letters*, vol. 1, p. 111.

7 See J. La Belle, 'A true love's knot: the letters of Constance Fowler and the poems of Herbert Aston', *Journal of English and Germanic Philology*, vol. 79 (1980), pp. 13–31.

8 Aston papers, folio 28v.

9 Aston papers, folio 30v; Clifford, *Tixall Letters*, vol. 1, p. 133.

10 Aston papers, folio 22v; Clifford, *Tixall Letters*, vol. 1, p. 94.

11 Aston papers, folio 23r; Clifford, *Tixall Letters*, vol. 1, p. 97.

12 P. Trolander and Z. Tenger, *Sociable Criticism in England, 1625–1725*, Rosemont, Cranbury, 2007, pp. 32–5.

13 Aston papers, folio 22v; Clifford, *Tixall Letters*, vol. 1, p. 94.

14 Aston papers, folio 21r; Clifford, *Tixall Letters*, vol. 1, p. 86.

15 I established this using M. Crum (ed.), *First-Line Index of English Poetry 1500–1800 in Manuscripts of the Bodleian Library Oxford*, 2 vols, Clarendon, Oxford, 1969; C. L. Day and E. Boswell Murrie, *English Song-Books 1651–1702: A Bibliography with a First-Line Index of Songs*, Bibliographical Society, London, 1940; S. Parks, M. Greitens and C. W. Nelson (eds), *First-Line Index of English Poetry 1500–1800 in Manuscripts of the Osborn Collection, Yale University*, Beinecke Library, New Haven, 2005; and A. Smyth, *Index of Poetry in Printed Miscellanies, 1640–1682*, online at http://cobweb.businesscollaborator. com/pub/english.cgi/0/5383492?op=rdb_view_database&search_items=&a_view1=- -All-Fields--&modifier_1=contains&ctp=9925984&htp=9925987&rtp=9925990&p age=1 (accessed June 2012).

16 H. Aston (ed.), manuscript verse miscellany, Beinecke Library, Yale University, Osborn MS B4 (c. 1634–50), folios 2v, 39r. 'Your meaner beauties' is the opening of the poem as given by Herbert; other MSS have 'You meaner beauties'.

17 H. Aston, verse miscellany, folio 26r, 'Art thou gon in hast and will forsake mee', from *The Thracian Wonder*, attributed to J. Webster and T. Rowley; folio 37v, 'Why art thou slow thou rest of trouble, Death', from P. Massinger's *Emperor of the East*, 1632.

18 Fowler, verse miscellany, folios 150r–2v, 155r–8r; Aldrich-Watson, *Verse Miscellany*, pp. 120–3, 128–33.

19 J. Donne, 'Elegy 16: On his mistress' ('By our first strange and fatal interview'), in A. J. Smith (ed.), *The Complete English Poems*, Penguin, Harmondsworth, 1971, p. 118, line 4.

20 A. Clifford (ed.), *Tixall Poetry*, Edinburgh, 1813, pp. 85–7, 94.

21 Ibid., pp. 45–51, 90–2.

22 Fowler, verse miscellany, folios 48v, 182v–4v; Aldrich-Watson, *Verse Miscellany*, pp. 96, 135–8.

23 Aston, verse miscellany, folios 49v–50r; Fowler, verse miscellany, folios 49r–52r; Aldrich-Watson, *Verse Miscellany*, pp. 97–103.

24 Fowler, verse miscellany, folio 185r; Aldrich-Watson, *Verse Miscellany*, p. 139; Smyth, *Index of Poetry*; A. Smyth, review of D. Aldrich-Watson (ed.), *The Verse Miscellany of Constance Aston Fowler*, in *Seventeenth-Century News*, vol. 60, no. 182 (spring–summer 2002), pp. 57–8.

25 Smyth, review of Aldrich-Watson, p. 58.

26 See chapters 8 and 9 in the present volume, by Margaret J. M. Ezell and Patricia Pender, for other examples of women's literary participation proceeding under differ-ent conventions from those applied to men.

27 In 1644 Fanshawe would marry his second cousin, Ann Harrison, who as Lady Ann Fanshawe composed her *Memoirs* in 1676. See P. Davidson, 'Fanshawe, Ann, Lady Fanshawe (1625–1680)', *Oxford Dictionary of National Biography*, Oxford University Press, Oxford, 2004–8, online at www.oxforddnb.com/view/article/9146 (accessed August 2013).

28 Clifford, *Tixall Poetry*, p. 215.

29 Fowler, verse miscellany, folios 187r–v; Aldrich-Watson, *Verse Miscellany*, pp. 144–5; lines 1–5.

30 Fowler, verse miscellany, folio 156v; Aldrich-Watson, *Verse Miscellany*, p. 130.

31 Fowler, verse miscellany, folio 11r; Aldrich-Watson, *Verse Miscellany*, pp. 11–12.

32 Fowler, verse miscellany, folio 12v; Aldrich-Watson, *Verse Miscellany*, p. 14.

33 E. Spenser, 'Prothalamion', in R. A. McCabe (ed.), *Edmund Spenser: The Shorter Poems*, Penguin, London, 1999, pp. 491–7, lines 37–9.

34 Fowler, verse miscellany, folios 185v–6r; Aldrich-Watson, *Verse Miscellany*, p. 141. Fanshawe's poem perhaps also alludes to the praise of the swans of Trent in 'The sheaphrd's sirena' by Michael Drayton, former client of Lord Aston.

35 Spenser, 'Prothalamion', line 6.

36 Clifford, *Tixall Poetry*, p. 215.

37 See H. Hackett, 'The Aston–Thimelby circle at home and abroad: localism, national identity and internationalism in the English Catholic community', in D. Coleman (ed.), *Region, Religion and English Renaissance Literature*, Ashgate, Farnham, 2013, pp. 123–38.

38 See T. S. Smith, 'The persecution of Staffordshire Roman Catholic recusants: 1625–1660', *Journal of Ecclesiastical History*, vol. 30, no. 3 (July 1979), pp. 327–51.

39 W. Shakespeare, *A Midsummer Night's Dream*, 3.2.200–12, in S. Greenblatt (gen. ed.), *The Norton Shakespeare*, Norton, New York, 1997.

40 W. Shakespeare, *As You Like It*, 1.3.67–70, in Greenblatt (gen. ed.), *The Norton Shakespeare*.

41 *The Tixall Library: Catalogue of Valuable Books and Manuscripts*, sale of 6–7 November 1899, Sotheby, London, 1899, p. 49, lot 592; p. 51, lot 610.

42 Ibid., p. 50, lot 599.

43 Ibid., p. 49, lot 598.

44 J. Donne, 'Upon the translation of the Psalms by Sir Philip Sidney, and the Countess of Pembroke his sister', in Smith (ed.), *The Complete Poems*, pp. 332–4, lines 14–16.

45 Fowler, verse miscellany, folio 28v; Aldrich-Watson, *Verse Miscellany*, p. 54.

46 Fowler, verse miscellany, folio 27v; Aldrich-Watson, *Verse Miscellany*, pp. 50–1.

47 Fowler, verse miscellany, folios 152v–4v; Aldrich-Watson, *Verse Miscellany*, pp. 124–7.

48 Allott (ed.), *The Poems of William Habington*, pp. xxiii–xxv; R. Wilcher, 'Habington, William (1605–1654)', *Oxford Dictionary of National Biography*, Oxford University Press, Oxford, 2004–8, online at www.oxforddnb.com/view/article/11833 (accessed June 2012).

49 Fowler, verse miscellany, folios 27v, 28v, 31r, 32v, 200v. For more on the doubtful authorship and hybridity of the two unattributed 'Castara' poems, see Hackett, 'Women and Catholic manuscript networks'.

50 Clifford, *Tixall Poetry*, pp. 45–51, 90–2; Fowler, verse miscellany, folios 152v–4v; Aldrich-Watson, *Verse Miscellany*, pp. 124–7.

51 V. E. Burke, 'Stafford [née Devereux; other married name Shirley], Lady Dorothy (1600–1636)', *Oxford Dictionary of National Biography*, Oxford University Press, Oxford, 2004–8, online at www.oxforddnb.com.libproxy.ucl.ac.uk/view/article/68096 (accessed June 2012).

52 Fowler, verse miscellany, folios 136r–v, 189r–200v; Aldrich-Watson, *Verse Miscellany*, pp. 105, 149–63.

53 Fowler, verse miscellany, folios 158r–v; Aldrich-Watson, *Verse Miscellany*, pp. 132–3.

54 Fowler, verse miscellany, folios 158v–9r; Aldrich-Watson, *Verse Miscellany*, p. 134.

55 V. E. Burke, 'Aston, Herbert (bap. 1614, d. 1688/9)', *Oxford Dictionary of National Biography*, Oxford University Press, Oxford, 2004–8, online at www.oxforddnb.com/view/article/68247 (accessed August 2013).

56 W. Montagu, *The Shepherds' Paradise* (ed. S. Poynting), Malone Society Reprints, vol. 159, Malone Society, Oxford, 1997, p. xiv, n. 41.

57 *The Tixall Library*, p. 49, lot 597.

58 E. Veevers, *Images of Love and Religion: Queen Henrietta Maria and Court Entertainments*, Cambridge University Press, Cambridge, 1989.

59 Aston papers, folios 23r–v, 26r–8v; Clifford, *Tixall Letters*, vol. 1, pp. 97, 109.

60 Aston papers, folios 26r–8v, 31v; Clifford, *Tixall Letters*, vol. 1, pp. 122, 136.

61 Fowler, verse miscellany, folio 150r; Aldrich-Watson, *Verse Miscellany*, p. 120; Clifford, *Tixall Letters*, vol. 1, p. 148.

CHAPTER 8

Late seventeenth-century women poets and the anxiety of attribution

Margaret J. M. Ezell

High-born Belinda loves to blame;
On criticism founds her fame:
Whene'er she thinks a fault she spies,
How pleasure sparkles in her eyes!
'Call it not poetry,' she says,
'No – call it rhyming, if you please:
Her numbers might adorn a ring,
Or serve along the streets to sing…'

Mary Barber, 'To a Lady, who commanded me to send her an Account in
Verse, how I succeeded in my Subscription' (1734)

ANNE Killigrew's literary reputation, as critics have pointed out, has
strangely suffered from her being immortalised by John Dryden. In
Dryden's famous ode, Killigrew (1660–85) is represented as the 'Youngest
Virgin-Daughter of the Skies', a 'Vestal' in a 'lubrique and adult'rate age',
a poet with a 'Heav'n-born Mind', but one untutored in her verse: 'Art she
had none, yet wanted none / For Nature did that Want supply / … / Such
Noble Vigour did her Verse adorn, / That it seem'd borrow'd, where 'twas
only born'.[1] Dryden's praise of her thus highlights her youth – although
she was twenty-five at the time of her death, not in her teens as one might
easily assume from this description – and her isolation from what he sees as
the polluting literary and court culture of the period. Dryden's depiction
of her seems to suggest she was just entering into public life and subsequent critics have followed suit, typically characterising her as a 'young'
writer, with its implied vulnerability. Earlier generations of critics found
Dryden's praise of her talents so hyperbolic, however, that they tended
to dismiss her out of hand; as recently as the 1990s, critics were reading
Dryden's praise of her as ironic and satiric.[2] More recent readers, however,
have reclaimed her for the study of women's engagement, through their
poetry, with the politics of royalist communities centred on the court and

as an example of women's participation in social authorship practices, in part based on her poem entitled 'Upon the saying that my VERSES were made by another'.[3] As Killigrew's life and works slowly become distinct from Dryden's hagiographic representation of her, her poems about herself as a writer and artist permit us to consider several models of authorship and women's participation in late seventeenth-century literary culture.

Central to models of seventeenth-century coterie or social authorship is the implicit assumption that the writer, male or female, was permitting their work to be read by a group of friendly readers, whether family members, neighbours or acquaintances selected for their shared interests. Grub Street writers might have their quarrels, Dryden and Shadwell might pursue each other through satires and lampoons, but in contrast to the competitive world of commercial authorship, coterie or social literary production is typically represented as avoiding such conflict and competition through the strategies of social decorum that shaped civil discourse. But is social circulation of texts and criticism ever that consistently smooth, controlled and civil? What might this model of the civility of social authorship hinder us from seeing? And can Dryden's 'young Probationer, / And Candidate of Heav'n' help us to revisit our existing models?

Although challenged successfully in some respects, J. W. Saunders' early and influential essay on the 'stigma of print' has had a long-lasting and in many ways highly beneficial impact on the recovery of manuscript texts that were circulated among readers outside of print.[4] Decoupling the notion of print from 'professional' in the sense of possessing greater literary merit, this model of authorship for early modern writers restored a more nuanced understanding of the flow of literary texts among writers and readers and its relationship to the establishment of a reputation as a writer. Later generations of critics continued to build on the concept that for those writing and reading well into the eighteenth century, there were viable and competing means for sharing one's literary work among a select circle of readers and establishing a literary reputation without venturing into print publication. These more recent studies, particularly of the literary text as a gift, suggest a multitude of functions that authorship based on mutual exchange of handwritten items among writers and readers might permit; as Helen Hackett convincingly demonstrates in chapter 7, the acts of exchanging of verses, collecting them and circulating them could serve as a way to confirm and to strengthen one's sense of identity and membership, in terms of both familial relations and religious identity.[5]

This validation of handwritten authorship practices has always also carried with it inherent assumptions about gender and authorship. While elite males might shun publications because of their distaste for commercial application of their creations, women of all classes, it commonly has been inferred, were particularly concerned to keep their names, if not their texts, out of the realm of print. Unlike Margaret Cavendish and Aphra Behn, who without hesitation declared in their published writings that they desired personal and lasting fame through their printed texts, studies of some of the principal women involved in so-called 'coterie' writing in the Restoration and into the late seventeenth century – Katherine Philips, Anne Finch, Countess of Winchilsea, and Anne Killigrew – rest on the assumption that even when publication did occur, there was considerable anxiety over the publication of the woman author's name.

Furthermore, there is the embedded expectation that women who wrote and circulated their verse in manuscript sought and stayed within a congenial circle. Carol Barash describes the general profile of late seventeenth-century women who preferred to publish in manuscript rather than with a bookseller as 'usually elite and well educated; their readers were assumed to be friends with shared political affiliations; and friends often imitated and even rewrote friends' poems in the manuscript mode'.[6] Kathryn King's exemplary critical study of the life and complicated literary career of another late seventeenth-century woman poet, Jane Barker, begins with an examination of the first stage of her long literary life, poems composed in the 1670s and 1680s for 'a small but sympathetic circle (or circles) of fellow amateur poets', resulting in 'pre-eminently social verse'.[7] Unlike Barash's perception of Barker's early verse as demonstrating a 'controlled – even willed – solitude', King argues that this early work shows 'a coterie poet whose literary métier was the expression of friendship ... this is not public poetry, in other words, nor is it especially political. It is occasional and familiar verse addressed to intimates.'[8] The nature of the content of the poems as well as the poet's relationship with her readers is thus tied to a friendly, familiar and contained group of readers.

Likewise, according to Trolander and Tenger's study of the art of sociable criticism in the seventeenth century, when poets circulated their works asking for amendment and correction as well as a response, 'the critical act is predicated upon personal relationships' between family members, close neighbours and like-minded friends.[9] Their description of this practice is worth quoting at length because it highlights the nature of the exchange as a social one governed by both the rules of polite conversation and familiarity:

> Because manuscript production was increasingly seen as embedded in social circumstances, critical activity around the manuscript text was envisioned as a reciprocal and collaborative process, involving at least one's close friend or associate and perhaps a small group or coterie using processes of selecting, recording, compiling, and amending to ready the manuscript for circulation beyond the author's immediate social circumstances. Regardless of the writers'

149

intentions as to the extent of the dissemination of their writings (that is, if they preferred to keep them close by or favored wider dissemination including through print or stage production), it was understood that critical activity ought to occur close to home, that is, in 'private' and personal social contexts.[10]

The discourses of polite civility, the acknowledgement of relationships and the friendly emendation thus shape the behaviours of both writer and critical reader. Manuscript texts of this period are described as being shared within a particular social dynamic and thus both the writer's text and the readers' responses are kept under control.

This connection between coterie, manuscript production and poetic form and subject matter is, of course, most marked in the ways in which Katherine Philips's society of friendship has been historicised. Carol Barash has argued:

> It may be that in such a period of change and in the face of great personal isola-
> tion and loss, imagined communities suggested new continuities, the hope of a
> collective response to a shared political crisis. From Katherine Philips's royalist
> 'Society of Friendship' to Finch's retreat to the landscape with a female friend
> who shares her political sympathies in 'petition for an Absolute Retreat', new
> female-centered communities are imagined as places of both political and
> emotional triumph.[11]

The notion that coterie or social textual circulation by women was confined to friendly readers also permeates classic studies such as Dorothy Mermin's, who declares that Aphra Behn, Katherine Philips and Anne Finch were members of 'a small social world that could be transformed into a fictional society that provided both context and material for verse'.[12] It is when handwritten copies escaped the control of the imagined circle of friendly readers, as with the 1664 publication of an unauthorised version of Philips's poems, that the hostile print reader had access to the work and, through her name, to the author and her public reputation, and it is this that generated the fear of public attribution for the seventeenth-century woman poet.

These studies are of critical importance for those interested in women's participation in literary culture, in that they have enabled the recovery of overlooked connections between women writers and the ways in which women poets were engaged with political issues, as well as the ways in which literary practice intersected with larger cultural notions of civility and conversation. However, what the general application of the model of coterie friendship (the civil exchange of manuscripts among like-minded individuals) obscures is the possible presence of rivalry and competition among the participants in this still social practice of authorship. On the other hand, the notion of friendly competition among male poets during this period and later is more commonly acknowledged. For instance, the literary competitions among the Cockney school poets in Leigh Hunt's circle in the early nineteenth century have been highlighted in Cox's study of the social yet competitive nature of their verse, while John Harold Wilson and Harold Love have explored the complicated literary exchanges among the Restoration court wits and their collaborative writings.[13]

That such competition and rivalry among early modern women poets may have gone unremarked in critics' representations of seventeenth-century women writers is not particularly surprising. 'Sisterhood' (in the 1970s feminist sense) has been conceived of as united in the tireless and too often unrewarded efforts made by earlier literary historians to recover the writings by these women from archival obscurity and critical dismissal, especially given the understandable reluctance to appear to be endorsing the savage misogyny directed at published women poets as squabbling sluts by satirists such as Alexander Pope. As Paula Backscheider correctly points out, one of the ways in which eighteenth-century women poets are marginalised is through the selection of particular types of poems to represent them: 'almost as popular is reprinting (and doctoring) poems in which women criticize other women, thereby perpetuating an "extreme and debilitating image of women" or writing "about girls the way blokes do"'.[14]

More recent scholarship, however, has begun to focus on the very real rivalries between women. Mary Ann O'Farrell's paper 'Sister acts', although looking at twentieth-century American musicals, nevertheless reminds scholars of earlier periods to consider that while sisterhood (whether defined by blood, shared experience or political perspective) is indeed characterised by unity and support, it also in many ways is struc-tured by envy.[15] Recently, critics working on professional women writers in the early eighteenth century have considered women writers' literary quarrels, but from the perspective of better illuminating the character of early commercial print culture rather than revealing the character flaws of the Grub Street women.

In this same vein of critique, Delarivier Manley's dismissal of an unpub-lished poem by Anne Finch is the starting point for Katharine Beutner's investigation of women writers and rivalry in the early eighteenth-century commercial literary marketplace. Manley has the character of Astrea (Aphra Behn's poetical name) critique Finch's poem 'The progress of life', which is embedded in Manley's *New Atlantis* (1709), by damning with faint praise: 'I presume she's one of the happy few that write out of pleasure and not necessity. By that means it's her own fault, if she publish any thing but what's good, for it's next to impossible to write much and write well'.[16] Likewise, Kathryn King has shone a light on the darker side of the coterie circle drawn to Aaron Hill in the early 1720s, analysing the tensions that existed between the professional women writers Eliza Haywood and Martha Fowke Sansom.[17] Instead of a lurid sexual triangle between Haywood, Sansom and Richard Savage, King interprets attacks by Haywood on Sansom as being primarily literary and commercial in nature, caused by a shift by Hill from Haywood to Sansom as his literary patron and benefactor, not mistress. As King concludes, 'literary rivalry can be a potent force as well, as we know from countless squabbles between Augustan male writers, and Haywood's [representation of Sansom] is, significantly, scathing in its assessment of Sansom's poetic abilities'.[18]

Interestingly, these two examples also demonstrate the complexities of the relationship between the realm of social, coterie groups and handwritten circulation and the sphere of paid authors and commercial print, too often represented as independent, almost segregated, practices. Manley can be dismissive of Finch for being a woman who did not publish and wrote for 'pleasure' and aggressively attack fellow commercial writers, including Mary Pix and Catherine Cockburn, demonstrating, as Beutner suggests, that 'different social meanings attended coterie manuscript poetry and printed Grub Street prose'.[19] Haywood is described by King as 'indeed stalk[ing] Sansom in print with a vindictive malice that certainly looks like sexual jealousy' over Sansom's perceived interference in Haywood's relationship with Hill and her participation in Hill's 'self-consciously modern poetic alternative to Augustan neoclassicism'.[20] In both of these examples, the overlap of the worlds of manuscript, coterie work and published commercial writing forms an area of contention.

Dryden's 'pious' Anne Killigrew might seem to be far distant from this example of literary stalking, as her poems were never printed during her lifetime and her precise coterie or literary circle has yet to be determined.[21] Her poems were collected together and published posthumously by her family as a memorial to the twenty-five-year-old poet and artist. While previously it was generally accepted that she served as a maid of honour in the court of Mary of Modena around 1683, even that biographical fact has recently been challenged.[22] In contrast, the court and literary career of Anne Finch, Countess of Winchilsea (1661–1720), and her manuscript poetry places her clearly in that court in 1682–84.[23] While there, Finch's concern, or anxiety, over having a reputation as 'a 'Versifying Maid of Honour', as she states in the preface to the manuscript collection of her verse, led her, according to her biographer, 'secretly to write'. Finch states 'it is still a great satisfaction to me, that I was not so far abandon'd by my prudence, as out of a mistaken vanity to let any attempts of mind in Poetry shew themselves whilst I liv'd in such a publick place as the Court, where everyone wou'd have made their remarks upon a Versifying Maid of Honour'.[24] Likewise, Killigrew's commentators highlight that 'we do not know exactly when Killigrew began writing poems, but she began attempting to make them public around 1680', suggesting a period of secret gestation before she permitted others to read her verse.[25]

Both of these women associated with the court of Mary of Modena in the early 1680s add to our understanding of the complexities not only of navigating one's way through the politics of the separate royal courts during a period of escalating political tensions, but also of managing the politics of coterie literary culture. In Barash's analysis, while for seventeenth-century women poets in general the 'new female-centered communities are imagined as places of both political and emotional triumph', Killigrew's 'poems repeatedly draw attention to the speaker's complicated position as one who is both insider and outsider at court'.[26] Killigrew's poem 'Upon the saying that my Verses were made by another' has been used as evidence of her involvement in a literary exchange circle and also as her indictment of the masculine court culture's ridicule of female ambition. Less attention has been given to Finch's 'The circuit of Apollo', a verse not included in the 1713 printed *Miscellany Poems, on Several Occasions*, but it, too, casts an interesting light on the dynamics of a semi-restricted literary circle.

My reading of these poems focuses more on the elements involved in being a member of a literary coterie, exchanging manuscripts and thus permitting others not only to know that one writes verse, but also to comment on it and critique it. Kristina Straub's reading of Killigrew's poem focuses on what she sees as a writer's sense of 'psychic violence' amounting to rape: 'the poem suggests that the social power conferred on her by class did not entirely cancel the vulnerability to oppression associated with her gender'.[27] As Straub points out, the poem follows the young poet's desire to write and then to be recognised for her writing, only to result in her 'feelings of being badly treated by an audience who refused to believe her the author of her own work'. In Straub's reading, the young female poet who initially is willing to sacrifice herself to the muse falls prey instead to the 'other', who 'gradually becomes explicitly identified with the male': 'her community insists that she has no right to what she thought was the pleasure and employment that would bring her honor'.[28] Barash, while disagreeing with Straub's reading of Apollo in Killigrew's poem as a rapist, seems to be in agreement that Killigrew, by letting others read her verses, loses control of them, such that her poems are 'no longer her own but the property of an aggressive and hostile court world', and that by 'giving herself over to Apollo puts the speaker into a complicated struggle with Fame: Apollo represents the male poets who provide the speaker access to a wider public, but whose possession of her poems means she can no longer claim them as her own'.[29]

Embedded in these two disparate readings of the poems are several implicit notions about participation in a coterie literary environment, especially a court one. Explicit in both readings is that a woman poet, after writing in secret and without an audience, would eventually permit her poems to be read by male readers in order to have them better presented to a larger coterie literary audience. The move from 'private' to 'public', in the sense that Anne Finch used the term in her preface, is marked by the poet encountering a hostile readership, presumably male. Killigrew's own narrative of her poetic steps, however, modifies that: before sending her poems out in search of 'Fame', she states 'I writ, and the Judicious prais'd my Pen' ('Upon the saying that my Verses were made by another', line 15). Who might the 'Judicious' be?[30] As Barash points out, Killigrew was indeed 'a very ambitious woman who came from a family of writers and courtiers'.[31] Her father, Henry Killigrew, was chaplain and almoner to the Duke of York, but he was also a polished and published playwright and translator, who would go on to publish several volumes of his own verse. Her mother, Judith (d. 1683), was a lady in waiting to the Queen and her inscribed copy of the second folio edition of Shakespeare now resides in the Folger Shakespeare Library.[32] Both her uncles were dramatists and poets: Sir William Killigrew and Thomas Killigrew were in the service of Charles II in exile and, after the Restoration, both became well established literary figures in both court and commercial literary circles. Thomas, significantly, was the manager of the King's Company at the Theatre Royal, one of the two patent theatres opened in 1660. In the 1670s through to early 1680s (before his death in 1683), Thomas was involved in bitter disputes with his son Charles over control of the theatre as well as with his authors and actors, including John Dryden, who broke with the Killigrews to join the Duke's Company, before the two merged in 1682 to form the United Company. Anne Killigrew thus was no novice in the world of coterie, courtier and commercial theatrical culture, with its intrigues and rivalries. With that literary pedigree and environment, if her family and relatives formed part of her initial audience, it is hardly surprising that she felt that, with their praise, 'Could any doubt Insuing Glory then?' (line 16).

Her decision to seek 'Fame' led her not to seek publication but to entrust her verses to 'some few hands'. But unlike the judicious early readers, 'ah, the sad effects that from it came!' she laments, 'What ought t'have brought me Honour, brought me shame!' The problem, however, was not that this wider circle of readers found her verses to be unskilful or immodest, as is suggested in the previous readings, but that she is accused of stealing them from others. Interestingly, while critics have dwelt at length over this section of the poem, Killigrew's chosen metaphor for her predicament – 'Like *Esops* Painted Jay I seem'd to all, / Adorn'd in Plumes, I not my own could call' – has gone unremarked. Essentially, Killigrew found herself accused of appropriating someone else's verses, exactly what she declares is being done with hers.

In the 1666 edition of *Aesop's Fables*, lavishly illustrated by Francis Barlow, the story of the Jay and the Peacock (fable 47) was put into English by Thomas Philipott:

> With gaudy feathers the Ambitious Jay
> Purloined from Peacocks, did her selfe array.
> And ye other Jays with coy neglect disdaines,
> Her selfe (mongst Peacocks mixt) a Peacock fayns.
> But they her borrow'd pride doe soone detect,
> And her disrob'd of her faiee [*sic*] plumes reject,
> When being confind againe to live with Jays,
> Her triviall pride each with Just scoffs repayes.
> Those yt to acts pretend they have not don
> Will n're ye guilt of pompous boasting shun.[33]

Assuming Killigrew selected her fable with some care, the charge being brought against her is not that she is a female seeking fame in a masculine court culture through verse, but that she is seeking fame by appropriating another's poems and thus pretending to be what she is not. As in the fable, her readers, like the peacocks, 'disrobe' her of her verses and attribute them to another: 'Rifl'd like her, each one my Feathers tore, / And, as they thought, unto the Owner bore' (lines 36–7). The question then arises, who did the readers think 'owned' the verses?

According to Killigrew, this poet already had achieved fame: 'An others Brow, that had so rich a store / Of Sacred Wreaths, that circled it before'. She concludes that, in the same way that a small stream is swallowed up and loses its identity when it merges with the 'Vast and Boundless Ocean', her small and emerging poetic reputation is extinguished in the presence of the more famous poet. There is no gendered pronoun, however, to guide us towards the poet whose existing reputation so engulfed Killigrew's efforts. Dryden, who wrote so effusively of her talents after her death, seems a possible candidate, but most courtiers could turn a verse as well. Are there other candidates suggested by Killigrew, carefully couched in indirect terms?

The next stanza, however, does directly reference Katherine Philips and her poetic fame. '*Orinda* (*Albions* and her Sexes Grace) / Ow'd not her Glory to a Beauteous Face'. Barash reads this turn as Killigrew comparing her own loss of face to Philips's success: 'Killigrew appeals to what Philips wrote, what she did as a political actor, not to the myth of her innocence upheld in the preface to Philips' *Poems* (1667)'. Barash observes, 'she depicted Philips participating in a war among poets, a war in which Philips triumphs ... Killigrew wishes a similar poetic glory for herself'. Although, according to Barash, both women had followed a similar path to literary fame through coterie literary exchange, Killigrew had a different goal: 'like Philips she depended on male friends to circulate her poetry at court. In contrast to Philips, however, she wanted it known that she was an author, and she lashed out at her audience for denying her control over her own writing'.[34] What this convincing reading leaves out is Killigrew's observation that Orinda's female readers treated her with respect and admiration: 'Nor did her Sex at all obstruct her Fame, / But higher 'mong the Stars it fixt her Name'.

What is confusing in the various later readings of this poem is that they seem to assert that Killigrew is dependent on masculine approval of her as a poet, versus her charge that it is people of her own sex who 'obstruct her Fame'. That the stanza describing how her poems are being attributed to a poet who has already won laurels is immediately followed by the reference to Orinda and her successes leads one to wonder if her unknown, apparently unjudicious, readers assume that certain types of verse must belong to 'Orinda' alone. 'What she did write, not only all allow'd, / But ev'ry Laurel, to her Laurel, bow'd!' 'Th'Envious Age', she concludes, 'only to Me alone, / Will not allow, what I do write, my Own'. It could be that, instead of encountering the friendly and civil response we expect of a literary coterie, especially one involving women, she discovered jealousy and envy, and saw the displacement of her poetic efforts onto a distant and deceased prominent female literary figure.

Envy, of course, is the bane of civil discourse and conduct, short-circuiting the friendly and sociable premise which may have inspired the writer to share her poems in the first place. While we are used to stereotypes of women being jealous or envious of other women because of their beauty or their social position, female verse envy seems to be less considered. In much the same way that 1970s feminism claimed 'sister' as the term to describe the nurturing and supportive relationship between women united in a shared cause, the analysis of women involved in coterie and social manuscript culture has highlighted the supportive and protective nature of such a readership.

Certainly, as referenced earlier, Anne Finch remembered feeling that the court of Mary of Modena in the 1680s was too 'publick' a place to circulate her verses, even though it is clear that she was indeed writing while there.[35] Did she have in mind Anne Killigrew's account of her reception as presented in 'Upon the saying that my Verses were made by another', where she relives the ridicule awaiting one with a reputation for being a 'versifying maid of honour'? Or was she one of the ones tearing out Killigrew's feathers? Finch, of course, is famous for her poems on her lack of ambition as a poet, at least as a poet performing in the public space of print, and the hostility she imagines will greet her poetry should it move outside the confines of her sociable circle because of her gender. As Backscheider has noted in her analysis of Finch's fable 'Mercury and the elephant', Finch mocks the 'self-absorption and ridiculous self-centeredness' of the elephant, concerned what the gods might be saying about it and by 'taking the position that she is as inconsequential to the London critical world as the elephant is to the gods, Finch frees herself to invoke an intimate circle of readers and poets who "for our Selves, not [critics], we *Writ*"'.[36] Barash offers a more challenging view of her overall career as a poet, which runs counter to Finch's own 'cultivated ... modest public identity in her poetry', seeing her instead as an 'ambitious, energetic poet both of political and religious extremity, and of lavish female communion'.[37]

As Backschieder, however, has also noted about the critical discussions of early women poets in general, 'neither agency nor ambition has been sufficiently studied'.[38] Barash invokes the court of Mary of Modena as a powerful female community where 'the Maids of Honour performed in court masques; they read, sang, and painted'; further, Barash stresses, 'they were schooled both in French and Italian translations of classical texts and in the heroic tradition of Tasso and Ariosto, and they were urged to make their own English translations of these works'.[39] One of Finch's biographers does not suggest that Killigrew and Finch were part of the same literary circles, instead simply stating that 'the extent of the friendship of these two young women is unknown', although she quotes an early biographer of Mary of Modena as saying they were both 'much beloved' by the future queen and 'alike distinguished for moral worth and literary attainments'.[40]

'The circuit of Apollo' is believed by critics to have been written around 1702, long after Finch had left the world of the court and was living in Kent with her husband as Jacobite exiles. This poem has drawn attention primarily because of its establishment of a type of female poetic genealogy based on contrasting Katherine Philips and Aphra Behn, with Behn apparently being Finch's preferred poet. Described by Charles Hinnant as being part of the 'session of the poets' genre, 'a popular, light-hearted, seventeenth-century genre' where Apollo creates contests in which witty male poets compete for the title of poet laureate, this sense of the piece as 'light-hearted' is shared by McGovern in her reading of it.[41] Hinnant also sees a dark side of the poem, one which deals with the dismissal of women as serious poets: Hinnant reads Apollo's decision that all four of the women poets in the poem equally deserve the bays as essentially declaring that none of them is deserving. Apollo's 'flattery ... appears to substitute an image that women have of themselves (e.g. as cooperative rather than competitive) for one that men have of women', that they are naturally jealous and hate to hear other women praised, especially by men.[42] Keith likewise points to the fact that Apollo's decision seems to be based on his 'fears that the contestants may be jealous if he declares one woman the winner (such is the stereotype of female jealousy), thus abandoning any real consideration of their qualities as artists'.[43]

Is Finch wielding her satiric pen to put the judgemental Apollo in his place or is she also writing about provincial literary life? The opening of the poem does not position Kent as the liveliest of poetic sites: when Apollo is passing through Kent as part of his 'circuit', historically a reference to judges travelling from town to town in a district to hear trials, he discovers that 'Poets were not very common' and, indeed, 'most that pretended to Verse, were the Women'.[44] Upon summoning all the poets of Kent to him to contest for the laurels, only four poets show up, all women. Resigned, he 'order'd them each in their several way, / To show him their papers, to sing, or to say, / What 'ere they thought best, their presentations might prove'. 'Alinda' is the first to compete with her 'song upon Love', which ravishes Apollo, and 'The Wreath, he reach'd out, to have plac'd on her head'. He is forestalled, however, by 'Laura', who 'quickly a paper had read / Wherin She Orinda has praised so high', which prompts Apollo to decide 'Who e're cou'd write that, ought the Laurel to wear'. 'Valeria' takes matters into her own hands, 'withdrew him a little from thence, / And told him, as soon she'd got him aside, / Her works, by no other, but him shou'd be try'd'.

'Ardelia', Finch's poetic name for herself, goes last. Ardelia is the most fully developed of the four and Finch makes it clear that Ardelia 'writ for her pleasure and not for the Bays' and uses poetry as a mean of passing 'a dull day, / In composing a song, or a Scene of a Play, / Not seeking for Fame, which so little does last'. As Apollo prepares to 'make an Oration', posing nicely with one foot artistically stretched forward and a lock of hair gracefully displayed, he remembers what happened to Paris on awarding the prize for the most beautiful woman and Apollo loses his nerve: 'Since in Witt, or in Beauty, itt never was heard, / One female cou'd yield t'have another preferr'd', he defers the judgement of the four women's poetry to a 'council of Muses ... / Who of their own sex, best the title might try'.

The pompous, and foppish Apollo is clearly a figure of mockery here, the male wit striking a suitable pose before thinking better of opening his mouth, then making an inglorious retreat. But are the women poets exempt from Finch's satiric eye? While some critics see 'Laura' as being a reference to Mary of Modena, this seems a distraction from the point of the poem, that this is an ironic portrait of provincial literary life, from the perspective of one who once enjoyed court culture. It is also a poem about Finch's self-declared rejection of competition, unlike the other women poets, and her representation of herself as one who writes for personal pleasure and really has no interest in 'winning' fame, indeed performing last because, modestly, she was 'expecting least praise'. Certainly, the character Ardelia behaves in a more dignified fashion than Valeria, demanding a private audience, or Laura, 'quickly' jumping in with her own work to forestall Alinda receiving the prize.

What these poems by the two women involved in the court culture surrounding Mary of Modena highlight for us is the complexity of the dynamic of social, coterie authorship. While it is still important to aid the further recovery of women's writings from this period to investigate the polite and carefully cultivated social nature of the literary circles in which they wrote and read, to use those connections between friends and relatives to reconstruct a woman poet's involvement in literary exchanges, to not discuss the complicated nature of literary exchange may lead us into difficulties in understanding women's participation in literary culture as it was developing in the latter part of the seventeenth century. The 1670s and 1680s saw the rise of the celebrity actress and an unprecedented number of women writing for the commercial theatre. To overlook or dismiss issues of rivalry or literary conflict among women writing in social literary circles may give us a slightly skewed point of view when we come to consider the issues surrounding women and literary fame or even celebrity in a more general context. Perhaps part of our surprise over Margaret Cavendish's supposedly anomalous repeated announcements in her publications in the 1650s and 1660s that she is writing only for 'fame' and literary glory arises because we have not paid as much attention to issues of women's competition and literary ambition as we have to their strategies for self-protection that deny any desire for fame or attention. Returning to the social milieu of Killigrew and Finch is another way to continue to study literary communities, seeing not only the existence of familial, 'sisterly' support but also the ways in which social authorship practices were used to manage untidy and often impolite impulses of rivalry, competition and ambition.

Notes

1 J. Dryden, 'To the pious memory of the accomplisht young Lady Mrs. Anne Killigrew, excellent in the two sister-arts of poesie, and painting', in *Poems by Mrs Anne Killigrew*, London, 1686, pp. av–b2v. All subsequent references to Killigrew's verse will be taken from this volume.
2 See H. Weinbrot, 'Dryden's "Anne Killigrew": towards a new pindaric political ode', in R. DeMaria (ed.), *British Literature 1640–1789: A Critical Reader*, Blackwell, Oxford, 2008, pp. 114–25, at n. 4.

3 See C. Barash, *English Women's Poetry, 1649–1714: Politics, Community, and Linguistic Authority*, Oxford University Press, Oxford, 1996; and M. J. M. Ezell, 'The post-humous publication of women's manuscripts and the history of authorship', in G. Justice and N. Tinker (eds), *Early Modern Women and the Circulation of Ideas*, Cambridge University Press, Cambridge, 2002, pp. 121–36.

4 J. W. Saunders, 'The stigma of print: a note on the social bases of Tudor poetry', *Essays in Criticism*, vol. 1, no. 2 (1951), pp. 139–64; for challenges to this model see S. May, 'Tudor aristocrats and the mythical "stigma of print"', in *Renaissance Papers* (1980), pp. 11–18, online at www.shakespeareauthorship.com/stigma.html (accessed July 2013).

5 See also P. Hammons, *Gender, Sexuality and Material Objects in English Renaissance Verse*, Ashgate, Aldershot, 2010; and E. Mazzola, *Women's Wealth and Women's Writing in Early Modern England*, Ashgate, Aldershot, 2009.

6 Barash, *English Women's Poetry*, p. 8.

7 K. King, *Jane Barker, Exile: A Literary Career 1675–1725*, Clarendon Press, Oxford, 2000, p. 29.

8 Barash, *English Women's Poetry*, p. 201; King, *Jane Barker*, p. 30.

9 P. Trolander and Z. Tenger, *Sociable Criticism in England 1625–1725*, University of Delaware Press, Newark, 2007, p. 28.

10 Ibid., p. 32.

11 Barash, *English Women's Poetry*, p. 15.

12 D. Mermin, 'Women becoming poets: Katherine Philips, Aphra Behn, Anne Finch', *English Literary History*, vol. 57, no. 2 (1990), p. 335.

13 J. Cox, *Poetry and Politics in the Cockney School*, Cambridge University Press, Cambridge, 2004; J. Wilson, *Court Satires of the Restoration,* Ohio State University Press, Columbus, 1976; and H. Love, *English Clandestine Satire 1660–1702*, Oxford University Press, Oxford, 2004.

14 P. Backscheider, *Eighteenth-Century Women Poets and Their Poetry: Inventing Agency, Inventing Genre*, Johns Hopkins University Press, Baltimore, 2005, p. 392.

15 M. A. O'Farrell, 'Sister acts', *Women's Studies Quarterly*, vol. 34, nos 3–4 (2006), pp. 154–73.

16 Quoted in K. Beutner, 'Writing for pleasure or necessity: conflict among literary women, 1700–1750,' unpublished dissertation, University of Texas, Austin, 2011, pp. 1–2.

17 K. King, 'Eliza Haywood, savage love, and biographical uncertainty', *Review of English Studies*, new series, vol. 59, no. 242 (2007), pp. 722–39.

18 Ibid., p. 739.

19 Beutner, 'Writing for pleasure or necessity', p. 6.

20 King, 'Eliza Haywood', p. 733.

21 See the introduction to my edition of Killigrew's poems for discussion of her possible literary and patronage circles, in M. Ezell (ed.), *Anne Killigrew, 'My Rare Wit Killing Sin': Poems of a Restoration Courtier*, Iter Inc. & Centre for Reformation and Renaissance Studies, Toronto, 2013.

22 D. Hopkins, 'Killigrew, Anne (1660–1685)', in *Oxford Dictionary of National Biography*, Oxford University Press, Oxford, online at www.oxforddnb.com/view/article/15530 (accessed October 2011).

23 B. McGovern, 'Finch, Anne, countess of Winchilsea (1661–1720)', in *Oxford Dictionary of National Biography*, Oxford University Press, Oxford, online at www.oxforddnb.com/view/article/9426 (accessed October 2011).

24 M. Reynolds (ed.), *The Poems of Anne Countess of Winchilsea*, University of Chicago Press, Chicago, 1903, pp. 7–8.

25 Barash, *English Women's Poetry*, p. 162.

26 Ibid., pp. 15, 162.

27 K. Straub, 'Indecent liberties with a poet: audience and the metaphor of rape in

Killigrew's "Upon the saying that my verses" and Pope's Arbuthnot', *Tulsa Studies in Women's Literature*, vol. 6, no. 1 (1987), pp. 27–45, at p. 30.

28 Ibid., pp. 31, 32.
29 Barash, *English Women's Poetry*, pp. 165, 166.
30 *Poems by Mrs Anne Killigrew*, pp. 44–7.
31 Barash, *English Women's Poetry*, p. 163.
32 Folger Shakespeare Library, shelf mark STC 22274, fo. 2, no. 31.
33 *Aesop's Fables* (trans. T. Philipott), 1666, p. 95.
34 Barash, *English Women's Poetry*, p. 164.
35 B. McGovern, *Anne Finch and Her Poetry: A Critical Biography*, University of Georgia Press, Athens, 1992, p. 5.
36 Backscheider, *Eighteenth-Century Women Poets*, pp. 58–9.
37 Barash, *English Women's Poetry,* p. 260.
38 Backscheider, *Eighteenth-Century Women Poets*, p. 396.
39 Barash, *English Women's Poetry*, p. 262.
40 McGovern, *Anne Finch* , pp. 21–2.
41 C. Hinnant, *The Poetry of Anne Finch: An Essay in Interpretation*, University of Delaware Press, Newark, 1994, p. 13; and McGovern, *Anne Finch*, p. 126.
42 Hinnant, *The Poetry of Anne Finch*, p. 14.
43 J. Keith, *Poetry and the Feminine from Behn to Cowper*, University of Delaware Press, Newark, 2005, p. 183 n. 40.
44 Reynolds (ed.), *The Poems of Anne Countess of Winchilsea*, pp. 92–4.

Part III: Narrative

CHAPTER 9

Rethinking authorial reluctance in the paratexts to Anne Bradstreet's poetry

Patricia Pender

ANNE Bradstreet's professions of inadequacy in much-anthologised poems such as 'The author to her book' and 'The prologue' make her exemplary of the modesty we have come to expect of early modern women writers. Her renditions of abject humility before literary tradition, her apparent objection to putting herself forward in print and her professed inability to complete the poetic projects she undertook have all helped to enshrine her as the quintessential woman writer who would not, or could not, call herself a poet.[1] This chapter reconsiders Bradstreet's now famous pronouncements of authorial reluctance in her two seventeenth-century printed publications: *The Tenth Muse Lately Sprung Up in America*, published ostensibly without her consent in London in 1650, and *Several Poems*, published six years after her death, but with material that she had clearly designed for publication, in Boston in 1678. If Bradstreet has traditionally been considered a prime example of the humble, submissive and self-effacing woman poet, this is partly due, I suggest, to overly literal readings of her modesty rhetoric and of the paratexts that accompanied her poetry into print. Reading these paratexts anew, and considering Bradstreet's modesty tropes as strategies of self-authorisation rather than heartfelt pronouncements of inadequacy, reveals instead a seventeenth-century female poet who was well versed in the specific literary traditions she selected to enter, effective in negotiating contemporary discourses of authorship and confident of her own claims to poetic skill and substance.

Studies of the transmission of early modern women's poetry can tell us much about the ways in which women's texts were produced in their specific literary-historical milieu and the ways in which they circulated as objects of textual exchange. Focusing on Bradstreet's two seventeenth-century publications, this chapter considers examples of the paratextual apparatus – the dedicatory epistles, commendatory verses and prefatory poems – that accompanied her entry into the public arena of print. Both the 1650 *Tenth Muse* and the 1678 *Several Poems* contain an elaborate rhetorical scaffolding that provides valuable clues about the ways in which women's poetry was imagined, promoted, denigrated and defended in its immediate historical context. The 1650 *Tenth Muse*, for instance, contains a number prefatory materials assembled to establish Bradstreet's credentials in various social, political and literary networks. An epistle to the 'Kind reader' by Bradstreet's brother-in-law, John Woodbridge, is followed by a poetic tribute signed by 'N. Ward' and Woodbridge's dedicatory poem, 'To my dear sister, the author of these poems'. These are followed by a commendatory poem, 'Upon the author, by a knowne friend', a four-line tribute signed with the initials 'C.B.', an untitled poetic tribute and a poem signed by 'N.H.' and entitled 'In praise of the Author, Mistris *Anne Bradstreet*, Vertue's true and lively Patterne, Wife of the Worshipful *Simon Bradstreet* Esquire'. There are then two more poetic tributes, 'Upon the author' and 'Another to Mris *Anne Bradstreete*, author of this poem', followed by two anagrams on Bradstreet's name ('Deer Neat *An Bartas*' and 'Artes bred neat *An*'). Anne Bradstreet's own dedication, 'To her most Honoured Father *Thomas Dudley* Esq; *these humbly presented*', is followed by 'The prologue'.[2] The 1678 *Several Poems*, printed in Boston by John Foster, largely replicates the prefatory apparatus from *The Tenth Muse*, but omits one commendatory poem and includes two new elegies, by John Norton and John Rogers, each of whom has been considered a plausible editor of this volume.[3] In the 1678 *Several Poems*, 'The author to her book' is placed after poems included in the 1650 *Tenth Muse* and precedes 'Several other Poems made by the Author upon diverse occasions' which were 'found among her Papers after her Death' and printed posthumously in 1678.[4]

Taken together, the paratexts to Bradstreet's 1650 and 1678 printed editions are complex and contradictory. The image of the poet that is offered by the commendatory verse assembled to introduce *The Tenth Muse*, for instance, is at odds with Bradstreet's own self-representation in the same volume. Her contemporary male supporters present her as reticent, reluctant and preternaturally gifted. She presents herself as truculent, determined and studied rather than sublime. Bradstreet certainly traffics in modesty rhetoric, yet she mobilises discourses of feminine inadequacy and anomaly with paradoxical ease and agility. This facility suggests not, as tradition has it, that she was cowed by a potentially hostile patriarchal culture, but that she knew her well read way around a literary disavowal. Sir Philip Sidney, Guillaume Du Bartas and, most ambitiously, Virgil were her chosen literary models in this respect. She was undoubtedly familiar with the modesty tropes of classical and contemporary literature. As Eileen Margerum contends:

Both the classical tradition of public poetry, which she learned reading the works of her predecessors, and the Puritan narrative tradition contain formulae for humility which writers were obliged to include in their works, regardless of personal feelings.[5]

Conventional modesty formulae are part of a literary lexicon that Bradstreet inherits, portions of which she selects to replicate in her own negotiations with literary tradition.

The critical tradition that sees Bradstreet as reluctant to print her poetry draws evidence primarily from material included in the printed books themselves, particularly from Bradstreet's poem 'The author to her book', first published in the second edition of her poems in 1678, and from the dedicatory letter and poem with which John Woodbridge introduced the first, unauthorised volume of her poems in 1650. Together, the persuasive rhetoric of these texts has produced a picture of Bradstreet as traumatised by seeing her own work in print. As the sentiments she and Woodbridge appear to express conform closely to the way we imagine an early modern woman writer might be expected to feel about printed publication in the period, the case for Bradstreet's authorial reluctance, promoted most effectively, it must be acknowledged, by herself, has seemed strong. It is significant, however, that there is little extra-textual evidence to support this assumption, and the textual evidence that does exist is not as transparent as it seems. This chapter focuses on Bradstreet's 'The author to her book' and Woodbridge's epistle to the 'Kind reader' as paratexts that can help us clarify, and distinguish between, attitudes towards manuscript circulation and printed publication that were presented by both Bradstreet herself and her public promoters.

In approaching 'The author to her book' from the perspective of authorial reluctance, the first thing we can note is that it is not, as it is so frequently represented, the apology for a work appearing in print: it is instead an apology for a previous work appearing in a badly produced printed edition. More specifically, it is an apology for what Bradstreet presents as the printing errors of the 1650 edition of *The Tenth Muse*, and is clearly designed to introduce a new, revised volume of poems that will better represent the poet's vision of her work to future audiences. The fact that her death preceded the publication of *Several Poems* by six years was of course out of the poet's control, but the poem that she crafted to introduce a future edition of her work needs to be considered as much for its negotiation with the conventions of the envoi – a genre in which the author addresses the book and its audience – as for the light it sheds on early modern women's poetic self-fashioning. In this context, Bradstreet's 'The author to her book' bears comparison to the envoi poems of the classical and contemporary poets she most admires, as a meta-textual meditation on the poet's creative practice.[6]

The poem begins with an apostrophe to the personified book, 'Thou ill-formed offspring of my feeble brain', and thus mobilises from the outset tropes of modesty – of deformity and incapacity – that strike a decidedly gendered note to modern readers.[7] The trope of parthenogenesis, of the text as child, also seems particularly apposite for a poet recognised today as the 'granddame' of American letters, and whose own oeuvre displays an abiding interest in themes of motherhood and maternity.[8] Yet the same trope that appears most firmly to gender Bradstreet's modesty rhetoric as traditionally feminine works in a different way to announce her literary credentials in a decidedly unapologetic fashion. Bradstreet's 'The author to her book' alludes in its first line to the famous sonnet sequence of the previous century's chief Protestant poet, Sir Philip Sidney's *Astrophil and Stella*. In this, one of the more wittily self-conscious envoi poems of the period, Sidney describes the painful labour he experienced attempting 'to paint the blackest face of woe' that results from his tortured love for Stella.[9] Sidney invokes the rhetoric of modesty in describing his travails 'in fain in verse my love to show' (line 1):

> But words came halting forth, wanting invention's stay;
> Invention, nature's child, fled step-dame study's blows;
> And others' feet still seemed but strangers in my way.
> (lines 9–11)

In the hyperbolic language of this sonnet, Sidney's desire to write meta-phorically impregnates him; the poet presents himself as 'great with child to speak, and helpless in [his] throes' (line 12).

In echoing Sidney's modesty rhetoric and reworking the trope of parthenogenesis that Sidney had used to great effect in *Astrophil and Stella*, Bradstreet positions herself and her new volume of poetry within an established, even revered, literary lineage, a position which her early elegy to Sidney had attempted to secure in a more straightforward, familial fashion.[10] Catharine Gray makes the important argument that Bradstreet's belated 'Elizabethan nostalgia' was actually 'part of a consistent poetic project':[11]

> Interweaving a public genealogy of neo-Elizabethan pan-Protestantism with private bloodlines, the poems of both Bradstreet and her male interlocutors figure her as a corrective addition to an Old World tradition of poetry and politics. In doing so, they position her at the center of a transnational counter-public of renewed critique and expansionism – one that exceeds the neat borders of geography and history.[12]

In claiming kinship with Sidney, whether through lineage or literature, Bradstreet 'imagine[s] a ghostly coterie in which ties of blood and ideology ultimately mix'.[13] She also speaks to Protestants transnationally, in an idiom they could both recognise and appreciate.

In 'The author to her book', Bradstreet claims that the work was 'snatched by friends less wise than true', who then 'exposed it to public view' (lines 3–4):

> And thee in rags, halting to th' press to trudge,
> Where errors were not lessened (all may judge).
> (lines 6–7)

The real crime, as Bradstreet presents it here, is not the actual act of publication but rather its botched execution. Bradstreet claims that printing has compounded the original errors of her manuscript, a fact that she expects her readers to be able to 'judge' – presumably through a comparison of both texts. This hardly seems the statement of a woman who was shy of publication or who wished to deny ownership of her works in print. It reads rather as a public articulation of her dissatisfaction with the 1650 *Tenth Muse*, and the confident presumption that those are interested in her work will be able to testify to the superiority of the new edition.

Like Sidney's before her, Bradstreet's envoi poem emphasises the struggle entailed in producing poetry – a strategy which seems to reinforce her claims of ineptitude but which succeeds in simultaneously foregrounding her determination and perseverance. The poem as a whole is minutely concerned with the processes of emendation and the challenges of creative practice. While lightly comic in tone, Bradstreet recalls her painstaking work of revision:

> I washed thy face, but more defects I saw
> And rubbing off a spot still made a flaw.
> (lines 14–15)

In doing so, she disparages her mistakes, but she also points out her credentials as a poetic practitioner and draws attention to her editorial work as literary labour:

> I stretched thy joints to make thee even feet,
> Yet still thou run'st more hobbling than is meet;
> (lines 16–17)

Apology for the quality of the work that is to follow is a common feature of early modern envoi poems, many of which mobilise the gentle self-mockery that is a feature of Bradstreet's poem. The deftness of Bradstreet's deployment of conventional modesty rhetoric, however, is lost if we read these lines as a genuine declaration of inadequacy. What Bradstreet demonstrates in these lines is that she is familiar with established poetic practice: she knows her craft and has worked at it. While the results are still not up to her standards, she implies, this has less to do with any constitutive incapacity on her part than the fact that her standards are particularly high – as high as Sidney's, in fact. Bradstreet is not only establishing herself as a competent practitioner in this poem but is also establishing her credentials as a knowledgeable reader and cultural critic.

For instance, when she writes of her poem 'In better dress to trim thee was my mind / But nought save homespun cloth i' th' house I find' (lines 19–20) she again employs a seemingly self-effacing gendered comparison: her poetry is homely, humble and distinctly domestic, as opposed to fine, fancy and fashionable. Yet such comparisons themselves have a long, illustrious literary history, going back to the use of *sermo humilis*, or the humble style, in the Bible.[14] This was a rhetorical style that, whether Bradstreet knew it or not, had been used effectively by women writers before her, such as Katherine Parr, Mary Sidney Herbert and Aemilia Lanyer. The modesty trope of simple humility triumphing over literary ostentation was one that earlier women writers in English had found particularly efficacious.[15] In Bradstreet's hands, this trope presents her poetry, rather disingenuously, as unadorned and makeshift, yet it also imbues her work with an independence and dignity that she is clearly proud of. It is likely that, to her contemporary readers, Bradstreet's claims of simplicity carried a 'New World' Puritan inflection as well. 'Homespun', in the right hands, carries the resonance of rebuke, showing up the superficiality and decadence of unnecessary adornment in a way that mirrored the reformed infant colony's defiant relationship with the corrupt mother country.[16] Proclaiming the modesty of her poetic offering in these lines, Bradstreet is also appealing to the moral and literary predilections of her religious milieu, in both Old England and New.[17]

The final sestet of the poem pursues this question of audience and conjectures about the afterlife of the work, an ambitious projection on the poet's part, but one that is in keeping with the genre of the envoi. Bradstreet suggests that their 'homespun' nature will allow her poems to venture into less travelled paths:

> In this array 'mongst vulgars may'st thou roam.
> In critic's hands beware thou dost not come,
> And take thy way where yet thou art not known;
> (lines 21–3)

Again, the surface logic of the modesty rhetoric employed here contains a more ambitious, even arch, subtext. Bradstreet seems to be suggesting that her homely poems deserve only a 'vulgar' audience and should 'beware' the judgement of critics. In suggesting that her poems should 'take [their] way where yet [they] art not known' she appears to disparage the idea of a continuing readership for her poetry, and to predict an audience that is obscure and, by extension, unvalued. But the familiar, even clichéd, moves of modesty discourse provide Bradstreet with the opportunity to defend her creative practice even as she seems to denigrate it. The alternative audience she projects is not necessarily an undesirable audience; it is merely a new, and possibly untried, audience. *The Tenth Muse* was, after all, the first collection of poetry by a New England poet to be published in the early modern period. If the 'vulgars' among whom her book will 'roam' include the poet's own 'homespun' local community, such an audience can seem not unvalued but rather, and more contentiously, *undervalued* by established literary standards. Securing such an audience in this context is not the literary failure it initially appears, but is more a poetic coup. Indeed, the subtext in this instance suggests that the failure of established poets – and poet-makers – to appreciate new communities of readers is in fact a shortcoming.

To be sure, Bradstreet also cautions her book to avoid critics, suggesting that she expects her poetry to fare badly at their hands. Following the implication of the previous lines, however, this is not necessarily because she doubts her own worth. It is equally possible that she doubts whether such critics are appropriately qualified to appreciate her worth. If we view Bradstreet's modesty about her poetry as nothing more than an appropriate and expected gendered response, we risk failing to appreciate her unusually critical stance towards the literary attitudes of her time. As late modern critics, we might expect this seventeenth-century woman poet to express humility and self-abnegation before a hostile critical literary tradition – as previous poets such as Aemilia Lanyer seem to do – and we have certainly found evidence to support this view. But Bradstreet is decidedly less abject in her relations with those who would judge her than we might expect. In several of her poems, she is scathing about contemporary tastes, and her references to critics in this poem warrant consideration in the broader context of her treatment of literary criticism as a whole. In her elegy to Sidney, for instance, she deems critics 'infatuate fools', 'men of morose minds' and 'beetle head[s]'[18] and in 'The prologue' she famously announces:

> I am obnoxious to each carping tongue
> Who says my hand a needle better fits,
> [...]
> If what I do prove well, it won't advance,
> They'll say it's stol'n, or else it was by chance.[19]

In the penultimate couplet of 'The author to her book', Bradstreet makes the unusual claim that the body of work this poem introduces has no father: 'If for thy father asked, say thou hadst none' (line 23). This claim is surprising given that *The Tenth Muse*, as published in 1650, was dedicated to Bradstreet's father, with the poem 'To her most Honoured Father *Thomas Dudley* Esq; *these humbly presented*'. Although this dedication remains in the 1678 edition of *Several Poems*, and is augmented by the elegy 'To the memory of Thomas Dudley, Esq.', in 'The author to her book' Bradstreet appears to shake off her male literary models quite explicitly. As Margerum has suggested, 'When she bids the "child" to acknowledge no father as it goes forth again, she is abandoning the role of junior poet and declaring herself free of the protection and influence of Du Bartas, of Sidney, and of her father'.[20] Far from being an unschooled and unself-conscious acknowledgement of unworthiness, then, 'The author to her book' is an extremely canny and careful negotiation with the conventions of the envoi genre.

Bradstreet's bids for authority and autonomy in 'The author to her book' – her claims that she is the sole author of her poems and that they have no father – acquire a heightened significance when we understand the extensive roles that a network of male figures played in the publication of the *Tenth Muse* in 1650. Bradstreet had apparently presented a manuscript of her poems to her father sometime in the mid-1640s, with the dedicatory poem, 'To her most Honoured Father *Thomas Dudley* Esq; *these humbly presented*'. It is a more developed version of this manuscript that Bradstreet's brother-in-law John Woodbridge presumably took to London when he travelled there in 1647. *The Tenth Muse* was printed by Stephen Bowtell at Bishop's Lane, London, and was compiled by John Woodbridge, possibly with the assistance of his younger brother, Benjamin Woodbridge, who was living in Salisbury, Wiltshire.[21]

John Woodbridge came from a ministerial family and arrived in New England in 1634 after studying at Oxford. He married Bradstreet's sister, Mercy Dudley, and became the first minister of Andover from 1645 to 1648. Woodbridge provided the epistle to the 'Kind reader' for *The Tenth Muse* and also the commendatory poem 'To my dear sister, author of these poems'. Benjamin Woodbridge had also travelled to New England in 1634 but returned to Oxford after completing his studies at Harvard in 1642. He is the author of the commendatory poem 'Upon the author, by a known friend', initialed B.W. in *Several Poems* but unidentified in *The Tenth Muse*.[22] Stephen Bowtell, a London bookseller known for his political publications, was probably recommended to Woodbridge by Nathaniel Ward, author of the second commendatory verse in *The Tenth Muse*, 'Mercury showed Apollo Bartas' book', and a family friend who knew the

Bradstreets well when they were his parishioners at Ipswich between 1634 and 1637.[23] Bowtell had published Ward's bestseller, *The Simple Cobler of Aggawam in America*, in London in 1647.[24] Kathryn Zabelle Derounian-Stodola suggests that Mercy Woodbridge also wrote a poem commending her sister's poetry, 'though it presumably circulated only privately' and is no longer extant.[25] All the paratexts that ultimately ushered Bradstreet's *Tenth Muse* into print in 1650, however, were written by Bradstreet's male relatives and their acquaintances – associates that Susan Wiseman describes as 'politically and spiritually linked, and geographically, both close, even local, yet also Atlantic'.[26]

John Woodbridge's epistle to the 'Kind reader', the first of the paratexts in both the 1650 *Tenth Muse* and the 1678 *Several Poems*, is a somewhat confusing text, even by the convoluted standards of seventeenth-century prefatory rhetoric. Woodbridge manages both to invoke and to subvert the generic conventions of the dedicatory epistle. If he possessed the wit of the author, Woodbridge writes, he would pen such a preface as would persuade the reader to peruse the volume.[27] He refuses this opportunity, he claims, because his lack of literary ability would lead the reader to believe that 'it is the gift of women not only to speak most but to speak best'. He fears it will be a 'shame, for a man who can speak so little, to appear in the title page to this woman's book' and rejects the task of recommendation, lest 'men turn more peevish than women, to envy the excellency of the inferior sex'. His solution to this dilemma is to leave all responsibility in the hands of the reader:

> I doubt not but the reader will quickly find more than I can say, and the worst effect of his reading will be unbelief, which will make him question whether it be a woman's work, and ask, is it possible.

Surprise, even stupefaction about the quality of the literary work being introduced is a commonplace of dedicatory rhetoric. But Woodbridge must deal additionally with the novelty of female authorship and the potential scandal of its printed publication. In preemptive response, Woodbridge provides his personal testimony not of Bradstreet's literary credentials, but of her diligence in fulfilling a more common understanding of the phrase 'women's work' – one that relates to her roles within the home and family. He writes:

> take this as an answer from him that dares avow it: it is the work of a woman, honoured, and esteemed where she lives, for her gracious demeanour, her eminent parts, her pious conversation, her courteous disposition, her exact diligence in her place, and her discrete managing of her family occasions, and more than so, these poems are the fruit but of some few hours, curtailed from her sleep and other refreshments.

At the end of this paean to appropriate womanhood, Woodbridge employs the classical modesty trope of nocturnal studies – a figure which presents the literary work as a sideline to the author's more pressing concerns and that serves to emphasise the effortlessness of composition as well as the author's nonchalant lack of investment in the resulting literary product. In chapter 8, Margaret Ezell considers Dryden's similar description of the 'untutored' verse of Anne Killigrew: 'Art she had none, yet wanted none'. A variant of this trope is also used by Sidney in *The Defense of Poesy*, when he refers to his career as a poet as his 'unelected vocation'.[28] Following the popularity of Baldassare Castiglione's *Il Libro del Cortegiano* (1528), this was a rhetorical strategy that early modern English writers would adopt under the rubric of *sprezzatura* – the display of effort so that it appears effortless.[29] However, Woodbridge's use of the nocturnal studies trope is not necessarily designed to suggest Bradstreet's *sprezzatura*; indeed, it seems distinctly literal. Given the context of his comment, it is likely that he is attempting to forestall possible criticism of the author for neglecting her traditional roles as wife and mother. Woodbridge's representation of Bradstreet's literary efforts as effortless nevertheless contrasts strongly with her own later representation of that work, in 'The author to her book', as determined literary labour.

Woodbridge then discloses that he has published Bradstreet's poems without her permission. At the conclusion to this epistle he writes:

> I fear the displeasure of no person in the publishing of these poems but the author, without whose knowledge, and contrary to her expectation, I have presumed to bring to public view, what she resolved should (in such a manner) never see the sun.

Woodbridge acknowledges that he has left himself open to the author's displeasure in publishing her poems without her consent. He describes this action as a presumption on his part that defies her 'expectation': Bradstreet was not expecting her brother-in-law to publish her poems; she had perhaps even voiced the expectation that no one would do so without her authorisation. But what is most significant in this narration is contained in parentheses: Woodbridge does not claim that Bradstreet had resolved that her poems should 'never see the sun', but merely that they should not see the sun 'in such a manner'. He presents Bradstreet not as averse to seeing her poems in print but, more precisely, to seeing them printed from the current state of her manuscripts. The enduring influence of what W. J. Saunders has described as the 'stigma of print', and more recent assumptions that women must have felt this stigma particularly, has meant that we have paid only selective attention to the terms of Woodbridge's actual claim – and indeed of Bradstreet's counter-claims in

'The author to her book'. In her 2009 monograph on the 'literary politics' of Anne Bradstreet and Phillis Wheatley, for instance, Kathryn Seidler Engberg states: 'The stigma of print made writing difficult for both male and female writers, although the vulgarity associated with print culture was particularly cruel to women writers who wanted to keep their modesty intact, which was important if one were to succeed socially'.[30] As we have seen, closer reading of Bradstreet's paratexts reveals that she does not apologise for her work appearing in print; she apologises for the corrupt state of her work in print. Similarly, Woodbridge courts his sister-in-law's displeasure, not for printing her work *per se*, but for printing it 'in such a manner', that is, in its current unauthorised state.

Woodbridge goes on to explain his reasons for publishing Bradstreet's poems without her authorisation:

> but I found that divers had gotten some scattered papers, affected them well, were likely to have sent forth broken pieces, to the author's prejudice, which I thought to prevent, as well as to pleasure those that earnestly desired the view of the whole.

Woodbridge refers here to the threat of literary piracy – what Ezell calls one of the more 'peculiar institutions of authorship' in the seventeenth century.[31] As Ezell points out, the term 'piracy' refers historically to the period after copyright had been consolidated, and its use to refer to un-authorised publication in the mid-seventeenth century is anachronistic in this strict sense. Nevertheless, the concept of a text published without the author's permission was undoubtedly familiar to early modern audiences. Woodbridge suggests that multiple or 'divers' readers had gained access to some of Bradstreet's poems and were likely to have these published 'to the author's prejudice'. By his own testimony, Woodbridge counters the threat of this unauthorised publication with his own unauthorised publication of Bradstreet's poems. As Ezell suggests, such situations reveal 'the negative aspects of print technology – imperfect, incorrect copy that does not involve the author – and simultaneously place it as the only remedy to the print-created problem'. Ironically, 'the author's involvement in yet another print production is the only way in which corrupt texts can be rescued from the literary pirates' (p. 48).

In Ezell's astute analysis, 'the subsequent preparation of an authorized text – literally a text prepared by the author for print – is thus the result of a desire to kill or nullify the pirated edition' (p. 47). She writes:

> Paradoxically, for the poet in particular to have his or her works printed seems to have been a matter of first creating through print a corrupt text and then rescuing it with a second 'authorized' print version that attempts to replicate the original scribal text. (p. 59)

While Ezell suggests that the subsequent text is not necessarily the result of 'the author's desire to bring to life a script text or to bring acclaim to his or her life as an author, or to find an audience' (p. 47), the preceding examination reveals that at least some of these sentiments seem to have animated Bradstreet in composing 'The author to her book'.

An instructive parallel to Bradstreet's publication history in this instance is provided by her near contemporary Katherine Philips, 'The Matchless Orinda'. On first recovering Philips as a significant seventeenth-century woman poet, scholars generally accepted her claims of violent shock and dismay at the unauthorised publication of her poems in 1664. Like Bradstreet, Philips's response to the piracy of her manuscripts is recorded in a preface to the second, posthumous publication of her *Poems*, in 1667. As with Bradstreet, however, the emotions Philips expresses in this preface need not be read as symptomatic of her reaction to the publication her work in general. As her 1997 editors note, for instance, a year previously Philips had permitted Roger Boyle, Earl of Orrery, to produce her translation of Corneille's *La Mort de Pompee* for the Dublin stage and to publish it in print in April of the same year. Philips's poetry also circulated widely in manuscript, both among her literary coterie and at court. Her response to the unauthorised publication of her poems in 1664 is thus more likely to have been prompted by the personal nature of the poems themselves, or by the volume's mistakes of transcription, that by exposure to print *per se*. Philips recalled the pirated edition in 1664 and went to London to oversee the publication of an authorised edition of her poems. While she died before she could complete this task, the 'authorised' posthumous edition of her poems was printed in 1667, probably with the assistance of her friend and mentor Sir Charles Cotterell.[32]

Bradstreet certainly did not rush to produce a corrected edition following the publication of *The Tenth Muse* in 1650, but she did continue to write and to revise her poems for over a decade and some of these clearly have a public audience in mind. This is true even of some poems printed in the first edition. Adelaide Amore has argued that, despite the extensive modesty rhetoric of the 1650 edition, her poem 'The prologue', which is included in both editions, is 'not the words of a humble, defenseless woman as some critics suggest. The entire prologue is meant to serve as an introduction to a book of verses; it is an appeal, both clear and traditional, by the author for a proper audience for her poetry.'[33] It is also significant that, unlike Philips, Bradstreet did not recall the first edition of her poems. As examined here, 'The author to her book' – a poem designed to introduce a revised, authorised volume of her poems – is clearly directed at publication and, as we have seen, relies for some of its rhetorical impact on readers being able to recognise the existence of a first edition. For Bradstreet's revised poems to travel "monsgt vulgars' and even before critics, they must indeed 'take [their] way where yet [they] art not known' – beyond the confines of their manuscript circulation. Presumably, Bradstreet's coterie audience would have little need to question who the 'mother' of the manuscript was, even if identification of the 'father' was less clear. As an envoi that derides an earlier print edition in favour of the current, still imperfect but much improved format, Bradstreet's 'Author to her book' bids her poetry 'roam' beyond the already extensive readership of the 1650 *Tenth Muse*, to audiences where her work is not yet known.

William London's *Catalogue of the Most Vendible Books in England*, printed in London in 1658, lists Bradstreet's *Tenth Muse* alongside her revered Du Bartas, 'Mr. Milton's poems' and 'Mr. Shaksper's poems'.[34] Only eight years after its unauthorised publication, then, Bradstreet's poetry had not only found favour in London, but was also being touted by early bibliographers for its popularity. It is possible that such evidence of her fame would not have been immediately accessible to Anne Bradstreet, at home in New England. It is likely, however, that the transnational coterie of family members and acquaintances who had ushered Bradstreet's work into print would have monitored *The Tenth Muse*'s fortunes and kept her family abreast of its progress. When in 'The author to her book' Bradstreet later assumes a new readership for her poetry that extends beyond that already garnered by *The Tenth Muse*, she is, despite her modesty rhetoric, imagining a significant audience indeed.

Bradstreet's claims of authorial reluctance can, in this context, be recognised as the knowing manipulation of the figure of the reluctant author and as strategic negotiations with the conventions of seventeenth-century printed publication, particularly the conventions of poetic paratexts. The paratexts that accompanied Bradstreet's poetry into print, first in 1650 and again in 1678 (and they are more extensive than the two examples considered here), provide us with new vantage points from which to assess her involvement and agency in the production and circulation of her poetic reputation. The fact that Bradstreet's poetry has yet to be reproduced in a modern critical edition that preserves its seventeenth-century paratexts has tended to blur distinctions between her two early modern printed publications, resulting in an overall flattening of her attitudes towards her work and its imagined audiences.[35] Our understanding of early modern women's attitudes towards printed publication, and their idiosyncratic engagements with literary tradition, stands to benefit from a more fully fleshed out Bradstreet, not one who is limited to the ingénue dilettante celebrated in the paratexts written by *The Tenth Muse*'s supporters. Bradstreet was, after all, a poet who wrote for the majority of her long life. A more historical understanding of her seventeenth-century editions will allow us to temper the image of the sensational 'New World' anomaly lauded in her supporters' paratexts with the image of the determined poetic practitioner, labouring at her craft, that she presents in her own.

Notes

1 Bradstreet expresses concern about finishing her poems on a number of occasions. The poem 'After some days rest' marks a gap between her completion of the first three of her *Four Monarchies* and the truncated final poem. 'An apology', appended to the fourth, Roman, monarchy, presents her inability to complete the poem due to ill-health, weariness and the fire that consumed her manuscript. Similarly, in her elegy 'In honour of Du Bartas', Bradstreet claims that she gave up writing the poems before she had even started: 'Knowing the task so great, and strength but small', she 'Gave o'er the work before begun withal' (lines 6–7). See J. Hensley (ed.), *The Works of Anne Bradstreet*, Harvard University Press, Cambridge, 1967, pp. 173, 177, 192. Such professions of reluctance within poems can be subjected to the same rhetorical analysis that this chapter provides for Bradstreet's paratexts. Susan Wiseman has considered expressions of authorial hesitation in *The Four Monarchies* as part of Bradstreet's response to contemporary political developments. See S. Wiseman, *Conspiracy and Virtue: Women, Writing and Politics in Seventeenth-Century England*, Oxford University Press, Oxford, 2006, pp. 188–99. On the work of conclusion – of completing a poem – in Bradstreet's poetry, see P. Kopacz, '"To finish what's begun": Anne Bradstreet's last words', *Early American Literature*, vol. 23 (1988), pp. 175–87.

2 The format of the 1650 *Tenth Muse* is reproduced in J. K. Piercy (ed.), *The Tenth Muse (1650) and, from the Manuscripts: Meditations Divine and Morall, Together with Letters and Occasional Pieces by Anne Bradstreet*, Scholars Facsimiles and Reprints, Gainesville, 1965. Work which considers the identity of Bradstreet's various dedicatees includes K. Z. Derounian-Stodola, '"The excellency of the inferior sex": the commendatory writings on Anne Bradstreet', *Studies in Puritan Spirituality*, vol. 1 (December 1990), pp. 129–47; C. Gray, *Women Writers and Public Debate in Seventeenth-Century Britain*, Palgrave, Basingstoke, 2007, pp. 143–81; and Wiseman, *Conspiracy and Virtue*, pp. 179–233.

3 For consideration of this question, see J. Hensley, 'The editor of Anne Bradstreet's *Several Poems*', *American Literature: A Journal of Literary History, Criticism, and Bibliography*, vol. 35 (1964), pp. 502–4; and J. Hensley, 'Anne Bradstreet's wreath of thyme', in *The Works of Anne Bradstreet*, pp. xxiii–xxiv.

4 Title page and editor's note from *Several Poems*, Boston, 1678.

5 E. Margerum, 'Anne Bradstreet's public poetry and the tradition of humility', *Early American Literature*, vol. 17, no. 2 (autumn 1982), pp. 152–60, at p. 152.

6 Among her acknowledged sources, Sir Walter Raleigh's *History of the World*, Joshua Sylvester's *Divine Weekes and Works* and the poetry of Sir Philip Sidney (discussed below) offer important precedents for Bradstreet's modesty rhetoric. See Margerum, 'Anne Bradstreet's public poetry'.

7 Bradstreet, 'The author to her book', in Hensley (ed.), *The Works of Anne Bradstreet*, p. 221. Further references to this poem will be cited by line number in the body of the chapter.

8 See, for instance, Bradstreet's poems to her children and husband in *Several Poems*. Adrienne Rich's 'Postscript' to her foreword, 'Anne Bradstreet and her poetry', included in the Harvard *Works of Anne Bradstreet*, reveals what Rich identified as the basis for her empathy for Bradstreet: 'she was one of the few women writers I knew anything about who had also been a mother' (pp. xx–xxi). Two of the more

recent contributions to scholarship on motherhood and maternity in Bradstreet's poetry are R. Hilliker, "'Engendering identity: the discourse of familial education in Anne Bradstreet and Marie de l'Incarnation'", *Early American Literature*, vol. 42, no. 3 (2007), pp. 435–70; and J. M. Lutes, 'Negotiating theology and gynecolgy: Anne Bradstreet's representations of the female body', *Signs* (winter 1997), pp. 309–40.

9   Sir Philip Sidney, 'Loving in truth, and fain in verse my love to show', sonnet 1 in *Astrophil and Stella*, in K. Duncan-Jones (ed.), *Sir Philip Sidney: A Critical Edition of the Major Works*, Oxford University Press, Oxford, 1989, p. 153. Further references to this poem will be cited by line number in the body of the chapter.

10 In the 1650 version of her elegy to Sidney, Bradstreet claims a family connection to her poetic hero. In the revised version of this elegy in 1678, this claim is omitted.

11 Gray, *Women Writers*, pp. 144, 143.

12 Ibid., p. 145.

13 Ibid.

14 On *sermo humilis* see E. Auerbach, *Literary Language and Its Public in Late Latin Antiquity and in the Middle Ages* (trans. R. Mannheim), Routledge and Kegan Paul, London, 1965; and P. Auksi, *Christian Plain Style: The Evolution of a Spiritual Ideal*, McGill, Queen's University Press, Montreal, 1995.

15 On the use of *sermo humilis* by these authors, see chapters on Parr, Sidney and Lanyer in P. Pender, *Early Modern Women's Writing and the Rhetoric of Modesty*, Palgrave Macmillan, New York, 2012.

16 This relationship is further explored in Bradstreet's poem 'A dialogue between Old England and New'. See Wiseman, *Conspiracy and Virtue*; Gray, *Women Writers*; K. Gillespie, "'This briny ocean will o'erflow your shore": Anne Bradstreet's "Second World" Atlanticism and national narratives of literary history', *Symbiosis: A Journal of Anglo-American Literary Relations*, vol. 3, no. 2 (1999), pp. 99–118; and P. Pender, 'Disciplining the imperial mother: Anne Bradstreet's *A Dialogue Between Old England and New*', in J. Wallwork and P. Salzman (eds), *Women's Writing, 1550–1750*, Meridian, Melbourne, 2001, pp. 115–31.

17 Wiseman suggests that 'the fifth monarchist inflection of Bradstreet's poetry and the political impetus of its millenarianism was welcome, indeed apparently familiar and acceptable, within [these] circles'. Wiseman, *Conspiracy and Virtue*, p. 205.

18 'An elegy upon that honourable and renowned knight Sir Philip Sidney, who was untimely slain at the siege of Zutphen, Anno 1586', in Hensley (ed.), *The Works of Anne Bradstreet*, pp. 26, 29–30.

19 'The prologue', in Hensley (ed.), *The Works of Anne Bradstreet*, p. 16, lines 27–32.

20 Margerum, 'Anne Bradstreet's public poetry', p. 158.

21 Derounian-Stodola, 'The excellency of the inferior sex', p. 134.

22 Ibid.

23 Ibid., p. 135.

24 [Nathaniel Ward] Theodore de la Guard (pseudonym), *The Simple Cobler of Aggawam in America*, London, 1647.

25 Derounian-Stodola, 'The excellency of the inferior sex', p. 134.

26 Wiseman, *Conspiracy and Virtue*, p. 202.

27 J. Woodbridge, 'Kind reader', in Hensley (ed.), *The Works of Anne Bradstreet*, p. 3. Further references to the epistle refer to this edition.

28 Sir Philip Sidney, *The Defense of Poesy*, in Duncan-Jones (ed.), *Sir Philip Sidney*, p. 212.

29 Baldesar Castiglione, *Il Libro del Cortegiano*, Venice, 1528.

30 K. Seidler Engberg, *The Right to Write: The Literary Politics of Anne Bradstreet and Phillis Wheatley*, University Press of America, Lanham, 2009, p. xxi. See also J. W. Saunders, 'The stigma of print: a note on the social bases of Tudor poetry', *Essays in Criticism*, vol. 1 (1951), pp. 139–64; and W. Wall, *The Imprint of Gender: Authorship and Publication in the English Renaissance*, Cornell University Press, Ithaca, 1993.

31 M. J. M. Ezell, *Social Authorship and the Advent of Print*, Johns Hopkins University

Press, Baltimore, 1999, pp. 45–60. Further references to this work will be cited by page number in the body of the chapter.

32 See J. Mitzmaurice, J. A. Roberts, C. L. Barash, E. E. Cunnar and N. A. Gutierrez (eds), *Major Women Writers of the Seventeenth Century*, Michigan University Press, Ann Arbor, 1997, pp. 177–80.

33 Adelaide P. Amore, *A Woman's Inner World: Selected Prose and Poetry of Anne Bradstreet*, University Press of America, Lanham, 1982, pp. xxv–xxvi.

34 J. Kester Svensen, 'Anne Bradstreet in England: a bibliographical note', *American Literature*, vol. 13 (1941), pp. 63–5.

35 Joseph R. McElrath Jr and Allan P. Robb's 1981 edition, *The Complete Works of Anne Bradstreet*, for instance, removes the paratexts to an appendix of 'Commendatory writings' and conflates paratexts from the 1650 *Tenth Muse* and 1678 *Several Poems*, thus effacing pre- and post-publication distinctions and revisions made by Bradstreet and her supporters. While variants between the 1650 and 1678 editions are noted in McElrath and Robb's apparatus, the editors' decision to sever the paratexts from their respective texts means that *The Complete Works* fails to offer the reader access to either the 1650 *Tenth Muse* or the 1678 *Several Poems* as they circulated in their contemporary contexts. A critical edition of Bradstreet's poetry that preserved its early modern paratexts would allow us to better understand such poems as 'The author to her book' and their location within the context of her oeuvre as a whole. A comparative edition of her seventeenth-century printed publications, of the kind recently made possible by advances in digitisation, would also allow us to more readily access the changes she made to poems from the 1650 *Tenth Muse* for later publication. Not only the elegy to Sidney and the revised 'Prologue' would benefit from such attention; as Wiseman (*Conspiracy and Virtue*) has demonstrated, Bradstreet's revision of long poems such as *The Four Monarchies* also rewards careful scholarship.

CHAPTER 10

A 'goodly sample': exemplarity, female complaint and early modern women's poetry

Rosalind Smith

IN 1596, Thomas Lodge wrote of the garrulous brothel-keeper Cousenage in *Wits Miserie*:

> Shee will reckon you vp the storie of Mistris Sanders, and weepe at it, and turne you to the Ballad ouer her chimney, and bid you looke there, there is a goodly sample: I wenches (saies she, turning hirselfe to hir maidens of yt second scise) looke to it, trust not these dissimulation men, there are few good of the[m], yt there are not.[1]

The story of 'Mistris Sanders' concerns the true-life murder of the London merchant George Saunders in 1573 by George Browne. Browne was the lover of Saunders' wife Anne, and the murder was part of a plot between George Browne, Anne Saunders, her friend Anne Drewry and Anne Drewry's servant Roger Clement. Twenty-three years later, in 1596, the story still had cultural currency: enough for Lodge to cite it as a 'goodly sample' to be hung over the chimney, talked about, wept over and taken as a warning. The case generated multiple textual responses to Anne Saunders' example, of which chronicle and pamphlet accounts survive, together with a ballad in the complaint form of gallows confession and (for the stage) the domestic tragedy *A Warning for Faire Women*.[2]

This chapter examines how the crime's enduring narrative and affective energy was mobilised through the rhetorical figure of exemplarity across these different forms of true-crime writing, but particularly in the ballad referred to by Cousenage, 'The wofull lamentacion of Mistress Anne Saunders'. Feminine exemplarity has a volatility in this text, and other gallows confessions like it, that raises the possibility that exemplarity might have offered not only a heuristic flexibility to readers but also a model to writers, including early modern women who incorporated a rhetoric of feminine exemplarity into their own complaints. Heroidean complaint has become newly central in early modern studies for understanding questions of gender, voice and authorship, yet, to date, early modern women writers' use of the complaint genre has received limited consideration. But as these gallows confessions indicate, the models of exemplarity, affect and inference at work in popular complaint could, at the very least, be imagined as a 'rhetoric of the possible' for women writers in the period.[3] This argument contests the current critical construction of the female complaint as a 'phobically imagined female vocality' that operated to control disruptive patterns of women's behaviour, to contain transgressive subjects and to allow female speech 'primarily as a means of silencing it'.[4] Instead, I examine what rhetorical possibilities popular complaint forms such as gallows confession might have opened up for early modern women writers of poetry, and explore the complex ways in which those possibilities were interpreted by male and female readers.

'The wofull lamentacion of Mistress Anne Saunders, which she wrote with her own hand, being prisoner in newgate' has survived only in a manuscript copy, in two hands, probably transcribed from a male-authored print text that is now lost. As such, it may seem a surprising inclusion in a volume on early modern women's relationship to the poem, divorced as it is from formulations of early modern women's writing that remain largely founded on the historical body of the female author. There have been some attempts to broaden the parameters of the field by adopting a performative model of gender that might involve the inclusion of texts circulated under female signatures as 'women's writing', and by recent developments in the history of the book that emphasise publication as a choral event, involving typesetters, printers, booksellers and readers as well as authors, in which early modern women might figure in multiple roles.[5] Such expanded definitions of publication include a revision of the idea of publication as a single, static instance, extending a text's publication to its retransmissions subsequent to an originary moment, which might take place over multiple modes, locations and times. However, at present, the field's foundational categories of 'women' and 'writing' remain relatively static, in ways that continue to occlude how the female lyric voice, whatever its origins, might be appropriated by other women, whether in redactive performance or through rhetorical modelling.

This is a particularly problematic critical lacuna in the case of poetry, which was the subject of both written and oral modes, read aloud, sometimes memorised and made the speaker's own in the moment of performance. Such histories of reading and redaction are difficult to retrieve, especially in the case of street literature, but, as Lodge's response to Anne Saunders' lamentation indicates, some traces of transmission history remain to illuminate the complex mechanisms of inheritance, circulation and exchange operating between poetic texts in the period. They point to the ways in which women as readers, writers and performers of poetry might have approached instances of female lyric subjectivity, whether male- or female-authored, as a resource to be appropriated, imitated or contested. Both Randall Martin and Frances Dolan have recently argued for a broader conception of the reception of popular literature: as Martin notes, 'the message transmitted was not necessarily the message received', and Dolan in particular argues for a range of reader responses to this material, a kind of 'mobile identification' that differs according to an individual reader's expectations.[6] The specific, fragmented history of transmission outlined here builds upon this work, suggesting that the genre of complaint, in both its popular and its elite manifestations, might be newly imagined as a site of possibility rather than limitation for early modern women poets in their reading and writing practice.

The multiple contemporary accounts of Anne Saunders' case give some indication of what lent the story its lasting appeal. Arthur Golding's 1573 prose narrative *A Briefe Discourse of the Late Murther of Master George Sanders* opens with the story's value as gossip: it 'ministreth great occasion of talk among al sorts of men', as well as generating 'muche diuersitie of reports & opinions' (A2r). While Golding acknowledges that these responses to the story might include revulsion, grief or the opportunity to reflect on human iniquity and divine mercy as a way to personal salvation, he chastises readers for what he perceives to be the dominant reason for their interest:

> that many delight to heare and tell newes, without respect of the certentie of the truth, or regarde of dewe humanitie, euery man debating of the matter as occasion or affection leades him. (A2r)

Golding's response is to make a truth claim for his text's own version of this narrative, straight from true-crime orthodoxy: his version is authoritative as it is unembellished, complete and from original sources – 'a playne declaration of the whole matter, according as the same is come to light by open triall of Justice' (A2v). Yet, almost immediately, the narrative excuses its incompleteness and its lack of detail as a refusal to 'feede the fond humor of such curious appetites as are more inquisitiue of other folkes offences than hastie to redress their own' (A2v). There is an anxiety here over the secular and spiritual applications of the story that belie Golding's claims to authority and that complicate recent readings of his account as solely popular Calvinist providentialism.[7] By 1596, in Thomas Lodge's use of the story, the sample is an ambivalent image: still 'goodly', it retains a didactic function in its warning against men's dishonesty, but it layers this with other, less predictable uses: for Cousenage, it works as a means of emotional, identificatory self-presentation in the liminal domestic and working space of the brothel – 'Shee will reckon you vp the storie of Mistris Sanders, and weepe at it'. Cousenage's response to the story of Anne Saunders indicates something of the unpredictable ways in which exemplarity might function, already shadowed in Golding's anxiety in 1573 about the ways in which his version of the narrative of Anne Saunders might be read.

The apparent transparency of example as a rhetorical figure means that its availability to multiple readings, as well the complexity of its ideological work, can be neglected. Yet, as Susan Wiseman has shown, the rhetorical figure of the example was a contested one in the period, with analyses ranging from Puttenham's view of example as the most persuasive and satisfying rhetorical tool, the shared and stable 'representation of old memories, and like successes happened in times past', to Montaigne's view of example as 'an uncertain looking glass, all-embracing, turning all ways'.[8] Yet even for Puttenham, example is a 'kinde of argument in all the Oratorie craft', a way of analysing and applying past experiences through reason to the present, and its successful persuasion rests precisely in the way it disguises the ideological complexity and ambivalence of that 'masse of memories' as a singular 'best course to be taken'.[9] While examples might work as persuasive tools in usefully overdetermined ways for writers, the way in which they were interpreted remains open, escaping the boundaries of paratextual scaffolding such as Golding's preface.

Timothy Hampton argues that early modern exemplarity relocates imitation from a writing to a reading practice: example is a 'marked sign that bears the moral and historical authority of antiquity and engages the reader in a dialogue with the past'.[10] This dialogue allows the example to figure both the authority of the past and the problematic uncertainty surrounding its interpretation in the present. It makes reading not only active but charged in ways that both are connected to the past and radically remake it, linking the hermeneutic procedures of humanism to its rhetorical practices. This is translated in Hampton's analysis of the rhetoric of heroism in Erasmus, Montaigne, Shakespeare and Cervantes, as 'a dialogue to be played out … on the stage of public action'.[11] The present chapter extends Hampton's model of exemplarity as imitation in reading practice to a quite different group of non-elite texts, and explores the ways in which this model's investments in both a collective sense of the past and individual interpretation in the present might be applied to street literature. The crime of 'Mistris Sanders' is hardly a narrative that would lend itself to imitative public action under the aegis of humanism. A different register of collective memory, a different kind of past, is invoked here. It is located in the domestic sphere and concerns affective relations between individuals that intersect with larger, institutional forces, of the church and state, in relation to which individual readers might position themselves, and which they might analyse and discuss in unpredictable ways, or, as Golding fears, 'as occasion or affection leades' them (A2r). To understand the ways in which these institutional and interpretative contexts might meet in the example of Anne Saunders, however, we need to know more about the crime itself.

According to Golding's detailed account, on 24 March 1573, the murderer, George Browne, received a letter from Anne Drewry informing him that George Saunders would be in a house in Woolwich belonging to John Barnes that night, and would be on foot heading towards St Mary's Cray the next morning. On 25 March, Browne attacked both George Saunders and his companion, the servant John Beane, near Shooters Hill. Saunders died instantly, but John Beane survived and was able to give information identifying Browne as his attacker. Browne immediately contacted Anne Drewry through her servant, Roger Clement, then went to her house as he became aware that he had been identified as Saunders' murderer. Unable to speak with her except through her servant Clement, Browne was paid £20, followed by a further £5 to flee. He was eventually apprehended and confessed to the murder, but claimed that it had been instigated by Anne Drewry, who had promised to facilitate his marriage to her friend Anne Saunders. All accounts speak of George Browne's excessive love for Saunders, evidenced by his maintenance of her innocence until his execution. Anne Drewry and her servant Roger Clement were arrested and, upon Clement's confession, so was Anne Saunders. Accused of procuring the murder and protecting the murderer after the fact, both women were condemned as accessories after the fact and executed; both confessed before execution. But it was Anne Saunders' initial protestations of her innocence that captured the public imagination, leading to support for her innocence or her ignorance of the criminality of her actions. As Golding asserts:

> And Mistresse Saunders ... stoode so stoutly stil to the deniall of all things, (in which stoute deniall she continued also a certayne tyme after hir condemnation) that some were brought in a blinde beliefe, that either she was not giltie at al, or else had but brought hir selfe in danger of lawe through ignorance, and not through pretended malice. (B1v)

Indeed, a 1580 account of the crime, *A View of Sundry Examples, Reporting Many Straunge Murthers*, focuses solely on George Browne's motivation and actions in killing George Saunders, with Anne Saunders' complicity mentioned only parenthetically as 'consent' to the act.[12] In Golding's account, however, among Anne Saunders' supporters was the Reverend Mell, who accompanied her from Newgate, fell in love with her on that journey and became convinced of her innocence. Using threats and bribery, he persuaded Anne Drewry to assume all the responsibility for the crime: Drewry then revoked her first confession and declared her guilt before the Dean of St Paul's. Unfortunately, Mell foolishly revealed this second plot to an outsider, who promptly reported him. Mell was pilloried at the same time as the two women's execution, with his crime inscribed on a paper pinned to his clothing: 'For practising to colour the detestable factes of George Saunders wife' (A4r). An unprecedented crowd gathered at the execution, filling the whole field and extending almost to Newgate. Golding claims that the crowd was so extensive that every available building was occupied even 'upon the gutters, sides, and toppes of the houses' and 'whole windowes & walles were in many places beaten down to looke out' (B2r).

Golding's account of this crime rehearses familiar themes of Renaissance accounts of feminine vice, particularly that of the false face of innocence masking sexual culpability. But as Golding's anxieties surrounding the reception of his account indicate, the tale of the murder of George Saunders is available to another set of readings that have little connection with the exemplary functions of warning, prescription or spiritual self-analysis. These readings are generated by curiosity, by the news value of a story about extreme love and its power to rewrite orthodox boundaries. Anne Saunders almost evaded responsibility for her crime twice, through the plots of men infatuated with her, and the crowd gathering for a sight of her might similarly generate posthumous tales of her innocence. Indeed, that is Cousenage's interpretation in *Wits Miserie*: she weeps at Saunders' naïve trust in 'these dissimulation men', and they, rather than Anne Saunders, are the villains in her version of the crime. In Golding's account, rather than showing only the just action of the law and God's purpose, as the narrator hopes, the narrative also exposes the law's vulnerability to corruption and manipulation by affect. In these accounts, although we do not hear Anne Saunders' affective and self-justificatory rhetoric, we see its power. However, we do have an instance where that rhetoric is given imaginative shape in a contemporary ballad in the form of gallows confession: 'The wofull lamentacion of Mistress Ann Saunders'.

In a number of recent studies of the genre of female gallows confession, the works themselves are almost exclusively seen to be simple and formulaic. In Katherine Craik's influential analysis, the ballad of Anne Saunders 'only momentarily' raises the possibility that 'complaint facilitates a new female vocality or authorship'; instead, it is dominated by a 'strain of ventriloquized self-enmity' that emphasises the speaker's contrition and what Craik perceives to be the ballad's didactic function.[13] In contrast, Shakespeare's 'A lover's complaint' is seen by Craik to be complex and open-ended, permitting a hermeneutic instability closed off in the gallows confessions:

> We know from the ballad-laments that exemplary (ventriloquised) female confessions expect and welcome the judgement of their audience by willingly acknowledging legal culpability and Christian sinfulness, by gracefully accepting punishment ('In burning flames of fire I should fry'), by quelling fears that the crime might be repeated ('Heauens graunt no more that such a one may be'), and by accepting promise of spiritual comfort ('Immortall blisse & Ioye/set fre from synne & blame'). But *A Lovers Complaint* dictates neither how the young maiden's complaint will be received by listeners within the fabric of the poem nor by readers outside it, for the double frame so suggestively opened in the initial stanzas remains finally unclosed.[14]

The binary established here is clear: female gallows confessions dictate readings that reinforce a didactic moralism, while the complaint attributed to Shakespeare is open to a broad range of hermeneutic possibilities. What, then, can be made of Thomas Lodge's representation of Cousenage's resistant reading of the 'storie of Mistris Saunders', a reading of sympathetic identification rather than moral condemnation? Even Craik's nuanced and detailed reading of Anne Saunders' lamentation is representative of a critical orthodoxy surrounding female gallows confession and early modern women's criminality that surprisingly continues to reinforce early new historicist ideas of containment and control in popular texts, while more elite texts are afforded a different level of complexity. In earlier readings, both Joy Wiltenburg and Sandra Clark view gallows confession with other sensational street literature of the early modern period through a providential lens, where the complexity their readings attribute to some of these ballads is again subsumed within their didactic and moral function.[15] If there is evidence, however limited, that any of these texts were read by early modern readers as contradictory, complex and open, then such closed modern interpretations might be rethought. I am suggesting that these ballads should be allowed the same range of heuristic possibilities afforded elite texts' depiction of the past and, in particular, their use of the rhetorical tool of exemplarity should be seen as not as fixed and didactic but as flexible and volatile.

Unpacking the assumptions surrounding popular literature, its genres and its modes of circulation allows us to reconsider the complex dynamics of Anne Saunders' lamentation in particular. While many gallows confessions were simple exercises in moral didacticism, ironically the Saunders ballad is an exception: it uses the volatility of negative and positive exemplarity in surprising new ways. As Craik points out, the sub-genre of female gallows confession presents the plainant's voice directly, without the mediating frames that characterise the genre of complaint more generally, creating an effect of authenticity around the speaker's voice. This is one of a number of devices comprising truth claims within the genre, together with an evocation of urgency, the detailed recreation of the events of the crime and the speaker's intense affective relationship to these events. The reader is placed in an intimate relationship to the speaker, overhearing her final words in the moment of extremis before execution. However, the association of these devices with authenticity is artificial, the product of conventions; the apparent transparency of these conventions testifies to their rhetorical efficacy, but not to their invisibility to the early modern reader. In the case of the Saunders ballad, the imaginative materialisation of Saunders' voice the evening before her death is a convention investing that voice with a veneer of authenticity and affective immediacy, not (as Craik suggests) a means of containing the threat of the sexually assertive woman by allowing her to speak 'only in order to silence her'.[16] Further, the multiple redactions of Saunders' story, in the surviving chronicle accounts, prose pamphlets and domestic drama, might be seen very differently to the model of a frail voice emerging only to be immediately extinguished. Early modern readers heard Saunders' voice directly ventriloquised again, in the 1599 play *A Warning for Faire Women*, and, as I have noted, the rhetorical power of her account of events at her trial is noted in the prose pamphlets that document its effect. Taking into account the multiple redactions that form the publication histories of early modern true-crime literature surrounding certain cases can help us understand the ways in which the complex and repetitive transmission histories of these cases shaped the ways in which they were interpreted. And even in isolation, the ballad form itself is one predicated on redaction across oral and printed forms. As the work of Adam Fox and Natalie Würzbach has shown, these ballads were widely circulated, read and performed; across the country, women and men would have spoken and sung laments such as Anne Saunders', pinned them above their chimneys and retold their version of their stories to their listeners.[17] Mimesis here must be considered spatially as well temporally: the cultural work performed by the ballads occurred multiply in different locations, within households, markets and streets, from 1573 to the end of the sixteenth century.

The Anne Saunders ballad begins with an epigram – 'I lament, I repent, I reioyce, / I trust in the lord christ, he will here my voice' – that provides a guide to the way in which the speaker's story is initially framed in this genre (8r).[18] The speaker's voice is that of the penitent sinner, borrowing from the traditions of penitential psalm meditation, and presenting a subject in despair, raising her tearful eyes to God. The first two stanzas outline the speaker's lament embodied in tears, transferred in stanzas 3 and 4 to her 'babes and children deare' and then to a broader audience of other 'tender mothers' who are invited to 'judge / and gushe out teares with me' (8v). Yet despite her remorse, the speaker emerges curiously innocent of the crime in this account. The ballad never gets close to attributing guilt to the speaker; in fact, in stanza 6 it uses the familiar Petrarchan metaphor of the ship subject to the elements, to distance her from her crime, even exonerate her, on the basis of her being subject to greater forces of evil in the world:

> I lyncked my selfe in love
> to hatefull bitter bale,
> Throughe whiche my barcke is ouertourn'd
> with quyte contrary gale.
> (9r)

These other, worldly sites of evil are embodied in the next set of stanzas, which open with the names of Anne Saunders' co-conspirators, Anne Drewry and Roger Clement, and their roles in the crime. They in effect take the blame for the crime, Drewry for inciting it and Clement for failing to stop George Browne from committing the murder:

> Anne Drewry woe to thee,
> wch drewe me to decaye:
> & woe the tyme I loved thy lure,
> woe me and wele away.

> Woe worth thy false entent,
> woe worth thy bloudy mynde:
> & woe thy flattering words wch made
> my doting hart so blynde.

> And Roger woe to the,
> in whome it was to staye:
> brownes hands from slaughter of my dear,
> & vs from this decaye
> (9r)

The speaker goes on to admit that she betrayed her husband, and that her 'race and end' serve a didactic function to other women readers – 'all honest wyves / and fynest london dames' – but this admonition is to 'beare to your husbandes trusty hartes', not to refrain from successfully plotting to murder them (9r–v). This works as a form of secular renovation in the ballad as preparation for the speaker's shift from negative to positive exemplar. By its conclusion, the speaker has moved from a worldly sinner tempted by false friends, to one tempted by Satan, to one whose redemption parallels Christ's. Christ's own 'Blodie harte' in stanza 15 echoes the speaker's 'wounded harte' in stanza 16, a parallel made explicit at the close of stanza 17: 'Christes bloud my bloudy facte hath clensde' (10r–v). She becomes God's 'child', 'set fre from synne and blame', dwelling with christe 'aboue the christall skyes' (10v). The ballad ends with the speaker commending, rather grandly, her friends to Christ – positioning herself as a renovated positive exemplar of Christian virtue:

> And therfore nowe farewell,
> all things corrupt & vayne:
> it is not longe til heavenly throng
> will make me vppe agayne,
>
> In this my very fleshe,
> to se christe wth myne eyes:
> & soule & body dwell wth him,
> aboue the christall skyes.
>
> For whome my friendes p[re]pare,
> & so I yow commend:
> to Jesus Christ who shall ye kep
> – & thus I make my end.
> (10v–11r)

The speaker shifts from penitence, to a partial confession that occludes her actual crime and mitigates her criminal complicity, to Christ-like ascension as moral exemplar, in ways that complicate assessments of her character as cautionary example and that present the reader with self-interested constructions of her character in both legal and spiritual contexts. While the reader may not accept these self-constructions, the shifts surrounding negative and positive exemplarity demonstrated here indicate the ways in which exemplarity could function in surprisingly open and inventive ways for the female subject, allowing the material of the immediate past to be at least partially remade in the present.

It must be said, of course, that, in this respect, 'The wofull lamentacion of Mistress Anne Saunders' is unusual: most female gallows confessions maintain the negative exemplarity of the female criminal as a warning to maidens and wives, especially those of the 'hasty kinde', as do the confessions attributed to male criminals.[19] For instance, in a ballad published in 1616, Anne Wallen is represented as a scold whose verbal abuse of her husband turns to physical abuse, and she finally throws a chisel 'amongst his intrailes', resulting in his murder. Her exemplarity remains negative: 'then wives be warn'd example take by me / Heavens graunt no more that such a one may be'. The ballad concludes with Wallen frying in 'burning flames of fire' and with the uncertain prospect of her redemption, merely a plea to 'Receive my soule sweet Jesus now I die'.[20] Alice Davis, who stabbed her husband in the heart with disturbing rapidity after a fight in which he asked her for money, is also burnt to death without stable renovation, praying for grace, in two ballads from 1628.[21] An exception, however, is Ulalia Page, who, like Anne Saunders, orchestrated a plot in which her husband was murdered by her lover, the intriguingly named George Strangwidge. Like Saunders, Page dies with her watery eyes fixed on heaven, guiltless, her crimes washed away by Christ's blood: she is transformed from negative to positive exemplar.[22] This contrasts with contemporary prose accounts of the crime, where her role was active and volitional: she had attempted several times to poison her husband prior to his murder, and paid a servant to £140 to assist Strangwidge in the murder.[23]

The heuristic flexibility at work in the Saunders and Page ballads has been thought through in another context, related to these texts' status as true crime, and linked to their participation in the legal rhetoric underpinning the genre of complaint. From the medieval period, the lover's complaint was aligned with legal plaint, echoing in its forms elements of the judicial process.[24] Recent work on early modern legal rhetoric locates the same connections between legal plaint and complaint, focusing on an interpretative flexibility which overturns any idea of fixed readings of particular circumstances, or crimes. In Barbara Shapiro's analysis of the Aristotelian concept of artificial proof, such proofs were constructed rather than uncovered by the orator; this mode of evidence in forensic oration depended upon an interpretation of signs that could be used for either the prosecution or the defence, according to the speaker's case.[25] The same set of circumstances could equally engender suspicion or remove it, creating narratives of good or bad character from the evidentiary material to hand.

As Lorna Hutson has argued in relation to Renaissance drama, the English jury system carried with it an implied epistemology associated with rhetorical structures of probability on which dramatists relied to produce plot and character. Juries were not bound to accept the testimonies of witnesses, but were free to interpret and evaluate their evidence according to their own knowledge of the facts.[26] Legal fact here is 'a contentious or conjectural issue', constructed by the speaker and interpreted by the audience, who assess the rhetorical probability of any given narrative.[27] Hutson revises the view that juries were passive instruments of the judiciary to emphasise their active participation in discourses of suspicion and probability, and further argues that 'participation in the justice system diffused concepts of fact finding and evaluation of narrative through the culture'.[28] The process of participation in pre-trial detection and in jury trials introduced lay people into ways of thinking about the presentation and evaluation of evidence that Hutson links to a similar kind of awareness in popular drama.

Extending Hutson's arguments to popular poetry, particularly that linked to historical crimes, I am suggesting that a similar awareness of the need for evaluation attaches to the exemplarity of the female plainant in gallows confession. In some cases, at least, the female speaker's unframed account presents an evidentiary narrative that invites the reader to evaluate the account of events that she describes and to assess its probability as grounds for determining character and weighing its exemplary force. Rather than simple exercises in didacticism, some gallows confessions offer persuasive narratives that invite readers to reinterpret their cases in ways that can startlingly diverge from the operation of the law and complicate the didactic cultural work with which they also engage.

In the case of Anne Saunders, the heuristic volatility surrounding the speaker's self-presentation in gallows confession enables the negative exemplarity promoted by legal judgement to be overturned and replaced by an individual and self-interested interpretation of scripture, which, although orthodox, works to highly unorthodox ends. In a way that exemplifies Hampton's idea of reading as imitation, placing the reader in active, interpretative dialogue with the past, one is invited to take the position of the deluded and besotted Reverend George Mell, led by the plainant's first-person account to abandon knowledge of her guilt for an endorsement of her Christ-like innocence. The reading experience generates a shadow of the erotic love charging Anne Saunders' power over her immediate circle, detaching her exemplarity from any institutional certainty, and exploiting interpretative instability to the point that guilt becomes innocence, and condemnation becomes affirmation. Hampton claims that exemplarity functions in the humanist project to import the authority of the past to a present of contemporary and unstable interpretation; I am suggesting that it functions in these popular texts in far more unpredictable ways. Rather than the authority of the past, what appears here is a fictive individual's ability to use interpretative instability for her own ends, to create a persuasive character invoking sympathy and the appearance of innocence.

These texts reinforce recent reformulations of early modern understandings of rhetoric, not as a rule-bound practical art, but as one reflexive to its own historical situation. It is able to characterise, in Daniel Gross's terms, 'how things might be otherwise'.[29] Yet, as we have seen, even the most recent criticism has assumed that such female complaints functioned in ideologically transparent ways and have applied Foucauldian regulatory analyses to these texts to suggest that men imitated female speech in order to silence it.[30] This means that the rhetorical possibilities opened up by such gallows confessions as those of Anne Saunders and Ulalia Page have never been considered alongside the texts that continue to make up the canon of early modern women's writing. Is it possible that the opportunities for self-invention provided by these complex and nuanced exercises in lyric self-invention might have penetrated the field of women's writing in ways that have not yet been considered?

Secure attributions of secular complaint exist for two women writers of the period – Isabella Whitney and Lady Mary Wroth – although other spiritual and secular female complaints exist in manuscript and print and were attributed to historical women, if not written by them.[31] Isabella Whitney's *The Copy of a Letter*, first published in 1567, draws from a range of precedents, of which popular complaints such as gallows confession might be part. This long poem uses selected histories from the *Heroides* as instructive examples to strengthen the speaker's case for her own virtue. This would be uncontroversial, except, like the Saunders and Page ballads, she borrows these examples in order to shore up a position outside convention, speaking as the lover of a man who is about to marry another. Like gallows confession, the complaint is staged on the eve of a crisis, imparting a sense of urgency to the persuasive evidence making up the speaker's case. As the three stanzas below show, Whitney's speaker makes a case for her own constancy in the hope of regaining her lover's attention and substituting herself as his wife:

> Whose constantnesse had never quaild
>   if you had not begonne:
> And yet it is not so far past,
>   but might agayne bewonne.
>
> If you so would: yea and not change
>   so long as lyfe should last:
> But yf that needs you marry must?
>   then farewell, hope is past.
>
> And if you cannot be content
>   to lead a single life?
> (Although the same right quiet be)
>   Then take me to your wife.[32]

Although not that of a convicted murderer, the speaker's status here shares a similar illegitimacy transferred to an erotic economy. She refuses to be a mistress, but she is not a wife, nor anymore her beloved's choice to be one; it is uncertain whether she is still even the object of his affections. The legitimacy of her position is entirely dependent upon the beloved's restoration of his attention. But, like the speakers of gallows confession, she seeks to reverse the uncertainty of her status by manipulating the resources of language to make a persuasive case for her legitimacy to both her beloved and the reader. She interprets any available evidence to her own ends, reverses the contingency of her position and replaces it with her own self-invented certitude; this parallels the rhetorical inventiveness and impulse towards self-invention found in Anne Saunders' lamentation. The speaker first addresses the beloved's 'falshood' and cites a range of examples from the *Heroides* of men's betrayal of women: Aeneas, Theseus and Jason (A2v–A3r). Typical of female complaint, these examples amplify the female speaker's woe, albeit through an Ovidian context specific to the late 1560s, where such examples would have had a freshness that they later lost. However, the poem moves away from this reproduction of woe to its reinvention, paralleling the rhetorically innovative strategies of some gallows confession. In imagining Jason's flight from Medea, the speaker conventionally attributes his safety at sea to Aeolus and Neptune's care, that 'might he boldly passe the waves / no perils could him stea' (A3v). But then, in Whitney's rewriting of the myth, another narrative is imagined – one of exposure and divine punishment:

> But if his falsehed had to them,
>   bin manifest befor:
> They wold have rent the ship as soone
>   as he had gon from shore.
> (A3v)

Not only this myth, but the entire raft of exemplars are then re-examined and reframed:

> For they, for their unfaithfulness,
>   did get perpetuall fame:
> Fame? wherefore dyd I terme it so?
>   I should have cald it shame.
> (A3v)

Exemplarity is curiously volatile here: what once was positive is swiftly rebranded as negative in a reversal that echoes the play on negative and positive exemplarity at work in the Saunders ballad. The speaker then goes on to build a case for her own positive exemplarity through a set of female classical examples also at times beset by a kind of volatility – Helen, for instance, exemplifies either virtue or vice, depending on interpretation: 'I rather wish her HELENS face, / then one of HELENS trade' (A4v). Nonetheless, these virtues of chastity, constancy and truth, figured through Penelope, Lucresia and Thisbie, are appropriated by the speaker to herself: 'Save Helens beauty, al the rest / the Gods have me assignd' (A4v). Speaking from this new, self-constructed position of divine virtue, she concludes that she need go no further: 'Thou knowst by prof what I deserve / I need not to informe thee' (A4v). As with the lamentation of

Anne Saunders, the poem concludes with the speaker aligning herself with God and commending her lover to join them after death: 'And after that your soule may rest / amongst the heavenly crew' (A5r). Spurned lover becomes a spiritual guide, reinventing her initially uncertain status to that of divine certainty in exact parallel to the reversals in exemplarity effected in the Saunders ballad. Rhetoric here is a resource manipulated to make things seem otherwise, to take back erotic power and to assert a kind of erotic exemplarity at odds with how things are.

A more complex instance of the transmission of popular complaint's rhetorical volatility to early modern women's writing can be found in the casket sonnet sequence attributed to Mary Queen of Scots and circulated in George Buchanan's *Ane Detectiovn*, which appeared in multiple editions from 1571.[33] Unlike Whitney's poems, its attribution problems mean that it cannot be read uncomplicatedly as the work of a historical woman writer, and these problems are compounded by the novelty of its female speaker. She is a mistress writing to her married lover, in a register that combines emotional masochism, sensation and jarringly detailed references to the material world. Most critics, reading the sequence through Petrarchism, find it baffling. This is not only because of its generic unfamiliarity, but also because it diverges dramatically from the more familiar types of early modern women's writing exemplifying constraint and textual control. The sequence is not the typical complaint of a lamenting queen, combining restraint with grief and demonstrating her virtue through 'the quality of her lamentation and the quantity – always decorous – of moisture clouding her eyes'.[34] Yet popular complaint provides this sequence with a clarifying context for its rhetorical strategies, its unrestrained speaker and its deployment of exemplarity, to the extent that it becomes typical rather than unrecognisable. This is possible, however, only if the genre of popular complaint can be read as a site of heuristic possibility rather than reduced to didactic moralism, and if Hampton's theory of exemplarity can be seen to extend beyond elite culture to the popular.

The female speaker of the casket sonnets uses her invidious position as mistress for her own benefit: like Whitney's speaker, her illegitimacy as mistress is seen as a marker of her 'true' devotion, in contrast to the wife's venal interest in status and wealth:

> Sche for her honour oweth you obedience:
> I in obaying you may receiue dishonour,
> Nat being (to my displesure) your wife as she.
> And yit in this point she shall haue na preheminence.
> Sche useth constancy for hyr awin profite:
> For it is na little honour to be maistres of your goodes,
> And I for luifing of you may receiue blame.[35]

This is the now familiar strategy of manipulating evidence to create a persuasive case, found in the Saunders, Page and Whitney complaints: a case for virtue made from material that suggests the opposite. Rather than lamentation underscoring an image of public piety and virtue, the casket sonnet speaker makes it clear from the second sonnet of the sequence that she is ruled by emotion, to the extent that she will give up her kingdom to make a persuasive case for her love:

> In his handis and in his full power,
> I put my sonne, my honour, and my lyif,
> My contry, my subiects, my soule al subdewit,
> To him, and has none vther will
> For my scope, quhilk without deceit,
> I will follow in spite of all enuie
> That may ensue: for I haif na vther desire,
> But to make him perceiue my faythfulness,
> (R2v)

Private passion overrides public duty here, in an abnegation of political responsibility at odds with good government. The speaker is more concerned with discrediting her rival: she casts her sovereignty aside in a single line but dwells for four sonnets (3–6) on the faults of the beloved's wife, pointing to her avarice, her infidelity, her coldness towards her husband and finally her falsity in love expressed through 'payntit words, hyr teares, hyr plaints full of dissimulation' (R3r). In the remainder of the sequence, the speaker seeks to override the wife's false expressions of love, as the speaker claims the beloved 'louest and beliuist hyr more than me' (R3r). In sonnets 7–11, the speaker shores up her case through repetition, creating a form of rhetorical excess in a project that is the antithesis of the struggle between restraint and grief characterising other royal women's plaints. Indeed, restraint militates against the casket sonnet speaker's project, that 'at length my loue sall appeare, / So clearly, that he sall neuer doubt' (R3v). The sequence concludes with the haphazard piling up of evidence for the speaker's love with increasingly strident claims for that love, which in sonnet 9 survives her rape, his injury and her forsaking her position:

> For him also I powred out many tearis,
> First quhen he made himself possessor of thys body.
> Of the quhilk then he had nat the hart.
> Efter he did geue me one vther hard charge,
> Quhen he bled of his bude great quantitie,
> Through the great sorow of the quhilk camd to me that dolour,
> That almost caryit away my life, and the feire
> To lese the onely strength that armit me.

For him since I haif despisit honour,
The thing onely that bringeth felicitie.
For him I haif hazardit greitnes & conscience
For him I haif forsaken all kin and frendes,
And set aside all vther respectes,
Schortly, I seke the alliance of you onely.
(R4r)

The sequence concludes in indeterminacy, as the speaker awaits her lover's response to her case for preference: 'You may tell who shall winne maist' (S1r). Yet this address to the beloved is itself a fiction conveying authenticity; it is the reader, not the beloved, who assesses the persuasiveness of the speaker's case. Her exemplarity is peculiarly open to a range of heuristic possibilities: simultaneously, her positive exemplarity as lover constructs her negative exemplarity as sovereign in a way that invites emotional identification from the reader as well as political condemnation. The speaker's unframed voice within the complaint invites the reader, like Cousenage, to weep with her, precisely as it makes a persuasive case for her unsuitability as queen.

Circulated by the Elizabethan court as a form of semi-publicity covertly damaging Mary's character, Buchanan's text prints the casket sonnets with other documents following his prose detection and forensic oration arguing for Mary's complicity in the murder of her first husband, Darnley, through collusion with her alleged lover, the Earl of Bothwell.[36] To be successful as propaganda, the sonnets had to be believable to the reader – that is, the plausible voice of a queen, albeit a foreign, murdering and adulterous one. There is some evidence that they were received as such. Norfolk provides an account of the sonnets' first, secret disclosure and comments that 'the said ballads do discover such inordinate love between her and Bothwell, her loathsomeness and abhorring of her husband ... as every good and godly man cannot but detest and abhor the same'.[37]

Norfolk's response indicates that the speaker's erotic exemplarity was read by at least some to imply the queen's criminal complicity. On the one hand, this indicates the limits to which a 'rhetoric of the possible' located in popular female complaint might have worked in practice for early modern women writers. While a rhetorical volatility existed to be exploited, it could not be controlled beyond the space of the page: the religious and legal institutions manipulated there continued to operate, and the connections that readers drew between textual worlds and their own were unpredictable ones that might work against the speaker's case as well as for it. On the other hand, Norfolk's reading of this erotic exemplarity as evidence of Mary Stuart's guilt also shows the extent to which the rhetoric of popular complaint deployed in the casket sonnets was also seen to be possible for a historical woman writer, a queen no less, and available for her use. The visceral, emotional and volatile poetic strategies of popular complaint were read by at least some sections of a contemporary audience as the plausible rhetorical voice of an elite woman writer.

Gallows confessions continued to circulate into the seventeenth century, and while all gallows confessions did not result in a transformation from negative to positive exemplarity, ballads such as that of Mistris Saunders remained in the popular imagination because of the volatile interpretative freedom that they offered their speakers: to remake the world as they will on the space of the page, even if the institutions of church and state remained inimical to their persuasion. Female complaint, particularly in its popular manifestations of gallows confession and broadside ballad, is a genre which has been oddly oversimplified in some recent criticism; its variety and complexity have been reduced to a didacticism that flattens the lyric possibilities afforded by some examples within the genre. In the late 1560s and early 1570s, at least, textual circulation and exchange occurred between female complaint forms such as gallows confession and women's writing of complaint, exchanges that indicate the genre may have facilitated women's lyric experimentation as well as supplied prescriptive models for feminine behaviour. The rhetorical figure of exemplarity did not suddenly cease to bear complexity when it was associated with the representation or practice of female lyric subjectivity. As these poems indicate, exemplarity and heuristic flexibility cannot be separated, as readers made assessments of the persuasiveness of example according to their own understanding of each case.

Notes

1 Thomas Lodge, *Wits Miserie*, London, 1596, p. 38.

2 Raphael Holinshed, *The Chronicles of England, Scotland, and Ireland*, London, 1577, vol. 2, pp. 1865–6; John Stow, *The Annales, or Generall Chronicle of England*, London, 1615, pp. 674–5; anonymous, 'The wofull lamentacion of Mistress Anne Saunders', British Library, Sloane MS 1896, folios 8r–11r; Arthur Golding, *A Briefe Discourse of the Late Murther of Master George Sanders*, London, 1573; Anthony Munday, *A View of Sundry Examples, Reporting Many Straunge Murthers*, London, 1580; anonymous, *A Warning for Faire Women*, London, 1599. Golding's contemporary narrative is cited henceforth in the body of the chapter.

3 D. Gross, *The Secret History of Emotion: From Aristotle's 'Rhetoric' to Modern Brain Science*, University of Chicago Press, Chicago, 2006, pp. 12–13.

4 K. A. Craik, 'Shakespeare's *A Lover's Complaint* and early modern criminal confession', *Shakespeare Quarterly*, vol. 53, no. 4 (2002), pp. 437–59, at pp. 439, 447–59.

5 For a broad definition of choral publication, see M. Cohen, *The Networked Wilderness: Communicating in Early New England*, University of Minnesota Press, Minneapolis, 2010, pp. 1–15.

6 R. Martin, *Women, Murder and Equity in Early Modern England*, Routledge, New York, 2008, p. 39; F. E. Dolan, 'Tracking the petty traitor across genres', in

P. Fumerton, A. Guerrini and K. McAbee (eds), *Ballads and Broadsides in Britain, 1500–1800*, Ashgate, Farnham, 2010, pp. 149–71.

7   See Subha Mukherji's recent reading of Golding's *Briefe Discourse* as extending God's work by 'plainly publishing the process of discovery'. S. Mukherji, *Law and Representation in Early Modern Drama*, Cambridge University Press, Cambridge, 2006, p. 110.

8   S. Wiseman, *Conspiracy and Virtue: Women, Writing, and Politics in Seventeenth-Century England*, Oxford University Press, Oxford, 2006, pp. 49–50.

9   George Puttenham, *The Arte of English Poesie* (ed. G. Doidge Willcock and A. Walker), Cambridge University Press, Cambridge, 1970, p. 39.

10 T. Hampton, *Writing from History: The Rhetoric of Exemplarity in Renaissance Literature,* Cornell University Press, Ithaca, 1990, p. 5.

11 Ibid., p. 23.

12 Munday, *A View of Sundry Examples*, folio B2r.

13 Craik, 'Shakespeare's *A Lover's Complaint*', p. 449.

14 Ibid., p. 457.

15 See J. Wiltenburg, *Disorderly Women and Female Power in the Street Literature of Early Modern England and Germany*, University of Virginia Press, Charlottesville, 1992, pp. 215–16; S. Clark, *Women and Crime in the Street Literature of Early Modern England*, Palgrave Macmillan, Basingstoke, 2004, pp. 91–2; S. A. Kane, 'Wives with knives: early modern murder ballads and the transgressive commodity', *Criticism*, vol. 38, no. 2 (1996), pp. 219–38.

16 Craik, 'Shakespeare's *A Lover's Complaint*', p. 450.

17 See A. Fox, *Oral and Literate Culture in England, 1500–1700*, Oxford University Press, New York, 2001; N. Würzbach, *The Rise of the English Street Ballad, 1550–1650*, Cambridge University Press, Cambridge, 1990.

18 Anonymous, *The wofull lamentacion of Mistress Anne Saunders*. All further references are to this manuscript and noted in the text.

19 Anonymous, 'Anne Wallens lamentation', Pepys 1.124–5, English Broadside Ballad Archive, online at http://ebba.english.ucsb.edu (henceforth EBBA) (accessed November 2010).

20 Ibid.

21 Anonymous, 'The unnaturalle wife', Pepys 1.122–3r, EBBA; anonymous, 'A warning for all desperate women', Pepys 1.120–21, EBBA.

22 Thomas Deloney, *The Sorowfull Complaint of Mistris Page*, London, 1635, p. 183; see also Thomas Deloney, *The Lamentation of Master Page's Wife* and *The Lamentation of George Strangwidge*, London, 1635.

23 Anonymous, *A True Discourse of a Cruel and Inhumaine Murder, Committed Upon M. Padge of Plymouth in Sundry Strange and Inhumaine Murthers, Lately Committed*, London, 1591, B2v.

24 See W. Scase, *Literature and Complaint in England, 1272–1553*, Oxford University Press, New York, 2007.

25 B. Shapiro, 'Classical rhetoric and the English law of evidence', in V. Kahn and L. Hutson (eds), *Rhetoric and Law in Early Modern Europe*, Yale University Press, New Haven, 2001, pp. 54–72.

26 L. Hutson, *The Invention of Suspicion: Law and Mimesis in Shakespeare and Renaissance Drama*, Oxford University Press, New York, 2007.

27 Ibid., p. 77.

28 Ibid., p. 80.

29 Gross, *The Secret History of Emotion*, p. 13.

30 Mirroring Katharine Craik's approach, Kate van Orden suggests that this genre offers not 'the expression of unofficial opinions' but 'prescriptions for women's behaviour'. K. van Orden, 'Female "complaintes": laments of Venus, queens and city women in late sixteenth-century France', *Renaissance Quarterly*, vol. 54, no. 3 (2001), pp. 801–45.

31 See for example S. Ross, '"Give me thy hairt and I desire no more": the Song of Songs, Petrarchism and Elizabeth Melville's Puritan poetics', in J. Harris and E. Scott-Baumann (eds), *The Intellectual Culture of Puritan Women*, Palgrave Macmillan, Basingstoke, 2010, pp. 96–107.

32 I[sabella] W[hitney], *The Copy of a Letter, Lately Written in Meeter, by a Yonge Gentilwoman*, London, 1567, folio A2v. All further references are to this manuscript and noted in the text.

33 George Buchanan, *Ane Detectiovn of the Duinges of Marie Quene of Scottes*, London, 1571.

34 Van Orden, 'Female "complaintes"', p. 824.

35 Buchanan, *Ane Detectiovn*, folios Q4r–S1r. All further references are to this manuscript and noted in the text.

36 See J. E. Phillips, *Images of a Queen: Mary Stuart in Sixteenth-Century Literature*, University of California Press, Berkeley, 1964, pp. 62–3.

37 Norfolk, Sussex and Sadleir to Elizabeth, 'Elizabeth: October 1568', *Calendar of State Papers, Scotland: Vol. 2, 1563–69* (1900), pp. 513–44, online at www.british-history.ac.uk/report.aspx?compid=44186 (accessed September 2011).

'The nine-liv'd Sex': women and justice in seventeenth-century popular poetry

Judith Hudson

Or rather Justice, with it selfe at strife
Judg'd the Wench worthy both of death and life.[1]

IN 1651, Thomas Arthur, a scholar at Christ Church, Oxford, penned the above couplet in a poem for the second edition of a pamphlet discussing the celebrated Anne Greene case, then the talk of the university. Greene, an unmarried Oxfordshire servant in her early twenties, had been condemned and hanged in the city the preceding December for the murder of her newborn child, a child fathered by the teenage grandson of her employer, and subsequent prosecutor, Sir Thomas Read. Her body, having been cut down from the gallows, was transported in its coffin to the house of one John Clarke, a local apothecary, whose home was the venue for regular meetings of men of science from across the university. There it was to be dissected as part of an anatomy demonstration with an accompanying lecture by Dr William Petty, the university reader in that subject. When her coffin was opened, however, Anne was seen to be breathing, and over the next few days she was nursed back to health by the very doctors who were to have anatomised her corpse.

Anne Greene's survival was almost universally interpreted as a providential revelation of her innocence, 'a contrary verdict from heaven', and a petition was raised for her pardon, supported by her doctors and representatives from across the university – and funded by the proceeds of an admission fee charged to the 'multitudes that flocked ... daily' to see this new celebrity on her sick-bed.[2] A review of the facts of her case revealed that the child she had been convicted of murdering had almost certainly been stillborn, delivered 'near the fourth month of her time ... not above a span long'.[3] It seemed, to a public very ready to believe in such redemption, that a miscarriage of justice had been averted.

Once she had fully recovered, Anne, her pardon obtained, left Oxford and returned to the country. She went on to marry and have three children, living for more than a decade after the execution of her sentence. Her afterlife as text, by contrast, was remarkable. Her case was first reported in that week's edition of the London newssheet *Mercurius Politicus* and inspired so much interest that a follow-up story, or 'further Accompt', appeared the following month, with the editorial comment 'we hope there will come forth a more full and entire relation of her [Greene's] Tryall, Sufferings, &c., to the end that this great work of God may be as fully and truly known, as becommeth so great a matter'.[4] The case was widely referenced throughout the second half of the seventeenth century, for instance in Thomas Fuller's *History of the Worthies of England* (1662), in James Heath's *Chronicle of the Late Intestine War* (1676) – wherein it was described as an occurrence 'very fit to be transmitted to posterity'– and in John Evelyn's diary for 1675.[5] Furthermore, it continued to be debated well into the next century, appearing, for example, in William Derham's *Physico-Theology* (1713), where it is described as 'still well remembered among the seniors' at Oxford.[6] The story of a twenty-two-year-old maid from the village of Steeple Barton in Oxfordshire, 'of a middle stature ... and an indifferent good feature', not only captured the imagination of her contemporaries, it would seem, but continued to resonate.[7]

This chapter focuses on a more immediate, if equally unexpected, response to events. It examines how Anne's story was told and retold in 'popular' poetic form, and asks how such poetry might work to construct a narrative about female subjectivity under the law. Three pamphlet accounts of Anne's case appeared in early 1651 and were reprinted repeatedly thereafter.[8] Of these works, two, William Burdet's *A Wonder of Wonders* and the anonymous *A Declaration from Oxford*, were issued by the London printer John Clowes for the sensation-hungry City market, but a third, *Newes from the Dead*, attributed to an Oxford 'scholler' called Richard Watkins, was produced by Leonard Lichfield, official printer to Oxford University. Watkins' pamphlet is a two-part document: it contains an account of the case, almost certainly drawn from William Petty's unpublished notes on the matter, but also a number of poems about the incident, written by students and fellows from colleges across the university.[9] The first edition of Watkins' text contains twenty-five short poems; the second, which followed almost immediately afterwards, a further sixteen. The poems are aimed at an audience who can read Latin, Greek and French as well as English and their authors include an eighteen-year-old Christopher Wren and the future antiquary Anthony Wood.[10]

Unlike the vast majority of works discussed in the present volume, then, the poems in *Newes from the Dead* are unquestionably authored by men. While a few of the poets imagine Anne's own voice, they make no claims to veracity and their ventriloquising is barely veiled. We cannot claim to recover an authentic, historical Anne at the heart of these works.

What do these texts have to tell us, then, in our exploration of the gendered place of the poem?

The presentation of the criminal, or criminalised, female in poetry is most usually via ballad or complaint, in verse forms associated with pamphlets, news-books and other ephemera – poetic works that are essentially narrative, exemplary and often providential in mode. In chapter 10, Rosalind Smith, writing on female complaint and exemplarity, questions our assumptions about contemporary responses to this genre and argues for a 'heuristic flexibility' in interpretation of gallows confessions, including the possibility of a transformation from negative to positive exemplarity.[11] What the *Newes from the Dead* poems seem to me to represent is a further step in this process, a complicating yet fundamentally celebratory move towards a very practical kind of redemption for Anne as a criminalised female. This is no simplistic apotheosis – Anne's transformation is inextricable from a re-reading of the facts of the case and it places her at the heart of legal process. Of course, *Newes from the Dead* is not a gallows testimonial: it is a text formed, as we shall see, in a complex conjunction of academic playfulness, medico-legal dissertation and what Alexandra Walsham describes as 'providential journalism'.[12] Yet it remains in essence a manifestation of a popular, cheap print mode, a mode which has most usually been seen as delivering a very clear formula, a mode in which, as Sandra Clark writes, 'the typical pattern ... is shaped by confidence in the providential revelation of the truth'.[13] In their transformation of their protagonist, the *Newes* poems disrupt that 'pattern', embedding a narrative about the integrity of law itself within popular discourses of crime and wonder.

This dynamic, I will propose, is enabled in part by the generic complexity of the *Newes* poems, and in part by the confidence that inheres in their 'elite' authorship. In this chapter, then, I will seek to demonstrate how an elite re-rendering of the narratives that surround criminal women may transform our understanding of a genre traditionally associated with strategies of simplification and containment. At the same time, however, I will also suggest that Anne's story is neither unique nor aberrant in encoding this redemption, and that we may find traces of her renewal in more traditional poetic texts on infanticide.

'Poore I the poorest now on earth'

EVEN to the modern reader Anne's story is dramatic, with its two compelling motifs of reversal: the false conviction for infanticide and the miraculous return from death by hanging – the latter thrown into further relief by the sinister promise of the anatomist's knife. This would seem an almost perfect hybrid of the moralised news reporting associated with the murder ballad and the providential sensation of the wonder pamphlet. Yet the text sits uneasily with either generic mode and, before we turn to the reporting of her case, it is worth exploring this disjunction with reference to contemporary print culture.

'Miraculous' tales of escape from hanging were not unknown. As Theresa Murphy and Peter Linebaugh, among others, have demonstrated, botched hangings were a relatively frequent corollary of the state execution system – and their interpretation as miraculous phenomena was not unknown.[14] In 1605, for example, Edward Alde of London had printed *A True Relation of Go[ds] Vvonderfull Mercies*, the story of John Johnson of Antwerp, erroneously convicted of robbery and hanged, but 'miraculously preserved' by God, so that after five days on the gallows he was still alive and able to plead his own cause.[15] As a miraculous feat, Anne's experience rather pales by comparison.

Equally, seventeenth-century readers of pamphlet and ballad accounts of infanticide (or 'newborn child murder' – for, as Mark Jackson reminds us, the term commonly used today was not current in the seventeenth century) were inured to, and indeed expected, far more lurid fare than Anne's story could provide.[16] In 1637, for example, Henry Goodcole had published *Nature's Cruell Step-Dames*, an account of the crimes of two mothers: Elizabeth Barnes, who slit her child's throat under alleged satanic influence, and Anne Willis, who threw her newborn child into a vault to die.[17] The simple fact of an infanticide conviction was rarely a subject for literary transformation; as Frances Dolan notes – 'pamphlets, ballads, and plays tend to ignore infanticide as the statutes defined it – as if there is not much of a story in it'.[18]

Where there is a story, at first glance it appears to be a very tightly structured tale. Two extant seventeenth-century poetic texts offer us accounts of acts of infanticide that are in many respects very similar to Anne's alleged crime. Both texts are first-person complaints and they run on a common theme. The first is 'Martha Scambler's repentance', published in 1614 as part of a pamphlet dramatically entitled *Deeds Against Nature and Monsters by Kinde*.[19] Martha, described as a 'lascivious young damsell' and 'graceless wanton', is condemned to die at Tyburn for smothering her newborn child and concealing his body in order to preserve herself from the scandal of his illegitimacy.[20] Her lament comprises a rueful and heavily moralised examination of her former 'follies', and tracks her descent into murder, claiming that she was urged on by the Devil to destroy her child.

> The Babe being borne and in my armes,
> I should have kept it from all harmes,
> But like a Beare or Woolfe in wood,

I with it smothered up in blood.
Whereat strange motions without feare,
From hell to me presented were
And bade me bury it in a Vault,
For none alive did know my fault.[21]

The second work, 'No naturall mother but a monster', a ballad attributed to Martin Parker, follows the story of another woman, known
only as Besse, hanged in London in December 1633 'for making away her
owne new borne childe'.[22] Like Martha, Besse is figured as having strayed
from the true path: 'my carriage was too wild / woe is me woe is me'.[23] The
consequences are inevitable; she is 'got with child' and, the father having
abandoned her, she seeks a means to remedy her 'woes':

How I my fault might hide,
still I mus'd, still I mus'd,
That I might not be spide,
nor yet suspected,
To this bad thought of mine
The Deuill did incline,
To any ill designe,
he lends assistance ...

... Being where none me saw,
Quite against natures law,
I hid it in the straw,
where it was smother'd.[24]

Each woman is posited as exemplar and warning: Martha, for example,
exhorts 'Both maides and men / Both yong and old / Let not good lives
with shame be sold'.[25] Similarly, the argument of each text rests firmly on
the premise of the providential revelation of sin – in Martha's case via an
extraordinarily persistent dog, which barks for three days and nights to
alert neighbours to her crime, and for Besse an inquisitive employer who
prompts her to confess. The message is clear: dark deeds will come to
light. As Besse notes ruefully, 'God that sits on high / with his all-seeing
eye' will reveal all.[26]

Rosalind Smith, in chapter 10, considers the possibility of 'evidence,
however limited, that any of these texts [gallows complaints] were read
by early modern readers as contradictory, complex and open'.[27] The
infanticide ballads seem to suggest a similar possibility, encoding alternative readings within their simple narratives. These works, with their
trajectory of repentance and remorse, have their own poignancy and,
beyond the condemnatory discourse of wantonness, it is possible to detect
an acknowledgement of the social and economic factors that underlie

neo-natal murder. As Garthine Walker comments: 'infanticide was some-times understood by contemporaries in terms of women's responses to unpropitious circumstances'.[28] Martha is 'Poore I the poorest now on earth', while Besse's desperation on finding her child's father 'fled' is forcefully conveyed.[29] Yet the overall message is clear: these women are justly condemned and, for them, redemption lies only beyond the grave.

'Variously and falsely reported amongst the vulgar'

NOT so for Anne. The unique conjunction of components in her story – the dramatic survival of the gallows and the distressing tale of an alleged child murder, of which she consistently maintained her inno-cence – was thrown into further relief by a third element, which had much to do with the time and place of her conviction. 'On one dead by Law but reviv'd by Physick' is the title of one of the early poems in *Newes from the Dead* (folio 14), and this is key. As we shall see, Anne's 'miraculous' story crystallised contemporary concerns about the legal treatment of alleged infanticides and, on one level, allowed those concerns to become part of a new, redemptive scientific discourse, to the greater glory of Oxford University. This process is manifest in *Newes from the Dead,* although it is not without complication: the pamphlet's very subtitle – *A True and Exact Narration of the Miraculous Deliverance of Anne Greene* – encodes this contradiction, and its opening paragraph furthers the point:

> There happened lately in this Citty a very rare and remarkable accident, which being variously and falsely reported amongst the vulgar (as in such cases is usuall) to the end that none may be deceived…, I have here faith fully recorded it, according to the Information I have received from those that were the chiefe Instruments in bringing this great worke to perfection. (folio 1)

Assertions of empirical truth, along with claims to be dispelling false and 'vulgar' reports with 'Information' from direct witnesses, are, of course, a classic feature of the 'wonder' pamphlet or providential murder text.[30] Yet, simultaneously, these textual devices function to move *Newes from the Dead* away from the 'wondrous' and towards the scientific, an identifica-tion that the piece itself at once embraces and resists.

We know only basic facts about Watkins himself. Anthony Wood iden-tifies him with the Richard Watkins, who gained his MA degree at Christ Church in 1647 and had a later career as a rector in Warwickshire and Gloucestershire.[31] *Newes from the Dead* itself emphasises his position as 'a scholler in Oxford' (folio 1). Undoubtedly, the pamphlet is a peculiarly 'Oxford' text, published in the city, produced by the university printer, and its poems, written by commoners, scholars, fellows and alumni from at least eleven different colleges, further endorse this status. It is unclear whether the poems were themselves produced as part of an academic exercise (perhaps unlikely, given the spread of colleges represented), or were anthologised by the author, the printer or a third party. If the identification is correct, Watkins was a student at Christ Church, and members of his college author at least three poems in the first edition and four in the second. However, New College and Queen's are both more significantly represented, while the majority of the new poems in the second edition are the work of student commoners at St John's. Whether or not Watkins was instrumental in the commissioning of the poems appended to his work, their juxtaposition with his core account sets up a particularly intriguing tension at the heart of this hybrid text.

Watkins' report begins conventionally enough, with a summary of Anne's discovery, conviction and execution. At the point at which she is observed to be still living, however, *Newes from the Dead* changes in mode. Not only does Watkins' language transform, now emphatically the discourse of the insider – 'Dr Petty ... *our* Anatomy-Professor' (folio 2, emphasis added) – but his time-frame slows to that of the scientific observer. From this point his pamphlet becomes, in effect, a meticulous account of a patient's treatment and recovery, and he documents each stage of the process rigorously, noting with fascination Anne's responses, her pulse rate and her routines:

> All this while her pulse was very low ... her arm being bound up again, and now and then a little cordial water powr'd down her throat, they continued rubbing her in several places, caused ligatures to be made in her armes and leggs.... Her face also began somewhat to swell and to look very red on that side on which the knot of the halter had been fastened. (folio 3)

He records what Anne ate, how long she slept and the gradual healing of her throat and tongue, which she had 'bitten ... in the time of her suffering' (folio 6). Undoubtedly, Petty is the source for this detail, but the meticulous and painstaking nature of Watkins' rendering of his information is evidence of aspiration to scholarship for his own text.

Once Anne is proved to have made a full recovery and retreats from the scene to the 'Countrey' (folio 6), Watkins turns to the scientific 'proofs' for her innocence of the murder of her child, presenting clear evidence that the child was miscarried or stillborn:

> it is evident that the child was very unperfect ... the Midwife said ... that she did not beleeve that ever it had life ... it is not likely that the Child was vital, the mischance happening not above 17 weeks after the time of her conception. (folios 6–7)

207

He offers a similar exposition of the reasons why Anne, as she asserted at her trial and in her gallows speech, did not know that she was pregnant, describing her menstrual patterns – 'she was not 10 weeks without the usual Courses of women' (folio 7) – and pointing to the scientific consistency of her testimony on this point.

During the course of his text, Watkins returns repeatedly to the point that Anne's body had originally been intended for the anatomist's hand, commenting upon the fact that her physicians 'missed the opportunity of improving their knowledge in the dissection of a Dead body' (folio 8). In her recovery Anne cheats the anatomists of their expected revelation – the 'science of seeing' described by Jonathan Sawday – but provides one still greater:[32]

> in the same Roome where her Body was to have beene dissected for the satisfaction of a few, she became a greater wonder, being reviv'd, to the satisfaction of multitudes that flocked thither daily to see her. (folio 6)

Watkins seems to offer his text as a materialisation of that greater revelation; he has codified Anne's survival as an alternative anatomy lecture.

Susan C. Staub suggests that 'Anne's body seems commodified and disciplined here', aligning the 'multitudes' of visitors paying their fee to see Anne with the observers of the anatomised corpse, yet its status in Watkins' narrative seems much more complex.[33] Quite apart from the fact that Anne uses the money 'earned' by her miraculous body to pay her physicians' bills and purchase her pardon, it is incorrect to assume that *Newes from the Dead* silences her actual voice in favour of the symbolic message of a dissected corpse. Despite her sore throat and injured tongue, Anne's voice is heard throughout Watkins' account – she is reported to have 'laughed and talked merrily ... complained of paine beneath the pit of her stomach; [and] of a deadness in the tipp of her tongue' (folios 4–5). Almost the first thing Petty and his associates attempt to do is to get her to communicate – 'bidding her, if she understood them, to move her hand, or open her eies' (folio 4). In fact, it is via Anne's commentary that the progress of her recovery is measured; she verbalises her own miracle.

It is clear that an element of Anne's celebrity arose from a happy conjunction with the careers of the men who oversaw her resuscitation. Her revival occurred at a significant moment for Oxford science: the group of medical men and natural philosophers who met at Clarke's shop would form the core membership of the Royal Society when it was founded in 1660. The 'wonder' of Anne's recovery proved a powerful piece of propaganda for William Petty in particular; in 1651 he became full professor of anatomy and the following year secured a coveted post in the Irish civil service. Quarter of a century later, John Evelyn referred in his diary to Petty as 'famous as for his Learning, so for recovering a poore wench that had been hanged'.[34] At its core, then, Watkins' project is to pay tribute to the success of Petty and his colleagues, 'those Gentlemen that freely undertook, and have so happily performed that Cure' (folio 8), but his account also celebrates its protagonist, and – whether intentionally or not – firmly establishes her as such. As we shall see, this schema is similarly adopted by his fellow scholars in their poetic tributes.

Just how successful is Watkins in his re-presentation of Anne's recovery as a discourse of scientific advance? In his discussion of *Newes from the Dead*, Joad Raymond describes the pamphlet as a 'serious, scientific publication ... discursively antithetical to the populist, cheaper pamphlets'.[35] However, Watkins' work remains an inevitably conflicted piece, unable quite to make the leap away from the seductive possibilities of the sensation text. In enumerating the various 'proofs' of Anne's innocence, for example, Watkins cannot resist including a final suggestion, one which plunges *Newes from the Dead* straight back to the level of that 'cheaper' print:

> There is yet one thing more.... That her Grand Prosecutor Sir Thomas Read died within three daies after her Execution; even almost as soon as the probability of her reviving could be well confirmed to him. (folio 7)

Watkins' hasty qualification, 'hee was an old man and such Events are not too rashly to be commented on', does little to redeem the pamphlet's descent into the discourse of signs and wonders.

When we turn to the *Newes* poems, we find this generic indeterminacy compounded further. Even as they endeavour to inscribe Anne's experience as a serious medical milestone, the poems also encode a range of other – and frequently highly partisan – responses, which simultaneously work against that endeavour. On one level, *Newes from the Dead* itself, with its muscular display of poetic prowess from across the colleges, represents a neat piece of scientific and literary assertion on behalf of Oxford: 'Oxford (the Arts Metropolis) ne're-knew/A rarer feat then was perform'd by you/ Brave Aesculapian friends!' (folio 14) writes Kingsmill Lucy of Christ Church. Certainly, a number of the verses are straightforward odes to the skills of Petty and his colleagues. Guil Fitzgerald's poem, 'To the physicians', is typical in its hyperbole:

> To raise a Pyramide unto your skill
> Were to mistrust experience, ...
> Yee are not mortall, nor need feare to dye:
> To conquer Death is Immortality.
> Yee have done that.
> (folio 7)

Yet it is really Anne herself who holds the poets' interest and, by the second edition of the pamphlet, some twenty-two of the forty-one poems are dedicated or explicitly directed to her. The Oxford poets treat her escape as a joyous conceit, plundering it relentlessly: for easy puns – 'Th' Hangman held her in *Suspense*' (folio 17), 'Sh'ad been cut up, if not so soon cut downe' (folio 22), 'Shee's a maid twice and yet is not dis-maid' (folio 22); for casual misogyny – 'Admire not, 'tis no newes, nere think it strange / T'were wonder if a Woman should not change' (folio 8), 'One thing both hang'd and sav'd her, shee was *light*' (folio 16); and for a catalogue of reversals, in which the hangman's rope is refigured as the 'thread of life' (folio 13) and the gallows become a regenerative force – 'The fatall Tree, which first began the strife / Sided with them, and prov'd a Tree of Life' (folio 10). Overall, the tone seems indulgent and irreverent, a celebration of ironic reversal and renewed life – that 'uncouth Paradox Resuscitation' (folio 9) – and far from a serious scientific endeavour.

While they bring the full scope of their learning – and a certain amount of academic posturing – to their task, the student poets certainly embrace the playful possibilities of the cheap print mode. The relationship between that mode, particularly the sensationalised crime story, and what we might perceive as a contemporary academic or elite culture is perhaps more complex than it first appears. As Sandra Clark points out: 'such productions were held in low esteem, regarded as trivial, time-wasting and damaging to serious literature'.[36] Nonetheless, and as Clark acknowledges elsewhere in her survey, this distaste was not universal, and as the seventeenth century progressed, these works became the stuff of collections such as those established by Anthony Wood, contributor to *Newes from the Dead*, and John Selden, among others.[37] The poets of *Newes from the Dead* seem comfortable with their participation in what, in essence, is a piece of mass market – albeit Oxonian mass market – ephemera.

This momentum towards the popular is only enhanced in the pamphlet's second edition, wherein much of the original Latin is 'Englished', suggesting an expanded target audience. In this edition, Watkins' prose account is moved to the start of the text, so that the poems function more obviously as commentary upon the case. The opening poem of the first edition, the rather ponderous 'In Puellam a Diutino Patibuli Cruciatu redivivam', is re-ordered to follow the newly entitled and rather more explicit piece, 'On Shee which was hang'd and afterwards recovered'.

In this opening verse Anne is compared to Eurydice, and the poet, Henry Perin, solemnly warns us that, 'Wives may deceive and do their best / To counterfeit in all the rest / Only let them not Dye in jest' (folio 9). Throughout the collection, womankind is figured as a 'nine-liv'd Sex' (folio 10), capable of endless deception – 'Women in this with cats agree,

I think/Both Live and Scratch after they have *tip't the Wink*' (folio 14); 'Well, for this trick Ile never so be led/As to believe a Woman, though shee's dead' (folio 8). Intriguingly, however, a number of the poems seem to display a grudging admiration for this fact; Anne is depicted as a 'Strange Sophister' (folio 10), a 'subtle Gamestresse' who plays Death at 'tick-tack' and emerges victorious (folio 15). In the verse created by Daniel Danvers of Trinity College she is even transformed into a military strategist – 'if with such art thou can'st thy Distaff rule/The Souldiers all to thee shall go to Schoole' (folio 8). Danvers describes Anne as 'thine owne *Clotho*' (folio 8), and indeed the sister fates appear repeatedly throughout the poems. In John Aylmer's 'On the death and life of *Anne Greene*', for example, the poet asks his subject 'Didst thou indent with Rigid *Atropos*,/To los't a while and then to quitte the Losse?' (folio 9), while in the piece immediately following, Peter Killigrew demands of 'Sportive *Atropos*', 'what, must we see/Some Hocus-tricks? The thread of life to be/Asunder cut, and yet entire remaine?' (folio 10).

Although Anne's duel with death takes a number of forms, it is to this fascinating collusion with, or defiance of, 'the *fatall Spinster*', as Anthony Wood terms it, that the poems return. This seems significant, and highlights what is an obvious and perhaps surprising omission from the *Newes* poems: unlike the editors of *Mercurius Politicus*, the student poets do not seem to regard Anne's survival as a 'great work of God'; while they deploy the occasional biblical reference, they seem not to feel that they must impose a Christian framework upon her story, and this confidence is liberating.[38] Indeed, their tropes are overwhelmingly classical, and while this may be an inevitable corollary of a group of undergraduates displaying their mastery of that mode, what is more noteworthy is that their imagery is predominantly feminine. Atropos and her sisters, Eurydice, the Furies: Anne is variously identified with and opposed to a range of classical female subjects, as she navigates her way between life and death. This may of course be simply another manifestation of the misogyny inherent in the poets' representations of the tricksy, inconstant 'nine-liv'd Sex'; certainly in the verse authored by Theodore Wynne of Jesus College, Anne's victory over a feminised 'Death' is portrayed as an act of gender treachery:

> The hungry grave hath lost a bitte,
> And yet still gapes, alas! I feare
> Death it selfe will be buryed there.
> Shee's sicke, and melts in her owne wo,
> The female Sex should cheat her so.
> (folio 18)

Yet, as we have seen, the poems undoubtedly concede a certain respect to their object and protagonist; this is bound up both with Anne's perceived victory over death and with a strain of imagery that links back to her original 'crime'. In the poem submitted by 'H.B.' of All Souls College, Anne is a model of fecundity and life-giving power – an 'Unchang'd Phoenix' who 'Offspring[s] Herself' and is 'Midwive to her Throwes' (folio 11). This imagery of Anne is oddly transformative, erasing her status as condemned infanticide and reinscribing her as something quite other. As we shall see, this empowering – and potentially troubling – revision of Anne's story may link to a number of difficulties around the status of her original conviction.

Perhaps inevitably, the poems exhibit an underlying preoccupation with Anne's sexual *status* – 'A Wench Re-woman'd!' (folio 14), 'twice a maid' (folio 11) – interestingly, however, this is frequently staged as academic disputation. The verse proffered by John Watkins of Queen's College, 'The woman's *case* put to the lawyers', wherein Anne, her own advocate, requests judgement, is typical:

> Mother, or Maid, I pray you whether?
> One, or both, or am I neither?
> The Mother dyed: may't not be said
> That the Survivor is a Maid?
> (folio 6)

Indeed, while they relish the intellectual dilemmas raised by her problematised status, the poets display little moral condemnation of Anne's sexual *activity*. This stance seems inextricably linked to the poems' conviction of her innocence of the crime for which she was tried. Just as the earlier infanticide ballads needs must present their guilty protagonists as morally reprehensible (even while tentatively acknowledging the difficulty of their situation), for the majority of the Oxford poets, Anne must be innocent of all crimes. This desire for full exculpation reaches its climax in the final poem in the pamphlet, which contains an oblique suggestion that Anne's pregnancy was the result of rape, a scenario for which there is no evidence whatsoever in any testimony, including Anne's own (folio 22). Certain critics, among them Frances Dolan, have noted possible implications of this – 'Watkins insists not only that she [Anne] did not perform the act for which she was convicted but also that she utterly lacked self-consciousness'.[39] Yet reading the poems, with their alternative model of Anne as laudable 'Champion' (folio 10), victorious over the law and death itself, must inevitably complicate this picture.

'Not consonant unto the Lawes'

T HE opening lines of the poem submitted by Robert Mathew of New College to the second edition of *Newes from the Dead* are addressed directly to Anne: 'Thou shalt not Swing again', they assert, 'come clear thy Brow / Thou hast the Benefit o' th' Clergie now' (folio 7). What this statement foregrounds for us is that the most curious reversal in Anne's case is not her journey from death to life, but from guilt to innocence. Why, having been convicted of murder, in a recognised court of law, and having accidentally survived an inept execution, was she not returned to the gallows forthwith? As we have seen, unsuccessful hangings were not uncommon and in fact a return to the gallows was their usual consequence, as Blackstone noted a century later:

> If, upon judgment to be hanged by the neck till he is dead, the criminal be not thoroughly killed but revives, the sheriff must hang him again. For the former hanging was no execution of sentence.[40]

This makes the granting of Anne's initial reprieve all the more surprising. Because all of the accounts assert Anne's innocence from the outset, as readers we are caught up in the momentum of renewal and vindication that is her narrative, a momentum that tends to obscure the practical question of her pardon. We know little about why she was granted that pardon in the face of a conviction for murder. Her involvement with Petty's circle can only have helped, of course, but one of the other pamphlets on her case, *A Wonder of Wonders*, suggests that it was popular rather than academic sentiment that saved her in the first instance. Anne's recovery, the account states:

> moved some of her enemies to wrath and indignation, insomuch, that a great man amongst the rest, moved to have her again carried to the place of execution, ... but some poor honest Soldiers then present, seemed to be very much discontented thereat, and declared, That there was a great hand of God on it, and having suffered the Law, it was contrary to all right and reason, that any further punishment should be inflicted upon her.[41]

We sense here an immediate readiness to believe in Anne's innocence, what seems like a popular discomfort with her conviction and a corresponding relief at her escape from the hangman. To fully understand the problematic nature of Anne's prosecution we must consider her alleged offence. Newborn child murder was a crime that had undergone a peculiar process of revision in the period. Prior to the seventeenth century, English law on neo-natal murder was at best unclear and achieving successful prosecution was complex. Cases were tried under common-law rules of evidence, which required it to be proven that the child in question had been born alive; an unborn child had no identity as victim in law – as Laura Gowing comments, such infants were 'still part of the mother; they were not, yet, separate legal subjects who could be injured'.[42] The difficulty of such proof was self-perpetuating, for without convictions there could be no precedent for the judge to offer the jury as a basis for deliberation.

This began to change in the late sixteenth century, with a growing focus on the concealment of infant death as a signifier of guilt. This idea crystallised a dual concern – about women who concealed their unlawful sexual activity, and about the economic cost of that activity manifest in illegitimate births. There is evidence that the rise of the concealment argument was linked to increasingly stringent attempts to control the poor, with bills dealing with infanticide first being heard in the Commons in the same period as the 1609 Poor Law, a statute which described bastardy as a 'great charge' to the country.[43] Yet alongside this socio-economic imperative, we seem to witness a corresponding fulfilment of a legal need. A dictat of concealment as an indication of guilt was legally very attractive; followed logically, it obviated much of the awkward uncertainty around proving infanticides, circumventing the need to codify the complex physical proofs previously required for conviction. Sure enough, in 1624 the concealment reasoning was made explicit in statute form. The text of 21 James I, c.27, runs thus:

> An Act to prevent the destroying and murthering of bastard children.
>   WHEREAS, many lewd women that have been delivered of bastard children, to avoid their shame, and to escape punishment, do secretly bury or conceal the death of their children, and after, if the child be found dead, the said women do allege, that the said child was born dead; whereas it falleth out sometimes (although hardly it is to be proved) that the said child or children were murthered by the said women....
>   II ... be it enacted by the authority of this present parliament, That if any woman ... be delivered of any issue of her body, male or female, which being born alive, should by the laws of this realm be a bastard, and that she endeavour privately either by drowning, or secret burying thereof, as that it may not come to light, whether it were born alive or not, but be concealed: in every such case the said mother so offending shall suffer death as in case of murther, except such mother can make proof by one witness at the least that the child ... was born dead.

The Act was clear; it targeted only mothers of 'bastard children', constructing them specifically as 'lewd women', establishing an immediate position of censure. Crucially, it shifted the onus of the evidentiary problem onto the accused, who must prove 'by one witness at the least' that the child was born dead. Suddenly, there was a neat chain of assumption for the jury – the unwed mother was a 'lewd' and sinful woman; she would naturally be secretive with regard to her sexual transgressions;

that very secrecy both practically and psychologically codified her moral turpitude and her responsibility for her child's death. Essentially, it was now a capital offence to conceal the death of an illegitimate newborn, regardless of whether the child had suffered any malicious action.

Turning back to 'Martha Scambler's repentance' and 'No naturall mother', we find that they inscribe the assumptions of the Act within their depiction of their protagonists' guilt. Martha, whose case would have been heard before the Act came into force, but while it was being debated, asserts that 'when my hour of labour came / To bring to light this fruit of shame / No Midwives help at all I sought'.[44] Equally, the lament ascribed to Besse records the fact that, at the time of her child's delivery, 'There was no woman than / neere to assist me'.[45]

Anne was prosecuted at the height of the Act's enforcement and the discussions of her indictment indicate how clearly the logic of her conviction mirrored the logic of the statute – 'she was delivered of a Man-child: which being never made known, and the Infant found dead in the house of office, caused a suspicion, that she being the mother had murthered it'.[46] For an unmarried woman, witnesses to a child's death were unlikely – a midwife present at the delivery would have been obliged to attempt to obtain the name of the child's father and to report the couple for fornication, for example – and this very failure to secure help of any kind during delivery was rapidly translated in the courts into a clear indication of intent to harm the child. Indeed, the seventeenth-century author and physician Peregrine Willughby commented on the prescience of having a midwife present at the birth 'to avoid all future suspicions and to free some of the looser sort from the danger of the statute-law', citing the case of a mother 'hanged for not having a woman by her, at her delivery'.[47]

Anne's conviction, then, was vindicated under the literal terms of the Act, yet, as we have seen, on the physical evidence it was deeply unsatisfactory and, judging by its reporting, observers were well aware of this potential disjunction in infanticide cases. The *Newes* poems undercut their verbal play with allusions, both subtle and overt, to the legal implications of the Greene case – herewith John Aylmer, Scholar of New College:

> Their Law would have some plea; were it to thee
> Who first the Malefactor Hang, then see
> Whe're t'were a just and equitable Cause
> Whether not consonant unto the Lawes
> (folios 9–10)

The poems make repeated reference to perceived deficiencies of the judicial process in the case – 'Whose scruples palsie-Juryes weigh amisse, / The Gallows her exacter balance is' (folio 19) – and indeed to the elision of medical evidence by the statute law – Anne is 'hang'd for her Abortive fruit' (folio 14), her 'Embryo's Birth's Abortive' (folio 12). In the verse authored by Walter Pope of Wadham College, this is made explicit, as the poet acknowledges the implication of concealment – 'Despightfull *Embryo* in secret plac't / By Her, by thee Shee's publikely disgrac't' (folio 16). Even Thomas Arthur, one of the few poets who feels obliged to acknowledge Anne's illicit sexual activity, contends that 'The crime was heinous, but (if you know all) / T'was not soe High as to be Capitall' (folio 16).

Garthine Walker has argued that, in fact, juries in infanticide cases 'regularly acquitted women whose cases rested on concealment alone' and, intriguingly, several of the poets seem to concur, highlighting the unfairness of the practice of denying women benefit of clergy – and thus the opportunity to mitigate a capital sentence – in such cases.[48] 'Clergie looke to it, for since shee / Was rob'd the benefit of thee', writes Anthony Wood (folio 21), while Robert Mathew offers Anne her *'Neck-Verse'* (folio 7), the text read by those who sought to assert their right to a clergyable reprieve. This is not without its own subtext of misogyny – for Mathew, it is a 'Strange Wench' who can be 'sav'd by *Booke'* (folio 7) – nonetheless, it represents an acknowledgment of the inequity of the judicial process.

In 1651, of course, the law that the Oxford undergraduates mocked was no longer a divinely ordained jurisdiction manifested in the person of the monarch. Law in interregnum Oxford was fraught with indeterminacy, its very authority in question, and the pamphlets pick up on this broader instability with disparaging references to a judicial system in flux: 'What hath the Law its power lost / Since th' English tongue hath it engrost?' (folio 18). Charles Capell's verse goes as far as to suggest that such a system may be vulnerable to the possibility of malicious prosecutions, with an overt reference to the death of Sir Thomas Read: 'Wee'l write on her Accuser, Here he *Lies'* (folio 18). In this context it is perhaps suggestive that at least one of the St John's poets, Francis Withins, invokes the possibility of an earlier, medieval, form of criminal trial for Anne – 'Death was thy Ordeal and Compurgatrix' (folio 15) – and, in his use of this particular variant of 'Compurgator', renders this redemptive process a feminine mode.

'Contradictions Legitimate'

IT is instructive to note that it is overwhelmingly the poems added to *Newes from the Dead* in its second, arguably more accessible, edition that evince this preoccupation with bad justice. So, while Richard Watkins looks to redeem Anne Greene via the scientific evidence in the case, his fellow scholars seem more closely aligned with the 'poor honest Soldiers' and their dissatisfaction with the mechanisms of the judicial process. Their 'discontent', however, is expressed with all the confidence that a classical education can provide, and it produces surprising results. 'The woman's *case*' is not only 'put to the Lawyers', as the title of John Watkins' poem relays, but the woman, liberated from the punitive discourses of a providential narrative, is placed at the heart of this process, requesting judgement on her own cause. The traces of doubt which we can identify in 'No naturall mother' and 'Martha Scambler's repentance' are here crystallised into a full engagement with a legal premise gone awry. Of course, what actually saved Anne was not the medical discourse Watkins proposes, but the ready belief in her innocence that her own 'victory' over law and death engendered, and the wave of opinion that that belief mustered. With their curious transformation of their protagonist from convicted infanticide to 'Unchang'd Phoenix' (folio 11), and in their tentative steps towards a feminised justice, it is to this victory that the majority of the poems pay tribute.

'Thy strange fate / Do's contradictions Legitimate' (folio 9) John Aylmer writes of Anne in *Newes from the Dead*, and this description might be said to apply equally to the text itself. A cheap print work that disrupts all our ideas of that genre, *Newes from the Dead*'s curious multivocality captures perfectly the diverse and conflicting responses provoked by the Anne Greene case, the competing discourses of science, law and sensation that surround the idea of newborn child murder in the period, and the anxiety that provokes. We see this anxiety both in the efforts of Watkins to reclaim truth via scientific fact, and in the quality of relief that subtends the celebratory mode of the poems. Ultimately, even the historical Anne participated in this; when, in 1651, she received her pardon and left Oxford, she took 'away with her the Coffin wherein she lay, as a Trophey' (folio 6).

While such a reading of the *Newes from the Dead* poems cannot claim to recover an authentic, unmediated female subjectivity, what it can and does do is shed light upon the complex possibilities that surround the literary presentation of early modern criminalised women. In part this may be enabled by the very particular circumstances of the poems' production: an elite, academic authorship and the modes of debate and enquiry associated with that group. Yet, as we have seen, this complexity is not confined to Anne's case; it is possible to detect traces of such questioning even within the most stylised of the popular infanticide ballads. As such, then, Anne's seemingly unique story may open up possibilities for more general enquiry; her 'strange fate' becomes a means to illuminate the 'contradictions legitimate' that form the subtext of a wider range of popular poetic works, unsettling our assumptions about the ways in which those texts may have been received and understood by those who encountered them.

Notes

1 Reproduced in R. Watkins, *Newes from the Dead. Or a true and exact narration of the miraculous deliverance of Anne Greene, who being executed at Oxford Decemb. 14. 1650. afterwards revived and by the care of certain hysitians [sic] there, is now perfectly recovered*, Oxford, 1651, itself reproduced in D. Wing, *Short Title Catalogue of Books Printed in England, Scotland, Ireland, Wales and British America and of English Books Printed in Other Countries 1641–1700* (2nd edition), 3 vols, Modern Language Association of America, New York, 1972–94, W1074, folio 16. The second edition of Wing has some errors in page numbering which are retained in my references, which appear in the text for most subsequent citations.

2 *Mercurius Politicus*, no. 28 (12–19 December 1650), p. 468; *Newes from the Dead*, folio 6.

3 *Newes from the Dead*, folio 6.

4 *Mercurius Politicus*, no. 32 (9–16 January 1651), p. 521.

5 T. Fuller, *The History of the Worthies of England*, London, 1662, in Wing, *Short Title Catalogue*, F2441, p. 341; J. Heath, *A Chronicle of the Late Intestine War*, London, 1676, in Wing, *Short Title Catalogue*, H1321, p. 279; J. Bowle (ed.), *The Diary of John Evelyn*, Oxford University Press, New York, 1983, pp. 252–3.

6 W. Derham, *Physico-Theology* (12th edition), Robert Urie, Glasgow, 1752, p. 159. See also J. Ward, *The Lives of the Professors of Gresham College*, London, 1740.

7 *Newes from the Dead*, folio 1.

8 As well as *Newes from the Dead*, cited above, these were: *A Declaration from Oxford*, London, 1651, in Wing, *Short Title Catalogue* (CD-ROM, 1996), D585A; and W. Burdet, *A Wonder of Wonders*, London, 1651, Wing, *Short Title Catalogue*, B5620.

9 For Petty's case notes, see W. Petty, *The Petty Papers: Some Unpublished Writings of Sir William Petty. Edited from the Bowood Papers by the Marquis of Lansdown*, vol. 2, Constable & Co., London, 1927, p. 157.

10 C. Wren, 'Wonder of highest Art!', *Newes from the Dead*, folio 13; A. Wood, 'I'le stretch my Muse', folios 16–21.

11 See page 191 of the present volume.

12 A. Walsham, *Providence in Early Modern England*, Oxford University Press, Oxford, 1999, p. 44.

13 S. Clark, *Women and Crime in the Street Literature of Early Modern England*, Palgrave Macmillan, Basingstoke, 2004, p. 24.

14 T. Murphy, *The Old Bailey*, Mainstream Publishing, Edinburgh, 1999, p. 63, for example; P. Linebaugh, *The London Hanged*, Verso, London, 2003.

15 *A True Relation of Go[ds] Vvonderfull Mercies in Preserving one Aliue, which hanged fiue days, who was falsly accused*, London, 1605, in A. W. Pollard and G. R. Redgrave, *A Short Title Catalogue of Books Printed in England, Scotland and Ireland and of English Books Printed Abroad 1475-1670* (2nd edition, revised and enlarged by W. A. Jackson, F. S. Ferguson and Katharine F. Pantzer), 3 vols, Bibliographical Society, London, 1976–91, 14668.

16 M. Jackson, *New-Born Child Murder: Women, Illegitimacy and the Courts in 18th Century England*, Manchester University Press, Manchester, 1996, p. 6.

17 H. Goodcole, *Nature's Cruell Step-Dames, or Matchlesse Monsters of the Female Sex*, London, 1637, in Pollard and Redgrave, *A Short Title Catalogue*, 12012.

18 F. Dolan, *Dangerous Familiars: Representations of Domestic Crime in England, 1550–1700*, Cornell University Press, Ithaca, 1994, p. 132.

19 *Deeds Against Nature and Monsters by Kinde*, London, 1614, in Pollard and Redgrave, *A Short Title Catalogue*, 809.

20 Ibid., sig. A2.

21 Ibid., sig. B2–B3.

22 M. Parker, 'No naturall mother but a monster', London, 1634, in H. E. Rollins (ed.), *A Pepysian Garland*, Cambridge University Press, Cambridge, 1922, pp. 425–8.

23 Parker, 'No naturall mother', p. 425.
24 Ibid., p. 426.
25 *Deeds Against Nature*, sig. B3.
26 Parker, 'No naturall mother', p. 427.
27 See page 187 of the present volume.
28 G. Walker, *Crime, Gender and Social Order in Early Modern England*, Cambridge University Press, Cambridge, 2003, p. 156.
29 *Deeds Against Nature*, sig. B2; Parker, 'No naturall mother', p. 427.
30 See, on this point, Walsham, *Providence*, chs 2 and 4.
31 Handwritten annotation to Anthony Wood's copy of *Newes from the Dead* in the Bodleian Library, shelf-mark Wood 515(12). See also J. Foster, *Alumni Oxonienses: The Members of the University of Oxford*, Oxford University Press, Oxford, 1891.
32 J. Sawday, *The Body Emblazoned: Dissection and the Human Body in Renaissance Culture*, Routledge, London, 1995, p. 219.
33 S. C. Staub, '"A wench re-woman'd": the miraculous recovery of Anne Greene', in T. Howard-Hill and P. Rollinson (eds), *Renaissance Papers 1997*, Camden House, Woodbridge, 1997, p. 110.
34 Bowle (ed.), *The Diary of John Evelyn*, pp. 252–3.
35 J. Raymond (ed.), *Making the News: An Anthology of the Newsbooks of Revolutionary England 1641–1660*, Windrush Press, Moreton-in-Marsh, 1993, p. 171.
36 Clark, *Women and Crime*, p. 4.
37 Ibid., p. 71.
38 *Mercurius Politicus*, no. 32, p. 521.
39 Dolan, *Dangerous Familiars*, p. 139.
40 J. W. Ehrlich (ed.), *Ehrlich's Blackstone*, vol. 2, Capricorn Books, New York, 1959, p. 524. Indeed, in May 1658 another maidservant was hanged for infanticide in the city, and was revived by the doctors who were to anatomise her. She was not so fortunate; the local bailiffs seized her by night and hanged her once again, on a tree in what is now Gloucester Green. See A. Clark (ed.), *The Life and Times of Anthony Wood, Antiquary, of Oxford, 1632–1695, Described by Himself*, Oxford Historical Society and Clarendon Press, Oxford, 1891, vol. 1, pp. 250–1.
41 Burdet, *A Wonder of Wonders*, folio 6.
42 L. Gowing, 'Secret births and infanticide in seventeenth-century England', *Past and Present*, vol. 156 (1992), p. 108.
43 7 James I, c.4.
44 *Deeds Against Nature*, sig. B2.
45 Parker, 'No naturall mother', p. 426.
46 Watkins, *Newes from the Dead*, folio 1.
47 P. Willughby, *Observations in Midwifery* (ed. H. Blenkinsop), H. T. Cooke & Son, Warwick, 1972, pp. 11–12.
48 Walker, *Crime, Gender and Social Order*, p. 153.

CHAPTER 12

The contemplative woman's recreation?
Katherine Austen and the estate poem

Susan Wiseman

On the situation of Highbury

So fairely mounted in a fertile Soile
Affordes the dweller pleasure, without Toile
Th'adjacent prospects give so sweet a sight
That Nature did resolue to frame delight
On this faire Hill, and with a bounteous load
Produce rich Burthens, making the aboad
As full of joy, as where fat vallies smile
And greater far, here Sicknes doth exile.
Tis an unhappy fate to paint that place
By my unpolisht Lines, with so bad grace
Amidst its beauty if a streame did rise
To clear my mudy braine and misty eyes
And find a Hellicon t'enlarge my muse
Then I noe better place than this wud choose
In such a Laver and on this bright Hill
I wish Parnassus to adorne my quill.

T HIS poem, printed here in its entirety, is probably the best-known
poem by Katherine Austen, a widow living in Restoration London.
Austen's sole surviving text, 'Book M', reveals her as pious, resourceful and
entrepreneurial, but also a curious thinker, writer and poet.[1] This chapter
takes 'On the situation of Highbury' as a starting place to reconsider the
place of the estate poem as one among several interlocking discourses of
land, property, place and money in Restoration London.

From the single, now isolated, manuscript book, 'Book M', researchers,
particularly Pamela Hammons, Sarah Ross and Barbara Todd, have begun
process of locating Katherine Austen in time (she lived from the late 1620s
to about 1683).[2] Building on that research, this chapter extends her web of
connections in a way that illuminates her place in London's literary and

social world, and in the Restoration development of the writing on land and property. The chapter aims to use close work on Austen in order to look again at the estate poem (discussed by critics from Alastair Fowler to John M. Adrian's work on the local) and tease out the conditions under which writers approached place at the Restoration.[3] In returning to the genre in the light of recent research on meditational writing, manuscript contexts and women's relationship to property, it becomes clear that, set in the context of other forms of writing with which estate poems habitually cohabited, such poems can become sources for new understandings of the way later seventeenth-century poetry represented the subject's relation to place. In 'modelling' the place of an estate poem at the Restoration, it is productive to take account of the genre's intellectual and poetic pedigree, but also to consider the nature of the written spaces around the manuscript poem and the published genres coexisting at that moment.

Accurately described by its editor, Sarah Ross, as a 'borderline literary text', 'Book M' offers a litmus test of life, money, land and literature as the 1650s become the Restoration. It also, as we will show, suggests a possible literary culture of circulation in and to the east of the City of London, articulating simultaneously aspirational and pious understandings of place. Austen's thinking on God's providence, widowhood, business and family fortunes gives 'M' quite strong thematic integration even as it is diverse in its modes and forms. The text is multifunctional and, accordingly, presented at a level of working formality that sits between 'presentation' and commonplace book. Among the modes it offers are: records of business and law; literary and meditational exploration; providential interpretation and recording; analysis of social relations and encounters; the copying or practising of letters. Whether or not she considered publication in print, or whether her writings did circulate in manuscript, is at present unclear, but she did anticipate readers and there is ambiguous textual evidence that she developed a sense of her poems as a sequence. Certainly, Austen's 'Book' uses the Bible, secular poetry, providence and business dealings in the world to register and explore her experiences – Austen usually draws her reading towards the significance of her own world.[4]

In the text's main span, from 1664 to 1666, three important struggles unfold: first, in this period Austen reinterprets providences given by God that had suggested that she would die at the same age as her husband (an age she would have reached in July 1664); second, she reconsiders the possibility of remarriage; and third, and most significantly for this chapter, she records her struggle to retain control of and fully possess the estate of Highbury Manor.[5] Some of the details of this legal wrangle are significant here, because of the long duration of the attempt to keep hold of the manor on the part of the Austen family, into which Katherine had married, and the highly contested nature of their claim, in which events reaching back to 1632 were challenged.[6]

The story of Highbury began when the crown gave it to Sir Allen Apsley, Lieutenant of the Tower (and father of the poet Lucy Hutchinson), in recompense for expenses he had incurred as victualler of the navy.[7] Apsley died in 1630, soon after the lands had been transferred to him, and, as one of Apsley's creditors, Thomas Austen legally secured Highbury. With Apsley's other creditors, Sir Allen Apsley, Lucy Hutchinson's brother, complained about Austen's practices.[8] However, the Austens hung on, and by 1653 Katherine's husband had inherited the rights. However, the wrangling began again after the Restoration, and in 1662 Katherine Austen appears in Chancery records seeking to secure the inheritance of her sixteen-year-old son, Thomas.[9] Apparent success was compromised by Highbury still being leased.

Laying hold of 'Louely' Highbury (111v, Ross, p. 167) would bring Austen's family a decisive upward leap in social and economic status in moving them, physically, from City-border Shoreditch to a potentially grand estate a little to the north, outside the fray. In the period of her book's composition, because of her changing expectation of life and death as she lived on beyond the date at which she had thought that a 'monition' had told her to expect to die, Austen's relationship to time changes. The struggle for Highbury, closely tied to her feelings about the future, also changes. While Austen is writing 'Book M', then, her relationship to land and property is articulated as a changing spiritual, financial and emotional drama. 'On the situation of Highbury' is the final poem in a long section headed 'Meditations on the Sickenes and of Highbury', apparently written in late autumn 1665 after a return to London from Tillingham, in Essex, where Austen had gone to escape the raging plague and where her suitor, probably Alexander Calendar, is recorded as dying.[10]

'Meditations on the Sickenes and of Highbury'

'Through six afflictions God has promised to carry his children, and in the seaventh they shall be delivered. Six I have passed.'[11] An identification with Job 5:19 opens this meditation, with a reference to plague. It continues with a monetary note:

Since August 1664 to Michaelmas 1665:

...

The renewing the Lease of Deane Hardy	80-0-0
The expence at Parliament	
The Looseing by a pecke pocket	14-0-0

The Lending money to Cosen Williame   336-0-0
in necessity onely for 2 months and vnpaid yet[12]

The splicing of biblical identification and anxious, detailed, attention to financial matters at this point in 'M' indicate both the intensity of Austen's attention to property and the many meanings it held for her. In the accounting year, Michaelmas, a quarter day, saw rents and bonds due, but not necessarily paid, especially in time of plague. Austen sees loss everywhere; however, as we turn the page, we find that 'At this time is arrived that most bounteous blessing of Highbury, which I hope will well wade me through. the residue of my expencive buildings, and disappointment of rents from a general.cause: stroak' (F99v–100r, Ross pp. 152–3). In the dramatic reversal of debt to wealth, the niggling, troubling, losses are overwhelmingly requited. This brief, almost theatrical moment, executed in the discourse of accounting, initiates a prolonged sequence of meditations which ends with more accounts and her secular poem on Highbury.

Earlier in 'Book M' Austen has told Fortune, 'I am not in thy power ... thy blind Lottery. that cannot distinie any thing to the wertuous' (F80r, Ross p. 130). In a world motivated by the divine, God's decision to give her Highbury eclipses the mere law by reframing the event and place within a limitlessly expanded field of faith and the ethics of a Christian life. 'How shal I endeavour to live a new life' is her question on Highbury coming out of lease. In response, it seems that she subjects the event to the method of 'occasional meditation', a Protestant meditational practice which recast quotidian events within a Christian frame, to ask how they illuminate the subject's relationship with God.[13] In this mode, which Raymond Anselment and Sarah Ross convincingly argue Austen employs, the acquisition of property is interpreted through the imperatives of the Christian life, using biblical texts in an apparently solitary struggle to comprehend and act on God's gift, and to determine how she should respond in thought and deed.[14] Crucially, such great worldly fortune registers on the overarching Christian schema as debt – and we see poems working through property within the problematic of bounteous debt beyond repayment. It is a spiritual mortgage of many generations' worth and, as such, fills Austen's heart with hope that she will indeed be sent 'deliverance' from plague and punishment, God 'dispencing his stroakes' (F101r, Ross p. 153). Her heart ought to be 'disposed and devoted to his glory' and she tells herself:

> Some worke of piety goe then and shew.
> A life of purity I ever owe.
> All humble thankes, a life of ful addres
> Vnto thy Alter pay, from me thats les

223

Than the least mit of what thy goodnes throwes.
Stil streams of boverty, sure a Mountain owes.
I never can dischardge so great a sume
Lord teach me *what* to doe.
(F101r, Ross p. 153)

Austen's explicit desire to produce a 'worke of piety', life 'of ful addres' to God in an impossible attempt to 'dischardge' the great debt of his gift inevitably encounters the problem of scale and power inherent in the Christian's self-dedication to God, an imbalance resolved, for Protestants, through grace. Austen later asks, 'O that Heaven wud direct me what I should doe whether I shal glorify his name by a contemplative private life. or by an active publike life' (105v, Ross p. 158). And it is not only her own life that is mortgaged: this is a debt which, as the benefit stretches on generationally, binds her children, too, to 'honour the God of their fathers' (F100r, Ross p. 153). Indeed, Austen had earlier warned her son against imagining himself subject to an estate 'flung upon you by the hands of Fortune' (92v, Ross p. 142). Highbury, so grand a gift, multiplied that filial duty many times.

Thus, shaping the future, the event of Highbury prompts Austen to review the past in the third poem addressing the topic:

Has Conduct carried me through seaven great yeares
Great in perplexities, and great in feares.
Great Griefes with Iob: could hardly be exprest
Neither by sighings, or by teares redrest
Six folded trials, and a seaventh as great.
By a perticuler and general waight.
(F102v, Ross p. 155)

For all the tremendous legal struggle to secure Highbury, its acquisition can be smoothly integrated into a vocabulary of biblical identification with the sufferings of Hezekiah, Job and the seven great trials of the Psalmist.[15] This framing of Highbury's acquisition through the struggles of Job, mapping Austen's personal and familial struggles as ending with the 'general' affliction of plague, effaces any culpability on Austen's part as deliverance and blessing are also an affirmation that she is an accurate reader of providences. Indeed, in the struggles of the world, Austen considers herself under divine 'conduct', safe conduct. 'Conduct', a significant term throughout her text, is used to describe how God protects her – guiding her like one escorted under guard to a 'Castle' on a 'hill'. As Reid Barbour notes, such heroic or romance vocabulary and dreams, two significant preoccupations of Austen's spiritual writing, figure in both the interests of the Great Tew circle, attempting to preserve Anglicanism, and Calvinist versions of Protestantism.[16] More significant, perhaps, for understanding Austen is her vicar, Francis Raworth, who has not previously been identified and discussed. Raworth, possibly from Kent, was at St Leonard's Church in Shoreditch and publishing in the 1650s, and taught at St Leonard's, where he remained until he died of plague in September 1665.[17] Raworth preached at St Paul's before the Lord Mayor, Titchburne, in 1656, and published at least three of his sermons in this period. Raworth, in his sermons, emphasises the difficulty of understanding God's providence. The published sermons emphasise works, and in his 1656 sermon on Margaret St John, the wife of an ex-MP, he notes 'those works that follow those that die in the Lord' include, especially, works of charity. The published sermons we have all appear in 1656, and each offers a version of a comment on hypocrisy and that 'Religion is now made a party by too many'.[18] And perhaps, given that this was Austen's church, it is helpful to bring this context, too, to her writing.

Certainly, such a desire, and unease, mark the final poem preceding 'On the situation'. This poem returns to worldly affairs:

> Ist true endead, to me and mine
> That many Blesings richly shine
> On the frail stock of flesh and blood
> Tis more than can be vnderstood.
> We exalted and made high
> Others in their Anguish lye
> We accessiones of this world
> They in penury are hurld.
> (F103v, Ross p. 158)

Even within the logic of occasional meditation, the bald socio-economic exaltation of the Austens as 'accessiones' at a time of plague makes a shocking contrast to those 'in their Anguish', 'hurld' in a hellish 'penury' – a deprivation to which the unpaid debts in her accounts attest.

Accounting to Michaelmas 1665, then, Austen's spiritually inflected economic vocabulary makes Highbury a 'bounteous blessing' (F100r), to be assayed in spiritual scales. As Sarah Ross reminds us, 'Even Austen's one secular poem is framed, physically and conceptually, by her providentialism' – and by her financial planning.[19] Highbury signifies a huge obligation for the future, a test of present humility – reminding her not to imagine 'a rest in an Earthly Paradise' (F103v, Ross p. 158) – and proof of the providential nature of past sufferings. If we think of manuscript writing, in Michel de Certeau's terms, as 'the artefact of another "world"', a space 'written on the nowhere of the paper', then these poems make a world that demonstrates the impact of property in discourses that seek to

225

integrate it into a world of benign religious experience.[20] As de Certeau argues, the nowhere, 'utopia', of the page also permits the temporary conquest and ordering of experience.[21] Yet, even as Austen seems to spin a world of financial and religious meaning from events, the self-enclosed nature of that conquest is exposed as temporary, fragile and troubled by the outward gaze upon 'anguish' of the poem preceding 'On the situation of Highbury'. In terms of manuscript space, the setting apart of 'On the situation of Highbury' marks Austen's return to the problem in another genre. Within this sequence, 'On the situation' is both separate from and coupled with a meditational understanding of land and the distinct conceptual world of poetic and public implications.

'On the situation of Highbury'

So fairely mounted in a fertile Soile
Affordes the dweller pleasure, without Toile

RETURNING to the poem with which we opened, we see Austen moving to a third discourse to discuss Highbury's meanings – that of the estate poem. As she composed, there was no house on the estate, and in many ways Austen's poem projects forward in imagining Highbury's potential.[22] In terms of poetic reference, however, the 'dweller' of her opening lines recollects Ben Jonson's famous ending in his address to the Sidneys' ancient house at Penshurst – 'But thy lord dwells'.[23] This backward glance places her poem neatly in relation to Jonson, whose poem, and particularly his conclusion, had become a touchstone in the pre-war poetry of place. Austen's 'dweller' claims a place for her poem in a long tradition of celebrations of place, and specifically the estate poem, and in doing so shows herself literate in secular verse.[24]

The overlapping concerns about 'dwelling', ease, labour and good estate management found in Austen's poem and 'To Penshurst' have been elucidated by Pamela Hammons.[25] Yet, even as Austen makes Jonson's 'dwells' her precedent, it is also true that, as her text makes us intensely aware, her own position is uncomfortably close to that of the innovating builders condemned by Jonson, rather than the ancient inheritance of the Sidney family. If Jonson's poem is concerned to link the bounty of the estate to the Lord's rule, then Austen's contrastingly Georgic emphasis is on the 'joy' given by the 'fertile Soile', 'bounteous load', 'rich Burthens' of the 'fat vallies'. Attitudes to labour are distinct, too – where Jonson's workers labour gladly, at a distance from the master they serve, in Austen's poem the dweller is rescued from work because Highbury, significantly, 'Affordes the deweller pleasure, without Toile'. This is consonant with

Austen's assessment of work elsewhere as 'too much stirring and walkeing', and 'cares and busneses', which left her mother's 'strong nature worne out', which 'retire-ment. wud have prolonged' (51v, Ross p. 94). Even as Austen pays homage, the poet–patron relationships and the valorisation of ancient antecedents structuring Jonson's poem have little to offer the problems Austen faced as a poet – such as the vexed question of how to represent, or efface, the potentially problematic perspective of a woman's successful legal struggle to acquire a manor; her poor relations with the court and 'courtiers'; and the fact of her family's startling movement up the social ladder. So, if 'Penshurst' and Jonson provided one way to consider dwelling, it was not in its specifics one that immediately resonated with Austen's circumstances or experience and, as we have seen, a marker of her reading style is her search for material productive in thinking through her own problems.

The first eight lines of Austen's poem ('So' to 'exile') discover nature's plan realised in Highbury, as if 'Nature did resolue to frame delight / On this faire Hill'. Much more strongly Georgic than Jonson's, Austen's poem sees Highbury as part of nature's planned improvements. It is 'fairely mounted', with a prospect, generating crops and, therefore, wealth. More, it is healthy (unlike the plague-ridden London in which she writes). As Andrew McRae has argued, the poetic landscape was made from 'conflict-ing networks of tradition' where concerns of genre were tested against moral imperatives derived from elsewhere; yet, in 'On the situation', as with other Restoration texts, we find a determined effort to blend, rather than polarise, distinct imperatives.[26] Nature's provision is bountiful, and the poet's task to emebellish and improve on it.

The last eight lines turn to the poet's task, to 'paint' the place with 'unpolisht Lines'. The laborious lack of inventive and imaginative flow is turned into a stream – as Hammons notes, both actual and poetic. Austen uses the modesty trope itself to initiate her clever turn, for the capitalisa-tion of 'Lines' might be a hint that the stream in her imagined garden of the gods is associated with Georgic understanding of a stream's purposed end in a lively and useful fishpond. If the capitalisation of 'Lines' might be a hint, 'Laver', too, turns out to be a useful word for Georgic speculation. A 'laver' is work; it is also a washing bowl, or place, the bowl of a fountain, a baptismal bowl and a mode of washing, and an edible sea-plant. It also, in an arcane and adjectival form, evokes blabbing. Inspired, the poet both works and is washed anew in the laver and labour she undertakes. Were she to have bathed her eyes in this stream, her poetic self, endowed with a poetic gift that can transform and enhance any place, would nevertheless choose to hymn Highbury. For this she asks the gods to 'adorne my quill'. The quill here, of course, is to be dipped in a clear river of poetic inspiration. Moreover, the kind of quills that were adorned were, clearly, those used for fishing rather than writing. Given the punning tendency of laver, implying work and the renewing of inspiration, and given the care taken over the rhyme and position of the final word, the stream of inspiration here is, it seems, both written and fished.

Finally, then, if the stream is indeed to be written and fished, this leaves the question of in what sense a 'Parnassus' might be an attractive adornment for quill pen or fishing quill. This noun describes the hill of the gods, indeed, and names poetic inspiration. It is also a plant, found in moist places and native to Cumberland (of which it is now the county flower) but also to Suffolk and to Essex, where Austen had recently been. In a Dutch herbal translated in 1578 we read that, 'Of the iuyce of this herbe is made a singular Collyrium, or medicine for the eyes, the which comforteth the sight, and cleareth the eyes, if you put unto it as much wine as you have the iuyce, and halfe as much Myrrhe, with a little Pepper and frankensence'.[27] Although John Gerard, in 1597, lists the plant and comments that those who see it as a grass must be 'blinde' in 'their understanding', neither he nor Thomas Johnson, whose herbal (an 'enlarged and amended' edition of Gerard's, of 1633) we might imagine Austen likely to be consulting during plague, mentions the properties for sight. Johnson does say it 'taketh away the desire to vomite', so we could distantly speculate, perhaps, that it might have been given to Austen when she was vomiting blood in Essex after her fall from a tree (F98v, Ross p. 150).[28] More certainly, she expects her audience to understand the punning possibilities of 'Parnassus' to evoke poetry, poetic inspiration and fishing.

Thus, the Parnassus grass takes us into the world and the circulation of the texts of Austen's contemporaries and the ways in which she seems to have read them. The poem uses the word 'Parnassus' to connect the world of poetry to the world of estate management and to the recreations appropriate to an estate, including fishing, as a way of relating to space. Condensing the place, or source, of poetry and poetic inspiration, the labour and inspiration of writing and the productive recreational labour of fishing, the 'Parnassus' focuses the reader's understanding of the world of Highbury as a question of poetic labour and achievement. Indeed, this relatively flamboyant poetic moment seems to signal some external connections likely to have been available to an immediate circle of readers but less apparent in the archival life of the manuscript isolated even from its own alphabetical series.

Katherine Philips, whose poetry is discussed by Gillian Wright in chapter 4, writes of 'courts content would gladly own, / But she ne're dwelt about a Throne'. And the apparently sole poem of her near contemporary and social superior, Elizabeth Delavel, praised 'A life retir'd' from 'croud's' and 'court's'. This version of retirement was used by many of Austen's contemporaries, particularly, it seems, women in the 1650s and Restoration. Lucy Hutchinson wrote 'freedom in the country life is found', where 'man's a prince' ruling over sheep and, as Elizabeth Scott-Baumann argues, Hutchinson's 'Elegies' explore the estate poem as place without content.[29] For all that Austen read poetry and may well have known Philips's *Poems* (pirated by Walton's publisher, Richard Mariot, in January 1663/64) and the pervasive presence of retirement in the writings of her contemporaries, just a brief consideration of these poems indicates that she is working to a different agenda. There were, however, texts that Austen was likely to have known that offer a context for her complex thinking about place in terms of the importance of poetic evocation, prospect and the viewing of the countryside, and the productive pleasure of relatively painless harvest. It may be that, just as the opening use of 'dwell' is a hint as to Austen's reading, so is the final couplet – 'on this bright Hill / I wish Parnassus to adorne my quill' – is another suggestion about the direction Austen is taking, and her reading.

There is a poem that Austen almost certainly knew that opens:

> Sure there are Poets which did never dream
> Upon *Parnassus*, nor did tast the stream
> Of *Helicon*, we therefore may suppose
> Those made not Poets, but the Poets those.
> And as Courts make not Kings, but Kings the Court,
> So where the Muses & their train resort,
> *Parnassus* stands; if I can be to thee
> A Poet, thou *Parnassus* art to me.[30]

Thus, John Denham's *Coopers Hill* begins with a sophisticated account of the role of the poet in mythologising the landscape. It also opens with two words, 'Parnassus' and 'Helicon', found in Austen's writing only in 'On the situation of Highbury', and it is at least possible that she is using them as markers of poetic affiliation, as she seems to be using 'dwell'. If Austen is thinking about *Coopers Hill*, that potentially invites some rethinking about her literary affiliations – so the evidence for whether, and how, she might engage the poem is worth exploring.

Besides 'Helicon' and 'Parnassus' there is further overlapping vocabulary. The opening sally of *Coopers Hill* (lines 1–59), which explores the landscape of the hill, Denham's 'emblem', has seventeen words in common with Austen's poem of under 130 words.[31] Less vocabulary is shared once the poem turns to the heroes of the English past and the Thames valley and there is no overlap in the hunt section (lines 240–348). Whereas it is hard to derive significance from such shared words (though the terms include 'Parnassus', 'stream', 'Helicon', 'hill', 'Muse', 'eie'), potentially more significantly, perhaps, though looser in specific linguistic connection, are the poems' shared emphases – on the prospect; the distinction between City and hill (lines 25–35); the role of the poet as an inventor, not recorder, of place and so the poem, not the world, being the place in which the subject's relation to place is made. In each case, the process of interpreting the landscape constitutes the poetic making of the world it 'describes'. The way in which each poem turns on the poet's, not the landholder's, ability to make place is a perhaps tenuous but potentially suggestive link and one which offers a relation between subject and place strikingly distinct from the relationships evoked in 'To Penshurst'.

Coopers Hill and its author were well known when Austen was writing. First published in 1642, the poem was much republished, celebrated and plundered. In 1664, the year that Austen began 'Book M', John Dryden described Coopers Hill as 'the exact Standard of good Writing'.[32] Its editor says it was first plagiarised in 1650, excerpted in Joshua Poole's popular poetic primer The English Parnassus (1657), imitated by Abraham Cowley and translated into Latin. So, the huge popularity of Coopers Hill in the eighteenth century was built on an already considerable cultural reach.[33] In the 1660s Denham himself was a London figure. He had become Surveyor of Works at the Restoration, a post which involved him financially and materially in the building of London, and a figure very likely to have impinged on Austen's entrepreneurial thinking. Moreover, in May 1665 Denham had been married for the second time, at Westminster Abbey – a public event in itself, and one in its disastrous consequences (for Denham) of interest to Austen in relation to her own concerns.[34]

Besides the author's London presence and the fact that it reached a wide readership, there were also specific reasons why Austen might have been aware of Denham's poem.[35] Katherine Austen's husband, Thomas, was at Oxford and, like Denham, at Lincoln's Inn (Denham went in 1634 and was called to the bar in 1639; Thomas went in 1646). Denham had lived at Egham, near the site of the local landmark.[36] And it is just possible that Katherine Austen herself trod the sacred slopes, for we know that in 1664 she visited her sister Mary in Twickenham, where she lived after her marriage to Joseph Ashe.[37] Whether or not Austen visited Cooper's Hill, just fourteen or so miles from Twickenham, her relatives probably knew the poem. In sum, Coopers Hill was much published and widely read; Austen had many reasons to know about it in her own life (a significant factor in her use of reading material) and Denham, himself, was a figure of high importance in her London world of property.

Most significantly, however, the poem also has potential for Austen's project and problems. As Brendan O Hehir comments, many of the readers of *Coopers Hill* took it, or mistook it, as a poem about hills and, certainly, Austen took as part of her task the articulation of the hill virtues of Highbury.[38] Besides this simple connection, though, if she was ready to receive it (and that is not clear) *Coopers Hill* had something a little more complex to offer Austen's attempt to situate her subject in an estate – most valuably in its poetic subject's outward orientation as an eye observing and defining, and mutually defined through, the conjuring of landscape. Denham's speaker contrasts with Jonson's in the nature of the power relations in which he is enmeshed; the power that Denham serves is diffused through the landscape as well as incarnated in parts of the poem. For any poet seeking a subtle way to connect owner and land, Denham's poem is a gift. For Austen, nature is an active agent in the framing of Highbury's virtues – she resolves 'to frame delight / On this faire Hill' – and Denham goes a step further in writing of nature being 'guided by a wiser power than Chance' in raising 'this ground' (lines 153, 156). Most significantly, perhaps, while both *Coopers Hill* and 'To Penshurst' explore place, they have very different understandings of the relationship between the poem's speaking subject, place and 'dwelling'. In Cooper's poem the subject evokes what is seen in prospect, not what is owned as property, arrogating to the poet the power to endow a landscape with meaning, and therefore not only to express its significant history but also, in many ways, to invent or reinvent it as a poetic landscape.

There is no proof that Katherine Austen was among the many readers of *Coopers Hill*, but we do know that Izaak Walton was. He owned a copy of the 1642 edition and the copy is corrected in a way that Brendan O Hehir argues indicates that the corrector had access to either the 1643 edition or, more intriguingly, a manuscript.[39] At the Restoration, as Austen was writing, Denham and Walton had both benefited substantially from the efforts of a shared patron, George Morley, who had ensured Denham's passage to be Surveyor of Works and who, when Bishop of Winchester, had employed Walton as his steward in that city.[40] Also suggestive is that a pamphlet panegyric to General Monck ascribed to Denham was published by Walton's publisher, Richard Mariot, in 1659.[41]

In this web of personal and literary connection, there is suggestive evidence that Katherine Austen had knowledge of Izaak Walton. And her connections with him are illuminating in terms of what she, herself, was reading. Alongside the recording in 'Book M' of extensive and intense religious reading of the Bible as well as sermons (particularly those by Jeremy Taylor and John Donne), we find hints of secular reading and records of material that is of interest to her from a very wide variety of sources. In the context of an assessment of dreams and portents she records a dream of John Donne:

When Doc Dun was in France, with Sir Henery Wotten: He left his wife in England big with child. One day the Docter was a siting a reading. in a passage Roome which had two dores. He saw his wife goe by him with a dead child in her Armes, and she lookt as paile as if she had been dead. This apparition did so affright him. that his hair stood up right: Sir Henry seeing him thus. did not regard any expence. immediately sent poast to England. And they found that about that very time. his wife was brought to bed of a dead Child. very hardly escaping her life. (F11r, Ross pp. 58–9)

Obviously speaking to Austen's personal interest in how to interpret signs, as a by-product, this passage gives a clue to the nature of Austen's reading and, ultimately, to her and Walton's apparently overlapping worlds. As Sarah Ross indicates, although Donne's *Sermons* were published in 1640 and in 1658, this anecdote did not appear in Walton's 'Life' of Donne, which prefaced the volume, until 1675.[42] Although Austen certainly returned to 'Book M' in subsequent years, there is no evidence that this is a retrospective addition. Moreover, her father's will records an Izaak Walton as living in his house in Chancery Lane in the later 1630s.[43] Austen's father, Robert Wilson, Walton and in Austen's own generation her brother-in-law Joseph Ashe were all drapers. R. C. Bald charts Walton's shop on Fleet Street, just two doors to the west of his lodging in Chancery Lane, and explores his involvement with St Dunstan's in the West, a parish at the border of the city and the Inns of Court. It is near here, too, that we find both John Donne and Walton's publisher, Richard Mariot.[44]

Taken alone, that Austen read Walton's life of Donne in manuscript is a slim connection – it implies only circulation of a significant text. However, Austen also indicates a knowledgeable interest in the Wottons (as Sarah Ross notes, Henry, for example, appears in this anecdote but not in the printed version) and the anecdotes of the family found in Walton's *Reliquie Woottonianae* (1651) also differ from Austen.[45] Izaak Walton was close to Wotton and repeatedly published his writings – and from here more tenuous literary connections multiply: John Donne, Henry King and Richard Corbet all appear in Austen's 'Book' and all were linked in life as well as letters. It seems, then, that Austen knew Izaak Walton well enough to read his writings and to know some of his London circle. If, as we know from her use of Henry King, Austen used secular texts to her own ends, it is at least possible that she knew Walton's book of London recreation – *The Compleat Angler; or, the Contemplative Mans Recreation*.

The Compleat Angler, like *Coopers Hill*, was rewritten and re-oriented in response to the Restoration. Given Austen may have been reading Walton's 'collections', it seems unlikely that she would miss *The Compleat Angler*.[46] We know Walton gave a copy of the 1661 edition to Anne King, and a version was published in 1664.[47] However, the connections between

'Highbury', specifically, and Walton are different from the potentially detailed reading of Denham's poem, being partly a matter of milieu, partly of simple theme (fishing) and partly of the evocation of movement and the liberated, pleasantly occupied, subject. Moreover, the attitude to fishing as an art of productive leisure or pleasurable labour is suggestively similar in each – although, obviously, much more developed in the prose text, where it is worth examination. As Walton indicates, angling is 'Art and Pleasure', where 'the very sitting by the Rivers side, is not only the fittest place for, but will invite the Anglers to Contemplation'. Famously punning on Anglicanism and angling, Walton's 'Conference betwixt an Angler, a Falconer, and a Hunter, each commending his recreation' expresses, explores and invents the social and imaginative associations of the River Lea to give a suggestive exploration of place, pedestrianism, pastoral. Flowing in to meet the Thames to the east of the city, and simultaneously offering a path out to the north and the Essex countryside beyond, the Lea or Lee was then, as it is now, a river by which London's residents could enjoy the pleasures of exercise and escape, to a place of recreations, between urban and rural – hawking, hunting and fishing. The journey in *The Compleat Angler* may represent a kind of secular pilgrimage; it is an evocation of an escape from toil to a place where pleasure and contemplation of landscape are perfectly intertwined with the exercise of skill and literary imagination. Towards the end of the first day of discourses, Walton introduces the figure of Sir Henry Wotton, first ascribing to him the aperçu that, in angling, there was an 'imployment for … idle time, which was then not idly spent', and 'a Moderator of passions, a procurer of contentedness', leading to 'habits of peace and patience'.[48]

Explicit about natural history and biblical intertextuality, Walton is less explicit about his pilgrimage away from London and the new Protectorate of Oliver Cromwell, and into the open air. Angling opens the book of nature in terms bound up with the Book of Common Prayer, at a point when that had officially been replaced by the Directory of Worship. That escape, however, structures the journey and allows a mental leeway that permits 'quiet' and an accommodation, if not an acquiescence, of the individual to government.[49] Thus, Piscator, the fisherman, is able to move, rest, fish and observe in his five-day walk up the River Lea towards the holiday destination of Ware. The implications of fishing in terms of status are fudged in the text, with emphasis being placed on pedagogy, skill and knowledge but in emphasising learned skill the text does constitute a subtle claim for an authority grounded in a skill that might be shared at the least between aristocrats and the prosperously leisured middling sort; there is an implication that fishing establishes an equalised community based on skill and special knowledge. The walk opens on Tottenham

Hill, just north-east of the Highbury estate, and there is a conversation, expanded in Restoration editions to a three-way conference among the fisherman, a hunter and a falconer. Piscator's broadly successful attempt to convey the virtues of angling to these interlocutors gives the *Angler* an appropriately loose, detailed, mobile and generically capacious structure so that the whole embraces biblical commentary, natural history (practical and marvellous), poetry and the valorisation of the 'practice' of fishing as fostering both social cohesion and song.

Walton asserts that the angler's relationship to riverine space fosters valuable moods of mind and spirit. He uses poetry to donate to the fisherman the 'art' and through the complex subjectivity supplied to the angler provides fishing with a tradition that includes Du Bartas, but also his peers John Donne and Henry Wotton, even stretching the topic to include Donne's 'The baite', where lovers '"new pleasures prove, / Of golden sands, and Christal brooks, / With silken lines and silver hooks"' and a female angler needs no art, being 'thy self art thine own bait'.[50] Walton primarily uses poems to evoke the patience, skill and accepting yet productive subjectivity of the angler, in Wotton's words, 'attending of his trembling quil', in time, place and weather – through 'showrs, the weather mild, / The morning fresh, the evening smil'd'.[51] For all Walton's claims concerning language and angling, the practical arts of the angler are as likely to have been of interest to a poet in search of an adornment for a quill.[52] The directions on how to make an 'Artificiall flye' are also directly relevant to Austen and, though sadly Walton does not recommend Parnassus grass, the directions offer a rich blend of borrowed feathers, drapers' silks and dexterity. He instructs the student to first 'arm your hook', then to 'take your Scissers and cut so much of a browne Malards feather as in your own reason wil make the wings of it, you having withall regard to the bigness or littleness of your hook', binding it 'three or four times about the hook with the same Silk, with which your hook was armed' and once the 'gold, or what materials soever you make your Fly of, do lye right and neatly; and if you find they do so, then when you have made the head, make all fast'; finally, 'with the arming Silk whip it about cross-wayes betwixt the wings'. Thus, overall, though compendious and growing from edition to edition, the Georgic usefulness of fishing is registered in Walton's careful construction of the sensibility of the moving, skilfully working and, therefore, located angler. The concept of dwelling in the outdoor world teased out by *The Compleat Angler* is far from the 'dwelling' of Jonson's grand estate, with its farmed ponds rather than mobile streams, and Walton promotes virtue through the careful evocation of the angler – moving and resting, catching fish in an activity somewhere between farming and hunting, sharing food, time, and a pastoral and sylvan freedom.

If Austen's flower is not, exactly, the confection of animal or insect, thread and metal that Walton is describing here, there is no doubt that she proposes a connection between poetry and fishing as an art that is very like his own. Indeed, in the capacious and richly intertextual *Compleat Angler* the fisherman-as-poet is an important analogy.[53] The angler acquires skill and an appreciation of space and climate. The patient, skilled work of fishing produces for the angler mobility and a direct, but not fixed, relationship to landscape where the estate is permissive, allowing the harvesting of fish, the movement of the subject, the exercise of skill and the mixing of social groups.

Austen's spiritual meditation on Highbury, as we have seen, draws accounts, experiences and profit through a process of spiritual assay in which the acquiring of Highbury is tested in relation to biblical identifications in a way that draws the significance towards the single (though, for Austen, of course all-important) point of spiritual self-assessment.[54] Arguably, this process isolates and conquers the experience of the acquisition of property by both facilitating its acceptance in integrating into an exemplary, typological, spiritual narrative of trials and transforming it, in that process, from bounty to debt. In doing this, or partially doing it, the estate poem performs a function of reaching outwards to articulate the subject's relation to place in terms familiar in past and contemporary writing, and using frames of reference that, repeatedly, reach outwards in doubling meanings (as in the pen and fishing rod, Parnassus the place and the flower) and in connecting Austen's articulation of property to that of other poets.

Land, laver, capital and enterprise

Finally, of course, the question is what this consideration of 'On the situation of Highbury' can tell us about wider issues – about the estate poem, about discourses of property, about gender and property and about literary culture. Economic historians, including most recently Paul Slack, have long characterised the Restoration as an originating moment of economic optimism qualified by moral scruples.[55] Away from the canon of economic treatises, Austen's vocabulary of cost, choice and political economy takes us as readers to more urgent experiences of affliction, fear, delight and acquisitiveness. Austen's 'Book M' discloses the world in a very different way from that audible to economics alone. 'On the situation of Highbury' tells us much – about the estate poem, about discourses of property, about gender and property and about literary culture.

In Austen's case, while it is clear that each discourse contributes to an understanding of the subject's relationship to place and property, it is equally clear that, rather than being blended, one or other genre is deployed in turn to articulate property. In what ways do those other texts – both those in the manuscript book and in the world – form a context for the reading of the lyric and what implications can we derive from the way land, place and subject are presented?[56] 'On the situation of Highbury' is both highly specific and, the evidence presented here suggests, richly bound to its historical moment. If Austen's dweller recalls Jonson's imagined estate then, simultaneously, the subject of her poem looks outward at the prospect, is full of Georgic movement and, above all, imagines a potential transformation of subjectivity in landscape. In returning to the estate genre, while Austen has clearly read 'To Penshurst', the conceptual apparatuses of Georgic and pilgrimage, with their associated genres of prospect and journey, are evidently influential. We know that Austen had a civic London life that impinged on her poetry, for, as has not previously been recognised, she memorialised the son of Colonel Alexander Popham, a neighbour making a successful path upward through society despite his Civil War allegiances, and who had an estate to the north of Shoreditch – both a landholder and part of an eminent and long-standing legal family.[57] Austen's concerns about land and landholding, citizenship and law are shared by the Restoration world in which she moved, and the research here suggests that her attitudes to them were shaped by her personal circumstances and beliefs, through the practice of occasional meditation and, as importantly, by the driving forces of her world. In this world everyone was sharply aware of the effect of the Civil War in producing multiple reversals of fortune and in making property, even land, contingent on what even providential Austen thinks looks alarmingly like fortune. Walton wrote explicitly about such reversals in his notes and 'lives'.[58]

The tortured compromises of poet and patron, familiar from Ben Jonson's generation, are part of the literary inheritance of the period and it is no accident that Walton seems also to have planned to write a life of Jonson. Yet, plainly, the rhetoric of 'restoration', and even the mobilisation of wits as royalist (as in the collections containing Corbet and King), encountered a world stubbornly reconfigured, a world in which impecunious landholder Sir John Denham made a mint as Surveyor of Works, overseeing and profiting from property transactions in London, while also paving the streets of Holborn. This was a world where a rich and pious widow might, against the odds, grasp and firmly hold an estate loosened from the hand of the aristocracy and, despite attempts at restoration, definitively participate in a market of land determined by legal and financial claim rather than by inheritance.[59] Of course, landholding had never been secure but the Civil War had made that visible. It seems likely that Izaak Walton, initiating his career by writing Donne's 'life' when the aristocrat, Wotton, failed in the duty, must be understood as in some ways tying Austen to a literary world. That world was not the competitive, overlapping court and town scene where, as the Duke of Monmouth's reuse of Katherine Philips's pastoral poem suggests, women were increasingly literary competitors among male peers, but to an overlapping circle, perhaps spanning the connections implied by Walton's London places of household, labour and leisure: the City on the border with the law and church, Chancery Lane, St Dunstan's in the West, Fleet Street, the Inns, the Ironmongers' Hall in Shoreditch, Clerkenwell, the path to modern Hertfordshire up the River Lee/Lea. If, as my research suggests, the 'Deane Hardy' of her lease account (quoted above) is indeed the Dean of Rochester, then it seems possible that her connections extended further west, to St Martin's – and Hardy knew both Apsley and Sir Charles Cotterell, Katherine Philips's connection at court.[60]

Whether or not she worked closely with the texts discussed, and the evidence suggests that she at least knew them, Austen's writings are clearly as bound to the genres of the 1650s and 1660s as to those of the 1630s. These genres in different ways register the mobility of people made so evident by the Civil War. They mark, particularly, the intensified market in that foundational claim and commodity (only, perhaps, partly recognised as such), land. If Austen's Georgic celebration effaces the commodity value of Highbury, the other vocabularies in 'Book M' both show Highbury as special and render it in some ways equivalent to other commodities, gains and losses; the discourses of law; accounting and money. Moreover, Highbury, as God's bounty, while experienced as particular, is rendered 'equal' as a worldly experience in its being subject to spiritual evaluation through meditation. Accounts and spiritual interpretation both assess Highbury, equalising it as an object and event whose value is interpreted within an overarching system.

In parallel to the availability of land as a transferable object weighed in the scales against Godly virtue, cash value, legal claim (or all three), the Civil War saw a counterbalancing emergence of genres focusing on the power of the individual to know and create through survey and mobility – the prospect poem (in which genre *Coopers Hill* can broadly be accommodated); the journey poem, reworked in prose melange by *The Compleat Angler*; and the emerging genre of guide and internal tourism of wonders.[61] But, just as earlier genres register the anxiety of landholding, in 'Book M' not only do we see several evaluative discourses operating simultaneously but also, within the writing of Highbury, the twin resolutions of landholding and poetic inspiration are conditional – 'if a streame did rise'. This 'if' is, certainly, used in the same way as Denham's 'if I can be to thee / A Poet, thou *Parnassus* art to me'. Skill, even virtuosity, lives in the angler (and arguably in some of the creatures Walton describes) but not in the land or landholder. So, when at the end of 'Book M' Austen writes that 'when I view over the assurances and hopes I have had in this book of my meditations' – for all that (at times) her writing suggests 'I have overcome my enemies and my feares' – more truly she sees:

> But such is the vnsurenes of every ground in this world to Anchor on. as I soone come to wade in deep places againe.
>   The moone hath not more variations then the affaires of this life. Then the ebes and flowes of Fortune. (112v; Ross p. 168)

The conditional, uncertain anchoring of the self, the need to analyse using the modes of meditation, poetry both secular and sacred, journal and providential retrospect show the subject of 'Book M' as deeply steeped in the knowledge of property as a commodity competed for, and the need for the subject to be alert to the very thing she earlier sought to stave off with the talisman of providence – 'the ebes and flowes of Fortune'.

Austen's fluid fortunes, and her knowledge of that fluidity, are a clear link to the need to move, the importance of the subject journeying to retain some understanding of and power over fortune. Her desire and failure to 'anchor', the sense that she imagined she had reached the 'haven', but 'was siting still in the storm' (112v; Ross p. 168) points us to a useful but unacknowledged literary relationship. Acknowledging the movement of land, Daniel Defoe's novel *Robinson Crusoe* (1719), notably named for its protagonist, not the nowhere in which he makes his empire, can be understood as restlessly revising the estate poem through journey and prospect. Shipwrecked Crusoe famously flees a potential encounter with a human: he sees 'the Print of a Man's naked foot on the Shore' and in 'Terror of Mind' retreats to 'my Castle, for so I think I call'd it ever after this'. 'On the Situation' (and its own larger situation in 'Book M'), *Coopers Hill* and *The Compleat Angler*, taken together, suggest a destination for the estate–journey–prospect poem in the articulation of land in Defoe's novel, just sixty years later. In this trajectory, then, we see clearly a place for women's writing of place neither in the framework of retirement from politics (which Austen seems to refuse) nor in the instituted literary culture of the Restoration in which men and women competed for favours in town and court, but in an aspiring, fractured and uneasy, articulate, complex city apprehension of a new conditional world where everyone's place rested on the 'vnsureness of every ground' (Book 'M' 112v, Ross p. 168).

Usually taken as a discrete genre, the estate poem has here been considered in terms of the other discourses with which it rubbed shoulders (and particularly their distinct yet adjacent ways of articulating relations among the subject, land and property). As Arthur Marotti has observed, 'Typically, lyrics were inserted in books given over to other sorts of texts', and so it is with Austen.[62] As suggested in the introduction, scholars see seventeenth-century writers as understanding manuscript as malleable. There is evidence that print, too, was more malleable than we have acknowledged. Certainly, the making of a somewhere out of other texts, as Austen partly does here, suggests not collaboration but a kind of reading that acknowledges both the agenda of another text (even as it may in use choose to override or ignore that agenda, as Austen does with Denham's royalism) but also a use of intertextuality to respond to conditions external to, though influencing, writing, and so Austen uses a notebook to make the mobile subject needed to tolerate – and fiercely compete in – London land markets and micro-politics. Accordingly, the desires for breathing space, laver, prospect and estate often shape her writing, as they do Denham's and Walton's. As Don E. Wayne implies in his discussion of 'To Penshurst', it is only in the later seventeenth century that the relationship between labour and property is articulated as close, a process of conversion of one into the other.[63] In sum, putting together 'On the situation', *Coopers Hill* and *The Compleat Angler* allows us to see mid-seventeenth-century connections between prospect, journey and land. As we see, not only does 'Book M' illuminate the situation of a London woman on the fringes of an emerging literary world at the Restoration, but also, in offering a newly visible grouping of texts or map of connections, it allows us to begin to see the way in which the loosening and losing of land in the period between 'To Penshurst' and 'On the situation of Highbury' are registered in the emergence of a discomfited, mobilised, non-elite Restoration writing on land.

Notes

Thanks to Dr Sarah Ross for productive and helpful comments and for sending me her edition of 'Book M' at an early stage in my research. Thanks to Mrs Pauline Batten for information on early modern Tillingham.

1 Katherine Austen, 'Book M', British Library, additional manuscript 4454, F104r. 'Book M' is reproduced in S. Ross (ed.), *Katherine Austen's Book M, British Library, Additional Manuscript 4454*, Medieval and Renaissance Texts and Studies vol. 409, Arizona Center for Medieval and Renaissance Studies, Tempe, 2011, the poem at pp. 158–9. The manuscript has multiple paginations; this chapter gives the British Library's pagination and the page number in Ross, henceforth within the text. In presenting Austen's text the present chapter in general follows Ross. However,

where Ross has coded her text to better represent the emphases and markings of the manuscript it has at times been necessary to silently remove her signals. Significant space, marking and juxtaposition of texts are used throughout Austen's manuscript.

2 R. Anselment, 'Katherine Austen and the widow's might', *Journal for Early Modern Cultural Studies*, vol. 5, no. 1 (2005), pp. 5–25; P. Hammons, '"Despised Creatures": the illusion of maternal self-effacement in seventeenth-century child loss poetry', *English Literary History*, vol. 66 (1999), pp. 25–49; P. Hammons, *Poetic Resistance: English Women Writers and the Early Modern Lyric*, Ashgate, Aldershot, 2002; P. Hammons, 'Rethinking women and property in sixteenth- and seventeenth-century England', *Literature Compass*, vol. 3, no. 6 (2006), pp. 1386–407; P. Hammons, 'Widow, prophet, and poet: lyrical self-figurations in Katherine Austen's "Book M" (1664)', in B. Smith and U. Appelt (eds), *Write or Be Written: Early Modern Women Poets and Cultural Constraints*, Ashgate, Aldershot, 2001, pp. 3–27; S. Ross, '"And Trophes of his praises make": providence and poetry in Katherine Austen's "Book M", 1664–1668', in V. E. Burke and J. Gibson (eds), *Early Modern Women's Writing: Selected Papers from the Trinity/Trent Colloquium*, Ashgate, Aldershot, 2004, pp. 181–204; S. Ross, '"Like Penelope, always employed": reading, life-writing, and the early modern female self in Katherine Austen's 'Book M', *Literature Compass*, vol. 9, no. 4 (2012), pp. 306–16; B. Todd, 'The remarrying widow: a stereotype reconsidered', in M. Prior (ed.), *Women in English Society 1500–1800*, Methuen, London, 1985, pp. 54–92; B. Todd, '"I do no injury by not loving": Katherine Austen, a young widow of London', in V. Frith (ed.), *Women and History: Voices of Early Modern England*, Coach House Press, Toronto, 1995, pp. 202–37; B. Todd, 'The virtuous widow in Protestant England', in S. Cavallo and L. Warner (eds), *Widowhood in Medieval and Early Modern Europe*, Pearson Education, Harlow, 1999, pp. 66–83; B. Todd, 'Property and a woman's place in Restoration London', *Women's History Review*, vol. 19, no. 2 (2010), pp. 181–200.

3 A. Fowler(ed.). *The Country House Poem: A Cabinet of Seventeenth-Century Estate Poems and Related Items*, Edinburgh University Press, Edinburgh, 1994; J. M. Adrian, *Local Negotiations of English Nationhood, 1570–1680*, Palgrave, Basingstoke, 2011.

4 Ross, 'Like Penelope'.

5 Austen considers herself to have had a predictive sign indicating that she would live to the same age as her husband, thirty-six years, two months and twenty-one days. Katherine Austen's birthday was 30 April 1628 and it seems therefore that she expected to die on 21 July 1664. She was thirty when her husband died. She started the book in April 1664, when she was due to have her thirty-sixth birthday.

6 *Calendar of State Papers Domestic 1625–1649*, pp. 246–7; Ross, p. 9.

7 Ross (ed.), *Katherine Austen's Book M*, pp. 8–10.

8 Ibid., p. 9.

9 This follows Ross, who cites London Metropolitan Archives Courts Leet and Baron ACC/2844/012. Ross, 'Introduction' to *Katherine Austen's Book M*, p. 10, especially n. 45.

10 Austen does not name her suitor but writes about him in ways that enable a very likely identification from the records of burial. Pauline Batten, archivist for the Church of St Nicholas, indicates that the burial records give 'Calendar Alexander, Doctour in Phisic' on 8 October. Other surrounding records designate by family connection rather than occupation; that this name stands out in the records in being designated by occupation, and that the dating and occupation coincide with Austen's account, make this a probable identification. The same identification is made without substantiation by Todd, 'Property and a woman's place'. John Donne's son, John Donne (d. January 1662/63 bequeathing his father's papers to Walton), held the living in Tillingham but did not reside there. R. C. Bald, *John Donne: A Life*, Clarendon Press, Oxford, 1986, pp. 548–52. Note the discussion of the importance of Walton's biography for Bald: D. Flynn, *John Donne and the Ancient Catholic Nobility*, Indiana University Press, Bloomington, 1996, pp. 10–11.

11 Ross, 'Introduction', pp. 16–17; F99v, Ross p. 151.

12 See F99v–F100r, Ross p. 152; and F105v, Ross p. 159.

13 M. L. Coolahan, 'Redeeming parcels of time: aesthetics and practice of occasional meditation', *Seventeenth Century*, vol. 22 (2007), pp. 124–5.

14 See Ross, 'Introduction', pp. 26–31; R. Anselment (ed.) *The Occasional Meditations of Mary Rich, Countess of Warwick*, Medieval and Renaissance Texts and Studies vol. 363, Arizona Center for Medieval and Renaissance Studies, Tempe, 2009.

15 On the Psalms see Ross, 'Introduction', pp. 26–31; her minister also advocates weighing the self against the Psalms – see F. Raworth, *Blessedness, Or, God and the World Weighted*, London, 1656, pp. 1–2.

16 R. Barbour, *Literature and Religious Culture in Seventeenth Century England*, Cambridge University Press, Cambridge, 2002, pp. 56–117.

17 'Sept. xiv. died Mr. [Francis] Raworth, minister of [St. Leonard's] Shoreditch; ex peste', quoted in F. Peck, *Desiderata Curiosa*, London, 1779, p. 544.

18 F. Raworth, *Work & Reward*, London, 1656. See also his *On Jacob's Ladder*, London, 1654. His best-received sermon appeared in *Monomaxia: Jacob Wrestling with the Ange ... with Jacob's Ladder...*, London, 1656, A4r–v; Raworth, *Blessedness*.

19 Ross, 'Introduction', p. 34; See also A. Smyth, *Autobiography in Early Modern England*, Cambridge University Press, Cambridge, 2010, pp. 57–9; E. Botonaki, 'Seventeenth-century Englishwomen's spiritual diaries: self-examination, covenanting, and account keeping', *Sixteenth Century Journal*, vol. 30, no. 1 (spring 1999), pp. 3–21, at p. 20.

20 M. de Certeau, 'The scriptural economy', in *The Practice of Everyday Life* (trans. S. Randall), University of California Press, Berkeley, 1988, pp. 134–5.

21 Ibid., pp. 134–5, 154.

22 Ross, 'Introduction', p. 9.

23 Ibid., and see 'To Penshurst', in Ben Jonson, *The Forest*, London, 1616. The latter is edited and introduced by C. Burrow, in M. Butler *et al.* (eds), *The Works of Ben Jonson*, Oxford University Press, Oxford, 2011, vol. 5, pp. 209–14; see also C. Burrow, 'Introduction', ibid., pp. 201–5.

24 P. Hammons, 'Katherine Austen's country house innovations', *Studies in English Literature*, vol. 40, no. 1 (2000), pp. 123–37. As a comparator for Austen in the use of Jonson see T. Lockwood, '"All Hayle to Hatfield": a new series of country house poems from Leeds University Library, Brotherton collection, MS Lt.q.44 (with text)', *English Literary Renaissance*, vol. 38, no. 2 (2008), pp. 270–303, at pp. 274–5 and poems.

25 Hammons, 'Katherine Austen's country house', productively discusses 'dwell', pp. 127–9, and the prospect, pp. 129–30.

26 A. McRae, *God Speed the Plough*, Cambridge University Press, Cambridge, 1996, p. 263.

27 H. Lyte, *A Niewe Herball, or Historie of Plantes* (trans. R. Dodoens), Antwerp, 1578, pp. 509–10 ('Of the grasse of Parnasus').

28 T. Johnson, *The herball or Generall historie of plantes. Gathered by Iohn Gerarde of London Master in Chirurgerie very much enlarged and amended*, London, 1633, book 2, p. 840. Gerarde is now more commonly rendered without the terminal 'e'.

29 P. W. Thomas (ed.), *The Collected Works of Katherine Philips, The Matchless Orinda: Volume 1, The Poems*, Stump Cross Books, Stump Cross, 1990, pp. 19, 91; see also 'A retir'd friendship to Ardelia', pp. 97–8 ('No trembling at the Great ones frowns', line 7; they 'Enjoy what princes wish in vain', line 36); E. Delavel, *The Meditations of Elizabeth Delavel* (ed. D. G. Greene), Surtees Society, Gateshead, 1978, p. 120; Lucy Hutchinson, printed in N. H. Keeble (ed.), *Memoirs of the Life of Colonel Hutchinson*, Everyman, London, 1995, pp. 389–40. For a discussion of Hutchinson's elegies productively elucidating their challenge to the form of the estate poem, see E. Scott-Baumann, '"Paper frames", Lucy Hutchinson's "Elegies" and the seventeenth-century country house poem', *Literature Compass*, vol. 4, no. 3 (2007), pp. 664–76.

30 I am extremely grateful to Sarah Ross for suggesting that I look at *Coopers Hill*.

31 Words common to the two poems include: 'chuse', 'Parnassus', 'stream', 'Helicon'/ 'Hellicon', 'hill', 'Muse', 'eie', 'fate', 'load', 'place', 'pleasure', 'sight' and 'eies', 'grace' ('Majestick' versus Austen's 'bad', but both qualifiers referring, in a sense, to authors). More distant matches include 'mist' and 'misty', 'Valley' and 'vallies' ('wanton vallies' also exist later, at line 160), 'Natures' and 'Nature'; 'toyl' occurs at line 176 of *Coopers Hill*, and 'Bounty' in line 177; 'fair' (line 188), 'clear' (though as a noun, line 191), 'beauty' (line 206), 'delight' (line 212); no vocabulary from the stag hunt; 'rais'd' (line 349) is quite a distant word from 'rise', though 'rise' is itself a noun at line 45 and used very differently by Denham, and 'dwells', in line 355, is a word which occurred earlier.

32 J. Dryden, 'To the Right Honourable Roger Earl of Orrery', dedication in *The Rival Ladies*, London, 1664, A4r. See also B. O Hehir, *Expans'd Hieroglphicks*, University of California Press, 1969, p. 295.

33 Hehir, *Expans'd*, pp. 294–7; in one of the British Library copies – *Coopers Hill. A Poeme*, London, 1643 (Cup. 407. Bb. 3) – a reader has marked sections which may also have been closely read by Austen, including 'eie' and the material on divine inspiration in choice of place.

34 B. O Hehir, *Harmony From Discords: A Life of Sir John Denham*, University of California Press, Berkely, 1968, pp. 154–62, 180–91.

35 See O Hehir, *Harmony*, p. 66–7; during the war a search was made for Denham's goods in Fleet Street; Sarah Ross, personal communication.

36 See O Hehir, *Expans'd*, pp. xxiii–xxviii.

37 See discussion and notes in Ross, 'Introduction', p. 79, 96, 111. The preacher Austen heard at St Mary's was William Hobson. Her sister and brother-in-law were associated with the church.

38 O Hehir, *Expans'd*, p. 7.

39 Ibid., p. 56.

40 O Hehir, *Harmony*, pp. 154–6.

41 Richard Mariot, *A Panegyrick on His Excellency the Lord General George Monck*, London, 1659; O Hehir, *Harmony*, pp. 152–3.

42 See Ross, 'Introduction', pp. 23–4.

43 Ross, 'Introduction', p. 21, cites Robert Wilson's will, National Archives, PROB 11/182.

44 According to Walter Thornbury, Walton occupied the house at 120 Chancery Lane from 1627 to 1644. See W. Thornbury, *Old and New London* (6 vols), Cassell, Petter and Galpin, London, 1872–78, vol. 1, p. 82. R. C. Bald notes that, at this point, Izaak Walton was 'a rising linen draper with a shop on Fleet Street two doors west of Chancery Lane' and 'got to know Donne via st Dunstan'; Bald, *Donne*, p. 503. Henry King, Donne's friend and editor, is another significant presence in Austen's text and King's editor, Margaret Crum, speculates that Izaak Walton could have been instrumental in the poems being published in 1657. This guess is worth noting, given other evidence suggesting that Walton might have had a connection with the Austens. See M. Crum (ed.), *The Poems of Henry King*, Clarendon Press, Oxford, 1965, p. 53. Walton inherited another house in Chancery Lane when Anne Grinsell died. See J. Bevan, 'Henry Valentine, John Donne, Izaak Walton', *Review of English Studies* n.s., vol. 40, no. 158 (1989), pp. 179–201, at p. 200.

45 See F12r, Ross, p. 60 n. 44, n. 45; Ross, 'Introduction', pp. 23–4, especially n. 97.

46 J. Butt, 'Izaak Walton's collections for Fulman's life of John Hales', *Modern Language Review*, vol. 29, no. 3 (July 1934), pp. 267–73.

47 J. Bevan, 'Introduction', in Izaak Walton, *The Compleat Angler* (ed. J. Bevan), Clarendon Press, Oxford, 1983, pp. 6, 33–7.

48 Izaak Walton, *The Compleat Angler*, London, 1653, p. 110.

49 As M. Swann argues, the *Angler* is indeed concerned with fishing but he is so not instead of the world of life and politics, as she suggests, but because fishing opens up a specific mobile, meditational, partly useful yet contemplative mode for the subject – fishing beneficially fashions a relation to space which in turn refashions the subject.

M. Swann, 'The *Compleat Angler* and the early modern culture of collecting', *English Literary Renaissance*, vol. 37, no. 1 (2007), pp. 100–17, at p. 101. J. Edwards, 'Thomas Hobbes, Charles Cotton and the "wonders" of the Derbyshire Peak', *Studies in Travel Writing*, vol. 16, no. 1 (2012), pp. 1–15.

50 John Donne, 'The baite', in Walton, *The Compleat Angler*, pp. 184–5.

51 Walton, *The Compleat Angler*, p. 34.

52 Thus he both simply associates nature with poetry (at one point noting the 'birds in the adjoining Grove seem to have a friendly contention with an Echo') but also explicitly draws an analogy between angling and the theory, versus practice, of rhetoric. Thus Piscator tells a parable of a borrowed sermon, the punch-line of which is that 'everyone cannot make musick with my words which are fitted for my own mouth' – returning the reader to the subjectivity and skill of the angler in terms of persuasive sound. Walton, *The Compleat Angler*, pp. 106–7.

53 See Bevan, 'Henry Valentine'.

54 de Certeau, *The Practice of Everyday Life*, pp. 134–7.

55 P. Slack, 'Material progress and the challenge of affluence in seventeenth-century England', *Economic History Review*, vol. 62, no. 3 (2009), pp. 576–603.

56 A. Marotti, *Manuscript, Print and the English Renaissance Lyric*, Cornell University Press, Ithaca, 1995, p. 17.

57 For an interesting discussion of the dynamics of displaced loss in the poem, see P. Hammons, 'Despised creatures: the illusion of female self-effacement in seventeenth-century child-loss poetry', *English Literary History*, vol. 66, no. 1 (spring 1999), pp. 25–49.

58 Butt, 'Izaak Walton's collections', pp. 267–73.

59 T. Raylor (ed.), *Wit Restor'd* (1658), Scholars' Facsimiles, Delmar, 1985.

60 See for example S. J. Wiseman, '"Public", "private", "politics": Elizabeth Poole, the Duke of Monmouth, "political thought" and "literary evidence"', *Women's Writing* vol. 14, no. 2 (2007), pp. 338–62; E. H. Hageman and A. Sunnu, '"More copies of it abroad than I could have imagin'd; further manuscript texts of Katherine Philips, "the Matchless Orinda"', *English Manuscript Studies 1100–1700*, vol. 5 (1994), pp. 127–69. Tai Liu, 'Hardy, Nathaniel (1619–1670)', *Oxford Dictionary of National Biography*, Oxford University Press, Oxford, 2004–8, www.oxforddnb.com/view/article/12287 (accessed August 2013).

61 See Edwards, 'Thomas Hobbes'.

62 Marotti, *Manuscript*, p. 17.

63 J. Locke, *Second Treatise*, sections 27 and 44, in *Two Treatises of Government* (ed. P. Laslett), 1960, revised edition, Mentor, New York, 1965, p. 328–9, 340–1, quoted in D. E. Wayne, *Penshurst, the Semiotics of Place and the Place of History*, Methuen, London, 1984, pp. 23–4. Wayne notes Locke's 'confusion', p. 192 n. 8.

Reading early modern women and the poem

Patricia Pender and Rosalind Smith

I N 2007, the journal *Women's Writing* dedicated an issue to early modern women's writing following the 2005 conference 'Still kissing the rod'. The papers published there highlighted both new directions in the field and issues central to the field's conception that remained unresolved. On the one hand, critical work on a rapidly increasing number of early modern women writers was seen to be transforming concepts of early modern authorship, transmission practices and histories of the book.[1] On the other hand, the field was perceived by at least one critic as persistently marginal, defined by its difference from and irrelevance to the early modern canon of male-authored writing.[2] Debts to the field's origins in the feminist project of recovery meant that a tension persisted between a focus on the difference of women's writing, attributable to the complex cultural matrix surrounding individual female authors, and a focus on the comparability of women's writing to that of their male counterparts. This tension between difference and similarity was directed towards the canon in Lorna Hutson's essay in that issue, which asked the larger question of whether work on early modern women writers could be absorbed into existing narratives of literary and cultural history, or whether it disrupted and re-constituted those narratives.[3] At stake here is the way gender is formulated and privileged: whether as a limiting or generative discourse, intersecting with the other cultural discourses making up a writer's experience.

In 2013, the chapters in this volume provide some measure of how, in the light of such assessments, critics are now approaching early modern women as writers, and more specifically as writers in the canonically charged mode of poetry. In this afterword, we would like to consider how this collection contributes to these debates and to the wider project of thinking about the place of early modern women poets within literary cultures, past and present. What changes might be perceived to have taken place in the field and in the relationship of that field to criticism on early modern writing more generally since 2007? How are the problems of a field defined by the gender of its writers approached and resolved? How is the field itself presently constituted? And what opportunities for further scholarship remain to be explored?

One of the most striking shared features of the chapters in *Early Modern Women and the Poem* is their careful delineation of the ways in which the sixteenth- and seventeenth-century poetry discussed participated in economies of inheritance and exchange, textual, social and political. From a complex deployment of the linguistic and imaginative patterns provided by classical rhetoric and writers such as Sappho, to an engagement with contemporary generic models provided by retirement literature, the estate poem, popular ballads or familial occasional verse, early modern women writers are seen to participate in a wide range of textual traditions and precedents. These might be male- or female-authored; an earlier critical anxiety over early modern women's restricted agency within particular generic traditions is here translated into a narrative of participation and inclusion, across a spectrum ranging from imitation to transformation of those generic conventions. The chapters map both histories of inclusion, with a use of precedents indistinguishable from that of male contemporaries, as well as analyses very conscious of the way in which gender inflects the insertion of a feminine lyric voice into generic conventions.

If a new modulation is at work here, considering generic traditions as they intersect with specific writers at particular historical moments, these chapters are still concerned with the question of whether women have a different relationship to literary precedent than men. For Line Cottegnies, reading the sonnets of Lady Mary Wroth, the answer is yes. She argues that Wroth revises and transforms a range of neo-Petrarchan precedents and classical models in order to construct a new female lyric voice within the highly gendered genre of the sonnet sequence. Similarly, Helen Hackett argues that women participated in verse miscellany culture under different rules from men. But for other writers in this collection, the answer is not so clear. Paul Salzman reads Wroth's engagement with the genre of satire through libellous verse exchange to be as rhetorically skilful as the exercises of her male counterpart, Lord Denny, even if that engagement was dismissively received by her seventeenth-century audience. Generic precedent is perceived to be available for use by the woman writer herself even if it is not valued by her contemporary readers. Suzanne Trill persuasively argues for Mary Sidney's rhetorical methods in revision of psalm translation as part of an unrecognised, divinely inspired project of collaborative authorship. Yet in her argument, Mary Sidney's gender is not the primary factor motivating either her rhetorical engagements or her collaborative approach. Similarly, Katherine Philips is seen by Gillian Wright as engaging with the androcentric norms of retirement poetry and male friendship poetry through a range of strategies varying from imitation to transformative self-assertion and critique. We would like to suggest that what can be perceived here, in apparent contradictions across this set of essays, is a critical shift in the field itself surrounding early modern women's engagement with genre. Assessed on a case-by-case basis, and alert to local exigencies, the relationship between gender and generic engagement has become contingent, subject to a number of determining factors, formalist, historical and political.

As Margaret Ezell points out in her chapter on social authorship, early modern women's experiences of coterie authorship are complex economies of rivalry and collaboration, enmity and friendship. The gender of their participants, particularly if those participants are women, does not automatically transform such coteries into places of 'political and emotional triumph'. Her observations indicate the extent to which criticism of women's writing can return to unacknowledged, normative models of gender, even in its most sophisticated of analyses. If the chapters here seem almost uniformly concerned with situating women's writing within networks, then the complexity of these connections naturally militates against single and uniform constructions of gendered effects. As the number of texts considered as early modern women's writing expands, across multiple genres and modes of transmission, the approach critics take to the way in which gender might function within those different works becomes less predictable. Such approaches are driven by the texts themselves, rather than assumptions about the historical woman writer who wrote those texts. Critics implicitly acknowledge the very different ways in which early modern women writers might be situated in terms of family, class, geography, religion and politics. Driven by the formalist turn in early modern studies more generally, the chapters indicate that a similar diversity is beginning to be attributed to early modern women's engagement with literary precedent, whether in terms of the classical inheritances of humanism or more contemporary models in the vernacular. This expectation of difference, maintaining a complex and historically nuanced idea of gendered intervention into genre, represents the very reconciliation of historicism and formalism through genre that Alice Eardley called for in her essay in *Women's Writing* in 2007.[4] Engagement with genre is a rhetorical engagement with a material literary history, and in this the volume participates very pointedly with the way in which such material histories are transmitted through rhetorical forms.

Under these more flexible formulations of the category of gender, some early modern women are seen to be writing in ways that are easily absorbed into existing narratives of literary history, while others are perceived to be writing against the grain and transforming the genres with which they engage. But perhaps a caveat might be offered here in response to such narratives of rhetorical triumph, in line with Ezell's more careful delineation of coterie authorship. When women writers are seen to transform the genres within which they participate, is this new iteration of generic convention part of the process of writing into genre engaged with by all writers, male and female? If, as Heather Dubrow argues, every generic intervention both draws upon a long history of convention and rebels against it, then to what extent can a woman writer's intervention within a genre be seen as either unusually transformative or attributable to her gender?[5] Again, it might depend on the genre and the historical moment at which a woman writer engages with that literary tradition. Mary Wroth's participation in the genre of prose romance is anomalous, radical and ground-breaking, in an English context at least, although tempered by other determinants, including familial exempla and political investments. Later in the seventeenth century, however, a woman writing a poem in the genres of familial elegy, spiritual meditation or even the estate poem, as Susan Wiseman's chapter shows, had a range of male- and female-authored exempla to draw upon. Genres are not always androcentric, and to insist that they are automatically reinforces women's exclusion from those genres. A more complex model at work in these chapters allows that women's writing might be pedestrian as well as ground-breaking, in the same way as men's writing within a genre ranges from conventional performances to radical revision.

A second, consistent point of return in these chapters is to the mechanisms and particular histories through which women's writing has been excluded or marginalised. Drawing upon a wider interest in the critical field on the textuality of reading, considered alongside the materiality of texts, a number of essays in this collection argue for specific cases where women's poetry has been suppressed through histories of reading, recording and circulation.[6] A broader conceptualisation of the imaginative and formal possibilities available to the early modern woman writer through textual example means that the question of her enduring marginalisation must be located elsewhere, outside the options available to her when confronted with the blank page and a range of textual precedents. Read collectively, the chapters suggest that such marginalisation of women's writing arises from the ways in which early modern women's poetry was received, redacted and valued. As Paul Salzman notes, the rhetorical sophistication of Lady Mary Wroth's satiric response to Lord Denny's libellous poem about the *Urania* was not, for John Chamberlain, 'worth the writing out'. The extent to which Chamberlain's assessment of Wroth's poem was aesthetic, personal or political is unclear (although the context of his letter suggests all three elements to be in play), but the impact of his choice not to make a copy is definitive in assuring that Denny's text is more widely read and culturally central than that of his female adversary. These contributions map a range of such assessments, from the sixteenth century to the present, which might collectively be seen to force early modern women's writing to the edges of the largely male-authored canon.

As Suzanne Trill argues through the example of Mary Sidney, such unacknowledged judgements still operate in the field. She deftly traces through the reception of the Sidneian Psalms an unexamined and continuing critical investment in individual authorship and ownership of texts, which has resulted in Mary Sidney's marginalisation as textual collaborator in favour of Philip Sidney's elevation as the Psalms' sole author. If early modern textuality has been understood in the last decade as increasingly collaborative, networked and social, that reconfiguration within male canonical writing in this case can be seen to be largely rhetorical, a kind of half-credence acknowledged yet not fully embraced. Lip service is paid to collaboration while leaving the single, inviolable and often canonical author intact. By detailing and analysing such histories of reading, these chapters suggest a way of approaching the problem of the marginalisation of women writers within the early modern canon. If early modern women writers remain little read, that marginality might be attributed to histories of reading that have seen women's poetry as 'not worth the writing out', or to formulations of textuality that continue to struggle with early modern women's particular engagements with authorship and textual transmission. We see the importance of keeping a dialectical model of early modern women's textuality alive here, one in which gender is one of a number of determinants that influence a writer's engagement with form. Such a model, alert to the possibility of both difference and similarity, allows early modern women's writing to be read in conversation with the male-authored field. It retains gender as a category of potential difference that might transform our understanding of the largely male-authored field at the same time as it might also underscore the ways in which male- and female-authored texts shared strategies, themes and forms.

In the readings provided by some of the chapters, the partial, collaborative or expanded models of authorship already at work in criticism of early modern women's writing offer the broader field exemplars of the ways in which authorship might be expanded. As the critical field surrounding early modern women's writing de-emphasises the historical woman writer in favour of a closer attention to her writing, it has also begun to review the field's connections between the body of the historical early modern woman writer and her text. Two chapters consider writing circulated as the work of women that was probably male-authored; indeed, as Judith

Hudson suggests in chapter 11, the ventriloquising strategies of some of these texts were barely concealed. It would be odd to imagine, however, that such examples of 'early modern women's poetry', whether in the form of popular ballads or Ovidian complaint, were not used by early modern women writers as enabling precedents for the female lyric voice. The availability of poetry that ventriloquised the voice of the early modern woman writer to historical women poets becomes clearer as we understand more of the links between oral and literate cultures in the period, together with the roles performance and collaboration played in poetic cultures.[7] As Matt Cohen suggests, early modern textual transmission was 'choral', the 'aggregate work' of writers, scribes, typesetters, editors, booksellers, readers and performers.[8] A single text did not exist in a unique iteration, but was remade in its subsequent transmissions and redactions in scribal, print and performance cultures. Just as participants in cultures of manuscript miscellany might remake a poem in the act of retranscription, so women readers and auditors of poetry might remake a poem in the act of recital. Such an expanded model of publication points to a much more dynamic and unfixed relation between the gendered bodies of historical women and poetry. Male- and female-authored poetry circulated in manuscript, print and oral cultures simultaneously, and while authorship could be ascribed and the gender of authors determined at some points within particular networks of transmission, these were not inviolable categories consistently applied by early modern men and women as readers or writers.

Such arguments, of course, can only be posited following a thirty-year tradition of scholarship devoted to unearthing early modern women writers, reversing negative assumptions about their work and understanding their place within literary cultures past and present. We acknowledge that arguments expanding the definition of early modern women's poetry to textual acts such as editing and performance are polemical, and that they have significant implications for an already marginal set of writers and works. But the project of restitution that initiated the field of early modern women's writing is creating larger methodological problems in the field. Specifically, it binds interpretative practices to models of gender and textuality that fit uncomfortably with new theories of the history of the book that are transforming our understanding of what constituted material texts, how they might have circulated, and the multiple ways in which they were read and redacted. In negotiating these new ways of thinking about text and history, early modern women's writing becomes an expanded group of texts and textual practices that is deeply imbricated with the corpus of male-authored writing. In this way, then, early modern women's writing is coterminous with men's writing, and should form part of its generic traditions and circulation practices across a range of responses, from imitation to disruption. It is difficult to conceive of women's writing always as different from men's writing, or always the same as men's writing, according to this model of publication, or to generalise about the impact of gender upon textual practice. These are questions that can be considered only locally and with genuine specificity in attempting to untangle the uses to which texts might be put.

The model of gender, author and text that we are positing here takes into account the multiple, flexible and often anonymous cultures through which texts circulated in the early modern period. These cultures challenge the single and inviolable status of both the most canonical authors in the period as well as the most marginal, in their emphasis on collaboration in authorship and extended, unpredictable transmission histories. In taking seriously revisions to the model of the single, inviolable male or female author, the chapters privilege sociality and exchange alongside ownership and control. Women participated across a spectrum of textual engagement as poets, with extremes of practice at either end: from Elizabeth I's careful dissemination of a poem such as 'The doubt of future foes' in manuscript and print as a way of marking her rhetorical and political skill, to the anonymous woman singer of a male-authored ballad in a marketplace.[9] It may seem that in insisting on the breadth and diversity of such a model, and in questioning the generalisations that might be made about gender, we may be left with an approach that again implicitly writes out women's textual engagements by default, one which returns to the bad old days where a level playing field was assumed and women's perceived lack of participation was naturalised. We take heart from the fact that a significant body of scholarship exists on early modern women as writers, and that the cumulative result of that work has been to form a new understanding of the diversity and range of women's diverse textual practices as poets, albeit in an expanded understanding of what that term might encompass.

This collection of essays on early modern women and the poem indicates that early modern women's writing might be thought about in terms that are beginning to break down the kind of binary surrounding similarity and difference at stake in the 2007 issue of *Women's Writing*. Then and now, this binary insists that women's writing is either different from the male-authored canon in ways that mean it disrupts and transforms that canon, or that its differences need to be downplayed in an effort to redress its marginality and to allow its integration into that canon. As these chapters show, canonicity cannot be an unproblematic aim, as the difference of women's writing is as much about reception as production, about histories of reading that have made the perceived marginality of early modern women and the poem normative. By attending to the mechanisms by which early modern women's poetry is valued, read and circulated, both at the originary moment of publication and beyond, as well as expanding conceptions of female authorship to a wide range of textual practices, these chapters move beyond generalisations about the canonical status of early modern women's poetry. Their cumulative effect is that women's engagement with poetry can be conceived across a spectrum, from imitation to transformative critique, and that an assessment of its relation to male-authored poetry, canonical or not, needs to be made on a case-by-case basis, according to differing historical, geopolitical, social and literary determinants. The chapters show both this possibility and its working out, as individual responses to understanding early modern women and the poem struggle to reconcile, with genuine specificity, writers' relations to literary canons, past and present. Without recourse to generalisations about similarity or difference, canonicity, marginality or centrality, the question of an early modern woman writer's status must be charted anew through her work. This means that the field might appear less coherent and more permeable. It also means that our understanding of early modern women's writing cannot be summed up in crude binaries. Women's relationship to the poem can be both different and comparable, delimited and generative, formally, socially and politically. If in 2013 we can locate a new uncertainty surrounding our assumptions about early modern women writers, it is an uncertainty built on a much broader and more flexible idea than once existed of the scale, content and forms of such writing.

Notes

1 See E. Clarke and L. Robson, 'Why are we "Still kissing the rod"? The future for the study of early modern women writers', *Women's Writing*, vol. 14, no. 2 (2007), pp. 171–93; J. Stevenson, 'Still kissing the rod? Whither next', *Women's Writing*, vol. 14, no. 2 (2007), pp. 246–69; and A. Eardley, 'Recreating the canon: women writers and anthologies of early modern verse', *Women's Writing*, vol. 14, no. 2 (2007), pp. 270–89.

2 N. Smith, 'The rod and the canon', *Women's Writing*, vol. 14, no. 2 (2007), pp. 232–45.

3 L. Hutson, 'The body of the friend and the woman writer: Katherine Philips's absence from Alan Bray's *The Friend* (2003)', *Women's Writing*, vol. 14, no. 2 (2007), p. 196.

4 Eardley, 'Recreating the canon', pp. 281–4.

5 H. Dubrow, *Genre*, Methuen, London, 1982, p. 117; see also A. Fowler, *Kinds of Literature: An Introduction to the Theory of Genres and Modes*, Clarendon Press, Oxford, 1982, p. 23.

6 See J. Richards and F. Schurink, 'Introduction: the textuality and materiality of reading in early modern England', *Huntington Library Quarterly*, vol. 73, no. 3 (2010), pp. 345–61; P. Salzman, *Reading Early Modern Women's Writing*, Oxford University Press, Oxford, 2006; and H. B. Hackel, *Reading Material in Early Modern England*, Cambridge University Press, Cambridge, 2005.

7 See B. Smith, *The Acoustic World of Early Modern England*, Chicago University Press, Chicago, 1999; and A. Fox, *Oral and Literate Culture in England 1500–1700*, Oxford University Press, Oxford, 2000.

8 M. Cohen, *The Networked Wilderness: Communicating in Early New England*, University of Minnesota Press, Minneapolis, 2010, p. 15.

9 For a discussion of Elizabeth I's transmission strategies see J. Summit, 'The arte of a ladies penne: Elizabeth I and the poetics of queenship', *English Literary Renaissance*, vol. 26, no. 3 (1996), pp. 395–413.

Index